"This is an important, timely and valuable contribution to the understanding of Islam in the world of today. Shepard succeeds in providing an accessible and empathetic introduction to Islam whilst also allowing for sufficient depth for the reader to go beyond the mere facts. The objectives for each chapter are clearly laid out and, with the discussion questions and additional website material, this results in a book that I will not hesitate in recommending to my students."

Roy Jackson, *University of Gloucestershire, UK*

"*Introducing Islam* is a fine, balanced and approachable text for bringing a basic understanding of Islam to undergraduates. Key issues in Islamic social and institutional histories, religious practices, scripture and theology are presented clearly and with an eye towards classroom activities and variable modes of syllabus organization. I've used this textbook multiple times – my students have appreciated its clarity, liked it, and learned from it."

Rocco Gangle, *Endicott College, USA*

"Shepard provides a comprehensive and intelligible study of Islam, from its origins in the seventh century to its dynamic developments in the medieval periods, providing insight into the manifestations of Islamic civilization beyond theology, such as on art, culture and rituals. Tracing Islam into the modern era, he sketches the complexity of how Islamic societies from the Middle East to Indonesia have confronted the tensions between traditional beliefs and contemporary expressions of Islam. Masterfully, this catholic and lucid discussion of Islam is accomplished without losing any of the sophistication of the topic."

Awad Halabi, *Wright State University, USA*

Introducing Islam

Second edition

William E. Shepard

Routledge
Taylor & Francis Group
LONDON AND NEW YORK

First edition published 2009, this edition published 2014
by Routledge
2 Park Square, Milton Park, Abingdon, Oxon OX14 4RN

and by Routledge
711 Third Avenue, New York, NY 10017

Routledge is an imprint of the Taylor & Francis Group, an informa business

British Library Cataloguing in Publication Data
A catalogue record for this book is available from the British Library

Library of Congress Cataloging in Publication Data
Shepard, William E., 1933–
Introducing Islam / William E. Shepard. – 2nd ed.
pages cm – (World Religions series)
Includes bibliographical references and index.
1. Islam. 2. Islam – History. I. Title.
BP50.S485 2014
297–dc23 2013027782

ISBN: 978-0-415-53342-3 (hbk)
ISBN: 978-0-415-53345-4 (pbk)

Typeset in Jensen
by HWA Text and Data Management, London

To my wife and children: Elza, Bill and Christina

Contents

Illustrations

Maps

Figures

Acknowledgements

It would be impossible to name all of those to whom I owe a debt of gratitude. These include Muslims and non-Muslims and include teachers, colleagues, students, friends, passing acquaintances who have taught me significant things in a brief time and many I have never met but whose writings I have read. Perhaps the one who most should be named is the late Wilfred Cantwell Smith, my teacher and dissertation advisor and one of the giants of our field. I believe that my approach considerably reflects his and I hope that it is worthy of him. Apart from him, to name any one of my teachers or colleagues without naming a host of others would be an injustice.

I should certainly mention the Muslim community here in New Zealand, who have provided my main living contact with the Muslim *umma* for over thirty years and have encouraged me in my research on them. If one person could stand for all of them it would be the late Abdul Rahim Rasheed, a lawyer who devoted so much time and effort to developing the community.

My appreciation is extended to those who have read all or part of the manuscripts of this edition and the first one, both those anonymous readers appointed by the publisher and the many who have responded to my requests for comments. They have made many excellent comments and suggestions and have steered me away from more than one pitfall. Appreciation is also due to the staff at Routledge, especially Amy Grant, with whom I worked most closely on the first edition and Faye Mouseley and Rebecca Shillabeer, with whom I have worked most closely on this one, but also others, many of whose names I will never know but whose work has been essential. Likewise, appreciation is due to Damien Keown and Charles Prebish for their initiative in undertaking the World Religions series, of which this book is a part, and inviting me to participate in it. Much of what is good is owed to all of these people. The weaknesses are my responsibility.

A debt of gratitude is also owed to my wife and children, who have encouraged me and often put up with my physical absence and my absence-while-present, so to speak, not only in writing this book but throughout my career.

World Religions series

Edited by Damien Keown and Charles S. Prebish

This exciting series introduces students to the major world religious traditions. Each religion is explored in a lively and clear fashion by experienced teachers and leading scholars in the field of world religions. Up-to-date scholarship is presented in a student-friendly fashion, covering history, core beliefs, sacred texts, key figures, religious practice and culture, and key contemporary issues. To aid learning and revision, each text includes illustrations, summaries, explanations of key terms, and further reading.

Introducing African American Religion
Anthony B. Pinn

Introducing Tibetan Buddhism
Geoffrey Samuel

Introducing Buddhism, second edition
Damien Keown and Charles S. Prebish

Introducing American Religion
Charles Lippy

Introducing Chinese Religions
Mario Poceski

Introducing Daoism
Livia Kohn

Introducing Judaism
Eliezer Segal

Introducing Christianity
James R. Adair

Introducing Japanese Religion
Robert Ellwood

Introducing Hinduism
Hillary Rodrigues

Introducing Islam

Just what is Islam and what does it mean to be a Muslim in the world today? Since the events of 9/11 and 7/7, Islam has become one of the most controversial and misunderstood religions in the world. *Introducing Islam* encourages students to put aside their preconceptions and explore this fascinating religion.

William Shepard traces the history of Islam from its origins in the life and career of Muhammad, through its classical expressions, to its interactions with the West in the modern world. A chapter is devoted to each major topic, including the Qur'an, Islamic law, Islamic theology, and the Sufi movement, as well as community rituals and Islamic art and culture. There is a survey of modern developments and four chapters are dedicated to individual countries: Turkey, Iran, Egypt and Indonesia.

Fully revised and updated, the second edition of this core textbook adds crucial material on contemporary issues such as women in Islam and democratization and human rights. Illustrated throughout, the book also includes learning objectives, a glossary of key Arabic terms, comprehensive further reading lists and critical thinking boxes, helping students to critically engage with the material in each chapter. Further teaching and learning resources are available on the companion website at www.routledge.com/cw/shepard. This book continues to be essential reading for students of Islam worldwide.

William E. Shepard is Associate Professor, Retired, of Religious Studies at the University of Canterbury, Christchurch, New Zealand. His previous publications include *The Faith of a Modern Muslim Intellectual: The Religious Aspects and Implications of the Writings of Ahmad Amin* (1982), *Sayyid Qutb and Islamic Activism* (1996) and numerous articles and translations.

Preface to the second edition

In this second edition of *Introducing Islam* I have made a number of minor changes and one major addition that I hope will increase the book's usefulness. I have corrected such typographical and factual errors as have been found and have rewritten some paragraphs for greater clarity or precision. I have added some material at points and updated some, especially in the chapters dealing with the modern period. I have also introduced a number of "critical thinking boxes" to encourage the reader to delve more deeply into aspects of the material presented in the book (see note on "Critical Thinking Boxes" below). The reading lists are somewhat expanded and brief comments are added to most entries. Indications of material on the website are also added. The major addition is the new chapter, chapter 21, which presents three topics that are currently under considerable discussion: gender, democracy and human rights. In comparison to the rest of the book, this chapter makes less effort to be factually complete and balanced and more effort to provoke reaction and discussion. I hope it will be found to be a useful addition.

About Introducing Islam

This book seeks to give a sympathetic presentation of Islamic religion and relevant aspects of the cultures of which it is a part without either ignoring or unduly emphasizing the negative elements that have attended them as they attend every human tradition. Over the last fourteen centuries Islam has guided millions of people to live full and productive lives and given consolation in misfortune and tragedy. If today Westerners tend to be more aware of the negative aspects of Islam, this is all the more reason why we need to stress the more positive aspects that have attracted so many to it and still do.

This book comes out of some forty years of my teaching and research about Islam within the context of Religious Studies. Although seeking to present the tradition in its fullness, it gives particular attention to the political aspects, insofar as these are closely related to religion, and to modern developments, because these have been

The author and publisher would like to acknowledge and thank the reviewers who provided valuable feedback throughout the writing process. They are:

Rocco Gangle, Associate Professor of Humanities/Philosophy at Endicott College, USA
Awad Halabi, Associate Professor, Departments of History and Religion, Wright State University, USA
Dr Jan-Peter Hartung, SOAS, University of London, UK
Dr Jocelyn Hendrickson, University of Alberta, USA
Aysha Hidayatullah, Assistant Professor, Department of Theology & Religious Studies, University of San Francisco, USA
Dr Thomas Hoffmann, Professor in Qur'anic Studies, University of Copenhagen, Denmark
Dr Roy Jackson, University of Gloucestershire, UK
Dr Nico J.G. Kaptein, Leiden University Institute for Area Studies
Dr Carool Kersten, Senior Lecturer in the Study of Islam and the Muslim World, King's College London, UK
Martin Nguyen, Assistant Professor of Islamic Religious Traditions, Fairfield University, USA
Olle Sundström, PhD, Associate Professor in History of Religions, Umeå University, Sweden
Alfons H. Teipen, Associate Professor of Religion, Furman University, USA

the main focus of my own effort. It is directed in the first instance at university-level students who have limited knowledge of the Muslim world and no knowledge of its languages. I hope, though, that others will also profit from it.

The introductory chapter discusses the appropriate approach to the subject and gives an introductory synopsis of Islam as a Muslim might give it. The first 14 chapters present the Islamic tradition as it has developed over the centuries, usually with some attention to modern developments at the end of each chapter. Of these, three chapters (2–4) give a historical overview from the pre-Islamic period to about 1700 and ten (5–14) deal with various aspects of the tradition, including the scriptures, the role of the Prophet Muhammad, sectarian divisions, religious scholars, religious law and mysticism. The remaining chapters (15–21) deal with the challenges of the modern period, with particular attention to religion and politics in Turkey, Egypt, Iran and Indonesia, with disparate aspects of what we call globalization and with selected topics of current interest.

I have used Western (Gregorian) dates throughout the book because most readers will presumably be unfamiliar with Islamic dates, which would therefore be an unnecessary additional burden. An explanation of Islamic dates is found in Appendix III. Transliteration of Arabic and Persian words follows a standard system as explained in the "Notes on Transliteration and Pronunciation" below; pronunciation is also explained for Turkish, Persian and Indonesian. I have tried to keep citations to a minimum and have used the Harvard system (abbreviated reference in parentheses in the text) where I have them. The sources for these will be found in the section labeled "References", at the end of the book.

Qur'anic references are given by chapter number and verse number, using Pickthall's versification; sources for *hadiths*, either the name of the collection from which they come or the source from which I got them, are usually given.

A book of this sort cannot avoid having a considerable number of names and technical terms that will be daunting to the student. To make things a bit easier, many of these are explained in the glossary. Also, words that are in the glossary are put in bold face the first time they appear in each chapter unless they are explained in the text at that point.

Critical thinking boxes

"Critical thinking" may be described for present purposes as careful assessment of statements or claims that includes considering the evidence for and against them, considering their implications and looking for contradictions or apparent contradictions, unstated motives or hidden assumptions. Beyond this, many of the boxes will call for the use of a disciplined imagination that may lead you to extend an idea, make connections with other ideas and facts, and perhaps find new approaches to a subject and new questions to ask. Most of the boxes will require some degree of research beyond general knowledge and the contents of this book, but they are not meant to involve a major research effort. (You should be able to discuss the topics for chapter 1, for example, without further research beyond reading, if possible, the article mentioned in one case.) While each topic is placed at the end of a particular chapter, in some cases relevant material is contained in other (usually earlier) chapters.

Companion website

A website accompanies this book and it is hoped that readers will make good use of it, in particular the parts labeled "Additional Information", "Further Reading" and "Useful Websites". The first contains passages from primary and secondary sources directly related to the material in the book and other information. The other two have additional bibliography and world wide web links, respectively. Some of its content is indicated at the end of each chapter. The URL for the website is: www.routledge.com/cw/shepard

Notes on transliteration and pronunciation

Proper pronunciation of Arabic and other languages can be learned only with specific instruction, so the following guide is designed to indicate to the speaker of English suitable approximations to the pronunciation of particular letters and combinations in the words that appear in this book.

Arabic

The transliteration of Arabic terms follows the system most commonly used today by scholars writing in English except that diacritics (macrons, and dots under certain letters) are omitted for the sake of simplicity in most of this book. Diacritics do help in pronunciation, however, and so they appear in this section and in the Glossary, and also at the first or first few appearances of a term in the text and sometimes later where there is a long lapse between appearances. Names of people and places are usually given in the commonly recognized form when such a form exists, e.g. Cairo instead of al-Qahira and Abdel Nasser instead of 'Abd al-Nasir.

Transliteration and pronunciation are based on Modern Standard (i.e. literary) Arabic; dialects vary considerably.

The following consonants are pronounced approximately as in English: *b, d, f, h, j, k, l, m, n, s* (as in sight, not rise), *sh, t, th* (as in thing, not this), *w, y, z*.

Consonants with underdots, *ḍ, ḥ, ṣ, ṭ, ẓ*, are pronounced distinctively in Arabic but may be pronounced like their undotted counterparts by the non-Arabist.

dh is pronounced like *th* in this.
kh is pronounced like the *ch* in *loch* (Scottish) or *ach* (German).
gh is voiced equivalent of *kh*, a bit like gargling. "Voiced" means the vocal chords are active; e.g. *g* (voiced) and *k* (unvoiced).

The letters in the combinations *sh, th, dh* and *kh* are pronounced separately if one or both of the letters has an underdot, e.g. *Aḍḥā* (pronounced *Aḍ-ḥā*). These cases are rare, however.

q is pronounced like *k* but is more guttural.
r is a tongue-flap, like the *r* in the Spanish or Italian *caro*, also somewhat like the *tt* in colloquial American pronunciation of *better*.
rr is a trill, like the *rr* in the Spanish *perro*.
ʿ represents the Arabic letter *ʿayn*, which has a very guttural sound that can be learned only with practice.
ʾ represents the Arabic letter *hamza*. The sound exists in English but is not represented by a letter. It is the breath we often make at the beginning of a word that begins with a vowel, and sometimes in other situations or in certain dialects: e.g. aʾ apple, liʾl (for little). The sign is not used when *hamza* is at the beginning of a word, thus *adhān*, not *ʾadhān*.

The Arabic letter *tā marbūṭa*, which appears only at the end of a word, usually is a silent *h* and in this book is not represented, but when it is constructed with a following word (called *iḍāfa* in Arabic) it changes to a *t* and is represented, e.g *shīʿa* (party) and *shīʿat ʿAlī* (party of Ali).

Some writers represent the *h* in the non-*iḍāfa* form, e.g. *shīʿah*.

Doubled consonants are actually doubled in pronunciation, i.e. stretched out longer.

The vowels are *a*, *i* and *u*, and the diphthongs are *aw* and *ay*. Long vowels are indicated by a macron, *ā*, *ī*, *ū*. These do make a difference to pronunciation; in particular the accent will usually be on the syllable with the long vowel. The macron is also occasionally needed to distinguish between words that would appear the same in transliteration without it but are different in Arabic, e.g. *Ḥajj*, the Pilgrimage to Mecca, and *Ḥājj*, the one who makes the Pilgrimage.

Long ā is pronounced like the *a* in *had*.
Short *a* is pronounced like the *u* in *but*.
Long ī is pronounced like the *ee* in *beet*.
Short *i* is pronounced like the *i* in *bit*.
Long ū is pronounced like the *oo* in *soon*.
Short *u* is pronounced like the *u* in *put*.
ay is pronounced like the *i* in *bite* or like the *ay* in *hay*.
au is pronounced like the *ow* in *how*.

The definite article (*the* in English) is always transliterated *al-*. Its pronunciation varies, however. The first letter may become *i* or *u* depending on the vowel at the end of the preceding word. (This need not normally concern the reader, however, because the transliteration does not usually indicate this vowel.) The second letter may assimilate to the first letter of the following word, e.g. *al-shīʿa* (the party) is pronounced *ash-shīʿa*. This happens with the following consonants: *d*, *ḍ*, *dh*, *l*, *n*, *r*, *s*, *ṣ*, *sh*, *t*, *ṭ*, *th*, *z*, *ẓ*. This pronunciation is reflected in some writers' transliterations and in the accepted spelling of many names, e.g. Abdurrahman, which in the transliteration normally used here would be 'Abd al-Raḥmān.

Plurals of transliterated words are usually made in this book by adding the English *s*, but occasionally Arabic plurals appear. These are made by adding *-ūn*, *-īn* or *-āt* to the word (e.g. *mu'min> mu'minīn*) or by changing the word in other ways (e.g. 'ālim> *'ulamā'*) but the latter cases will be explained if necessary where they occur.

The word *Abū* (father) in names is sometimes *Abī* for grammatical reasons, e.g. *'Alī ibn Abī Ṭālib* (see Appendix IV on names).

Accent: words with no long vowels are usually accented on the second or third last syllable; words with one long vowel are usually accented on that syllable; words with more than one long vowel are usually accented on the last long vowel.

Persian

Persian names and terms are not transliterated according to a single scholarly system here but according to common usage in scholarly and journalistic writing. Diacritics are not used here. Something like the Arabic *iḍāfa* exists in Persian and is represented by *-i* (pronounced something like the *a* in *ate*, but very short), e.g. *vilayat-i faqih* (the governance of the jurist), the Arabic equivalent is *wilāyat al-faqīh*.

As this example also illustrates, the *w* in Arabic becomes *v* in the transliteration of Persian.

q and *gh* are pronounced like the *gh* in Arabic (some words may be transliterated with either *q* or *gh*, e.g. *faqih* or *faghih*).

Persian words are usually accented on the last syllable, e.g. *Khomeiní*.

Turkish

Modern Turkish is written in Roman script and for present purposes should present few problems. Note, however, the following, which appear in this book:

c is pronounced like *j*.
ç is pronounced like *ch*.
ğ is silent, but lengthens the preceding vowel.
ş is pronounced like *sh*.
ö and ü are pronounced as in German or *eu* and *u* in French.

Names and terms from before the 1920s are often transliterated as if they were Arabic: e.g. *shaykh al-Islam* instead of *şeyhülislam*.

The Arabic *tā marbūṭa* becomes *t* in Turkish, e.g. *şeriat* for Arabic *sharī'a*.

Indonesian

Indonesian is also written in Roman script and also should present few problems. Note the following:

c is pronounced like *ch*.
sy is pronounced like *sh* (e.g. *Syariah* for *Shari'a*)
dl in recent writings is pronounced like *d* (e.g. *Nahdlatul Ulama*)

The Arabic *tā marbūṭa* usually becomes *h*, sometimes *t* (e.g. *Syariah, Syariat*)

Previously Indonesian was romanized according to Dutch orthography and this often appears in names (though these are also often updated), e.g. *Soeharto* instead of *Suharto*, *pantjasila* instead of *pancasila*, *sjariah* instead of *syariah*.

1 *Introduction*

Approaching the subject

This chapter discusses the approach to Islam taken in this book, in particular the goal of "empathetic understanding". It also provides an introductory overview of Islam from a Muslim perspective.

In this chapter

- Who represents Islam?
- What is Islam?
- Is there a "true Islam"?
- Empathetic understanding
- Apologetics
- Two problematic pairs
- From Orientalism to Islamic Studies
- The role of the media
- Issues of language and related matters
- Dates
- An introductory overview of Islam

Who represents Islam?

Islam has been very much in the news in recent years but all too often for the wrong reasons. Media attention to high profile terrorist actions such as the destruction of the Twin Towers in New York on 11 September 2001 ("9/11"), wars in Iraq and Afghanistan and political turmoil in other places, has led many to associate Islam with violence and fanaticism. We hear much less about the vastly larger number of Muslims who express their faith by going quietly about their work or household chores, educating their children, donating to charity, lending a helping hand to their neighbors and working for their communities, as well as performing their prayers and participating in other prescribed practices. This book seeks to give its primary attention to this latter group, which is certainly more representative of the Muslim community as a whole, but will not neglect the more radical and violent elements, both past and present.

What is Islam?

We may begin by saying that Islam is the religion of those people who have for some fourteen centuries followed the teachings of the Prophet **Muhammad**. Today they number more than one-and-a-half billion, living throughout the world but concentrated particularly in the swath of lands stretching from Morocco eastward to Indonesia and from Central Asia southward to sub-Saharan Africa.

Going further, we may understand the word "Islam" at three levels. At the most basic level it means submitting or committing oneself to God, essentially an inward mental action though with outward consequences. The one who does this is termed a Muslim. This was the earliest meaning of the terms Islam and Muslim. At the second level Islam refers to a religion, that is, a system of beliefs and practices believed to be ordained by God, and Muslims are the adherents of this religion. At the third level Islam may refer to a culture and a civilization, indeed several cultures and civilizations, created by Muslims over the course of time but also shared by many non-Muslims. Islamic civilizations integrated into themselves ideas and practices from other civilizations, including those of Greece, Iran and India, and were among the great civilizations of human history. Today, particularly, there are some who may be called "cultural Muslims" – who sit loosely by the religion but are heirs to the culture and civilization and identify with them.

According to conventional history Islam in the first two senses began with the career of the Prophet Muhammad (c. 610–632 CE), although Muslims say that it began much sooner, as we shall see later. Islamic civilization also began to develop at this time but took two or three centuries to reach its first full flowering. Islam as a civilization is a constantly developing tradition, varying from one time and place to another. Many, including the author of this book, would say this is also true of Islam as a religion, although most Muslims would say that the essentials of the religion of Islam do not change.

This book will focus primarily on Islam as a religion, presenting the symbols, ideas, practices and institutions of which it is composed and tracing their historical development as much as possible. It will also deal with culture and civilization because religion is embedded in these and the line between them and religion is often hard and sometimes impossible to draw. The precise form of the religion of any particular group of Muslims will depend considerably on its cultural context. The diversity of culture has resulted in considerable diversity of belief and practice throughout the Muslim world, with the result that many scholars prefer to speak of "Islams" rather than "Islam". Nevertheless, there is still considerable agreement among Muslims on the core elements of the religion.

In fact, however, it is not the religion or the culture that are most important. It is the people. Religion and culture exist only in the people who practice and participate in them. Apart from people they are abstractions. Because the people commit themselves with varying degrees of conviction and consistency and with diverse interpretations, there is enormous diversity at the personal level. We can almost say that there are as many "Islams" as there are Muslims. While we cannot avoid the abstractions and generalizations of religion and culture, especially in an introductory presentation, we must always try to see or imagine the actual people.

Is there a "true Islam"?

Many Muslims believe that there is a "true Islam" or a "real Islam", which is properly followed only by some. They differ, however, as to exactly what this true Islam is. What is essential for some is heterodox or mere culture for others. This question is of understandable concern to Muslims, but it is one that as scholars in Religious Studies (or in most other academic disciplines) we do not ask or seek to answer. The closest we come is to note that certain beliefs and practices are more common or agreed upon, and thus more "mainstream", while others are less common and more contested. Having said this, though, we do take account of the Muslims' interest in the "true Islam" in our efforts at understanding.

Some non-Muslims may also claim that there is a true Islam, which consists of certain beliefs and practices that they wish to privilege for reasons of their own. Some stress the more attractive aspects of Islam in order to defend it and some stress the more violent practices in order to justify their claim that Islam is a threat, something we often see in the **Western** media today. We try to avoid both agendas.

In principle every form of Islam is for us significant and worthy of attention. In practice, of course, we will give more attention to those beliefs and practices that are "mainstream", but we will not ignore the less widespread beliefs and practices. We will also give more attention to some forms of Islam than their numerical following would dictate because they are interesting or important in some way. One example is Islamic philosophy (***falsafa***), which mainly involved a small elite but is intellectually interesting and had considerable influence on both later Islamic and Western thought. We will likewise give more attention to contemporary terrorists than their numbers dictate because of their impact. We will take them seriously as representing one form of Islam, though one that is quite aberrant in relation to mainstream forms.

Empathetic understanding

If we do not ask which is the true Islam, we also do not ask whether any version of Islam is true. We do not, at least initially, pass any theological judgment on the doctrines and practices or the people and groups we study, nor usually any moral judgment. Our first and most important task is simply to understand them, as well and as fully as possible, from their own perspective. This is not always so simple. In the first place, we must get the facts. For example, what do Muslims (or some particular group of Muslims) actually do when they pray? Second, and crucially, we must try to understand what the facts mean to the people. What does praying mean to Muslims (and to particular Muslims)? To find this out we also need to know some of the social and historical circumstances of those involved.

This understanding must be at least an empathetic and, if possible, a sympathetic understanding. By empathy I mean imaginatively entering into the experience of another person and seeing the world as they see it. Sympathy adds to this a favorable attitude toward them and their experience. In either case, we try mentally to walk the proverbial mile in their moccasins. In order to do this we must often temporarily set aside many of our own beliefs and disbeliefs, values and presuppositions, and ask what would follow if the beliefs, values and presuppositions of those we are studying were in fact true. This is called "bracketing", because we bracket off for the time being our own views. It may lead us to appreciate that if we were in the situation of those we are considering we would have done what they have done, or at least been tempted to do so. This is possible because we and those we study are all human and on that common humanity understanding can be built. Likewise, our cultures are human cultures and we can usually find parallels that will illuminate any case, although these parallels must be handled carefully, as we shall see. This, of course, applies to the study of all religions and, ideally, to all human beliefs and practices.

Undoubtedly this is difficult with some, such as the perpetrators of 9/11. This is an extreme example and yet for that reason a good "test case" for the possibility of empathy. Is sufficient information available about their beliefs and attitudes and the forces playing on them? I believe so. Were they human with recognizably human motivations? We may wish to say no, but the answer is yes. Bracketing our revulsion will not be easy, but for that reason will be all the more necessary. Can we find parallels in our own culture that will help us? The answer is yes, if we recognize that they were ideologues and "soldiers" willing to die for their cause, and that our culture, too, has its ideologies and those who are willing to die for a cause. Sympathy is undoubtedly out of the question in this case, but empathy is possible and very much needed. An effort to do this will be made in chapter 20.

Fortunately, almost all of this book will deal with less extreme cases, where sympathetic as well as empathetic understanding is attainable. We should note, though, that situations and elements in Islam that appeal to us or seem familiar present their own challenges for understanding. We may think we understand them before we do. For example, as we shall see, the Qur'an is the Muslim scripture, so it is natural for Westerners initially to draw comparisons with the Jewish or Christian Bible. These are helpful to a point, but soon we learn that in some ways the Qur'an is more to be compared with the person of Jesus Christ in Christian thinking than with the

Bible. Drawing analogies from our own culture and experience is one of the methods of attaining empathy, but it must be done with care. It should be noted that while empathy requires imagination and even intuition, it also requires critical thinking to sift the information on which they are based and to discipline their outcomes.

Empathetic understanding, of course, does not preclude our making moral judgments and acting on them. In the case of 9/11 and many others, we must sooner or later remove the brackets, judging and acting in terms of our own values and beliefs. Likewise, those whose actions and beliefs accord with our values often deserve our open approbation and support. The point is to do these things *after* we have achieved as much empathetic understanding as we can. The process of empathetic understanding, itself, must be as little influenced by our own values as possible.

Empathetic understanding, likewise, does not mean that we reject the critical study of Islamic religion and history that has been carried out by mainly Western scholars over the last two centuries. Their accomplishment is impressive and this book relies heavily on it. Muslims have often viewed Western critical study as an attack on Islam (and in some cases they have been right) but there has been some acceptance. Critical study is not inconsistent with empathetic understanding, but it applies it in its own way. For example, if a critic gives a radically novel interpretation to the first generation of Muslim history (see chapters 3 and 5), this critic is (or should be) undertaking an empathetic understanding of the Muslims of that generation, not the present one. For an empathetic understanding of the present generation of Muslims one has to recognize that most of them do not accept Western critics' radical reinterpretations of some parts of Muslim history. Where there is a significant difference between most Muslims' views of some matter and the views of (mainly) Western academic critics I shall attempt to explain both. In fact, today many Muslims participate in the (Western) academic study of Islam and accept many of its critical views and methods, as noted later.

Apologetics

A distinction has to be made between empathetic understanding and apologetics. Apologetics is the effort to defend a particular view or position and recommend it to others, frequently by overstating the virtues of that position and understating its defects while doing the reverse with opposing positions. Often it proceeds by contrasting one side's ideal with the other side's reality. Christian apologists may contrast Christ's teachings of love and forgiveness with the violence of Muslim conquest while downplaying the violence in Christian history. Muslims may do the reverse. In fact, there has been a lot of apologetic writing among modern Muslims, as we shall see in the later chapters of this book. Apologetics has a legitimate place in religious life but is separate from religious studies. Empathetic understanding seeks to be much more balanced. Nevertheless, the critical study of apologetic writings can help us in our quest for empathy.

Two problematic pairs

Writings on Islam, including this one, commonly contrast "Islam" with the "West" (i.e. Europe, mainly Western Europe, and the societies deriving historically from them) and tradition with modernity. This language is unavoidable in my view but carries serious dangers. In the first place it suggests that all four of these are more monolithic and unchanging than is the case. Second, it tends to suggest a certain picture of history in which the West and Islam have mainly been in conflict and in which modernity, which is secular and derived from the West, is now displacing tradition, which is associated with Islam and with religion generally. This picture is simplistic at best and has been very much put into question by the events of recent decades, as we shall see. Third, it obscures the degree to which terms of each pair interpenetrate each other. The most traditional person is modern in some respects (e.g. use of technology) and the most modern (or post-modern!) person is conditioned by the tradition they come out of, often in ways they do not recognize. Islam and the West have not only interacted and influenced each other but today there are many who are both Muslim and Western. This could be said of many educated Muslims who have adopted Western ways of thinking and acting and even more of the many Muslims who live in the West, particularly those born in the West. Nevertheless, all four of these terms denote important realities and suitable replacements have not been found. So the reader is urged to bear these things in mind when these terms appear in this book.

From Orientalism to Islamic Studies

Until about the middle of the twentieth century or a bit later, those who engage in the academic study of Islam were usually called "Orientalists" and their discipline "Orientalism". In more recent years, and particularly since the publication of Edward Said's book, *Orientalism*, in 1978, this term has become associated with a kind of scholarship that focuses on the study of written texts, tends to treat Islam as if it were unchanging over time and unvarying from place to place, and often intentionally or unintentionally supports and justifies Western imperialism. Still, it has to be said that the Orientalists produced a vast quantity of valuable scholarship and today's scholars presume much of this accomplishment and stand very much on their shoulders.

Most scholars of Islam today seek to avoid or at least minimize the negative tendencies associated with Orientalism and call themselves "Islamicists" and their discipline "Islamic Studies", terms appropriate not only for scholars in Religious Studies but also those in other fields, such as History, Anthropology, Political Science and others, who focus primarily on some aspect of Islam. Most of them have sought a significant level of empathy with Islam and Muslims. The term "Islamicist" should be distinguished from "Islamist", which refers to one who calls for an Islam state and society, a position discussed in Part III. (See text box on "Tendentious terms" in chapter 15.)

An important recent development is the increasing number of Muslims who are participating in what has been Western Islamic Studies and accepting many or most of its critical views and methods. Their commitment and experience enriches the field and provides for a level of dialogue and mutual understanding that has not been possible in the past. This is another example of the interpenetration between Islam and the West and also between "tradition" and "modernity" since many have had "traditional" educations upon which they build.

The role of the media

Much of our information about Islam and Muslims inevitably comes from the media, whether newspapers and magazines, radio and television or the internet in its various forms. In and of itself this is not to be disparaged, since the media usually provide our first information about new developments and often about other aspects of Islam. Unfortunately, however, the media tend to sensationalize, oversimplify and play to existing prejudices in order to get and hold an audience. They often stress what is dramatic, violent, happening today and perceived as directly affecting us (whoever "us" may be in any situation). Historical, cultural and linguistic background sometimes appears but is likely to take second place.

An example can be found in the reporting of Muslim efforts to have the **Shari'a** recognized in Western countries. What tend to be emphasized are the harsh punishments and unequal treatment of women in traditional interpretations of the Shari'a. Rarely does one see much on the varying interpretations of the Shari'a or the complexities around the definition of Shari'a that are such as to raise questions as to what the recognition of the Shari'a in the West would mean.

In defense of the media it has to be said that they have to report what people are interested in if they are to stay in business and reporters often do not have much time to get the necessary background on breaking stories. Some media sources are more dependable than others and it is usually possible to find out which these are in any place. It is hoped that this book will help the readers to sort out the wheat from the chaff in media reports.

Issues of language and related matters

Challenges to understanding arise from the problems of translation. For example, one of the most important practices is called ***ṣalāh*** in Arabic (also written *salat*) and *namaz* in Persian, Urdu, etc. These words are usually translated "prayer" or "worship", but neither English word gives an adequate idea of what actually happens. In this case one has simply to learn what Muslims do and, if at all possible, use the Arabic or Persian term. In other cases an English term may be more or less adequate but is still likely to mislead. For example ***fiqh*** is often translated as "law" or " jurisprudence", but given the differences between the Islamic and Western legal traditions I prefer usually to use the Arabic word. Still another sort of problem is illustrated by the word "Islam" itself. I translate it as "submission" or "commitment". The former is the usual translation and linguistically the most accurate, but "submission" for most English speakers has a negative connotation, whereas for Muslims "Islam" never does. Therefore, I think "commitment" often comes closer to the force the word has for Muslims.

I shall therefore introduce and use the Arabic (or other Islamic language) words for the most important terms and encourage the reader to become familiar with them. With proper names I sometimes use the recognized Anglicized form, e.g. **Umayyad** (proper transliteration is Umawi), and sometimes use the Arabic form in preference to a recognized Anglicized form, e.g. Ibrahim for Abraham, Salah al-Din for Saladin, depending on my sense of the appropriate compromise between precision and familiarity.

Dates

With dates I opt for familiarity over precision and use Western dates almost exclusively rather than Muslim dates, although it is important for an understanding of Islam to have an awareness of its calendar. Appendix III contains information about the Islamic calendar. When appropriate, CE (Common Era) or BCE (Before the Common Era) will be used because they are a bit more ecumenical than AD (*Anno Domini*, The Year of the Lord) and BC (Before Christ). If a Muslim date is given it will be labeled *Hijri* or H.

An introductory overview of Islam

As has been suggested, there are almost as many Muslim views of Islam as there are Muslims. The following is one such view that might be given by an educated person with fairly good knowledge of the West. (It has been written by the author but shown for comment to several Muslims. Since it is putatively by a Muslim, it is in the first person, "we".) Although this is only one of many possible statements, and in particular presents a Sunni perspective (discussed in chapter 8), I believe it can serve as good starting point in the quest to understand Islam, but not an ending point.

Islam means submission or commitment to God and what this involves is stated in the words by which we witness to our faith, known as the *shahāda* or "Formula of Witness": "There is no god but God; Muhammad is the Messenger of God." The rest is commentary, but commentary is necessary.

God is the source and ruler of the universe and nature submits to Him. The stars in their galaxies, the sun and its planets, the mountains, the plains, the rivers and oceans, the plants and animals, large and small, all follow the courses of action He has laid out for them. In fact, the orderliness of nature is one of the most powerful evidences of the existence of one God. The main exception to this is human beings. Our bodies obey God as do other natural things, but when it comes to moral decisions we have the power to disobey God and we often do. In short, nature is always *muslim* (submitting to God) but humans have to choose to be so. God placed the first man and woman in a paradise, but they disobeyed and so he placed them here on earth, where life is a struggle. They expressed sorrow for their disobedience and God forgave them but they remained on earth where their descendants continue the moral struggle, to be rewarded or punished after death depending on their faith, their actions and God's grace.

How do we know what God wants us to do? In part we can discover this from the laws of nature and also from our human nature insofar as we are born with a God-given inclination to worship and obey Him (called *fiṭra*), though our lower impulses and our society draw us away from this to a greater or lesser degree. God has therefore also sent us prophets and messengers to inform and remind us of His will. The first messenger was the first man, Adam, and others have included Nūḥ (Noah), Ibrāhīm (Abraham), Mūsā (Moses), Dāwūd (David) and ʿĪsā (Jesus). These and many others brought messages from God to their societies. In all cases the core of the message was that there is no god but God, that no idols or natural forces or human rulers should be considered worthy of worship or complete obedience, which are due only to God, and that we should not give undue rein to our personal desires or to worldly success. In addition they brought specific moral and social rules that varied slightly due to differences among their societies. Some received scriptures from God for their people, such as the *Tawrā* (Torah) given to Moses, the *Zubūr* (Psalms) given to David and the *Injīl* (Gospel) given to Jesus. Their later followers, however, made changes in their teachings. Jesus, for example, was a messenger, but his followers made him into the son of God and part of a divine trinity, something that we reject.

Some six centuries after Jesus, God sent his final messenger to confirm the messages of the previous messengers and clarify points where disputes and misunderstanding had arisen. This was Muhammad, the son of Abdullah, who was born in the city of Mecca, in Arabia, in 570 CE and received his first revelation from God in 610. For the next thirteen years he preached God's message to a small group of followers in the face of increasing opposition and persecution from the Meccan leaders. In 622 he had the opportunity to move with most of his followers to another city, which we now know as Medina. This event is called the *Hijra* or "Emigration" and was the turning point in his efforts. In Medina he was able to create what amounted to an Islamic state in today's parlance. He could not avoid armed conflict with his Meccan opponents, whose forces were initially stronger than his, but after eight years of struggle he prevailed. He then received the Meccans into his community, forgiving even his most bitter opponents. He died two years later, in 632. Under his immediate successors the rest of Arabia accepted Islam.

Muslim armies then spread Muslim rule beyond Arabia until, within a century, it covered a large stretch of land from Spain in the west to what is now Pakistan in the east. These lands were now open to the preaching of Islam although their inhabitants were not compelled to become Muslims. Eventually, however, the attractions of Islam, including its pure monotheism and its concern for human brotherhood and social justice, led most to accept it. In time Islam spread further, mainly through peaceful activities of merchants and others, and an Islamic civilization developed with accomplishments in philosophy, science, art, architecture and social organization that made it one of the great civilizations of all time. Later Western accomplishments in philosophy and science have been built on foundations laid by Muslims.

For Muslims God's will, as well as other knowledge, is revealed through the Qur'an and the *Sunna* (teaching and example) of Muhammad. The Qur'an consists of the verbatim words of God, revealed gradually to Muhammad over the twenty-three years of his career, memorized by him and others and written down by scribes. God has preserved it from any modification. The *Sunna* consists of words and deeds of Muhammad, which were also recorded and somewhat later collected as we have them now. These are not direct revelation in the sense that the Qur'an is, but God protected Muhammad from error. The Qur'an and the *Sunna* are the basic sources for the Sharī'a, the law of God by which we are called to live.

Scholars have interpreted these sources in order to apply them to new situations and this interpretation is called *fiqh* (literally "understanding", more often translated as "law" or "jurisprudence"). We believe that God has guided these scholars though not to the same level as the Holy Qur'an and the *Sunna*. Islam is also concerned for the inner spiritual life and this has been expressed especially in the Ṣūfī movement, whose teachers provide guidance for individuals in their personal quest for God, as well as providing for certain social needs.

The central beliefs of Islam are belief in God, His angels, His scriptures, His messengers, the Last Day, when all will be raised from the dead and judged, and His determination of good and ill. The most important practices, or Pillars, of Islam are affirmation of the *shahāda*, *ṣalāh* (a structured form of prayer five times a day, often written *salat*), fasting in the month of Ramadan, giving *zakāh* (alms or poor tax, often written *zakat*), and performing the *Ḥajj* (pilgrimage to Mecca) at least once in one's lifetime if one is able. To this some would add *jihād*, striving in the path of God whether in war or in moral and spiritual struggle. *Jihād* is undoubtedly important but most do not include it among the Pillars.

Islamic practice is not limited to these, however. In fact, we believe that the Shari'a applies to all areas of life, whether worship, personal and family life, economics, politics and all forms of culture. We are called on to discover God's will and follow it in all areas of life and to do this, not only as individuals but also as societies.

Some speak of giving to Caesar what is Caesar's and to God what is God's, but in reality everything is God's. Therefore, politics is important to Islam. In fact, the major division between Muslims, that between Sunnis and Shi'is, began with political differences among Muhammad's followers. Although important differences continue between them, they generally agree on the most basic things. While the Shari'a guides all areas of life, it is not unduly restrictive because it takes account of human weaknesses and its interpretation is sufficiently flexible to deal with all situations. God in the Qur'an tells us that He has not made our religion hard for us.

Over the last two centuries Western domination and influence have resulted often in putting Western secular institutions and practices in the place of Islamic ones. Today there is an effort to re-Islamize society. For many this means establishing Islamic states, i.e. states governed according to the Shari'a, and also using Islamic banks, wearing Islamic clothing and other things. Others believe it is not necessary to go so far and believe many Western-derived practices are in accord with God's will. It is also worth noting that many Westerners have been attracted to Islam and find it meets their spiritual needs.

Ever since Adam and Ḥawwā (Eve) were expelled from paradise, human life has been a struggle. We hope for material success in this struggle, but the real success is to struggle in the way God wants us to. The person who calls us to *ṣalāh* says, " ... come to *ṣalāh*, come to success".

Key points

- The violence associated with Islam in the media in recent years does not represent most Muslims.
- Islam exists at three levels, personal commitment, religion as a system of beliefs and practices, culture and civilization.
- We do not here concern ourselves with whether Islam is true or what is the "true Islam".
- Our goal is at least empathetic, usually sympathetic, understanding of Islam and Muslims.
- Translations of key terms can be misleading, so we must consider carefully what is being said.
- Islam means submission or commitment to God and no worship of anything else.
- Muhammad was the last of a series of messengers from God. His scripture, the Qur'an, and his *Sunna* constitute the basic sources of authority for Muslim life.
- The Shari'a in principle applies to all areas of life, including politics.

Discussion questions

1. What would you say to someone who claims that Islam is a violent religion and cites various media reports?
2. Can we speak of an "essence" of Islam? If so, what might it be?
3. The Bible and the Qur'an are both scriptures. Would you assume that Muslims are keen to translate the Qur'an into as many languages as Christians have been with the Bible? (The answer will come in a later chapter, but see what you think now.)
4. "Islam is not a religion and Muhammad is not its founder" (G. Jensen, *Militant Islam*, London and Sydney: Pan Books, 1979, 17). What do you think?
5. On the basis of this chapter, what do you think will be the most interesting and the most difficult things in your efforts to understand Islam?

Critical thinking box 1.1

In an article about teaching the Bible in schools entitled "Religion Without Truth" Stanley Fish questions whether we can actually "bracket" the truth claims of religion given that these truth claims are central to religions such as Christianity, Judaism and Islam. "The secular project ... counsels respect for all religions and calls upon us to celebrate their diversity. But religion's truth claims don't want your respect. They want your belief and, finally, your soul. They are jealous claims. Thou shalt have no other God before me."

Does this represent a valid criticism of the position taken in this chapter's text?

For Fish's whole article see http://select.nytimes.com/2007/03/31/opinion/31fishs.html (accessed 5 September 2013).

Critical thinking box 1.2

Reread carefully the section on "An introductory overview of Islam" and ask yourself what questions this raises in your mind and/or in what ways this statement challenges your own personal beliefs.

Companion website

Includes some basic statistics and a brief but important quote on empathy.

Further reading

Al-Faruqi, Ismail R. (1979) *Islam*. Niles, IL: Argus Communications. (Basic introduction by a prominent Muslim scholar and leader in the United States.)

Haeri, Shaykh Fadhalla (1989) *Living Islam: East and West*. Shaftesbury, UK: Element Books in association with Zahra Publications. (By a contemporary spiritual leader. Moral and spiritual approach, organized topically.)

Haeri, Shaykh Fadlallah (2004) *The Thoughtful Guide to Islam*. Winchester and New York: O Books. (Historical approach. Also under the title *Elements of Islam*.)

Mahmud, Abdel Haleem (1978) *The Creed of Islam*. London: World of Islam Festival Trust. (Basic introduction by a leading traditional Egyptian scholar.)

Mawdudi (Maududi), Abul A'la (1960) *Towards Understanding Islam*. Lahore: Idara Tarjumanul-Quran. (By a leading Islamist, very readable.)

Martin, Richard C. (ed.) (1985 [2001]) *Approaches to Islam in Religious Studies*. Oxford: Oneworld. (Foreword and chapter 1 provide a critical history and survey of the field to the mid-1980s, with a brief updating in the Preface. Other chapters deal with particular aspects of the study of Islam and will be relevant to later chapters.)

Ernst, Carl and Martin, Richard (eds.) (2010) *Rethinking Islamic Studies: From Orientalism to Cosmopolitanism*. Columbia, SC: The University of South Carolina Press. (The Introduction provides a good discussion of the recent history and current state of the field, though a bit advanced for the beginner. Other chapters relate more to the later chapters of this book.)

Ernst, Carl (2004) *Following Muhammad: Rethinking Islam in the Contemporary World*. Edinburgh: Edinburgh University Press. (Chapters 1–2 deal with our approach to Islam; other chapters deal with the sources of Islam, ethics and spirituality.)

Online resources

Please refer to the electronic resources listed in the further reading section on pp. 405–6 and also the websites listed at the end of some chapters.

Part I

History of the community

2 *On the eve of Islam*

The Hellenistic–Iranian world

> The Greeks have been vanquished in a nearby land, but after defeat they will be victorious in a few years. Such is God's command both the first time and the second.
>
> (Qur'an 30:2–4a)

Historically Islam may be said to have had two major roots, one in central Arabia and the other in the lands surrounding it, from Iran to Greece to Egypt and Ethiopia, which we may call the Hellenistic–Iranian world. The first will be dealt with in the next chapter and the second in this one. The political face of the Hellenistic–Iranian world was relatively simple, with two major "superpowers". Its religious and cultural face, however, was extremely diverse with a multitude of religious groups, of which this chapter will describe the most important. It is difficult to present so many diverse groups in a few pages and the reader may find it confusing, but the very awareness of this diversity is a step toward understanding, and most of the groups described here will be mentioned in later chapters. While Islam represented a major break with this world in many ways, it represented a continuation of it in others.

In this chapter

- Two "superpowers"
- Religion in Iran
- Byzantine Christianity
- Other forms of Christianity
- Jews
- Philosophers and Gnostics
- The Axial Age

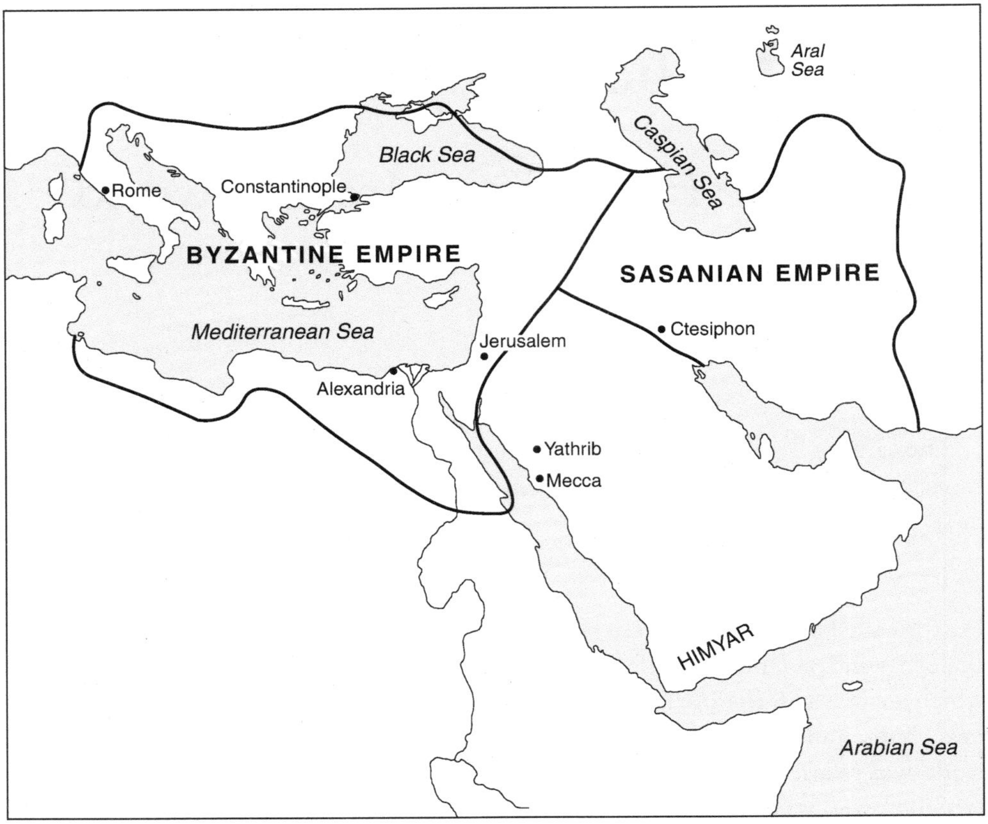

Map 1 The Hellenistic–Iranian world

Two "superpowers"

On the eve of Islam much of the land north and east of Arabia was divided between two large empires, the Sasanians and the Byzantines, two regional "superpowers", we might say. The Sasanians were Iranian in language and culture and the Byzantines were Greek, but both ruled over other ethnic groups also. These included Aramaic-speaking people in Iraq ruled by the Sasanians and Aramaic speakers in Syria (then including what is now Syria, Lebanon, Israel/Palestine and Jordan) and Coptic speakers in Egypt, ruled by the Byzantines. A third but lesser center of power was in Ethiopia.

The Sasanian Empire had been founded about 246 CE and was quite consciously heir to an Iranian imperial tradition going back to Cyrus the Great and the Achaemenid Empire (c. 550–331 BCE) and a cultural tradition going back much further. Iran had, however, known a period of Greek rule following the invasion of Alexander the Great (331 BCE) and had been subject to Greek cultural influence, against which the Sasanians were reacting. The Byzantine Empire was the eastern half of the Roman Empire, which had survived the collapse of the western half in the fifth century and would continue until the fifteenth century. Its beginning can be dated from the fourth century, when the capital of the Roman Empire was shifted from Rome to Constantinople and Christianity was first tolerated and then became the religion of state. The Sasanians and the Byzantines were in frequent conflict with each other and from 603 to 628 – during the Prophet Muhammad's lifetime (see Qur'an 30:2–4a, above) – they engaged in a particularly destructive war that weakened both empires in the face of the Muslim challenge that was shortly to come.

If the overall political configuration was fairly clear, the religious picture was extremely complex. Each of the empires had an official religion, which may be considered the "orthodoxy", but beside these was a host of other religions, philosophies, sects and movements, many of which were disaffected from the ruling power or at least not greatly committed to it. Many of them survived into Islamic times, some for centuries, and influenced Muslim culture and religion.

Religion in Iran: Zoroastrianism

The official religion of the Sasanians is known to us as Zoroastrianism, so named after the Iranian Prophet Zarathushtra (Greek, Zoroaster). It is also called Mazdaism or the "Good Religion". Zarathushtra had undertaken a major reform of traditional Iranian religion sometime before 1000 BCE. The early history of his religion is not well known but it is clear that the Achaemenid kings were Zoroastrians, although they tolerated other forms of worship and often supported the religions of the other peoples they ruled over. It was the Achaemenid Cyrus II ("the Great") who permitted the Jews to return to their land from exile in Babylon in 537 BCE. It was only under the Sasanians (c. 226–651 CE) that Zoroastrianism became fully the state religion, and they were rather less tolerant, although numbers of Jews lived peacefully for the most part under their rule and Christianity spread especially in Iraq, sometimes in the face of persecution.

In its developed form Zoroastrianism taught a cosmic dualism of good and evil. There were two primordial spirits, Ahura Mazda, "The Wise Lord", later known as Ormazd, and Angra Mainyu, "The Evil Spirit", later known as Ahriman. At the beginning of time Ormazd chose truth and goodness and Ahriman chose falsehood and evil. They have been and will be in conflict until the end of time. To assist him in the struggle Ormazd called into being a number of lesser deities or *yazatas* and created the world along with its inhabitants. Ahriman is assisted by spiritual beings called *daevas* or *divs*. The task of humans is to side with Ormazd and struggle for the good "in thought, word and deed", as it is commonly put. At the end of time a cosmic savior will herald the final victory of good over evil, the dead will be raised, the wicked annihilated and the righteous will enjoy eternal happiness in a transformed earth. These doctrines are to be found in the Avesta, the Zoroastrian scripture, part

Figure 2.1 Bas-relief representation of the Zoroastrian symbol known as *faravahar* on the Apadana (columned hall) built by the Achaemenids at Persepolis (later one of the Sasanian capitals). *Faravahar* is currently thought to refer to the *fravashi*, a guardian spirit (*yazata*) and also the eternal aspect of each person or thing, but may have earlier refered to the *khvarr* or even to Ohrmazd. © Alireza Firouzi/Alamy

of which goes back to Zarathustra, as well as in other later writings. This religion is in principle a universal religion but due to historical circumstances it became in effect an ethnic Iranian one. These Zoroastrian conceptions, however, contributed to Jewish, Christian and Muslim conceptions of a cosmic struggle between good and evil with angels, demons and a dramatic end of time.

The state plays an important and positive role in the cosmic struggle. The shah (king) is the symbol of Ormazd, who has bestowed part of His sovereignty on him and granted him the *khvarr* (a kind of divine effulgence or blessing). The prosperity of the people and even the wellbeing of nature depend on the character of the shah. Assisting and advising him is the priesthood, which was very strong during the Sasanian period. A well-known adage was that religion and government are twins, each depending on the other. Central to Zoroastrianism is a concern for purity and ritual, and particularly important is the cult of the sacred fire, since fire is believed to be the symbol of Ormazd and the purest element created by Him. Muslims and others have called Zoroastrians fire worshippers, but the Zoroastrians deny that they actually worship fire. The positive attitude toward both royalty and worldly life is illustrated by the following statement from a late text: "The principal characteristic of kings is pleasure ... pleasure is consonant with kingship provided it is rooted in greatness. Pleasure rooted in greatness does not pass away" (Zaehner, 1961, 299). Consistent with this was the considerable luxury and ceremonial that surrounded the shah and was to be continued by many Muslim rulers.

Over the four centuries following the Muslim conquest most Iranians became Muslims but a small community of Zoroastrians continues in Iran today and a larger one, called Parsis, in South Asia, especially Mumbai (Bombay).

Other Iranian religions

An influential Iranian "heresy" was Manicheism, founded by Mani (216–276 CE), who claimed to be a prophet and a successor to Zarathushtra, Buddha and Christ, whose true teachings he claimed to restore and complete, a claim similar to that to be made by Muhammad in relation to previous prophets. Like the Zoroastrians he taught a cosmic struggle between good and evil but unlike them he identified matter with evil. In a complex series of cosmic events sparks from the realm of light have become captive in material human bodies and can only escape through a strict asceticism, including celibacy and vegetarianism. Only the "elect" are capable of this but others can benefit by following a less rigorous regime and supporting the elect. Mani was favored and protected by one of the Sasanian shahs but was later put in prison at the instance of the chief priest and died there. His movement, however, continued for some centuries, spreading into Central Asia, where it was adopted by the Uigur rulers from 763 to 840, and even to China. It also spread into the Roman Empire, where it presented a significant intellectual challenge to Christianity. It was severely persecuted in most places and was seen as a dangerous challenge by Muslim authorities but lasted more than a thousand years.

Similar in some ways to Manicheism was the movement led by Mazdak, who taught a peaceful way of life and sought a fairer deal for the poor, including some redistribution of property. His detractors claimed that he wanted property, including women, held in common. He received support from the shah for a time, probably as a means of weakening the nobility, but in 528 he and many of his followers were killed. The movement survived underground into Islamic times and reappeared in the form of several radical religio-political movements, while for the ruling classes Mazdak's movement symbolized social disruption.

Byzantine Christianity

Christianity had begun in Palestine in the first century as a Jewish sect, made up of those who believed that Jesus of Nazareth was the Messiah (Christ in Greek), the hoped for king and savior of the Jews. He had been crucified but they believed he had been raised from the dead, taken up into heaven, and would return to establish the reign of God. While the first Christians were Jews, the movement soon attracted gentile (non-Jewish) converts and became a predominantly gentile movement. It spread rapidly through the Roman Empire and beyond and attracted sporadic persecution. In the fourth century, however, the emperors made it the official religion, as mentioned earlier. The Patriarch of Constantinople became head of the Byzantine church and in the eleventh century formally separated from the Western Church, headed by the Pope in Rome. (We now speak of three main divisions of Christianity: Eastern Orthodoxy, Roman Catholicism and Protestantism, the latter two being forms of Western Christianity.)

Christian theology developed amidst considerable controversy using Greek and Latin categories of thinking, which were significantly different from the Semitic categories of the Jews. The three most important doctrines developed were those of the trinity, incarnation and atonement. According to the first two in their "orthodox" formulations, God is three "persons", Father, Son and Holy Spirit, in one godhead and the man Jesus was the Son present in human flesh. According to the doctrine of the atonement, Jesus' death and resurrection have opened the way for humans to be saved from the power of sin and death and to receive eternal life, but this was not as clearly defined doctrinally as the others. Islam was to very consciously reject all of these.

The doctrines and rules of the official church were worked out in seven "ecumenical" councils, between 325 and 787. Especially important were those of Nicaea (325) and Chalcedon (451). At the first council it was affirmed that the Son and the Holy Spirit are fully part of the Godhead, over against the Arians, who said that Christ was the highest of God's creations but not divine. At the other it was affirmed that Christ is fully human and fully divine, the two natures being inseparably united, over against the Nestorians, who seemed to want to separate the natures, and the Monophysites ("one nature-ists"), who believed that the human nature of Christ was transformed and absorbed into the divine nature. (We will see analogues to these debates in Muslim theology, in chapter 11.)

The Eastern Church has a strong sense of the mystery of the divine and its sacramental presence in the material world, of the importance of the Christian community as a community both in worship and in worldly life, and of Christ as the Risen Lord and ruler of the cosmos (by contrast, Western churches give more emphasis to the crucified Christ). These characteristics are reflected in the Eastern liturgy and church buildings. The church is divided by a partition called the *iconostasis,* so called because icons are placed on it. Behind it is the altar where the priests perform the sacramental actions by which the bread and wine become the body and blood of Christ. The sense of mystery is enhanced by the fact that most of the sacramental action is performed out of the sight of the laity. The differing actions of the clergy and laity are seen as complementing each other and forming an orchestra of worship to God. Most churches have a dome, which symbolizes heaven,

Figure 2.2 Byzantine coin with head of Christ, probably from the tenth or eleventh century. The image of Christ is partly derived from the icon of Christ as *Pantokrator*, an image familiar to the people. The reverse (not available for this coin) may have a cross and the statement "Jesus Christ, King of Kings". The coin reflects both piety and propaganda. Courtesy of Shutterstock

and at the top of the dome, looking down on the people, is the figure of *Christos Pantokrator*, Christ the ruler of all. Of major importance are icons, which are pictures of Christ, his mother or saints, and are painted according to a traditional format. They are powerful symbols and are described as "windows on eternity". An effort was made to eliminate them during the "Iconoclastic Controversy", in the eighth to ninth centuries, an effort partly stimulated by the presence of Islam, which tends to reject such images. It failed, however, because of their popularity.

After it became Christian, the empire came to be seen as an icon or image of the Heavenly Jerusalem and the emperor an icon on earth of God's rule in heaven. Church and state were distinct but not separate and the Emperor played an important role in the church though he could not dictate its teachings. One notes here a similarity, at least in general terms, to the situation in the Sasanian Empire, though state and "church" were more closely linked in the latter case. This close relation between state and what we may call "orthodox" religion was to continue under Islam.

Monasticism was also an important aspect of church life. Those who wished to devote themselves fully to contemplation and prayer renounced normal life to become either hermits or monks living in a community. Monasticism began in Egypt in the fourth century and became widespread. It is sometimes described as a form of martyrdom, replacing the martyrdom of blood of the age of persecution. Monasticism suggests that in its attitude toward the material world Christianity stood in between the world-affirming stance of Zoroastrianism and the world-rejection of Manicheism. Monasticism was to be rejected by Islam, although ascetic practices were to be important for some Muslims.

The Byzantine Church was culturally Greek. Though its followers in Syria generally spoke Syriac (a form of Aramaic), and later spoke Arabic, they were ministered to by a Greek-speaking clergy. They came to be known as Melkites (from the word for "king", i.e. following the emperor's religion). When in time Orthodox Christianity spread beyond the empire to eastern Europe, however, it organized itself along national and ethnic lines, as the Russian Orthodox Church, Serbian Orthodox Church and so on. These were united with the Byzantine Church in doctrine and worship but were self-governing. They used their own national language and provided an important element of the national identity. Those under Islamic rule constituted autonomous communities (later called ***millets***) often governed by their patriarchs and bishops.

Other forms of Christianity

Those whose views were rejected at the councils did not simply recant or pass out of existence, but constituted strong movements for some centuries. While the term "orthodox" tends to be used for the religions recognized by the state or dominant in some other way, the groups discussed next consider themselves no less orthodox in the generic sense (i.e. rightly believing and worshipping).

The Nestorians, or the "Church of the East" as they call themselves, were forced out of Byzantine territory after the Council of Chalcedon but the churches under Sasanian rule accepted the Nestorian creed; the Nestorian church would prosper for many centuries under Muslim rule and Nestorians would make significant contributions to Islamic civilization. It also spread northeastward into Central Asia and for a brief period into China. It gained many adherents among the Mongols, who invaded the Muslim lands in the thirteenth century. After the Mongol ruler converted to Islam at the end of that century, however, the Nestorians lost ground and after the invasion of Timur (d. 1405) they were reduced to a small minority. Today they call themselves Assyrians and are found in Iran and, at least until recently, in Iraq, as well as in immigrant populations throughout the world.

There were, and are, several Monophysite churches. The Church of Armenia, which was independent of Byzantium and the Sasanids and had become Christian even before Rome, was Monophysite. Also Monophysite was the Coptic Church in Egypt, to which virtually all the native population adhered. Among other things it was noted for a strong monastic tradition. This church was to diminish under Muslim rule but still represents today about 10 percent of the Egyptian population. Coptic Christianity spread south to Ethiopia, whose Christian ruler was to play a role in Muhammad's career, and where it is still the official religion. A third Monophysite church was the Jacobite Church, to which a large proportion of the population of Syria adhered. This church continued strong until it suffered successively from the Crusades and the activities of the Mongols and Timur.

Another distinct group were the Maronites of the Lebanese mountains, who look back to a fifth-century saint, St. Maron, and developed as a church in the seventh century. They later assisted the Crusaders and had contact with Rome from the fifteenth century, eventually accepting Roman Catholicism. Today they play an important role in Lebanese politics.

In practice, cultural and ethnic differences were no less important than theological differences. The Armenian and Coptic churches used their native languages and have been major bearers of their respective national identities, while the Nestorian, Jacobite and Maronite churches used the Syriac language and represented a Semitic culture, in contrast to the Greek culture of Byzantium. They enshrined a political and cultural challenge to the Byzantine Empire, which was probably the main reason why they suffered persecution from time to time, a persecution that was particularly intense on the eve of the Muslim conquest.

Jews

While some Jews, as mentioned earlier, followed Jesus as Messiah, most did not but continued the main lines of Jewish belief and practice with some significant developments. They looked back to Abraham (c. 1700 BCE?) as their "father" and Moses (c. 1300 BCE) as their greatest prophet and teacher, who led them out of slavery in Egypt and mediated a special covenant with God. They also looked back to a period of independence in the Land of Israel (geographically today Israel/Palestine) and of greatness under Kings David and Solomon (c. 1000?–931 BCE). This period of independence ended, however, after they were defeated and exiled, some by the Assyrians in 721 BCE and others by the Babylonians in 587 BCE. Some of them returned after Cyrus II of Iran conquered Babylonia but they lived under foreign empires, Iranian, Greek and Roman–Byzantine except for a brief period (Maccabees, c. 169–63 BCE). Their temple to God was destroyed by the Babylonians in 587 BCE, rebuilt and then destroyed again by the Romans in 70 CE during a revolt (66–73 CE). This rebellion and another (132–35 CE), along with the later Christianization of the empire, led to the decline of the community in the Land. Even before then most Jews lived outside of the Land of Israel in diaspora (dispersion) and by the sixth century Jewish cultural and religious leadership had passed to the diaspora, particularly to the community in Babylonia (Iraq).

Most came to accept that these catastrophes were punishments from God because they had violated the covenant and disobeyed God in various ways. Prior to their failed revolts many Jews believed that God would support an uprising to restore their control of their Land, or that God would intervene in human history in a dramatic, apocalyptic way. Apocalyptic thinking continued after this in some Jewish and Christian circles (and has also been present among Muslims), but most Jews came to accept that God intended most of them to live in exile for an indeterminate period and that the coming of the messiah and their return to the Land could be furthered mainly by faithful practice of Torah. Since the other main link to God, the sacrifices of the Temple, had ended, Torah became the centerpiece of Jewish religion.

Torah refers in one usage to the first five books of the Bible, those believed to have been revealed to Moses, but in a broader sense it refers to all authoritative religious teaching, particularly the moral and ritual rules for living, as developed and elaborated by the Rabbis. The two most authoritative compendia of Rabbinic teaching are the Mishna, compiled about 200 CE, and the Talmud, compiled in two versions from the fifth to seventh centuries. These interpret and complement the Bible (consisting for Jews of the Torah, in the first meaning mentioned earlier, and two other collections, the Prophets and the Writings, called the "Old Testament" by Christians). The Babylonian Talmud is the more important one. The Mishna and Talmud are to the Bible, in many respects, what the New Testament is to the "Old Testament" for Christians. This emphasis on Torah predominated until the nineteenth century, and gave Jews a moral basis for living under the rule of others. The Muslim conquests simply meant a change of masters and, on the whole, a change for the better. Since the nineteenth century various modern movements, particularly Zionism, the movement to regain the Land, have shifted the focus for most Jews.

Philosophers and Gnostics

Related in one way or another to most of the movements discussed so far was the tradition of Greek philosophy. It flowered in the fifth and fourth centuries BCE with Socrates (d. 399), Plato (d. 347) and Aristotle (d. 322), the best known figures. Socrates was its martyr, who chose to die rather than recant views that offended the populace. He believed that all knowledge is innate within us and can be elicited by proper questioning, hence the "Socratic method". Plato was his defender and apologist. Among other things, Plato held that the physical world consists of imperfect copies of "ideas" or "forms" that exist in a higher realm. The soul is immortal and before its descent into the body it contemplated the forms. Through intellectual discipline it can perceive them again. Plato's idea of the immortality of the soul became part of Christian thinking about the future life, and eventually, though to a lesser degree, Jewish and Muslim thinking. It sat somewhat uneasily beside the alternative conception, the resurrection of the body. Aristotle, who was the tutor of Alexander the Great, focused on the empirical world but found that it depended on a perfect God, who is "thought thinking itself" and who does not intervene in the world directly but motivates it by its attraction to him. These philosophers also had important ethical, social and scientific ideas. In fact Greek philosophy dealt with most of the areas, e.g. physics, that we assign to science today. Generally these philosophers continued to participate in the worship of the many Greek gods, viewing this worship as good for society and the gods as lesser beings than the intellectual realities with which they concerned themselves or as symbols of these realities. For them there was a clear distinction between philosophy and religion.

In time the tradition spread beyond the Greeks (though largely done in Greek or Latin) and took on a more religious character. Among the later philosophers the most famous was Plotinus (205–c. 270 CE), whose views are known as neo-Platonism. According to him the universe emanates from "The One", which is transcendent and even beyond being, but also present within it. Emanation is illustrated by a comparison with the sun and its rays. The human goal is to realize one's unity with The One by turning away from the material world, which is conceived not as evil but as imperfect. Evil is non-being; everything insofar as it exists is good. Some of the early Christians rejected philosophy but others sought to use it in the service of the faith, and neo-Platonism made a major contribution to Christian theology. After the empire became Christian the pagan tradition of philosophy diminished and finally ended in the empire after the school at Athens was closed by the emperor in 529. Nestorians, however, continued the tradition in Sasanian territory and it was established in Baghdad under Muslim patronage in the ninth century and then continued by Muslims (see chapter 11). Some Jews took an interest in philosophy in ancient times, such as Philo of Alexandria, but most Jews turned away from it after the disasters of the first and second centuries. Later, under Islam, a significant philosophical tradition would develop among Jews, with Maimonides as its leading figure, and Jews would play an important role in transferring philosophical knowledge to Western Christians.

There were also, from the second century CE, a number of movements that we call Gnostic, drawing to some extent on philosophical ideas or images, some identifying themselves as Christian and some not. These movements were quite diverse, but commonly they believed that salvation was possible only through esoteric knowledge (*gnosis*) imparted by a teacher to initiates. This *gnosis* was usually knowledge of one's true self, which had fallen from the highest spiritual realm and become trapped in the world of matter.

The explanations of how *gnosis* was attained were very complex. Often it was believed that a messenger or savior had come from the highest realm to bring *gnosis* to humans. Christian Gnostics identified this figure with Christ and sometimes held that Christ did not have a physical body or did not actually die on the cross, but merely appeared to do so, a view known as docetism (from a Greek word meaning "to appear").

In Gnostic movements Christian ideas are often inverted. For example, the God of the Old Testament is said to be an imperfect or evil being who created this imperfect world, while only the God of the New Testament is the true God. The serpent in the Garden of Eden may be seen as offering true wisdom rather than deceptive claims. There are Gnostic gospels, such as the Gospel of Thomas, which give their version of the life and teachings of Christ. Manicheism is commonly considered a form of Gnosticism although its dualism is more complete than most of the others. A non-Christian Gnostic movement that has survived, just barely, to the present day in Iraq is that of the Mandeans, who are sometimes identified with the Sabeans mentioned in the Qur'an (2:62; 5:69). Most Gnostic groups were esoteric, limiting knowledge of their teachings to inner elite, and partly for this reason they probably had relatively little direct political impact. As far as we know, most Gnostic groups had died out by 600 CE, but their ideas have had some influence on later Jewish, Christian and Muslim thinking.

The Axial Age

The concept of an "Abrahamic religion" is often used these days to indicate the common heritage of Judaism, Christianity and Islam, since all of them look back to Abraham (Ibrahim in Arabic) as a seminal figure. For our purposes here, however, what some scholars call the "Axial Age" is more illuminating, since all of the movements described in this chapter can be seen as products of it. It can help us to situate them in relation to the rest of the world and to Islam.

The Axial Age is the period from about 800 to 200 BCE when radical changes in human thinking began to take place along similar lines but apparently independently in Greece, Israel, Iran, India and China. The most important of these changes was the conviction that behind the multiplicity of the world there is one ultimate reality, whether conceived personally as God or more impersonally as a force or principle, and this reality radically transcends the world. Under the old polytheism gods, humans, animals and other beings functioned within the same worldly system. Gods, for example, were nourished by the ritual sacrifices made by humans, who in turn depended on the gods for help. The one God or the ultimate force is the source of the universe but is not part of it and does not need sacrifice in this way. The gods are demoted to the status of (or replaced by) subordinate deities or angels, or are converted into demons, or are deemed not to exist. Where a personal God is involved, the new thinking tends to be intolerant of any other worship. In general there is a heightened sense of a cosmic struggle between good and evil, darkness and light.

Since the transcendent power is one, religious systems relating to it are in principle universal, not limited to a particular tribe or nation. In practice this was often not fully realized in the "post-Axial" religions, since, as we have seen, Zoroastrianism, Judaism and, to a lesser degree, Christianity remained ethnic in practice. Greek philosophy in its later phase transcended ethnicity but was limited to the educated classes. The individual becomes more important since the individual can in some way relate directly to Ultimate Reality and will meet his or her final destiny as an individual. Because of the greater gap between the divine and the human there is often a sense of alienation, reflected in the Christian sense of sin, the Jewish idea of exile and Gnostic ideas of a primordial fall, and need is felt for a mediator, such as Christ for Christians, Torah for Jews and a redeemer for Gnostics.

These various changes at first were largely limited to a spiritual or cultural elite but over time they spread outward geographically and down the social scale. Christianity, Zoroastrianism and Judaism, and to some extent Gnosticism, represent the extension and popularization, and often the reformulation, of Axial Age thinking, inevitably with some compromises with earlier thinking and practice.

One place that Axial Age thinking may not have reached in a very significant way by this time was the Arabian peninsula, particularly central Arabia. In the next chapter we will observe a shift from pre-Axial to Axial Age thinking there and what can be considered the last major reformulation of Axial Age thinking.

Key points

- There were two major imperial powers in the Hellenistic–Iranian world on the eve of Islam, the Sasanians and the Byzantines.
- In both of these religion and the state were closely connected. Orthodoxy basically meant following the state religion.
- There were a large number of religions, sects and movements other than the state religions, some of which represented a rejection of the existing order.
- In contrast to the earlier paganism, most of these religions and movements, orthodox or otherwise, believed that the universe has its source in a single, transcendent God or Principle, were at least potentially trans-ethnic, and gave greater prominence to the individual.

Discussion questions

1. In what ways were the Sasanian and Byzantine Empires similar to each other and in what ways different?
2. One might say that "orthodox" groups are generally the ones that "won out" in past doctrinal and political struggles. Would you agree? Among which groups did "orthodoxies" develop in the period covered by this chapter?
3. Which of the religions described in this chapter might be said to reject the existing social or political order. Did it matter?
4. How does each of the religions or movements described in this chapter fit or not fit the description of the Axial Age?
5. It could be argued that Muslims and Westerners (including secularists) are all the spiritual heirs of Zarathushtra. What do you think?
6. Can the situation as presented in this chapter be seen as preparing the way for Islam? How?

Critical thinking box 2.1

Consider the relationship between religion and political institutions advocated (explicitly or implicitly) by each of the groups or movements described in this chapter. In what ways are they similar and in what ways different? Can you place them on a scale of types? Are there any that seek a separation between religion and politics?

Companion website

Includes information, readings and weblinks for most of the groups discussed in the chapter and some others, as well as material on the Axial Age.

Further reading

Rose, Jenny (2011) *Zoroastrianism: An Introduction* (*I.B. Tauris Introductions to Religion*). London: I.B. Tauris. (A fairly detailed discussion of the beliefs, practices and development of the religion, structured historically. Chapter 4 gives a good account of the Sasanian period.)

Nigosian, S.A. (1993) *The Zoroastrian Faith: Tradition and Modern Research*. Montreal, etc.: McGill-Queens University Press. (A clearly written account of Zoroastrian history, scriptures, beliefs and observances organized topically.)

Yarshater, Ehsan (ed.) (1983) *Cambridge History of Iran*, vol. III/2. Cambridge: Cambridge University Press, see chapter 23, "Zoroastrian Religion" (by J. Duchesne-Guilleman), chapter 24, "Jews in Iran" (by J. Neusner), chapter 25, "Christians in Iran" (J.P. Asmussen), chapter 27a, "Manichaeism" (G. Widengren), chapter 27b, "Mazdakism" (by Ehsan Yarshater). (Generally very scholarly and thorough; detail is sometimes confusing, especially in chapter 23.)

MacCulloch, Diarmaid (2009) *A History of Christianity: The First Three Thousand Years*. London; New York: Allen Lane. (A massive volume; chapters 6–8 will provide helpful background to this chapter, especially on political and ecclesiastical matters.)

Atiya, A.S. (1968) *A History of Eastern Christianity*. London: Methuen (Reasonably informative study of the various churches; does not include the Greek Orthodox Church).

Ware, Timothy (1997) *The Orthodox Church*. Harmondsworth: Penguin. (Well-written study of the doctrine and history of orthodoxy. First published in 1963.)

Brown, Peter (1971) *The World of Late Antiquity*. London: Thames and Hudson. (Evocative and insightful study; presumes some prior knowledge; see especially chapters XIII, XV, XVI.)

3 *The beginnings of Islam*

Muslim history to about 700 CE

When God's help and victory come, and you see the people entering the religion of God in droves, then sing the praises of your Lord, and seek his forgiveness.

(Qur'an 110:1–3a)

An observer about 600 CE would probably have predicted that in due time Arabia would become Christian or Zoroastrian or, less likely, Jewish. He or she would hardly have predicted what actually happened, that the Arabs would develop their own form of post-Axial religion. This chapter seeks to present the pre-Islamic period in Arabia, the career of the Prophet Muhammad, and the initial spread of Islam into the Iranian and Hellenistic world as something of a unit. For the critical historian most of this period is problematic; what is presented here is an imperfect consensus about what happened or probably happened. More radical views are discussed at the end of the chapter.

In this chapter

- The Arabs before Islam
- The career of the Prophet Muhammad
- Conflict and conquest after Muhammad
- Some scholarly reservations

The Arabs before Islam

The Arabian peninsula lay on the periphery of the lands ruled by the **Byzantines** and the **Sasanians**, not part of them but not uninfluenced by them. Both empires sought to control the border tribes of northern Arabia and in the sixth and early seventh centuries the kingdoms of the Ghassanids and the Lakhmids served as buffer states for the Byzantines and the Sasanians respectively. They were Christian in religion, Monophysite in the first case and Nestorian in the second.

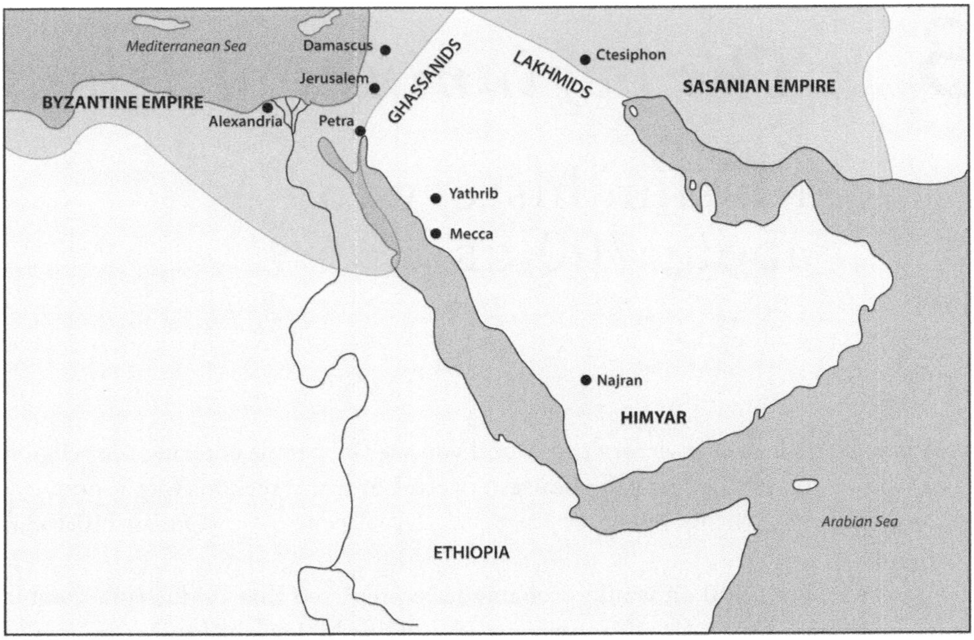

Map 2 Arabia before Islam

In earlier centuries the Nabateans, of Arab origin but Aramaic and Greco-Roman in culture, had created a sophisticated kingdom (c. 200 BCE–200 CE) in the north with Petra, the rock hewn city, as it capital.

South Arabia, present-day Yemen, was the site of a significant civilization from about 1000 BCE but by the sixth century CE it was in decline and subject to intervention by the Ethiopians and the Persians. In the fourth century Monophysite Christianity had established itself at Najran and in the early sixth century these Christians were persecuted by the king of Himyar, in south Arabia, who had Persian support and had accepted Judaism, an event possibly referred to in the Qur'an (85:4–9). About 525 the Ethiopians invaded the area, while the Persians controlled it from about 575 to 631.

In central Arabia were tribes, mostly nomadic but many living in agricultural settlements or trading towns. Prominent among the latter was **Mecca**, which was settled by the **Quraysh** tribe about 500 CE and became prosperous through the caravan trade.

These Arabs worshipped spirits associated with natural features such as stones and trees, and possibly stars, but this worship was highly pragmatic and contingent upon the spirits delivering what was asked for. There were also *jinn* (called "genies" by Westerners), invisible beings that could help or harm humans, that could possess a person and make him crazy (*majnūn, jinn* possessed), or could inspire a soothsayer (*kāhin*) or a poet. They also recognized higher gods, usually connected with particular tribes, and distantly in the background, rarely invoked, was the creator god, Allah. The Quraysh believed that Allah had three daughters, who could be called on to intercede with him. There were sanctuaries used by several tribes, of which the most important was at Mecca, a pilgrimage site that, according to tradition, had been founded centuries earlier by Ibrahim (Abraham) and his son Isma'il (Ishmael). It included a building known as the *Ka'ba*, which is said to have housed 300 idols and had a black stone set in the wall at one corner that was believed to have come from heaven.

The Arabs' ethical values were not closely related to these spirits and gods, but rather to the tribe, which was the primary focus of loyalty and identity and usually the only source of security in a difficult environment. Each tribe's way of life, or *sunna*, was laid down by tradition and exemplified in the poetic accounts of the exploits of its past heroes. The most important values were generosity (the word *karīm* means both noble and generous), courage, fortitude and loyalty. There was no belief in personal immortality; immortality consisted in being part of a tribe that continued after one's death. There were, however, just before Muhammad's time, people known as *ḥanīfs*, who appear to have been religious seekers, monotheists but not part of a religious community.

Tribal members were roughly equal economically though some families had more prestige. The tribal leader, or *shaykh*, would come from a leading family but had to be acceptable to the tribe as a whole and ruled largely by consensus. His successor would usually be chosen from his family but would not necessarily be his eldest son. Since the tribe was the highest loyalty, a kind of anarchy reigned among tribes (in some ways like international relations today!). They frequently raided each other for plunder but usually took few lives. This state of anarchy was tempered by traditions of hospitality to outsiders and by the law of blood revenge, according to which if a person was killed or injured by members of another tribe, any member of that tribe could be killed or injured in retribution. A similar rule applied between families within a tribe. Gender relations varied. Unwanted girl babies might be killed and wives might be inherited as part of their husbands' estates, but some women clearly had considerable independence and power, not least Muhammad's first wife. The primary literary expression was poetry, which developed into a very fine art and also served as a means of propaganda for individuals and tribes.

This period came to be called the ***jāhiliyya***, conventionally translated as "Age of Ignorance", but the word also implies wild or excessive behavior. This could be excess in fighting, or in seeking revenge, or in drinking wine, or in violating sexual rules, or even in generosity. The story is told of Hatim al-Tayyi who made a name for himself by giving away all of his father's camels to provide hospitality for visitors. Another, Imru al-Qays, is pictured as a hard drinking vagabond, adventurer and womanizer. When his father was killed, he first caroused for seven days, saying, "wine today, business tomorrow" (Nicholson, 1969, 105). Then he swore to eat no meat, drink no wine and touch no woman until he had accomplished his vengeance. Even when an oracle forbade him to act, this did not deter him. He had many adventures in his effort but little success. Eventually he found his way to the Byzantine court, where he was killed for seducing the emperor's daughter. Such stories may be more legend than history, but they illustrate the idea of *jahl*, excessiveness. *Jahl* could be positive and even necessary at times but needed to be counterbalanced by *ḥilm*, self control. A poet sang: "Although I be in need of *ḥilm*, of *jahl* I am at times in greater need" (Stetkevych, 1996, 8). In Islamic times *jahl* and *jahiliyya* came to be seen as purely negative, the opposite of Islam.

The career of the Prophet Muhammad

About 570 the Ethiopian governor of Yemen mounted an expedition against Mecca that came to grief, miraculously it is claimed (Qur'an 105 is said to refer to it). In this same year, according to the most widely accepted reports, Muhammad ibn (son of) Abdullah was born into the Hashemite clan of the Quraysh. His grandfather was at the time the custodian of the *Ka'ba*, but the clan was not as strong as it had been. Muhammad's father had died before he was born and his mother died when he was about six years old, so he was left an orphan in care of relatives, under the protection first of his grandfather and then of an uncle, Abu Talib. In this situation his basic needs were taken care of but his prospects were limited. Some scholars believe that commercial prosperity in Mecca was causing social strains and weakening tribal solidarity as the gap between the wealthy and the poor was increasing and the wealthy were less inclined to look after the poor than had been the case. Muhammad may have suffered from this. Later in life Muhammad is reported to have told his followers that he, like previous prophets, had looked after sheep when he was young. While still young he traveled to **Syria** in a trade caravan and along the way it is said that a Christian hermit stopped them and recognized that he would be a prophet. He gained a reputation for honesty and was known as *al-amīn* (the faithful one). It is said that once when the black stone fell out of the wall of the *Ka'ba* and the tribes could not agree on who should have the honor of replacing it, Muhammad solved the problem by putting the stone on a blanket and having a representative of each tribe take hold of the blanket and raise it to its position. Financial security came when Khadija, a wealthy widow engaged in the caravan trade, made him her agent and then married him. He was 25 years old at the time and she is said to have been 40. The marriage was a happy one and produced several children. He did not take a second wife while she lived though he took a number later (see Appendix V).

At some point Muhammad began to make periodic retreats for spiritual reflection in a cave near Mecca called Hira'. During one of these, possibly in the year 610, he had a vision in which an awesome figure appeared to him and commanded: "Recite in the name of your Lord Who created, created humans from a clot; recite, for your

Lord is the most generous, Who taught by the pen, taught humans what they did not know" (Qur'an 96:1–5). Unnerved by this and afraid he was becoming a poet or a *majnun*, he was reassured by Khadija and a Christian relative of hers that this was a genuine message from God brought by the angel Gabriel. After a time he received further messages and began to gather a small group of followers, the first being his wife, Khadija, others including his cousin **'Ali ibn (son of) Abi Talib** and his friend **Abu Bakr**. The first messages spoke of Allah's goodness and power but did not ban the worship of other deities. This ban came shortly, however, and provoked increasing opposition from the Meccan leaders. Muhammad was protected by his clan, even though the leader, his uncle Abu Talib, was not a believer in his message. Some of his followers, however, who did not have such protection, suffered for their faith and Muhammad, perhaps in 615, sent some of them to Ethiopia for a time, where the Christian ruler welcomed them. Soon after this, Muhammad's whole clan suffered considerably when it was boycotted for two years but nevertheless stood by him out of clan solidarity. Probably in 619 death took both Khadija and Abu Talib, whose successor as clan leader was not sympathetic to Muhammad. Thus he was suddenly deprived of major moral and material support. Soon after this, however, he experienced, possibly in a vision, a miraculous journey one night to Jerusalem (*isrā'*) and from there an ascent to heaven (*mi'rāj*), which consoled him spiritually and was to become important for Muslim devotional life (discussed further in chapter 6).

Muhammad now began to seek support outside Mecca. He went to the nearby town of al-Ta'if but was rejected by them and also by some other tribes he approached. Eventually he was approached by representatives from Yathrib, a city some 210 miles (338 kilometers) to the north of Mecca. Yathrib, a farming oasis, was divided by serious tribal conflict and after some negotiations Muhammad was invited to come as a mediator. In 622 most of his followers gradually left Mecca for Yathrib and in September Muhammad himself, along with Abu Bakr, made the move, just avoiding an effort by his enemies to kill him. This event is known as the *Hijra*, or Emigration, and is considered the most significant event of Muhammad's career, indeed, of human history. The year of the *Hijra* was to become Year One of the Muslim (*hijrī*) calendar. Yathrib was henceforth to be known as *Madīnat al-Nabī* (the City of the Prophet), or Medina, for short.

Muhammad went to Medina as mediator but over time became its effective ruler and formed a union of tribes called an *umma*, a new kind of entity that would become the Muslim community. Medina under his rule is commonly viewed today as the first Islamic state, i.e. the first polity to try to govern itself by God's laws. Those who came from Mecca were known as the Emigrants, *muhājirūn*, and their Medinan supporters as the Helpers, *anṣār*. There was also a party whose support was undependable, labeled the Hypocrites, *munāfiqūn*. Finally, although Muhammad had probably hoped for support from the Jews, they refused to recognize him as a prophet and the three main Jewish tribes came to oppose him.

Muhammad's position in Medina would not be tenable in the long term unless he could deal successfully with the Meccans, whose influence with the surrounding tribes was considerable. Also, the Emigrants had no means of support in Medina. So he planned raids against the Meccan caravans, a time-honored method in Arabia of gaining income by booty and weakening the enemy's prestige. The first efforts yielded little success but in 624 they undertook to raid a large caravan and when the caravan escaped they engaged with a contingent sent to protect it. This was the battle of Badr, in which they defeated a much larger Meccan force. This they ascribed to divine aid. According to the Qur'an, "You did not kill, but Allah killed them; you did not shoot when you shot, but Allah shot" (8:17). In Mecca the Muslims understood that God did not want them to respond to their enemies with violence, but in Medina they received different orders:

> Permission to fight is given to those against whom war is made, because they were wronged (surely God is able to help them), who were expelled from their homes for no cause, except that they say "Our Lord is God."
>
> (22:39–40)

There is reason to think that the Muslims in fact were averse to fighting, as suggested by the following passage from the Qur'an:

> Fighting is ordained for you, though you hate it; but you may hate a thing that is good for you and love a thing that is bad for you. It is God who knows, not you.
>
> (2:216)

While rooted historically and culturally in the old tradition of raiding, fighting is now raised to a higher ideological level; it is to be done mainly for God rather than booty or tribal honor.

The following year the Meccans returned for revenge and defeated the Muslims at the battle of Uhud, even wounding Muhammad, but failed to follow up on it. In 627 the Meccans again advanced on Medina but the Medinans dug a trench, it is said on the suggestion of a Persian convert, Salman al-Farisi, a tactic hitherto unknown in Arabia, and the Meccans were foiled. During this period Muhammad managed to eliminate the opposing Jewish tribes, who were considered a threat. Two were expelled, one after each of the first two battles. The third was accused of treachery in connection with the battle of the Trench and the men were killed while the women and children were enslaved. This treatment was harsh, but was in response to perceived treason in the midst of a life and death struggle. As such, it was not out of line with existing moral standards (the main issue for those involved seemed to have been whether loyalty to the *umma* should be put above loyalty to the clan protecting the Jews).

In 628 the Muslims sought to make a pilgrimage to Mecca but the Meccans refused to allow this. They agreed, however, in the treaty of Hudaybiyya, to allow the pilgrimage the following year and to make a ten-year truce. Muhammad and his followers duly made the pilgrimage and the truce allowed Muhammad to spread his message among the surrounding tribes and seek their allegiance, with the result that his following increased considerably. By 630 Muhammad's position had become so strong that, when an attack upon some of his allies allowed him to break the treaty, he marched on Mecca. The Meccans capitulated with almost no fighting in return for a general amnesty and the safety of their possessions, an outcome mediated by Abu Sufyan, one of the Meccan leaders and the father of one of Muhammad's wives. The leading Meccans soon swore allegiance to Muhammad and became at least nominal Muslims. This was followed by expeditions against opposing tribes and an expedition in the direction of Syria, while deputations came from surrounding tribes to profess allegiance. In March 632 Muhammad made what is called his "Farewell Pilgrimage to Mecca", and set the precedents for the conduct of future pilgrimages. From this

Figure 3.1 The attack on Medina, sixteenth-century manuscipt (H1223), Topkapi Palace Museum, Istanbul, Turkey. © Sonia Halliday Photographs/Alamy

time on non-Muslims were not allowed to make the Pilgrimage; it was strictly a Muslim affair. About this time, the following *sura* of the Qur'an was revealed:

> When God's help and victory come, and you see the people entering the religion of God in throngs, then sing the praises of your Lord and ask His forgiveness, for He is ever ready to forgive.
>
> (110)

Muhammad, however, was in poor health and he died in June of the same year. At this stage a number of the tribes of Arabia had professed Islam but not all.

As a result of Muhammad's career the Arabs passed from what I have called in the last chapter pre-Axial to post-Axial Age thinking, but in a new formulation both attuned to its original Arabian environment and capable of universal appeal. Allah, the remote high god of the previous period, was now recognized as fully transcendent but also directly involved with and in control of His creation. The individual related directly to Him, making *shahada*, a personal witness to his faith, and being personally responsible to Him on the Last Day. He was thus less immersed, morally and psychologically, in his tribal context. At the same time he was part of a potentially universal community, the *umma*, united in its allegiance to God, and he was at least in principle equal to all other members of the community. Mediating between humans and God, primarily to make God's will known, were the revelations that had come to Muhammad, the Qur'an, as well as the example of Muhammad's actions, his *Sunna*, and to some extent his person (see chapters 5 and 6). There were other mediating figures for some as we shall see in later chapters. Much from the Arabian environment was retained, usually in a modified form. For example, generosity was still a virtue, but not extreme generosity. Raiding for booty was transmuted into striving, *jihad*, in the path of God, and thus given a new purpose. (On *jihad* see the box in the next chapter.) Of course, the older tribal mentality did not die immediately, especially among the more nominal Muslims, but continued to influence events over the next century and beyond. From a secular point of view, one of the main reasons for Muhammad's success was the fact that the Arabs were at that point in time ready to make this transition. The other reason would be Muhammad's own visionary and leadership qualities. Though military victories were involved, military strength was hardly the main factor.

Conflict and conquest after Muhammad

Once the tribes were united and given a higher purpose their combined energy would be directed outward, to "open" (*fatḥ*) the lands beyond Arabia for their rule in the name of God (in Western parlance, to conquer them). But there were also issues of leadership to be sorted out.

According to the majority of Muslims and critical scholars, Muhammad did not appoint a successor. After his death, 'Umar ibn al-Khattab, an early convert and one of the leading figures in the *umma*, convinced the community to pledge allegiance to Abu Bakr, who is reported to have said, "Obey me so long as I obey Allah and His Messenger." Abu Bakr thus became the first caliph (*khalīfa*), or successor, of the Prophet, and also took the title *amīr al-mu'minīn* (commander of the faithful). He ruled for only two years (632–634) but during this time the rest of Arabia was brought into the Islamic fold. He also dealt successfully with two or three copy-cat prophetic movements that had arisen in Arabia and successfully fought certain tribes that refused to pay ***zakah*** (at this time a tax paid to the leader of the *umma*) after Muhammad's death since they viewed their allegiance as being to Muhammad personally, not to his successor. Abu Bakr considered this to be *ridda*, or apostacy, and compelled them to pay. In so doing he averted threats that could have disintegrated the *umma* right at the start.

Abu Bakr designated as his successor 'Umar, who ruled from 634 to 644. He is remembered by most Muslims as quite a strict and upright leader (some stories make him stricter than Muhammad). During his caliphate Muslim armies conquered Syria, Egypt and Iraq and moved into Iran. Key precedents were set for settling and taxing these lands. Thus a considerable proportion of Byzantine and Sasanian lands came under Muslim control and the Sasanian state was soon to disappear. 'Umar was assassinated by a Persian slave and, on his death bed, chose six men as a ***shūrā***, or consultative council, to choose one of their number to succeed him. The person chosen was 'Uthman ibn 'Affan, also an early convert but a member of the Umayyad clan, one of the leading Meccan clans most of whose members had accepted Islam only near the end of Muhammad's career. It was under 'Uthman that the Qur'an was compiled in its present form, according to the most generally accepted account. One reason for doing this was that variations in the text of the Qur'an had appeared and it was felt that such variations could lead to disunity in the *umma*. Conquests continued at a diminished rate under 'Uthman. 'Uthman was not able to resist the pressure of his Umayyad relatives for favors, or so it was perceived, and this led to increasing discontent and finally to a mutiny in 656 in which 'Uthman was killed.

This resulted in the first *fitna* or civil war (*fitna* means temptation or trial, and it has been suggested that this was seen as a trial from God to see if they would choose the right leadership). The people in Medina chose as caliph 'Ali ibn Abi Talib, the cousin of the Prophet and the husband of his daughter, Fatima. Many of 'Ali's supporters, in fact, claimed that Muhammad had designated him as his successor, but that the first three caliphs had usurped his position and he had acquiesced for the sake of the unity of the *umma*. Others, however, including 'A'isha, the Prophet's youngest and favorite wife, demanded that 'Ali punish 'Uthman's killers, something he was unable to do. 'A'isha gained the support of two of Muhammad's close associates, Talha and Zubayr, who fought 'Ali at the Battle of the Camel (named after the camel on which 'A'isha was seated, watching the battle) but were defeated. Meanwhile, the governor of Syria, Mu'āwiya, who was a member of the Umayyad clan like 'Uthman and also a son of Abu Sufyan, a leader of the former Meccan opposition to Muhammad, took up the call for vengeance for 'Uthman and refused to recognize 'Ali as caliph. His army met in battle with 'Ali's at Siffin in 657. The fighting was inconclusive (or according to some sources 'Ali's side was winning) and Mu'awiya's side raised copies of the Qur'an on their spears and called for arbitration, which 'Ali was forced to accept but which did not, finally, produce a satisfactory conclusion. Meanwhile, some objected to the arbitration on religious grounds and rebelled against 'Ali. They came to be known as Khārijīs, seceders or rebels. He defeated them in battle but in 661 one of them assassinated him. In later times 'Ali has often been viewed as the model of a chivalrous and idealistic figure (and more than this by his partisans, the **Shi'is**, as we shall see) while Mu'awiya has been viewed as the shrewd and practical politician.

After 'Ali's death, Mu'awiya was able to gain recognition as ruler of the whole *umma*. Al-Hasan, 'Ali's eldest son, had made claims but was, in effect, bought off. Mu'awiya was the first of the Umayyad dynasty, which lasted until 750. He was an effective leader, who strengthened the power and finances of the central government and under whom conquests continued in northwestern Iran and in North Africa (the Maghreb). He is said to have styled himself *khalīfat allāh* (the deputy of God) but his power largely rested on more mundane things: a loyal army in Syria, his ability to symbolize the unity of the *umma*, so desired after the excesses of the *fitna*, and his style of governing, much like that of the old Arab *shaykh*, conciliating tribal and other interests where possible. The old tribal mentality and tribal loyalties continued to condition politics to a considerable degree. Nevertheless, in order to run a large empire, Mu'awiya and his successors had to override tribal independence in ways that seemed quite oppressive by the older standards. Moreover, during his lifetime Mu'awiya insisted on having his son, Yazid, recognized as his successor. Undoubtedly he saw this as necessary to guarantee the harmony of the *umma*, but he has been criticized, then and since, for turning the caliphate into a hereditary monarchy. Indeed, for the pious, the Umayyads represented a cruel irony, for with them there had come to power the descendants of the very people who had so bitterly opposed Muhammad. Still, these were probably the only ones who had the skills and connections to run the empire that the Muslim realms had become.

As we shall see in later chapters, out of these events arose the main sectarian divisions of Islam. Those who accepted the way things had developed and did not oppose the Umayyads were to become the Sunnis, the majority group. Those who rejected the Umayyads out of allegiance to 'Ali and his family were to become the Shi'is. The Khārijīs were to form a third division, much smaller in number.

Mu'awiya's son, Yazid has had a bad press, viewed by Shi'is in particular as grossly dissolute and oppressive, though others describe him as skilled and capable. His brief reign saw the beginning of the second *fitna*. Husayn, the second son of 'Ali, revolted against him and was slaughtered with a small group of followers at Karbala' in Iraq in 680. This was to become a major event in the minds of the Shi'is. Soon afterward there was a movement to avenge his death among some of his followers who repented for not being with him at Karbala', but this came to nothing. It was followed by a "populist" revolt by a Shi'i leader, Mukhtar, in the name of another of 'Ali's sons, Ibn al-Hanafiyya. Khariji groups were also active in Iran and Arabia. The most serious threat, however, was the revolt based in Mecca and Medina in 681 under Ibn Zubayr, whose father had died at the Battle of the Camel. He briefly gained widespread recognition as caliph and held Iraq for some time. Meanwhile, the Umayyads regrouped first under Marwan (684–685), a cousin of Mu'awiya, and then his son, 'Abd al-Malik (685–705), who finally terminated Ibn Zubayr's movement in Mecca in 692.

'Abd al-Malik made major administrative reforms, drawing on Byzantine and Sasanian models while at the same time underlining Islamic identity and strengthening the state as an institution (as distinct from the person of the caliph). These reforms included the introduction of Arabic as the language of administration in place of the languages of the previous empires, Greek and Persian, which had been used until then. Likewise, coins with Qur'anic phrases replaced the Byzantine- and Sasanian-style coins that had continued in use (replete with pictures of the emperor or shah and Christian or Zoroastrian motifs). He also built the Dome of the Rock in Jerusalem, a symbol of Muslim pre-eminence (see pp. 42, 216).

Figure 3.2 Umayyad dynasty, silver *dirham*, 79 H/ 698–99 CE, struck at Al-Kufa, Iraq, the first of the reformed Islamic silver coinage. On the obverse (front) field is the statement "No god but God, He has no companion", with the mint location and date in the margin. On the reverse (back) in the field and around the margins are Qur'anic inscriptions from *sura* 112 (in the field) of the Qur'an and *sura* 9:33 (around the margin). © The Trustees of the British Museum

Figure 3.3 Dome of the Rock in Jerusalem. Built by 'Abd al-Malik. Courtesy of iStockphoto

These measures signified the distinctiveness and permanence of the new Islamic order and symbolized its claim to be the successor to the previous empires. They also constituted the first steps in the building of an Islamic civilization. Islam, however, was still very much an Arab affair. Outside of Arabia, where 'Umar had decreed only Muslims should live, the Arab Muslims constituted a small ruling class superimposed on the subject population and little or no effort had yet been made to convert these. They were *dhimmis*, people with a covenant of protection, required to pay special taxes and recognize Muslim pre-eminence in other ways but otherwise self-governing in their own affairs. In Iran this arrangement represented a continuation and formalization of the arrangements the shahs had had with non-Zoroastrians. In general most *dhimmis* found Muslim rule less oppressive than that of their previous overlords. For some time their life continued much as it had before and the archeological record shows little evidence of the Muslims or of any destruction wrought by them.

Some scholarly reservations

This account is largely based, indirectly or directly, on sources that in the written form in which we have them date from about 800 CE or later, that is, one to two centuries or more after the events described. They are often, moreover, partisan and contradictory. Among these is the *sīra* or biography of Muhammad, written by Ibn

Ishaq (d. 770) and revised by Ibn Hisham (d. 833), which provides the generally accepted outline of the Prophet's life, as well as other historical writings, *ḥadīths* of the Prophet Muhammad and records of pre-Islamic poetry. Most critical scholars have assumed that with careful critical sifting these sources can be used to discover what happened with reasonable accuracy, although there will always be uncertainty and differing opinions on specific matters, as has occasionally been suggested above. They generally agree that little about Muhammad's career before the *Hijra* can be known with certainty, and even for the latter period most of what is written above could be questioned to some degree. (See also chapter 6.)

Since the 1970s, however, a number of critical scholars commonly called "revisionists" have presented more radical reconstructions of this period of history. Some argue that the traditional Muslim sources are far too late and tendentious to be of any historical value. Even the Qur'an provides little historical information on its own, since it usually alludes to events without identifying them. Some turn rather to more contemporary sources, such as non-Muslim writings of the time, coins, papyri, inscriptions and other archeological material, and more radically critical analyses of the Qur'an than have been attempted heretofore (see chapter 5). Some of these reconstructions have Islam originating in northern rather than central Arabia or even in Iraq or Syria. Some hold that the essential beliefs and practices, and even the text of the Qur'an, developed gradually over about two centuries. Others hold that Muhammad's Meccan opponents were monotheists, though of a "defective" sort, or even Christians. According to all of these interpretations Islam in its formative stage was much more closely involved with the milieu of the Iranian and Hellenistic world than is usually thought and the presence of considerable Jewish and Christian material in the Qur'an is understood in the light of this.

While some of this work is quite impressive and raises important (and sometimes uncomfortable) questions, their reconstructions of early Muslim history are speculative, diverse and often mutually contradictory. Critical scholarship in general has rejected some of their conclusions and been cautious about the rest (details about specific critics and their views can be found on the website).

However it may be for critical scholars, we must bear in mind that most Muslims hold to some form of the traditional view in these matters. Few have adopted even the more moderate critical views, much less the revisionist ones. As for the future, as Muslims say, *Allāhu aʿlam* (God knows best). In fact, the traditional accounts of the period covered in this chapter may be described as the "founding myths" of Islam, using the term "myth", as we do in Religious Studies, to mean a story that may or may not be true but that conditions peoples' world views and motivates their actions in a major way. (See also the comments on myth at the end of chapter 21.) Most Muslims, though in varying degrees, look to this period for their image of what it is for individuals and societies to be truly Muslim.

Key points

- The pre-Islamic Arabs had a distinct set of values focused on the tribe.
- While the pre-Islamic Arabs knew of Allah, Muhammad insisted that worship be focused on Allah alone.
- The key event in Muhammad's life is generally understood to be the *Hijra*, after which he became the head of what may be considered the first Islamic state.
- The *Hijra* is also the event from which the Islamic calendar begins.
- The period following Muhammad's death was marked by military success but considerable turmoil in the community.
- Islamic civilization, as distinct from Islamic religion, begins with the reforms of 'Abd al-Malik, about 690.

Discussion questions

1. In what ways did religious thinking in the *jahiliyya* differ from that in Islam?
2. Can Muhammad be described as a violent man?
3. It has been said that Islam grew up "in the full light of history". Is this true?
4. If you were a Christian in Syria about 660, what might you have thought of your Muslim rulers and their religion? (Note that prior to the end of the First World War Syria usually refers to what is now Syria, Lebanon, Israel/Palestine and Jordan.)
5. Look up the Qur'anic *sura* 9:33, which is on the coin pictured in Figure 3.2. What does this suggest about the attitude of the Umayyad rulers?

Critical thinking box 3.1

"There is nothing new under the sun." (Ecclesiastes 1:9)

Does early Islam refute this? Was the Islamic empire of the first two centuries something quite new and different or was it basically similar to previous empires?

(You will need to bear in mind the material from the previous chapter and also the next chapter through the early Abbasid period.)

Companion website

The additional information includes material on pre-Islamic figures and primary source material on the first revelation to Muhammad. The further reading has an extensive list of items on the critical and revisionist views of the period and the website provides weblinks to images of Umayyad coins.

Further reading

Lapidus, Ira M. (2002) *A History of Islamic Societies*, 2nd ed. Cambridge: Cambridge University Press. (Recent edition of a "classic" study. Introduction to chapter 4 corresponds to this chapter.)

Nicholson, R.A. (1907, reprint 1969) *A Literary History of the Arabs*. Cambridge: Cambridge University Press. (A "classic" study, still useful in my view.)

Shahid, I. (1970) "Pre-Islamic Arabia", Holt, P.M., Lambton, A.K.S. and Lewis, B. (eds.), *Cambridge History of Islam*, vol. I. Cambridge: Cambridge University Press, pp. 3–29.

Watt, W.M. (1961) *Muhammad, Prophet and Statesman*. London: Oxford University Press. (A summary of his two long works, *Muhammad at Mecca* and *Muhammad at Medina*. Watt is particularly known for his theory about the growing gap between the rich and the poor in Mecca, mentioned earlier.)

Peters, F.E. (1994) *Muhammad and the Origins of Islam*. Albany: State University of New York Press. (Important critical study, more critical than Watt but less than Crone and others.)

Armstrong, Karen (1991) *Muhammad: A Biography of the Prophet*. London: Gollancz. (Well-written, popular, appreciative account, not particularly critical.)

Cook, Michael (1983) *Muhammad*. Oxford and New York: Oxford University Press. (A brief, readable study of early Islam. Chapter 7 gives an introduction to the revisionist approach.)

Reynolds, Gabriel Said (ed.) (2008) *The Qur'an in Its Historical Context*. London, Routledge. (The introduction and chapters 1–4 have good discussions of current critical and revisionist theories.)

Hawting, G.R. (1987) *The First Dynasty of Islam: The Umayyad Caliphate AD 661–750*. Carbondale, IL: Southern Illinois University Press. (A good account that clearly indicates the uncertainties and varying opinions surrounding many events.)

Donner, Fred M. (2010) *Muhammad and the Believers: At the Origins of Islam*. Cambridge, MA: Harvard University Press. (A well-written account of the Islamic movement and its spread to about 700 CE, aimed at both specialists and non-specialists. His thesis about the "believers" movement is attractive but novel and as yet not generally accepted.)

See also: Knysh, *Islam in Historical Perspective* (Chs 1–4) [F]; Esposito, *The Oxford History of Islam* (Chs 1, 7) [F]; Brown, *A New Introduction to Islam* (Chs 2–3, 7–8) [F]; Crone, *God's Rule* (Chs 1–4) [8].

Note: The items under "See also" in this and following chapters are items for which publication information and comments are given elsewhere. The number in brackets indicate the chapter at the end of which these appear. [F] refers to the Further Reading section at the end of the book. For example, further information about Crone, *God's Rule* will appear at the end of chapter 8. Chapters 1–4 (in parentheses) are the parts of Crone's book that are relevant to this chapter.

4 *Expansion and flowering*

The history of Islam from about 700 to 1700 CE

> You are the best *umma* ever brought forth to humankind, enjoining right conduct, forbidding indecency and having faith in God.
>
> (Qur'an 3:110)

This chapter provides a skeleton overview of Islamic history from the end of the second *fitna* to the eve of the modern period, about 700 to 1700 CE. It is intended to provide a framework that will be helpful when reading the later chapters. The reader should concentrate on the main trends and the overall picture more than on the names and other details, many of which will appear in later chapters.

In this chapter

- The later Umayyad period
- The early Abbasid period
- Independent or autonomous realms
- The later Abbasid period
- The Crusades and their effects
- The Mongol invasions and after
- The three great empires: Ottomans, Safavids and Moghuls
- Central Asia, China, Southeast Asia and Africa

The later Umayyad period

After the second *fitna* order was restored under Marwan and his successor while administrative reforms, drawing considerably on Byzantine and Sasanian models, strengthened the Umayyad state. A greater degree of force was used to keep the tribes in line. Judges (*qāḍīs*) were appointed by the government while independent scholars studied the **Qur'an** and ***Hadith*** and began to develop the other religious sciences, such as jurisprudence (*fiqh*) and theology (*kalām*). These would develop

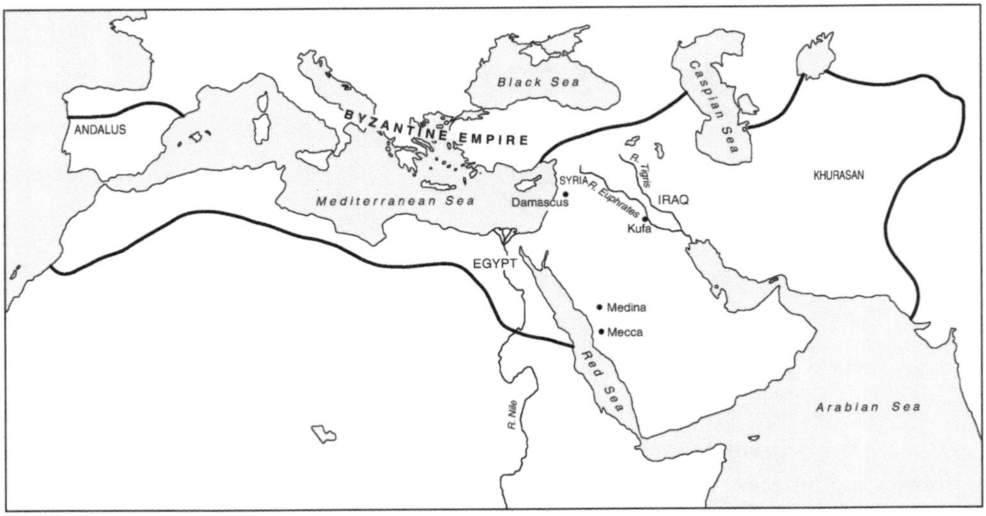

Map 3 Muslim lands about 800 CE

into the social grouping known as the *'ulamā'* (lit.: knowers, learned). Conquests were resumed and by 750 the Islamic realm extended to Spain in the west, into central Asia and to the Indus Valley in India.

Conversion to Islam by non-Arabs increased but these converts had to become clients (*mawālī*) of an Arab tribe, effectively accepting a second class status after conversion. This continued through the rest of the Umayyad period. Hence both *mawali* and disaffected Arabs supported a revolutionary movement mounted in Khurasan (northeastern Iran) in the name of 'Ali's descendants. In fact, when it was successful, in 750, it brought to power not 'Ali's direct descendants but the Abbasids, indirectly related to Muhammad by a different line.

The early Abbasid period

The Abbasids ruled, at least in name, until 1258. If the Umayyad rule could be considered Arab as well as Islamic, under Abbasid rule Arab and non-Arab Muslims were treated equally, and equally judged by their loyalty to the ruler. The empire's capital was shifted from Damascus to Baghdad, located near the former Sasanian capital, and Iranian administrative and court procedures continued to be adopted, while Arab and Iranian courtiers competed for cultural influence. Administration became more complex and in time was headed by a *wazīr* (vizier). The caliph was presented as chosen by God and legitimated in Iranian as well as Islamic terms. The peak of Abbasid political power was reached under the caliph Harun al-Rashid (r. 796–809) of "Arabian Nights" fame. Under the Abbasids a distinctively Islamic high culture, both secular and religious, flourished for the first time. During their first two centuries the authoritative Sunni collections of *Hadith* were compiled, the best known biography (*sīra*) of Muhammad was written, and the "founders" of the main schools of Sunni *fiqh* (jurisprudence) were active, as were the ascetics and mystics who represented the early stage of the Ṣūfī movement. The rulers sponsored

Jihad

The word *jihād* is usually translated as "holy war" and in recent years has become particularly associated with the most radical and violent Islamists (see chapter 15 for a discussion of this term), often called *jihadis*. In reality, matters are not so simple.

Jihad literally means "striving" and in the Qur'an is often said to be "in the way of God". There the word sometimes refers to fighting and sometimes does not. Often it appears to refer to both. As the tradition developed and is reflected in the *Hadith* and in *fiqh*, however, *jihad* did come mainly to refer to fighting. Rules were elaborated that could in some ways be compared to the Western idea of "just war". Here are some. If Muslims intend to attack ***kāfirs*** they must first invite them to Islam and attack only if the *kafirs* refuse to accept Islam or *dhimmi* status. They are not to kill non-combatants. Spoils may be taken and there are rules for its distribution. Prisoners might be enslaved, ransomed or freed. This kind of *jihad* is an obligation that need be carried out only by some Muslims (*farḍ kifāya*). If, however, the *kafirs* invade Muslim territory and the ruler so proclaims, *jihad* becomes a duty of everyone (*farḍ 'ayn*) and a wife, for example, may fight without her husband's permission. The degree to which leaders stressed the idea of *jihad* and the armies actually followed these rules varied, as with just war in the Western case. In modern times most resistance to Western imperialism has been considered defensive *jihad* (see chapters 15–20) and in recent years the term *jihadi* has been used, both by Muslims and others, for those who resist by violence and especially by what is considered terrorism.

There is, however, a *hadith* according to which Muhammad said on returning from battle that they had come from the lesser *jihad* to the greater *jihad*, the battle against the lower self. This idea has been popular among Sufis and others, and today there are many who believe that this is the most important form of *jihad*. In modern times many Muslims describe economic development and nation building as *jihad*. Iran has an agency called the Jihad for Construction.

Thus *jihad* is a multi-valent term whose range of meanings makes it comparable to the Western word "crusade", which may be a religious war but may also refer to a strong moral campaign for a variety of secular goals.

the translation of philosophical works from Greek and Syriac, mainly by Nestorian translators, building on the work that they had been doing under the **Sasanians**. There were also organized disputations between scholars of various religions and sects. These were one factor in the development of Muslim theology or *kalām*.

The Abbasids slowly replaced the Arab tribal levies of the previous period with paid soldiers directly loyal to them and about 840 began to recruit Mamlukes (slave soldiers) from the Turks of central Asia, beginning a practice that was to be repeated by many Islamic states. The Mamlukes initially were useful because they had no connection with any local faction, but in time they gained considerable power themselves and often made and unmade caliphs. In the provinces the caliphs faced numerous revolts and eventually lost control in most places to rulers who were independent, in fact, though sometimes formally acknowledged the caliph's authority.

Independent or autonomous realms

Andalus, as Islamic Spain is called, had been conquered between 711 and 718 and its rulers had never given allegiance to the Abbasids. It was ruled by an Umayyad dynasty that created a unified realm from the mid-eighth to the early eleventh centuries. It was also the seat of an Islamic culture and civilization that rivaled Baghdad's and was to serve as an intermediary between the Islamic world and the West in both material technology and ideas. Independent dynasties arose in North Africa in 789 and 800 and in Egypt the governor, Ahmad ibn Tulun, made himself independent in 868.

Several independent dynasties arose in Iran beginning in 821. Of these the Saffarids (873–900) were the first to stimulate the renaissance of Persian literature, now in an Arabized and Islamicized form, a development that was carried further by the **Samanids** (900–999) and the **Ghaznavids** (see below). Persian was to become the language of administration and culture for much of the Islamic world.

The fourth century of the *Hijra* (912–1010 CE) has been called the "Shi'i century". It was during this period that the different **Shi'i** groups took definitive form, although the distinctions among these and between **Sunnis** and Shi'is were still not as clear as they were to become. During this century Shi'i religious scholarship began to flourish and the authoritative collection of *Hadith* for the Twelver Shi'is (the largest Shi'i group, see chapter 8) was made. There were several important political movements.

In 905 the Shi'i Hamdanids established themselves in northern Mesopotamia and later Syria and become noted as patrons of poets and scholars. They continued until 1003 but there were other Shi'i dynasties in the area until about 1150. From 945 to 1055 the Buyids (or Buwayhids), who were Twelver Shi'is, were the effective military rulers in Baghdad. They took Iranian titles, even *shahanshah* (king of kings), for themselves but left the Sunni caliph in place as a legitimating figurehead. About

Figure 4.1 Inside the Mosque of Ibn Tulun, in Cairo, ninth century. The minaret resembles that of the Great Mosque of Samarra in Iraq, built by the Abbasids. Courtesy of the author

900 the Qarmatis, an **Isma'ili** movement (a different variant of Shi'ism), established a republic in Bahrain and eastern Arabia that lasted until 1077. At one point they carried off the Black Stone from the **Ka'ba** in Mecca (since they considered it idolatrous). Another Isma'ili movement, the Fatimids, took power in Tunis in 909 and in Egypt in 969, remaining in power in Egypt until 1171 and claiming the caliphate of the whole Muslim world. Isma'ili missionaries established themselves in Syria, Iraq and Iran with a mountain fortress at Alamut, south of the Caspian Sea, separating from the Fatimids in 1094. They waged a decentralized revolutionary struggle against the Abbasid rule, assassinating key leaders. The name "Assassins", given to them, derives from their falsely alleged use of hashish (*ḥashshāshīn*, hashish users). They continued their efforts until the Mongols destroyed Alamut in 1256.

The later Abbasid period

The fourth century of the *Hijra* (1010–1107 CE) saw what has been called the "Sunni revival". Baghdad returned firmly to Sunni rule in 1055 when the Saljuq Turks took control there. The Saljuqs had come into Muslim lands earlier in the same century, having been converted to Islam in central Asia, probably by wandering Sufis. For a brief period they established their control over an area from Syria to western Afghanistan in the name of the Abbasid caliph, who was still mainly a legitimating figurehead but had more scope under them than under the Buyids. In 1071 they defeated the Byzantine army at the battle of Manzikert and added part of Anatolia to their realm. Turkish rule in one form or another was to continue in much of the Muslim world for centuries and with it Turkish culture was added to the existing cultural mix. Meanwhile the Ghaznavids (961–1186), an agressive Sunni dynasty, had established themselves in Afghanistan and at their peak they controlled much of Iran and of northwest India. Though independent, they recognized the Abbasid caliphate as a source of legitimacy. They patronized scholars, including Firdowsi (d. c. 1020), who wrote the great Persian epic, *Shahnameh* (Book of Kings), about the pre-Islamic kings of Iran.

The Crusades and their effects

In 1099 an army of Western European Christians, called "Franks" by the Muslims, captured Jerusalem, carrying out an enormous slaughter of its inhabitants, and established a number of small states along the Mediterranean coast of Syria. These were the Crusaders, who had come to rescue the Holy Land from "infidel" rule. At the time, this part of the Muslim world was disunited and weak. The Fatimid dynasty, which had controlled the area, was well past its prime and most of the area consisted of very small feuding political entities. The Crusaders held Jerusalem until 1187 when Salah al-Din (Saladin) unified the Muslims and led them to victory, pointedly sparing Jerusalem's defenders and inhabitants. The Crusaders continued to hold some territory until 1291 and even regained Jerusalem from 1229 to 1244.

The Crusades had a considerable influence on Western Europeans, since the Crusaders encountered a culture much more advanced materially and intellectually than their own and learned much from it. Even Salah al-Din appeared as a model of chivalry. For the Muslim world, apart from the areas directly affected, the impact was much less at the time. They were just one more "barbarian" invasion and ultimately more ephemeral than most. In fact, those under attack were unable to get help from their fellow Muslims outside the immediate area.

One effect in the immediate area, however, was to reinvigorate the ideal of *jihad* and the *ghāzī* rulers (frontier warriors) who led it. Another was to make Muslims less tolerant of the eastern Christians that lived among them, who had sometimes cooperated with the Franks but often suffered from them. The Crusaders were, in fact, much more of a threat to the **Byzantine Empire**, which they initially came to support. In the Fourth Crusade (1203) they sacked Constantinople and the Empire never fully recovered from this. In the modern period, however, many Muslims were in retrospect to view the Crusades as the first step in Western imperialism. Western powers are often called "crusaders" today. Salah al-Din has come to be seen as a hero not only of Islam but also Arab nationalism (although he was in fact a Kurd). His defeat of the Crusaders after eighty years of occupation is seen as a symbol of what Muslims and Arabs might accomplish against Israel. The term "Frank", in varying dialectical forms, has been a common Muslim term for Westerners until the present.

Another effect in the immediate area was the establishment of a unified center of power in Egypt and Syria. Salah al-Din had been able to confront the Crusaders successfully because he had taken control in Egypt and then extended his power to Syria. In 1171 he formally ended the Fatimid dynasty and returned Egypt to Sunni allegiance. His successors ruled as the Ayyubid dynasty until 1250, when the Mamlukes, slave soldiers brought in by the Ayyubids, took over. A woman, Shajarat al-Durr, linked the two dynasties, being wife of the last Ayyubid and of the first Mamluke. She ruled briefly in her own name and organized a successful resistance to the Sixth Crusade led by King Louis IX of France. The Mamlukes ruled until 1517, when the Ottomans took control. The Mamlukes are noted for some strikingly monumental mosque architecture and also for driving out the last of the Crusaders in 1291.

Western Christian moves against Islam were more successful in Sicily and **Andalus**. Between 1061 and 1091 the Normans took Sicily from the Muslims, who had ruled it since the ninth century. In Andalus, the eleventh century saw the beginning of the long Christian reconquest that finally ended with the termination of the last "Moorish" kingdom by Ferdinand and Isabella in 1492.

In spite of the considerable political instability in the Muslim world during this period, culture in its various forms, both secular and religious, continued to flourish. The breakdown of political unity did not necessarily discourage cultural activity and sometimes encouraged it. The Fatimids had built al-Azhar in Cairo, initially to train Isma'ili propagandists, but it became a Sunni institution under the Ayyubids and continues to this day as the most prominent institution of Islamic learning. *Madrasas*, schools for *'ulama'*, were first founded in the tenth century in Khurasan but were patronized and spread especially under the Saljuqs and became the pivotal institutions for the *'ulama'* throughout the Muslim world. The Sufi movement also began to become somewhat more institutionalized. A number of Sufi scholars sought to reconcile Sufi spirituality with Shari'a-oriented legalism. Of these the best known was al-Ghazali (d. 1111, see chapter 13), who worked under the Saljuqs. The twelfth and thirteenth centuries saw the careers of several of the "founders" (mostly eponymous) of the Sufi *ṭarīqas* ("orders") that were to dominate the religious scene in the following centuries. Perhaps the best known of these is the Mevlevi *tariqa*, known as the "Whirling Dervishes", founded by Jalal al-Din Rumi (1207–1273). The greatest of the Sufi spiritual theorizers, Ibn 'Arabi, died in Damascus in 1240.

The Mongol invasions and after

If the Crusades were a localized challenge, the Muslim world faced a large-scale disaster when the Mongols appeared. In the early thirteenth century Chinggis Khan (d. 1227) unified the Mongol tribes in Central Asia and his successors soon ruled an empire from northern China to Eastern Europe and extending south into the Muslim world. Their brutality and devastation in the face of resistance was legendary and served as a means of terrorizing their enemies. In Nishapur they slaughtered all the inhabitants and built pyramids of their skulls. In 1258 they took Baghdad, sacked it and executed the caliph, effectively ending the Abbasid caliphate, though one of the caliph's relatives was able to take refuge with the Mamlukes in Egypt and maintain a very shadowy claim.

The Mongol advance was stopped by the Mamlukes at 'Ain Jalut in Syria in 1260. The devastation wrought by the Mongols set back the affected lands economically and culturally for some time. In fact, many modern Muslims view the Mongol invasion as one of the main causes for the (supposed) decline of the Muslims.

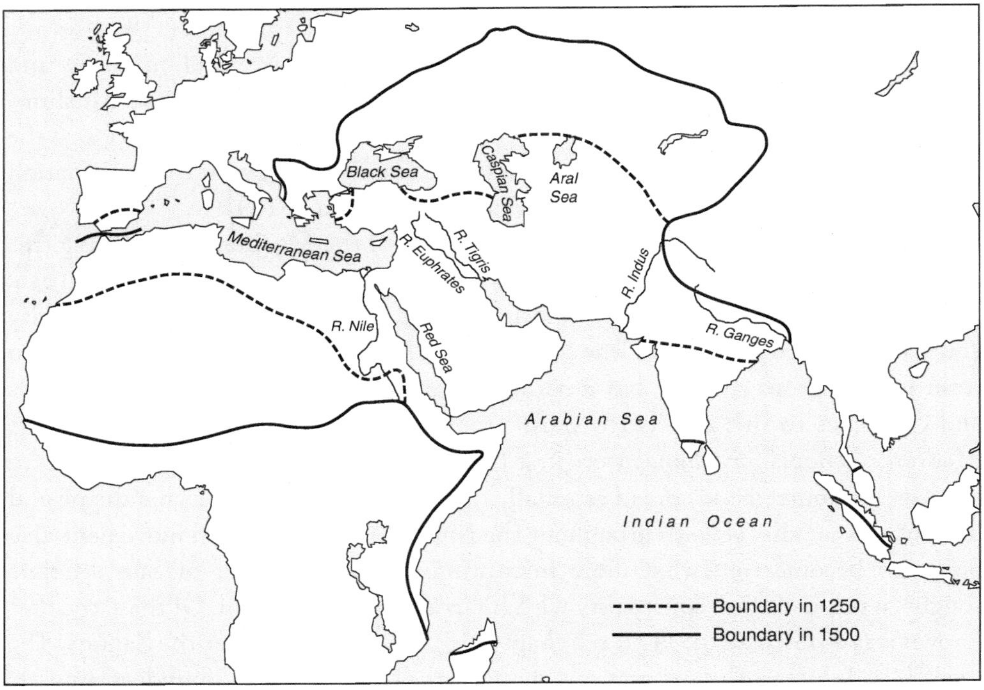

Map 4 Muslim lands in 1250 and 1500

The Mongols have become a by-word of horror for Middle Easterners not unlike the Nazis for Westerners. The Mongols were not Muslims. Some of their leaders were Nestorian Christians and some were Buddhists, while most followed their traditional shamanist belief. This prompted some European Christians to dream of a link-up of Christians against the Muslim world. It was during this time that Marco Polo made his famous journey. In 1295 the Il-Khan (deputy of the Great Khan) Ghazan converted to Islam and within a decade the rest of the Mongols followed suit. Buddhist monks were driven out and the Nestorians entered difficult times. The Mongols then began to patronize Islamic culture and contributed further to its blossoming. The Il-Khanid dynasty continued to 1336, after which its lands were divided among various regimes. Many of the Mongol rulers were sympathetic to Shi'ism and important Shi'i scholars flourished under them. Sufi *tariqas* also flourished under them.

Another notorious conqueror was Timur, a Turk imbued with Mongol ideals. His conquests from 1379 to 1402 began in Central Asia, extended to Iran, and then to India in one direction and Anatolia in the other. These conquests, though brutal, were carried out in the name of Islam and commonly supported by the *'ulama'*. His successors, for about a century, were also important patrons of Islamic culture.

Figure 4.2 Timur's capture of Delhi in 1398, one of his greatest military achievements. It was followed by an uprising of the inhabitants and the slaughter of many of them. From the *Zafarnama* by Sharaf al-Din, 1533 (vellum). Courtesy of British Library/Robana via Getty Images

Conversion to Islam

Westerners have often had a picture in their minds of Muslims spreading their religion with sword in one hand and Qur'an in the other. As this chapter makes clear, this is far from an accurate picture. What was spread with the sword during the first century of conquest was Muslim rule, while most of the conquered people became *dhimmis* and retained their religion. Later on Sufis and merchants spread Islam as often or more often than military conquerors.

In most of the areas conquered in the first century the population became half Muslim or more after about two centuries. In India and the European parts of the Ottoman Empire Muslims never achieved a majority, while in Java superficial conversion was nearly complete by two-and-a-half centuries after the end of the last Hindu kingdom.

The main factors leading to conversion seem to have been the following (not necessarily in order of importance):

- The attraction of Islamic doctrine and practice, which may have seemed to many a simplification and purification of Christianity and Judaism.
- The military and political success of the Muslims, which would have convinced many that they had God's favor, just as previous empires had made similar claims.
- The desire for economic and social advancement by joining the dominant group, especially since that group was open to entry.
- The desire to escape the disadvantages of *dhimmi* status. How great these were is hard to generalize about. In principle *dhimmis* were second-class citizens, their lives and properties were protected but they were subject to a special tax, the *jizya*, and various disabilities, such as wearing distinctive garb, not riding horses, and not being allowed to build or repair their places of worship. In practice the situation varied considerably. *Dhimmis* often prospered in trade and rose to high positions in government but they were also sometimes persecuted by rulers and sometimes suffered from mob violence. It was generally understood that their status was meant to be inferior to that of Muslims (Qur'an 9:29). In general their position was unsatisfactory by current Western standards of human rights but better than the Western treatment of minorities in the Middle Ages and often since then.
- Once Islamic civilization had developed, its predominance and attractiveness undoubtedly provided a context that encouraged conversion.

- The proportional increase of Muslims was also assisted by the fact that conversion is almost entirely in one direction in an Islamic society, since the Shari'a forbids conversion away from Islam and popular attitudes likewise strongly oppose it.

Over time *dhimmi* populations in many places maintained themselves but in relatively small numbers. In Egypt and Greater Syria Christians have been about 10 percent of the population since the fourteenth century, though decreasing in Palestine–Israel since 1948. Their proportion has been smaller in Iran, and probably larger in Turkey until the population exchange of the 1920s. On the other hand, as we will see, *dhimmis* remained a majority in the Balkans and India. Jewish communities maintained themselves from Morocco to India but since 1948 most have emigrated to Israel.

The three great empires: Ottomans, Safavids and Moghuls

Timur almost nipped in the bud what was arguably the greatest Islamic empire. The Osmanlis, or Ottomans, were a Turkish dynasty of ***ghazis*** founded in 1281. They were also very strongly Sunni and took seriously their role as defenders of the faith. They conquered northwestern Anatolia and moved into the Balkans, winning a number of battles of which the best known and most symbolic was against the Serbs at Kosovo Field in 1389. Bouncing back from defeat at the hands of Timur, they continued their expansion, finally conquering Constantinople in 1453 and bringing to an end the Byzantine Empire. After defeating the Shi'i Safavids (see below) they took over the rest of Anatolia and northern Mesopotamia. In 1516–17 they took over the Mamluke Empire in Syria and Egypt, though local Mamluke rule in Egypt was allowed to continue under the Ottoman aegis. They built a strong fleet in the Mediterranean Sea that contended with European powers and they took control of Tunis, Algiers and other North Africa ports (not Morocco) as well as Cyprus and Malta. They also contended with the Portuguese in the Indian Ocean. They expanded beyond the Balkans into Hungary and Romania, besieging Vienna unsuccessfully in 1529, and they also expanded north against the Russians.

The Ottomans developed a strong bureaucracy and, more than any other pre-modern Muslim state, incorporated the *'ulama'* into this bureaucracy and made them into a hierarchy. Certain Sufi *tariqas* were close to the governing elite, such as the Bektashis, **Mevlevis** and Naqshbandis. A distinctive Ottoman variation of the idea of Mamlukes was the *devshirme*. Under this system boys were recruited from non-Muslim villages, converted to Islam, and trained to become part of an elite military corps known as the Janissaries, who were directly responsible to the sultan.

They also systematized dealings with the *dhimmis* by creating what is known as the *millet* system. The various *millets*, Christian and Jewish, were dealt with through representatives, often religious leaders, and managed their own internal affairs. In general the *millets* supported the government and were supported, and to some extent controlled, by it. The *millets* generally prospered commercially under this system and many Christians and Jews had high positions in the government. Although Anatolia had become 90 percent Muslim by the fifteenth century, most of the European parts of the empire remained predominantly Christian to the end. The empire reached its height under Suleyman the Magnificent (or the Lawgiver, 1520–1566). After this it gradually weakened internally and externally. In 1683 the Ottomans once again besieged Vienna unsuccessfully but they ultimately lost the war and at the Treaty of Carlowitz in 1699 for the first time made peace as the defeated party. It was a harbinger of things to come.

The Safavid movement began as a Sufi *tariqa* in northeastern Iran under Shaykh Safi al-Din (1252–1334), a Sunni teacher, but later adopted Shi'i allegiance. In 1501 they invaded Iran under Isma'il (1487–1524), who declared himself shah. Twelver Shi'ism was imposed by force on the populace, who were mostly Sunnis at the time, and Shi'i *'ulama'* were brought in from Arab areas such as southern Lebanon, southern Iraq and Bahrain to instruct the people. Thus a link with the *'ulama'* of these areas was established that continues to the present. A system of *madrasas* was also established so that scholarship flourished. Sufis, however, were persecuted since they represented a potential challenge to Shi'i authority and the Sufi movement weakened. The imposition of Shi'ism was so successful that an effort to make Sunni and Shi'i Islam equal in the eighteenth century failed. If one seeks evidence that religion can be imposed by force of authority, Safavid Iran provides it. The Twelver *'ulama'* also claim to be deputies of the Hidden ***Imam*** and thus were potential competitors with the shahs for authority in a way that Sunni *'ulama'* never have been. At first and for some time the shahs held the upper hand, in part because the *'ulama'* were initially outsiders. In time the *'ulama'* began to assert their claims but the full development of this was to be seen only in the nineteenth and twentieth centuries. The Safavid period witnessed a major cultural flowering, especially under Shah Abbas I (r. 1588–1629), as can be seen in the impressive mosques and palaces of the Iranian capital, Isfahan. It was said, "Isfahan is half the world." It also saw the development of a form of philosophical mysticism known as *'irfan*, whose greatest representative was Mulla Sadra (d. 1640).

Until 1639 the Safavids fought frequently with the Ottomans and Sunnism and Shi'ism became important ideological markers in this contest. It was probably only in this context that Sunni and Shi'i Islam become as clearly distinct from each other as they are now. The Safavid Dynasty declined in the seventeenth century and was ended in 1736 by the Afghans.

In India, Sind had been conquered under the Umayyads in 712–13. The Ghaznavids took Lahore in 1030 and their successors, the Ghurids, extended their control as far as Delhi. In 1209 one of the Ghurid generals founded what became known as the Sultanate of Delhi, ruled by several Turkish or Afghan dynasties, some of whose members were Mamlukes. These dynasties extended Muslim rule to cover almost all of India. Both the Mongols and Timur raided India but did not establish themselves there, although a number of scholars came to India fleeing the Mongols. The existing social system was left largely intact. Hindus were treated as *dhimmis* and their chiefs often cooperated with the Muslim rulers, who functioned as a ruling caste in a society organized by caste. The Sufis and their *tariqas* flourished in India and were instrumental in converting about 25 percent of the population of the whole subcontinent, a majority in much of the north, especially since they were prepared to adapt their message to the needs of the local population. This was probably facilitated by at least apparent similarities between Sufism and various Hindu ideas and practices such as the devotional movement known as Bhakti. One result of the cross fertilization between these was the Sikh movement, inspired by the devotional poems of Kabir (1440–1518) and organized as a separate religion in the sixteenth and seventeenth centuries.

The Mughul dynasty first came to power in 1526 and was stabilized and made into an empire by its greatest ruler, Akbar (r. 1556–1605), who was a tireless warrior and dedicated reformer. He is known especially for his tolerance in religious matters. He abolished the *jizya* tax that non-Muslims had to pay and established a "house of worship" where theologians of different schools of thought and religions (including Christians) discussed and debated their views. He was particularly respectful of the Chishti Sufi teachers and later formed a kind of universalistic *tariqa* with himself as teacher and with a limited number of disciples.

Akbar was followed by three successors covering the period to 1707. One of these, Shah Jahan, built the well-known Taj Mahal as a mausoleum for his wife. The last of these three, Awrangzeb, adopted a stricter religious policy, reimposing the *jiyza*, among other things. In order to accede to the throne Awrangzeb had set aside his brother, Dara Shikoh, who had written a treatise to show that the Hindu Upanishads contained the same truths that the Sufis taught. In contrast, an important Sufi thinker during Awrangzeb's time, Ahmad Sirhindi, opposed compromises with Hinduism and also criticized the teachings of Ibn 'Arabi, which seemed to efface the boundary between God and humans. Akbar and Dara Shikoh, on one hand, and Awrangzeb and Sirhindi on the other, have been seen as symbols of the two attitudes Muslims might take toward Hindus, conciliatory or dominating. The eventual separation of Pakistan from India in the twentieth century may to some extent be seen as a victory for the latter tendency. After Awrangzeb's death, Mughul power declined rapidly although formally the dynasty continued until 1857.

Central Asia, China, Southeast Asia and Africa

In Central Asia in the sixteenth century a confederation of Uzbek Turks ruled a realm that included major centers of learning such as Bukhara and Samarqand. Uzbek rule continued less firmly until the nineteenth century. Islam penetrated China with merchants and Sufis via Central Asia and with merchants in Chinese seaports. The descendants of the latter group along with others are called the Hui and are Chinese in language and culture. The Uigurs and other Muslims of Xinjiang were brought under Chinese rule in the eighteenth century but have maintained their ethnic identities and have been less happy to accept Chinese rule, as recent events have attested.

Islam came comparatively late to Southeast Asia, but today this is a very important part of the Muslim world, both numerically (Indonesia has the largest Muslim population of any country) and in other ways. Islam appears to have been brought by traders and Sufis from both India and from the Arabian Peninsula sometime before 1300 and spread south along the coasts of Sumatra and the Malay Peninsula, and thence to Java, where the last Hindu kingdom was replaced by a Muslim state by 1550. The Portuguese took Malacca in 1511 and were replaced about a century later by the Dutch, who in time took full control. The presence of Europeans in fact stimulated the spread of Islam as a form of cultural and political resistance. *Jihad* became a form of anti-imperialist struggle, as would happen elsewhere. Islam spread as far as the southern Philippines, where it was blocked by the Spanish.

In Sub-Saharan Africa, as a general rule, merchants and Sufis first brought Islam, which was later accepted by the rulers. Among the most important Muslim kingdoms in the western part of Sub-Saharan Africa between the eleventh and the sixteenth centuries were Ghana, Mali and Songhay. Timbuktu was the leading religious and commercial center in this area. Further east, the Hausa rulers became Muslims in the fourteenth century and made Kano a center of learning. Traders brought Islam to the East African coast and Somalia from the ninth century but the coast suffered under Portuguese domination in the sixteenth century. To the north between the twelfth and early sixteenth centuries, Muslims pushed south from Egypt and north from the Blue Nile area, conquering Christian kingdoms. Ethiopia, however, resisted the Muslim push and continues to do so to the present, although a considerable proportion of its population is Muslim.

An observer considering the state of the world in the year 1000 of the *Hijra*, 1592 CE, would surely have been most impressed by the physical and cultural strength of the Muslim world. In the center it was dominated by three large empires that were at or just past their prime, while on its periphery it was expanding, especially to the south and southeast. As for the European "Franks", they had admittedly made some progress from their barbaric state at the time of the Crusades and they were demonstrating political and intellectual vitality, but they were also dissipating much of this in internecine religious wars. The intellectual and political creativity that would change the world in the future would have been less evident to the outside observer. For the moment, and indeed for another century, the Muslim world was on top.

Key points

- Military conquest extended the realm of Islam to Spain in the west, central Asia to the north and the Indus Valley in the east. Later the realm was extended much further partly by war but more by traders and teachers.
- Until about 750 Islam was predominantly an Arab affair. After that it became multiethnic.
- Various aspects of religious scholarship and culture began under the Umayyads but reached their first maturity under the Abbasids.
- This culture combined Arabian, Persian and later Turkish and other elements in a distinctive cultural mix.
- Under the Abbasids many provincial rulers had de facto independence although they formally recognized the caliph's authority.
- The Crusades briefly destabilized one part of the Muslim world but were ultimately more important to Europe, and as a memory to modern Muslims.
- The Mongols posed a major challenge to Muslim civilization but soon became Muslims and supported it.
- From the sixteenth to the eighteenth centuries the central part of the Muslim world was ruled by three large empires, the Ottoman, the Safavid and the Mughul, that at first were far stronger than any European state.
- Islam spread into Sub-Saharan Africa from the eleventh century and into Southeast Asia from the thirteenth century.

Discussion questions

1. Many people think of Islam as an Arab religion. Are they right? For what reasons might they think so?
2. Where I live we have a rugby team called "The Crusaders". Some Muslims object to this. Why, do you think? Are they justified?
3. It is common to divide the period of history covered in this chapter at the Mongol invasion. Do you agree? Why or why not?
4. What political developments or institutions described in this chapter strike you as most unusual?
5. How long was the Muslim world united politically? What do you think held it together after that?

Critical thinking box 4.1

In modern usage the Arabic word *umma* often refers to the modern nation (e.g. in the Arabic for "United Nations"). To what extent can the *umma* as described in chapters 3 and 4 be considered a "nation"? (You may find it interesting to use Benedict Anderson's concept of "imagined community". There is some information about this on the website.)

Critical thinking box 4.2

Read the charter of protection confirming the election of a catholicos (patriarch) of the Nestorian Church by an Abbasid caliph at: http://www.nestorian.org/a_charter_of_protection.html (accessed 5 September 2013) and also the charter of protection in Donner, *Muhammad and the Believers*, p. 117. What do these suggest to you about the relationship between Christians and Muslims in these times and places?

Companion website

Includes reading and (mainly) weblinks relating to just war, some Muslim leaders, *dhimma* and Serbian reactions to Ottoman victories.

Further reading

Sonn, Tamara (2004) *A Brief History of Islam*. Oxford: Blackwell. (Chapters 1 to 3 survey pre-modern Islamic civilization with some interesting observations.)

Bennison, Amira K. (2009) *The Great Caliphs: The Golden Age of the Abbasid Empire*. London: Tauris. (Interesting and informative study of Islamic society to the time of the Mongols. Chapter 1 surveys the political developments; other chapters deal with cities, trade, the various social groupings and philosophy and theology.)

Bonner, Michael (2006) *Jihad in Islamic History: Doctrines and Practice*. Princeton, NJ: Princeton University Press. (A good survey of the idea and practice of *jihad* throughout Islamic history.)

See also: Knysh, *Islam in Historical Perspective* (Chs 7–8) [F]; Lapidus, *A History of Islamic Societies* (Chs 4–21) [F]; Robinson, *The Cambridge Illustrated History of the Islamic World* (Chs 1–3) [F]; Esposito, *The Oxford History of Islam* (Chs 1, 7–10) [F]; Donner, *Muhammad and the Believers* [3].

Part II

Aspects of Islam

5 *The Qur'an*

God speaks

> We have revealed it as an Arabic Qur'an so that you may understand.
>
> (Qur'an 12:2)

The Qur'an is the Muslim scripture and the primary authority for Muslim life. It is comparable in some respects to the Christian and Jewish scriptures. An English-speaking non-Muslim who first approaches it will probably find some of the content familiar, but the form and the style will often seem strange. This chapter will focus on how Muslims understand their scripture and the influence it has on their life and culture.

In this chapter

- What is the Qur'an?
- The Qur'an in Muslim culture
- The main teachings of the Qur'an on God, faith, prophecy, other spiritual beings, the Last Day, social teachings
- Interpretation of the Qur'an
- Modern critical approaches to the Qur'an

What is the Qur'an?

For Muslims the Qur'an consists of the verbatim words of God, conveyed in the Arabic language to the Prophet **Muhammad** by the Angel Gabriel, and not modified by Muhammad's personality. The Qur'an commands Muhammad to say, "It is not for me to change it of my own accord. I follow only what is revealed to me" (10:16). The messages were conveyed in relatively short sections over the twenty-three years of his prophetic mission in response to his needs and those of the ***umma***. Muhammad's own words and deeds are also important for Muslims and will be discussed in the next chapter, but the distinction between his words and God's words is kept clear.

This view is held by virtually all Muslims today although a few modernists have sought ways to say that the Qur'an is human as well as divine (see chapter 20). Non-Muslims usually treat the Qur'an as Muhammad's words, but this can be offensive to Muslims. When quoting the Qur'an, it is best to say, "The Qur'an says ... " rather than "Muhammad said ... ".

As passages of the Qur'an were revealed to Muhammad, whom most Muslims believe to have been illiterate, he recited and memorized them and others wrote them down on materials that were available. It is claimed that from time to time Muhammad reviewed with Gabriel the content of what had been revealed, but at the end of his life it was still scattered on "pieces of papyrus, flat stones, palm-leaves, shoulder-blades and ribs of animals, pieces of leather and wooden boards, as well as [in] the hearts of men" (Watt, 1970, 40), as one source puts it. The "hearts of men" refers to the fact that many had memorized part or all of it. From the beginning the Qur'an was transmitted both in written form and in memorized form. The memorized form was the more important since the society of the time was one in which literacy was limited and which therefore relied mainly on memory. The heritage of pre-Islamic poetry was also memorized and was only written down much later. Moreover, the Arabic script of the time was very primitive and did not distinguish all of the letters (e.g. *b*, *t*, *th*, and sometimes *y* and *n* were written the same way), so that it was mainly useful as an aid to memory. It would take two centuries before it was to be fully adequate to record the Qur'an.

The best known account of the compilation of the Qur'an is as follows. In a battle the year after Muhammad's death a number of those who had memorized the Qur'an were killed and **Abu Bakr**, the first caliph, decided that the whole should be collated and recorded. This was done by Zayd ibn Thabit, who had been one of Muhammad's secretaries, and the text was eventually passed to Hafsa, the daughter of **'Umar** and widow of Muhammad. Under the third caliph, **'Uthman**, as the *umma* spread geographically, it became evident that different people were writing and reciting the Qur'an in slightly variant ways. This he considered a threat to the unity of the *umma* and so he had Zayd and others produce a definitive edition and sent copies of it to the main centers, ordering all others to be destroyed. In this edition there are 114 chapters, or *suras*, of quite unequal length, the shortest having three and the longest 286 verses, or *āyas*. Except for the short first *sūra* (quoted below), the *suras* are placed roughly in order of length, from the longest to the shortest, not in the order in which they were revealed nor in any clear thematic arrangement. Many Muslims believe that at least two of these copies still exist, one in Tashkent and one at the Topkapi museum in Istanbul. Most critical scholars, however, doubt the authenticity of these. In spite of 'Uthman's effort, there came to be some seven to ten different "readings" of the Qur'an that vary in details but are all judged to be acceptable. Some hold that all of these were revealed to Muhammad, possibly to accommodate different dialects of Arabic. Muslims do not consider that these variations compromise the integrity of the text, which they believe has been protected by God from distortion. In recent years most printed editions of the Qur'an follow the edition authorized by the Egyptian government in 1925.

If the Qur'an is the verbatim speech of God, it can only be so in the Arabic language, in which it was revealed. A "translation" into any other language is merely an imperfect effort to convey some of its meanings. Therefore, the Qur'an is always recited in Arabic and serious study of it is done in Arabic. Even apart from this "theological" point, it is a fact that Arabic generally is difficult to translate into English and the Qur'an, with its particular style, is even more so. It is usually not possible to render all of the ideas, allusions and emotions present in a Qur'anic passage adequately into English.

In fact, Muslims insist that the Qur'an is a literary miracle that cannot be equalled as literature. The Qur'an, indeed, makes this claim for itself (2:23–24) and Muslims have devoted a considerable literature to elaborating this claim. It is said that 'Umar, who was to be the second caliph, had been a bitter opponent of Muhammad but was converted after reading a page of the Qur'an. It is believed that every prophet's mission was confirmed by a miracle from God and Muhammad's main miracle, according to many his only miracle, was the Qur'an. The miraculous aspect is heightened by the fact that he is believed to have been illiterate.

This literary claim is not easy for the outsider to appreciate. The parts of the Bible Westerners most often read have a fairly straightforward narrative, poetic or doctrinal line and the whole has a fairly clear organization. The Qur'an by contrast often jumps unexpectedly from one topic to another, tells only part of a story and elliptically omits words and phrases. (It should be noted, though, that some of the prophetic books of the Bible are closer to the Qur'an in this respect.) Apart from the decreasing length of the *suras* it is hard to discern any overall principle of organization. Thomas Carlyle, who was one of the first writers in English to write favorably of Muhammad, spoke for many who approach the Qur'an for the first time when he described it as "a wearisome confused jumble, crude, ... endless iterations, long-windedness, entanglement ... ", though he also went on to say that in it "there is a merit quite other than the literary one. If a book come from the heart, it will contrive to reach other hearts; all art and authorcraft are of small amount to that" (Carlyle, 1910, 86–87). One problem, of course, was that he had to read the Qur'an in English, and in a poorer translation than those available today. Even in Arabic, though, the Qur'an's style and organization often appear fragmented. It is important, however, to bear in mind that the Qur'an is more recited and listened to than read and is mostly recited in relatively short sections, so that the power of the words and the immediate content is more important than the logical coherence of the larger context in which it is set. Muslim scholars have devoted considerable attention to the rhetorical features of the Qur'an. Many have also claimed to discern coherent organization in the text though this may be a different sort of coherence from what

Westerners look for. In any case, incoherence can be only apparent, for God has undoubtedly given the Qur'an the form it has for a good reason.

Since Muslims view the Qur'an as the actual speech of God, it is for them the point where God is most fully present in the mundane world. The significance of this can be underlined by a comparison with Christianity. It would seem obvious to compare the Qur'an with the Bible, but on closer reflection we may conclude that the person of Christ provides a closer parallel. For orthodox Christians it is not the Bible but the person of Jesus Christ, the incarnation of God (God "in the flesh"), who is the point where God is most fully present in the world. There is a confirmation of this point in the history of Muslim theology, where the debates over whether the Qur'an was created or uncreated (see chapter 11) resemble the Christian debates over the nature of Christ (see chapter 2). Orthodox Jews, on the other hand, will find that the Muslim view of the Qur'an is fairly close to their own of the written Torah (first five books of the Bible) given to Moses on Mount Sinai.

Being the speech of God, the Qur'an has *baraka*, a spiritual or almost magical power (we shall see this term again later). This is illustrated at the popular level by such practices as putting a passage of the Qur'an into a small container and hanging it around one's neck as an amulet to ward off bad luck or evil forces or writing a passage on paper and dissolving the ink in water to drink as a medicine. There are stories such as one that the horse of a Companion of the Prophet bolted when someone recited the Qur'an. One should be ritually pure before touching a copy of the Qur'an or reciting it. Arabic copies of the Qur'an usually have on the title page the following, which comes from the Qur'an: "a well guarded book which none may touch except the purified" (56:78–80). It is also worth noting that the word *āya*, used for a verse of the Qur'an, also means sign or even miracle. It is used in the Qur'an for God's activity in creation, e.g. the rain, the winds, the alteration of day and night (2:164), for a victory in battle such as Badr (3:13) and for "miracles" such as Moses' rod turning into a serpent (7:106, cf. Exodus 4:3 and 7:10 in the Bible). All of these are signs of God and so is, pre-eminently, each *āya* of the Qur'an.

The Qur'an in Muslim culture

The Qur'an penetrates Muslim cultures to a degree even greater than that to which the Bible used to penetrate Western, especially Protestant, cultures. Muslim names are commonly drawn from the Qur'an, as we shall see later. Phrases such as *al-ḥamdu li-llāh* (praise be to God), *inshā'allāh* (if God wills) and *Allāhu a'lam* (God knows best) are constantly on people's lips. Muslims recite a portion of the Qur'an in their regular prayers (*salah*) and on many other occasions during the day. The *Fātiḥa*, the opening chapter of the Qur'an, is recited on many occasions, such as the closing of marriage contracts. The Qur'an also generates what Westerners would call "art forms". One of these is calligraphy. The Arabic script, which has been developed in several styles,

Figure 5.1 Boy reading the Qur'an. Courtesy of iStockphoto

lends itself particularly well to graceful presentation. One finds Qur'anic calligraphy often on the walls of mosques and other public buildings, as well as on posters and in pictures in people's homes and elsewhere (see chapter 14).

Since the Qur'an is primarily a book to be recited and listened to, recitation also gives rise to something like an art form. Until modern times recitation of the Qur'an, along with its use in learning to read and write, was the mainstay of Muslim primary education. Many people memorize and recite the Qur'an even though they don't know Arabic and cannot understand the words; they and their listeners still benefit from the *baraka*. Those who memorize the whole of the Qur'an are called *ḥāfiz* and have considerable prestige. For some, recitation becomes a profession. They will be called on to recite at weddings, funerals, and various other religious, civic and family occasions. (See *Online Resources for Qur'an Recitation* under Further Reading at the end of this chapter and also on the website.) For purposes of recitation and also learning, the Qur'an is divided into thirty "parts" of equal length and each of these into two *ḥizb*; this is separate from the division into *suras* and *ayas*. There are two styles of recitation, *tartīl*, which is fairly plain, and *tajwīd*, which is more ornamental and "musical" (Qur'anic recitation is in fact not considered "music" by Muslims) and more difficult to master. It may be said that a leading Qur'an reciter has a status comparable to a leading opera singer in the West and evokes an intensity comparable perhaps to a rock star. Kristina Nelson describes a dramatic moment in the public recitation of the Qur'an in Cairo in terms that suggest both art and *baraka*:

> Suddenly the power of the phrase seizes the scattered sensibility of the crowd, focusing it, and carrying it forward like a great wave, setting the listeners down gently after one phrase and lifting them up in the rising of the next. The recitation proceeds, the intensity grows. A man hides his face in his hands, another weeps quietly. Some listeners tense themselves as if in pain, while, in the pauses between phrases, others shout appreciative responses to the reciter. Time passes unnoticed.
> (Nelson, 1985, xiii)

The main teachings of the Qur'an

God

The main teachings of the Qur'an relate, of course, to God, **Allah**. The Qur'an does not introduce Allah, since the Arabs already knew of Him, but it has much to say about Him. First and foremost, He is One and has no partner. "Say: He is Allah, One, Allah, the Eternal; He has not begotten nor has he been begotten, and none is equal to Him." (Qur'an 112). The recognition that Allah is one is called ***tawhīd*** (literally, considering [Allah] to be one), a very important term in the Muslim lexicon. Moreover, Allah is the creator and sustainer of everything. He created the universe in six days and "settled on the throne" (32:4 and elsewhere). He did not rest on the seventh day, as the Bible claims, but immediately took charge of His universe. He created humans to praise and obey Him and He guides them. On the Last Day He will dramatically bring the universe to an end and judge humankind.

Most of these themes are captured in the *Fātiḥa,* the opening *sura,* and the one most often recited by Muslims.

> In the name of Allah, the Merciful, the Compassionate.
> Praise be to Allah, Lord of the worlds
> The Merciful, the Compassionate
> Master of the Day of Judgment
> You only do we serve; to You only do we turn for help
> Guide us in the straight path,
> The path of those whom You have blessed,
> Not of those with whom You are angry,
> Nor of those who are astray.

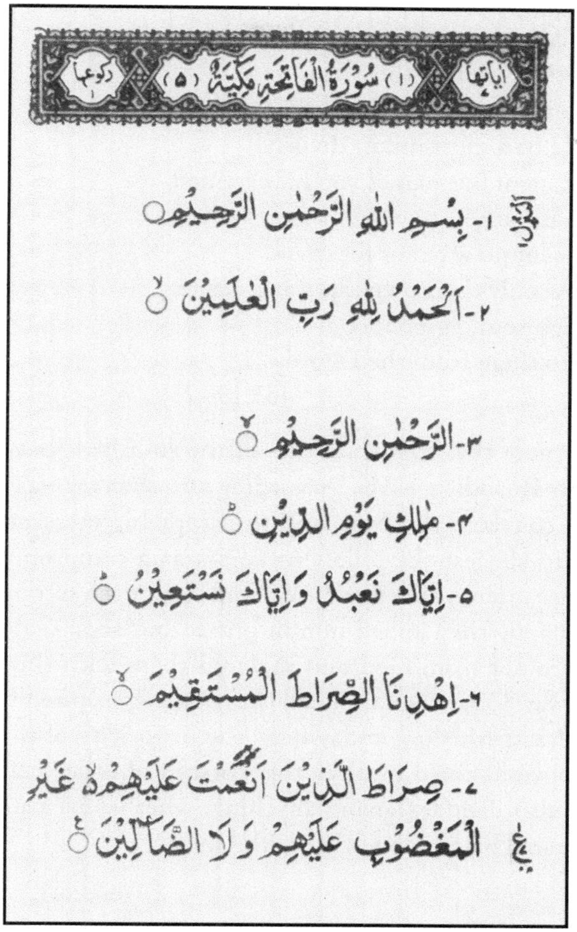

Figure 5.2 Calligraphy of the opening *sura* of the Qur'an, the *Fatiha*

The Qur'an has a number of epithets or names for Allah, and from these Muslims have compiled lists of ninety-nine names (they vary slightly), of which the first two are the Merciful (*Raḥmān*) and the Compassionate (*Raḥīm*), mentioned in the *Fatiha*. These names are often recited and appear in calligraphy in pictures and posters. They also appear in Muslim names, such as 'Abd al-Rahman, servant of Merciful One, 'Abd al-Nāṣir, servant of the Helper (name of the former president of Egypt, usually known in the West as Nasser), and of course, 'Abd Allah (usually transliterated Abdullah), servant of God.

The opposite of *tawhid* and the most serious sin humans can commit is *shirk* (commonly and slightly inaccurately translated "polytheism"), meaning to ascribe partners or associates to Allah, something the Meccans did with three of their pagan goddesses, whom they considered to be daughters of Allah, as the following passage indicates:

> Have you considered al-Lat and al-'Uzza,
> and that other, Manat, the third?
> Are you to have sons, and He only daughters?
> That would be a most unfair division!
> They are naught but names you have named,
> you and your fathers.
> Allah has sent no warrant for them.
> They follow only their own ideas and desires,
> Even though sound guidance
> has come to them from their Lord.
> (53:19–23)

It is interesting to note that this is the site of the so-called "Satanic verses", made famous by Salman Rushdie's novel. According to some reports Muhammad was overly anxious to convince the **Meccans** to accept his message and Satan took advantage of this to suggest the following verses as a compromise: "They are the exalted swans whose intercession is to be desired" (after the second line, above). The Meccans were so happy they joined him in prayer, but soon Gabriel appeared and told him these were not from God and replaced them with the present text. The Meccans turned away. Gabriel guaranteed that nothing inspired by Satan would be allowed to stand. Most Muslims today deny the historicity of this account. While *shirk* in its most obvious form involves the worship of other gods, most Muslims would say that it also includes giving anything, whether pleasure, wealth, career, family, or nation, equal place in one's life with God.

Faith

The most important requirement for humans is faith, *īmān*. In fact, the word *mu'min* (believer) is the most common word used in the Qur'an to denote Muhammad's followers, the word *muslim* being comparatively rare. Even today, *mu'min* is preferred by many. The term *iman* became the subject of considerable theological discussion and we will return to it in chapter 11. The opposite of *iman* is ***kufr***, unbelief or, more precisely, the refusal to recognize and act on the blessings of Allah. It carries the strong connotation of ingratitude and is perhaps the most forceful negative term in the Islamic vocabulary.

Prophecy

Allah's power and mercy can be perceived in the universe by those with eyes to see but He conveys his commands and moral standards to humans primarily by way of prophets (*nabī*) and messengers (*rasūl*) (the relation between these terms is too complex to enter into here). The Qur'an names some twenty-five of these and makes it clear that there are many it does not mention. Muslim traditions suggest that there have been as many as 124,000 prophets over the whole course of history. Most but not all of those named correspond to Biblical figures. In most cases the accounts of each prophet are scattered through the Qur'an with each account giving part of the story from a particular perspective. We will consider a few here.

Although Adam, the first man, is not specifically called a prophet or messenger in the Qur'an, Muslims have generally taken him to be such. Adam was created to be God's *khalīfa,* or deputy, on earth (2:30–39 and elsewhere). This is the same term that is used in a different context for the later leaders of the *umma*, in their case commonly transliterated "caliph". Adam and his wife, not named in the Qur'an, are placed in paradise (called "the garden", *janna*) and told not to eat of a certain tree, but they disobey and are therefore expelled to the earth. There is no indication that Eve first disobeyed and then tempted Adam; they appear to have disobeyed together. Adam then repented and was forgiven and received "words of guidance". While they are put on earth where they will face temptation and difficulty, sin consists of specific acts of disobedience to God, not the corruption of their moral nature (as in the Christian doctrine of original sin). They have the ability to obey.

Nuh (Noah) and several other prophets, including Arabian prophets such as Hud and Salih, who are not in the Bible, convey a warning from Allah to their communities (*ummas*), most of whose members reject the message and are destroyed by Allah, while only the prophet and a few followers escape. The story of Nuh's ark is presented in the Qur'an and fits this pattern (11:25–48 and elsewhere).

Ibrahim (Abraham) is particularly important. The Qur'anic Ibrahim was raised in an idolatrous family, discovered the truth of *tawhid* while observing the heavens (6:75–80), destroyed his father's idols (21:51–67), was thrown into a fire from which Allah saved him and migrated to Palestine (29:24–26 and elsewhere, the term ***Hijra*** is used here). After this, among other things, he was commanded by God to sacrifice his son, who was ransomed at the last minute (37:102–11). The Qur'an does not say which of his sons this was but Muslims believe it was Isma'il (Ishmael), not Ishaq (Isaac). He also traveled with Isma'il to Mecca where they built, or rebuilt, the ***Ka'ba*** (2:125–28) (some think it was built originally in Adam's time). Ibrahim's descendants, Ishaq, Isma'il, Ya'qub (Jacob) and Yusuf (Joseph), were all prophets. The people of Israel (Banu Isra'il) were descended from Ishaq, Ya'qub and Yusuf, and the Arabs from Isma'il, though the Qur'an is not explicit on the latter point.

The story of Musa (Moses) has much in common with the Biblical account. He is saved from death as a baby (28:4–13 and elsewhere), flees after killing a man (28:15–21), is called to by God from a burning bush (20:9–24 and elsewhere), and sent to confront Pharaoh, who is more consistently evil than in the Biblical account, and who is drowned as Musa's people escape (2:50 and elsewhere). Musa receives the

Torah from God, but the people worship the calf and prove disobedient in other ways (2:51–54 and elsewhere).

'Isa (Jesus) is understood to be a messenger sent to the people of Israel and is explicitly stated not to be Son of Allah or part of a Trinity (19:35; 5:73–78). He is born of a virgin and there are accounts of the annunciation and the birth that differ considerably from the Biblical ones (3:42–47; 19:16–34). He receives a scripture, the *Injīl* (Gospel), preaches, performs miracles, and raises the dead. His enemies try to crucify him but fail as Allah raises him to Himself (4:157–58 but see 19:33).

The Qur'an calls Jews and Christians "People of the Book" (*ahl al-kitāb*) and in some places seems to put their faith on the same level as that preached by Muhammad, whose message is said to be the same as theirs and as all the other prophets (2:136; 42:13 and elsewhere). Elsewhere they are criticized for disobedience, for changing their scriptures (4:46 and elsewhere) and for rejecting Muhammad. Though critical of both, the Qur'an is more consistently critical of Jews while having some favorable things to say about Christians (5:82). The Qur'an says, "No compulsion in religion" (2:256), but it also calls on Muslims to fight the People of the Book until they are humbled and pay *jizya*, a special tax (9:29).

Many of the elements in the accounts of the prophets that are not found in the Bible are found in other Jewish and Christian sources, one example being Ibrahim breaking the idols. This has led many Western scholars to speak of Jewish and Christian influence on Muhammad and even to speculate whether Muhammad was more influenced by Judaism or Christianity. For Muslims all these stories come from Allah. They and others were undoubtedly circulating in the environment; otherwise the Qur'anic versions, which are usually highly elliptical, would not have been understood. God in the revelation confirmed what was true in the material being circulated and discarded what was false, as well as adding new material.

These stories are still very much alive in Muslim societies, just as Old Testament stories are alive in Christian circles. "Stories of the prophets" is and always has been a very popular literary genre. These works collate the Qur'anic accounts of each prophet and fill in the gaps. In the process, a considerable amount of Biblical and other Jewish and Christian material is often included. For example, in these works, contrary to the Qur'an, usually Eve's name is given (Ḥawā' in Arabic) and she is first tempted and then tempts Adam, as in the Bible. Many Muslims are named after these prophets and allusions are often made to events in their lives. Khomeini, the leader of the Islamic revolution in Iran, was given the epithet "idol breaker", alluding to Ibrahim's action. Several rulers, including the Shah of Iran and President Sadat of Egypt, have been labeled "Pharaoh" by their enemies (see chapters 17 and 18 on these).

Other spiritual beings

In addition to Allah, the Qur'an speaks of other spiritual beings. Angels are servants and messengers of Allah who praise Him and do His bidding. *Jinn* (singular: *jinnī*) are beings made of invisible fire who may harm or help humans and may be believers or unbelievers. The Qur'an gives an account of a group of *jinn* who were converted by hearing it recited (46:29–31). *Jinn* are, of course, the "genies" who supposedly are let out of bottles and grant three wishes. Among the *jinn* is Iblis (devil) or Shaytan (satan), who was commanded along with the angels to bow down to Adam, after he was created, but refused. For this he was thrown out of heaven, but has been allowed to tempt human beings (17:61–65).

The Last Day

Some of the most dramatic passages of the Qur'an deal with the Last Day. For example:

> When the heaven is split open,
> When the stars are scattered,
> When the seas are poured forth,
> When the tombs are overturned,
> Then a soul shall know what it has done,
> And what it has left undone.
>
> (82:1–5)

Descriptions of Paradise and the Fire (hell) are likewise vivid, including the heavenly maidens (*houris*) who will attend those in Paradise (no number is given in the Qur'an). Feminists complain that the description of Paradise is very male oriented. Interestingly, it is reported that some of the women of the time thought so, too, and complained to Muhammad. Following this he received the following verses: "Muslim men and women, believing men and women, obedient men and women ... for them God has prepared forgiveness and a mighty wage" (33:35). In this worldly life social rights and duties differ but in the final accounting gender, like other social distinctions, falls away.

Social teachings

Many of the Qur'an's social and moral teachings will be dealt with in later chapters, but it is worth mentioning three that underline the contrast between the Qur'anic ethos and the *jahili* ethos of the pre-Islamic Arabs.

As mentioned in chapter 3, the highest loyalty of the pre-Islamic Arabs was given to the tribe. The *jahili* poet Durayd ibn Simma sang:

> I am of Ghaziyyah: if she be in error, then I will err;
> And if Ghaziyyah be guided right, I go right with her.
> (Nicholson, 1969, 83)

By contrast, the Qur'an says:

> O, humankind,
> Surely, We have created you from a male and a female,
> and made you into nations and tribes
> so you may know each other.
> Surely, the most noble of you in God's sight
> Is the most pious.
> (49:13)

That the *jahili* attitude of Durayd lives on is suggested by the following statement of the American Stephen Decatur in 1816: "Our country! In her intercourse with foreign nations may she always be in the right; but our country, right or wrong!" This supports the view of many Muslims today that modern nationalism is the moral equivalent of *jahili* tribalism and is *shirk*. The same Qur'anic passage also signals a shift in what it means to be noble (*karīm*). For the *jahili* Arabs nobility meant having noble ancestry and demonstrating this by noble deeds such as bravery in battle and generosity. For the Qur'an nobility is piety, which requires no ancestry.

As also mentioned in chapter 3, *jahiliyya* meant not so much ignorance as a glorying in extreme behavior, as illustrated by the accounts of Imru al-Qays, with his drinking, womanizing and then persistent quest for vengeance and Hatim al-Tayyi giving away all of his father's camels as an act of hospitality. The Qur'an, by contrast forbids fornication, gambling and wine drinking, and calls for the limitation of vengeance or, preferably, forgiveness (5:45). As for generosity, "be neither miserly nor prodigal" (17:29).

For the *jahili* Arabs the motive of ethical action was essentially honor, especially the honor of the tribe. Hatim says to his father,

> Oh my father, by means of [the camels] I have conferred on you everlasting fame and honor that will cleave to you like the ring of the ringdove and men will always bear in mind some verse of poetry in which we are praised. This is your recompense for the camels.
>
> (Nicholson, 1969, 86)

As for a future life, the Qur'an quotes them as saying, "There is this life and no other. We live and die; nothing but Time destroys us!" (45:24). For the Qur'an, on the other hand, the primary motive is precisely the "mighty wage" of the future life:

> Say: "It is God who gives you life and later causes you to die. It is He who will gather you all on the Day of Resurrection. Of this there is no doubt. ... As for those who have faith and do good works, their lord will admit them to His mercy. Theirs shall be a glorious triumph. To the unbelievers. ... The evil of their deeds will manifest itself to them and the scourge at which they scoffed will encompass them ... ."
>
> (45:27–33)

Out of fear for honor or fear of poverty *jahili* Arabs would sometimes bury their girl babies (16:58–60). The Qur'an forbids this, "Do not kill your children, fearing poverty. We shall provide for them and for you. Killing them is a great sin" (17:31).

Interpretation of the Qur'an

Like all scriptures, the Qur'an needs interpretation. Indeed, some interpretation is involved in the material presented above. A basic level of interpretation has been the effort to determine the temporal order of the Qur'anic material. Muslim scholars have distinguished between *suras* revealed in Mecca and those revealed in Medina. In general the first group are shorter and more poetic while the latter are longer, more prosaic and more likely to deal with legal material. Beyond this there has been an effort to determine the order of the *suras* within each group and this appears in the chapter headings of the Egyptian edition. It is recognized, though, that in some cases a *sura* includes material from different periods. One reason the temporal order is important is the idea that sometimes a later passage abrogates an earlier one. This is one explanation of apparent contradictions and is also important for applying the Qur'an in practice. In such cases it is important to know which is the later passage. For example, Qur'an 2:219 says that wine is of some value but greater evil but Qur'an 5:90, which is later, unreservedly forbids it.

An important part of interpretation is the effort to determine the "occasions of revelation" (*asbāb al-nuzūl*), that is the specific circumstances under which a passage was revealed and the issues that were being addressed. Much of the Qur'an cannot be understood without this information, since the Qur'an usually does not provide the context of its statements or at most alludes to it without giving the details. The case of the women questioning about paradise is an example of this.

The commentaries to the Qur'an that follow the order of the text are called *tafṣīrs* and a considerable number have been written. These are sometimes divided into those based on transmission (especially of *hadiths*, statements of the Prophet, see the next chapter) and those that make greater use of rational opinion. The most famous of the first group is that of Ibn Jarir al-Tabari (d. 922) and of the second that of al-Zamakhshari (d. 1144), condensed and edited by al-Baydawi (d. c. 1286). These and other traditional *tafsirs* usually contain a considerable amount of linguistic analysis and other technical material, as well as discussion of "occasions of revelation" and stories of the prophets, and much else. *Tafsirs* continue to be produced in modern times, some of them ideological in character, such as those of Mawdudi and Sayyid Qutb (see chapters 15 and 17 respectively) and some especially concerned to relate the Qur'an to modern science, such as that of Tantawi Jawhari (1940). These are generally less technical and more accessible to the general reader. A distinction is also often made between *tafṣīr* and *ta'wīl*. The former is a straightforward, exoteric interpretation, while the latter seeks hidden, esoteric meanings. An example of *tafsir* is the interpretation of "Lord" in the *Fatiha* as meaning not only master but also nurturer, based on the root of the Arabic word. An example of *ta'wil* would be the interpretation of the first letter of the same *sura* as symbolizing the beginning of creation and also 'Ali, the first Shi'i *Imam*.

One can see that the scholarly interpreter of the Qur'an faces a considerable task. He or she must master the various approaches just described as well as the fine points of the Arabic language and sciences related to the *Hadith* described in the next chapter.

Modern critical approaches to the Qur'an

Most Western scholars accept that the present text of the Qur'an is essentially what Muhammad presented as divine revelation, though they raise some questions at particular points and question the traditional accounts of its compilation. The German scholar Nöldeke (1836–1930) developed an analysis of the *suras* that divided them into three Meccan stages and one Medinan. This analysis has been extremely influential though more recent scholarship questions whether the *sura* can be the unit of analysis, since many *suras* contain material from different periods. Indeed, many doubt whether the temporal sequence of the Qur'anic material can in fact be determined. In a refined form, though, Nöldeke's approach is still used by most Western scholars and many Muslims. A Muslim scholar has recently developed a highly sophisticated analysis of stylistic elements, discerning seven chronologically ordered groups of material.

Western scholars have also come up with different interpretations from traditional Muslims on specific points. For example, traditionally the word *ummī* when applied to Muhammad is taken to mean "illiterate". Westerners, by contrast, generally take it to mean something like "gentile", i.e. belonging to a community that has not received a scripture.

Since the 1970s the "revisionists" mentioned at the end of chapter 3 have developed a much more radical criticism. John Wansbrough and others have applied to the Qur'an methods of literary criticism that have long been applied to the Bible. Denying any historical value to the traditional accounts of the compilation of the Qur'an and stressing the piecemeal and, in their view, contradictory nature of its contents, they conclude that the Qur'an was authored and edited over a period of some two centuries before it reached its present form and does not all come from Muhammad. Less radically, others note that the earliest surviving written passages of the Qur'an date from the late seventh century and often have wordings that are not standard (e.g. in the Dome of the Rock and a large number of ancient Qur'an fragments discovered in Yemen in 1972). Even though these variations are minor they are significant in a text whose wording is supposed to be sacrosanct and they suggest that the text was still developing long after the Prophet's death. If, as is commonly held, the orally transmitted version was (and is) the most authoritative minor written discrepancies would not prove much. These critics, however, claim a greater role for the written text even in the early period and argue that the existence of the discrepancies makes the existence of an authoritative oral version unlikely. Some critics argue that much of the Qur'an is in, or closely related to, the Aramaic language. One, going under the pseudonym of C. Luxenberg, has gained considerable media attention by claiming on this basis that the *houris* are not heavenly virgins but really white grapes, a view hardly accepted by other scholars. Other scholars, however, have argued on critical grounds that the Qur'an as we have it substantially goes back to Muhammad and question the idea of 'Uthman's compilation.

These various revisionist views are not accepted by most Western scholars, much less by Muslims, but they have had some influence and have to be taken seriously. For the purposes of this book, however, it will usually be appropriate to assume that the Qur'an is at least from Muhammad.

Key points

- The Qur'an is central for Muslims; it is the verbatim word of God and the point where the divine comes most in contact with earth.
- For Muslims the recited form of the Qur'an is of particular importance and Qur'an reciters are highly respected.
- Muslims consider the Qur'an to be a literary miracle.
- The Qur'an insists on the unity and centrality of Allah.
- The Qur'an tells the stories of a number of prophets, including Ibrahim (Abraham) and 'Isa (Jesus).
- The Qur'an rejects tribal honor as the central goal of life.
- Critical Western scholars have questioned the traditional understanding of the Qur'an in diverse ways.

Discussion questions

1. A comparison between the Qur'an and Jesus has been suggested. How convincing is this? What are its implications?
2. What difference would it make if the Qur'an were read and studied in its written form rather than mainly memorized and recited?
3. What might a Muslim say in response to Carlyle's statement, "If a book come from the heart, it will contrive to reach other hearts; all art and authorcraft are of small amount to that."
4. What are some of the points on which the Qur'an differs from the Biblical tradition on God and prophets? What is the significance of these?
5. Why do most Muslims hold that the Qur'an cannot be adequately translated into another language?

Critical thinking box 5.1

Discuss the quotations from Durayd and Stephen Decatur from a historical, social and ethnical point of view. Are they tribal/nationalistic chauvinists? (There are some helpful references on the website.)

Critical thinking box 5.2

Examine the passages dealing with the prophet Ibrahim (Abraham) in the Qur'an. How is he presented? What is his story? Does this story develop from earlier to later *suras* in the Qur'an? How does this story differ from that found in the Bible? How does he illustrate the general message of the Qur'an? (A list of the passages is on the website. You may also consider the accounts of Ibrahim in the "Stories of the Prophets" literature. See the website for some examples.)

Critical thinking box 5.3

"To historicize the Koran would in effect delegitimize the whole historical experience of the Muslim community," says R. Stephen Humphreys, a professor of Islamic Studies at the University of California at Santa Barbara.

> The Koran is the charter for the community, the document that called it into existence. And ideally – though obviously not always in reality – Islamic

history has been the effort to pursue and work out the commandments of the Koran in human life. If the Koran is a historical document [i.e. at least to some extent a product of human history], then the whole Islamic struggle of fourteen centuries is effectively meaningless.

(Lester, Toby, "What Is the Koran?" *The Atlantic Monthly*, January 1999, 283(1): 43(1). Online: http://www.theatlantic.com/magazine/archive/1999/01/what-is-the-koran/304024 (accessed 17 August 2013)

To what extent do you agree? (The article from which the quote is taken will be of help on this.)

Companion website

Features considerable additional information and reading lists relating to the Qur'an, including additional translations, and websites for the names of God and other items.

Further reading

Translations of the Qur'an; Concordance

The Koran Interpreted (1980) trans. A.J. Arberry, reprint. London: Allen and Unwin. (The translation most used by Western scholars, at least until recently, seeks particularly to convey the literary quality of the original, both in wording and formatting but has some odd usages at points.)

The Qur'an: A New Translation (2008) trans. M.A.S. Abdel Haleem. Oxford: Oxford University Press. (Straightforward attractive prose translation, easy to understand. Emphasizes comprehension over literal fidelity to text. Paragraph format aids understanding, hinders emotional appreciation. Good for the beginner.)

The Meaning of the Glorious Koran (1953), trans. M.M. Pickthall, reprint. New York: New American Library. (Long and popular translation in which it is easy to find chapter and verse; King James style English impedes appreciation; has some notes based on traditional Muslim scholarly interpretation.)

Holy Qur'an (1975) trans. A. Yusuf Ali, reprint. Lahore: Sh. Muhammad Ashraf. (Used a lot by Muslims; English is somewhat stilted and there are a lot of interpretive interpellations; has a modernist commentary that is omitted in some editions. My edition has the Arabic text in parallel column.)

The Qur'an With a Phrase-by-Phrase English (2004) trans. 'Ali Quli Qara'i. London: Islamic College for Advanced Studies Press. (Phrase-by-phrase translation with

Arabic text beside; translation is quite precise but also reads well and captures some of the literary quality. Chapters, verses and parts are clearly marked. Author is Shi'i.)

Approaching the Qur'an: The Early Revelations (1999), trans. Michael Sells. Ashland, OR: White Cloud Press (accompanied by an audio CD). (Includes *suras* 1, 53 (part), 81–114. Translation with a scholarly commentary that seeks to convey the Qur'an's distinctive "combination of majesty and intimacy".)

Kassis, Hanna (1983) *A Concordance of the Qur'an*. Berkeley: University of California Press. (Concordance to Arberry's translation.)

"The Qur'anic Arabic Corpus" http://corpus.quran.com. (Accessed 5 September 2013; if you click on "Translation" on the sidebar you will come to a page from which you can get seven different English translations of each verse of the Qur'an, including Pickthall, Yusuf Ali, Shakir and Arberry, as well as a recitation.)

About the Qur'an

Denffer, Ahmad von (1983) *Ulum al-Qur'an: An Introduction to the Sciences of the Qur'an*. Leicester: Islamic Foundation. (A fairly standard Muslim discussion of issues relating to the Qur'an and its use.)

Watt, W.M. (1970) *Bell's Introduction to the Qur'an*. Edinburgh: Edinburgh University Press. (This is a considerable revision of an earlier work and for many years the "standard" study in English of matters related to the Qur'an; still very useful.)

Esack, Farid (2002) *The Qur'an: A Short Introduction*. Oxford: Oneworld. (Covers much the same ground as this chapter though in greater detail and from a Muslim modernist perspective that critically engages in a positive way with Western scholarship while remaining definitely Muslim.)

Cook, Michael (2000) *The Qur'an: A Very Short Introduction*. Oxford: Oxford University Press. (Begins with modern use and interpretation of the Qur'an and works more or less back to a mildly revisionist understanding of its origins, discussing various important issues along the way.)

Gätje, H. (1976) *The Qur'an and its Exegesis*. London: Routledge & Kegan Paul. (A wide sampling of Qur'an commentaries from various times and perspectives with a brief introduction to the history of Qur'an commentaries.)

Rahman, Fazlur (1980) *Major Themes of the Qur'an*. Minneapolis, MN: Bibliotheca Islamica. (A high-level discussion of topics such as God, man, nature, prophethood, etc. from a Muslim modernist perspective that largely accepts the presuppositions of modern Western scholarship. See page 336 for his view of revelation.)

McAuliffe, Jane Dammen (ed.) (2006) *The Cambridge Companion to the Qur'an*. Cambridge, UK and New York: Cambridge University Press. (Articles by various scholars on topics related to the Qur'an, including its history, literary characteristics and interpretation. Chapters 1–3 provide basic accounts of traditional and critical views of the compilation and development of the Qur'an, with chapter 3 having a particularly concise and clear summary of the main revisionists. Chapter 11 provides a basic survey of Western scholarship from the Middle Ages to the revisionists.)

See also: Renard, *Seven Doors to Islam* and *Windows on the House of Islam* (Ch. 1) [F]; Knysh, *Islam in Historical Perspective* (Ch. 5) [F].

Online resources for Qur'an recitation (accessed 2 September 2013)

http://www.youtube.com/watch?v=B74JX-kcGKo&feature=related. (By the well-known Qur'an reciter Abd al-Basit; there are several others linked to the same page including a very nice one by a young woman, another by a child and a recitation of the names of God.)

http://www.mp3quran.net/ajm.html. (Has the whole Qur'an recited by Ahmad al-Ajami; each section has one *sura*, click on the left-hand column. Unfortunately for some the labeling is in Arabic, but the *suras* are in order, so the first one is the *Fatiha*.)

6 *The Prophet Muhammad*

"The best of all creatures"

The Prophet is nearer to the believers than they are to themselves.

(Qur'an 33:6)

The Messenger of God said, "None of you is a believer till I am dearer to him than his child, his father and the whole of humankind."

(Muslim)

If the Qur'an is the Book of God, Muhammad is the person through whom that book came to humanity and his words and deeds are the first and most important commentary on it. In his lifetime he was prophet, arbitrator, political leader and moral exemplar. It is this last role, moral exemplar and model for his followers, that has primarily continued after his death. In addition, though, he has also come to be seen as a spiritual intermediary and intercessor and as a focus of emotional attachment. All of these aspects of the Prophet are discussed in this chapter, as well as a distinctively modern role as "hero". The historical outline of Muhammad's career has been given in chapter 3 and will not be repeated here.

In this chapter

- Muhammad is human, but special
- Muhammad's example as recorded in *Sunna* and *Hadith*
- How authentic are the *Hadith*?
- Muhammad as intercessor and spiritual being
- Modernist views: Muhammad as hero

Muhammad is human, but special

Muslims agree that Muhammad was a human being and not an incarnation of God, as Christians claim for Jesus. He is in no sense to be worshipped. The Qur'an commands him to say, "I am a human being like you. It is revealed to me that your God is one God. Let him that hopes to meet his Lord do what is right and worship none beside him" (18:111). After Muhammad died some were saying he could not have died, so Abu Bakr checked and then said: "O men, if anyone worships Muhammad, Muhammad is dead, but if anyone worships God, God is alive and does not die." Then he recited from the Quran: "Muhammad is no more than a messenger: other messengers have passed away before him. If he die or be slain, will you turn back on your heels?" (3:144). As a human being he was subject to human failings and the Qur'an even reprimands him on one occasion for turning his back on a poor man who approached him while he was trying to win over a rich man (80:1–10).

Muslims insist, nonetheless, that if the Prophet was human he was a very special human, like a gemstone in comparison to ordinary stones. The Qur'an shows its respect for him in the following terms: "God and His angels bless the prophet. O believers, do you also bless him and grant him peace (*or* give him greetings of peace)" (33:56). From this is derived the formula: "May God bless him and grant him peace", which regularly follows the name of Muhammad in Muslim speech and writing. This phrase is used only for Muhammad, while other phrases are used for other prophets and for Muhammad's companions, typically "Peace be upon him" and "God be pleased with him", respectively.

It stands to reason, of course, that God would have chosen only the best of humans to receive His final message and Muhammad is described in some devotional formulae as "the best of all creatures". In fact, most Muslims believe that Muhammad had God's protection (*'iṣma*) from error. Minimally, this is protection from error when reciting the Qur'an and from major sins after he became a prophet, but most Muslims believe it is protection from all sins over his whole life. Therefore, most believe that he did not participate in **Meccan** idolatry even before his prophetic call, though Western scholars are inclined to believe that he did, a view apparently supported by the Qur'an when it says to Muhammad, "Did He not find you erring and guide you?" (93:7). Commentaries, however, argue that "erring" in this case does not mean sin and also that this refers to the period before he was a prophet. In any case, the Qur'an says, "He who obeys the Messenger obeys God" (4:80) and, "You have a good example in God's Messenger" (33:21).

Sunna *and* Hadith

This "good example" is the *Sunna* of the Prophet. The word *sunna* means literally "a trodden path" and was originally used to refer to the ideal way of life of a pre-Islamic Arab tribe (see chapter 3). In the Qur'an the *sunna* of God is the way God invariably acts in dealing with humans. After the coming of Islam it was for a time used to refer to the norms recognized by the Muslim *umma* or by parts of it, e.g. the *sunna* of the people of Medina. The predominant usage, however, came to be the *Sunna* of the Prophet, the values, norms and laws implicit or explicit in what the Prophet said, did or knowingly allowed to be done. To be a Muslim is to follow the *Sunna* of the Prophet. The opposite of the word *sunna* is *bid'a*, innovation, which is the usual Muslim term for heresy.

The *Sunna* is known through the *Ḥadīth*. A *hadith* is a report or a piece of news, specifically about an action or statement of the Prophet. In its complete form it has two parts, the *sanad* or *isnād*, which gives the chain of transmitters back to the first witness, and the *matn*, which gives the actual report. Here is an example:

> [*sanad*:] 'Abdallah ibn al-Aswad told me: Al-Fadl ibn al-'Ata' told us: 'Isma'il ibn Umayya told us on the authority of Yahya ibn 'Abdallah ibn Sayfi that he heard Abu Ma'bad, the freedman of Ibn 'Abbas, say: I heard Ibn 'Abbas say: [*matn*:] When the Prophet, may God bless him and grant him peace, sent Mu'adh to the Yemen, he said to him: You will come upon some of the People of the Book, so the first thing you will call on them to do is to profess the Oneness of God. When they have learned that, inform them that God has prescribed for them five ritual prayers a day. When they have made the ritual prayers, inform them that God has imposed *zakat* on their possessions, to be taken from the rich and given to the poor. When they have accepted all this, then take the tax from them, but leave them their most precious possessions.
>
> (Al-Bukhari as quoted in Williams, 1963, 68, slightly modified)

There are thousands of *hadiths* and they cover almost every conceivable area of concern. They include commentary on the Qur'an, details of what is permitted and forbidden (legal *hadith*), details of ritual action, theology, accounts of creation and eschatology, personal etiquette, descriptions of the Prophet's character and activities, and more. It is these that flesh out the often terse or general statements of the Qur'an. Without them, essential guidance in many areas would be lacking. Therefore, where some Christians say, "back to the Bible", comparable Muslims say in effect, "back to the Qur'an *and* the *Sunna*".

Here are some examples of *hadiths*:

> God is beautiful and loves beauty.
>
> (as quoted in Schimmel, 1975, 291)

> None amongst you is a true believer until he likes for his brother or for his neighbor what he likes for himself.
>
> (Muslim)

> When any man says to his brother, You *kafir* (infidel), one of the two deserves the name.
>
> (Bukhari as quoted in Williams, 1963, 72)

> I asked 'A'isha what the Prophet used to do at home. She said: He used to be at the service of his family, i.e. he would act as their servant (by performing domestic tasks), and when the prayer times came around he would go out to prayers. ... Never did the Apostle of God strike anyone with his own hand, neither his wives nor his servants, though he fought vigorously in the way of God. Never was there any wrong done to himself for which he took vengeance on the one who did it, but when there was the slightest violation of the respect due to God he would avenge that for God.
>
> (Mishkat al-Masabih, as quoted in Jeffery, 1958, 31, slightly modified)

> The Apostle of God was neither dissolute nor immoderate in speech. He was not one who talked loudly in the streets, nor did he return evil for evil, but rather he would pardon and forgive.
>
> (Mishkat al-Masabih as quoted in Jeffery, 1958, 31, slightly modified)

> I saw the messenger of God eating fresh dates and cucumbers.
>
> (Al-Bukhari as quoted in Williams, 1963, 73)

> Abdullah reported that the Messenger of God (peace be upon him) had a signet ring fashioned of gold but kept its stone on the inner side of his palm as he wore it; so the people had such rings fashioned. Then one day as he sat on the pulpit he pulled it off, saying: "I wore this ring and kept its stone towards the inner side." He threw it away, and said: "By God, I will never wear it." So the people threw their rings away.
>
> (Muslim)

> The great and glorious Lord said (to the angels): Whenever my servant intends to commit an evil, do not record it against him, but if he actually commits it, then write it as one evil. And when he intends to do good but does not do it, then take it down as one act of goodness, but if he does it, then write down ten good deeds.
>
> (Muslim)

The last of these is a *hadith qudsi* (divine saying), one of a group of *hadith* in which God is the speaker. The previous two are "legal" in that they may influence action in specific ways. Some of the strictest wanted to follow the *Sunna* to the point of eating only what the Prophet was known to have eaten. The *hadith* therefore permits dates and cucumbers. The *hadith* about the ring leads many to the view that a man should not wear a gold wedding band. I have heard this argued vigorously.

The Biography of the Messenger of God (*Sirat Rasul Allah*) by Ibn Ishaq (d. 768) revised by Ibn Hisham (d. 833), mentioned in chapter 3, is essentially a compilation of *hadiths* with both *isnads* and *matns*.

The angel Gabriel teaches Muslims their religion

The Prophet – May God bless him and grant him peace – was one day appearing publicly to the people when a man came to him and asked, "What is faith (*iman*)?" He answered, "Faith is that you believe in God, in His angels, in the meeting with Him, in His messengers and believe in the resurrection." "Then what," asked the man, "is Islam?" He answered, "Islam is that you worship God, giving Him no partner, that you observe *salah*, pay the *zakah* that is incumbent, and that you fast during Ramadan." "And what," asked he, "is it to do good (*iḥsān*)?" He answered, "To do good is to serve God as though you saw Him, for though you do not see Him, He assuredly sees you." "And when will the Hour be?" He answered, "He who is asked knows no more about it than he who asks, yet I shall inform you of the signs of it. It is when the handmaiden gives birth to her master, and when boorish camel-herds comport themselves arrogantly in fine houses. This is one of the five things which no one knows save God." Then the Prophet recited, "Surely God has knowledge of the Hour" (Qur'an 31:34). At that, the man turned and went off. The Prophet called out, "Bring him back!" but they saw nothing. He said, "That was Gabriel." He had come to Muhammad to teach people their religion.

(Al-Bukhari as quoted in Jeffery, 1958, 73–74, slightly modified)

How authentic are the Hadith?

If the Qur'an is considered authentic by virtually all Muslims (and by most Western scholars), the situation is different with the *Hadith*. Muslim traditionists, the experts on *hadiths*, have always recognized that in the two centuries following Muhammad's death a number of *hadiths* were fabricated and put into circulation to support various political and other interests. They therefore expended considerable critical effort to determine the authenticity of *hadiths*. In investigating a *hadith* some attention was given to the *matn*, where it seemed problematic, but primary attention was given to the *sanad*. Could this chain of narrators be accepted? Was each one known to have been in contact with the next one, or at least was this possible? Was each of them a person who could be depended on to tell the truth? This, interestingly, spawned a whole scholarly discipline called "the science of men", designed to gather the necessary information. This in turn led to the creation of biographical dictionaries. We may note that for most until about 1050 CE it was important to actually hear a *hadith* from its transmitter, given the importance of oral transmission in the culture and the limitation of early Arabic script. Written collections were made but were not authoritative at first. Therefore many scholars traveled considerable distances to

Figure 6.1 Two pages from an edition of the *Hadith* collection compiled by Muslim ibn al-Hajjaj. Courtesy of British Library/Robana via Getty Images

hear *hadiths*. One who did this was called a "seeker after knowledge" (*ṭālib al-ʿilm*), knowledge here being knowledge of *hadith*. The word *ṭālib*, seeker, came to mean student in general and still does in Arabic and other Islamic languages (e.g. Taleban in Afghanistan). The *hadiths* were graded into several categories, of which the most important were weak (*ḍaʿīf*), good (*ḥasan*) and sound (*saḥīḥ*). Within the last category is the subcategory of *mutawātir*, *hadiths* that are attested by many chains of transmitters all of whom are strong. These *hadiths* are considered to be certain. The result of all this effort was six major collections of *hadiths* recognized as canonical among Sunnis. The two most important are the *Sahih* of al-Bukhari (d. 870) and the *Sahih* of Muslim (d. 875). The others are by Abu Da'ud (d. 888), al-Tirmidhi (d. 892), al-Nasa'i (d. 916) and Ibn Maja (d. 886). There are later collections that largely draw from these such as the *Mishkat al-Masabih*. Among Shi'is *hadiths* also include those attributed to the *Imams*, as well as the Prophet. The main collection is that of al-Kulayni (d. 940). Al-Bukhari claimed to have examined some 200,000 *hadiths* to find about 7,397 sound ones, a number further reduced to about 2,602 when duplications or variant versions are accounted for (Brown, 2009, 32). In fact, though, many purported *hadiths* are in circulation that are not found in these collections.

Did these traditionists, then, get it right? Muslims generally believe that they did. Non-Muslim Western scholars mostly believe that they did not. The latter, following particularly from the work of Ignaz Goldziher and Joseph Schacht, argue from the evident expansion of the number of *hadiths* over the first two centuries and from the fact that the earliest examples of *hadiths* do not have *isnads* or have incomplete ones. They have also felt that the traditionists put too much emphasis on the *isnads* in comparison to the *matns*. It has been argued that much of the material had been transmitted by story tellers, whose commitment to entertainment or moral edification was often greater than to historical truth. Their view has been that the *hadiths* represent the views of Muslims of the second to third centuries of the *Hijra*. There may be some that go back to Muhammad but it is impossible now to tell which they are. Not all are so extreme, however. Some argue that there is evidence for both written and oral transmission of *hadiths*, particularly within families, resulting in a firm body of written *hadiths* by the end of the first century.

If the followers of Goldziher and Schacht are right, then we have very little hard evidence for the career of the Prophet. As indicated in chapters 3 and 5, the Qur'an alludes to a number of events but without saying much about them and therefore is not sufficient.

The views of Goldziher and others have had some reception among Muslims. The Ahl-e Qur'an in India and Pakistan reject all *hadiths* while other modernists feel free to reject many accepted *hadiths* (see chapter 15). The view of Fazlur Rahman (see chapters 15 and 20) is that the close and public relationship between the Prophet and his community guaranteed a continuity of the substance and ethos of his *Sunna* even though the *hadiths* may not be strictly historical. Traditional Muslim scholars reject Western-style *hadith* criticism but have become more willing to reject some *hadiths* or ignore them in practice. Traditional forms of *Hadith* criticism are used in a strict way but sometimes with novel results by the ***Salafi*** thinkers such as Nasir al-Din al-Albani (d. 1999).

Muhammad as intercessor and spiritual being

For most Muslims Muhammad has not only been the prime model for living, but has also functioned on a higher spiritual and metaphysical level. He is viewed, with some Qur'anic justification, as an intercessor with God for his people. "Who is he that intercedes with Him (Allah) save by His leave?" (2:255). The passage suggests that someone will be allowed to intercede and surely the most likely candidate for that is "the best of all creatures". This theme became extremely important. A popular prayer (*du'ā'*) goes, "O God, appoint our lord Muhammad as the most trusted of speakers ... and the first of intercessors ... and cause him to intercede acceptably for his nation and his people, with an intercession in which the first and the last are included" (Padwick, 1961, 42).

Figure 6.2 The Prophet's mosque in Medina. Courtesy of iStockphoto

Also, God worked miracles through or for Muhammad. While the Qur'an is seen as the most important miracle, attesting his status as a prophet, and some would say it is the only one, other miracles have been attributed to him or connected with him and have been important in popular piety. Here are some, in some cases said to be connected with passages from the Qur'an. When his mother was pregnant with him a light went forth from her womb by which she could see distant palaces. At his birth the palace of the Iranian shah was damaged and the fires in the **Zoroastrian** temples went out. When he was young, angels opened up his chest, washed his heart and removed a black spot from it (Qur'an 94:1–2). He split the moon at the demand of the Meccans (Qur'an 54:1). When he and Abu Bakr were traveling from Mecca to Medina during the *Hijra*, they hid in a cave and a spider wove a web across the opening, putting his enemies off the scent. It is believed that Muhammad still appears to people in dreams and any such dream is veridical because Satan cannot assume Muhammad's form.

Particularly important is the Night Journey (*isrā'*) and Ascent to Heaven (*mi'rāj*) (Qur'an 17:1 and possibly 53:13–18). According to the traditional account this happened during the year before the *Hijra*, when things were going badly for Muhammad since he had lost his wife, Khadija, and his uncle and protector, Abu Talib. He was carried, along with the angel Gabriel, by a miraculous animal, called Buraq, from Mecca to Jerusalem, where he prayed with Abraham, Moses, Jesus and other prophets. He then ascended through the seven heavens where, after a look at hell, he met various prophets at different levels and finally was taken into paradise.

It is debated whether this was a physical event or more of a dream vision. 'A'isha, his favorite wife, is reported to have said that Muhammad's body never left his bed but many take the event as physical. Mystics, and perhaps also Dante, have found in it a model for their own spiritual ascent.

It has also been held that there is prophetic Light that passed from prophet to prophet, beginning with Adam and coming finally to Muhammad (for Shi'is it continues through the *Imams*). It is said that it was visible on the forehead of his father before he was conceived. Muhammad came to be seen by many as a manifestation of the Perfect Man (*insān kāmil*) or the Essence of Muhammad (*ḥaqīqa Muḥammadiyya*), a cosmic principle linking the world with God, something like the *logos* in Greek philosophy and Christian theology, and it was with this that some of the later mystics sought union. A *hadith* says, "He was prophet when Adam was still between water and clay." Nevertheless, he never ceases to be the servant of God.

These various themes appear in poems of praise composed in honor of the Prophet. Two of the best known are the "Mantle Poem" (*Burda*) composed in Arabic by al-Busiri (d. 1294), which he is said to have written after having a dream in which the Prophet threw his mantle over him, and the "Noble Birth" (*Mevlid-i Sherif*), composed in Turkish by Suleyman Chelebi (d. 1421). Both are recited on the occasion of the *mawlid*, the Prophet's birthday, a major celebration for most Muslims (see chapter 7), as well as on other occasions. A few passages from the "Noble Birth" will illustrate their contents.

> On [Adam's] brow first God set the Light of Prophets,
> Saying: This Light belongs to my Beloved.
> Long years the Light shone there, nor ever wavered,
> Until the prophet's earthly life was ended.[81]

[The Light passes in order to Eve, Seth, Abraham and Ishmael]

> From brow to brow, in linkèd chain unbroken,
> The light at last attained its goal, Muhammad.
> The mercy of the worlds appeared, and straightway
> To him the Light took wing, its journey ended.
> Know first that never did that sacred body
> Cast shadow on the earth, not e'en at noonday
> The Friend of God in twain the moon divided,
> Though he but gestured towards it with a finger.

[During the *mi'raj*, God offers to grant Muhammad's wishes. Muhammad says:]

> What shall become of these thy halting people,
> How shall they find their way into thy presence?
> By night and day their deeds compass rebellion;
> I fear lest the Abyss should be their portion.

> O Majesty, this is my sole petition –
> My people, may they be by thee accepted.
> From Truth Supreme a loving cry resounded:
> "I grant them all to you, my friend, Muhammad!"
> You are the glass which mirrors my reflection;
> Your name have I inscribed with mine together.
>
> (Chelebi, 1943, 19–37)

Muhammad is here the friend of God. He is also the beloved of God and the beloved of his followers. As the *hadith* says, "None of you is a believer till I am dearer to him than his child, his father, and the whole of mankind." An early mystic, Rabi'a, said she had no space in her heart for any but God, but a century later another mystic gave this answer when he saw the Prophet in a dream and received the reply, "He that loves God must have loved Me."

Modernist views: Muhammad as hero

Many Muslims in modern times see Muhammad largely as their ancestors did, and these poems of praise are still popular. Others, generally called "modernists", undertake to depict Muhammad in a way that is congenial and acceptable to the outlook of modern people. This writing is usually apologetic, that is, it undertakes to respond to and refute Western criticisms of the Prophet, and of Islam generally, and to demonstrate the superiority of Islam to Christianity and other Western doctrines. This writing generally stresses the worldly more than the supernatural accomplishments of Muhammad. It strongly rejects most or all of the miracles traditionally associated with him other than the Qur'an, which is one that does not violate the natural order. Revelation tends to be understood as an inward voice or vision, though no less veridical, and the *mi'raj* is seen in the same terms. Muhammad, thus, relied essentially on rational persuasion, although the previous prophets performed physical miracles. Muhammad thus represents a significant historical step in the direction of modern rationalism and his religion is best suited to modern rationality. (See chapter 15 for more on modernism.)

Muhammad is also presented as a reformer who considerably raised the social and ethical level of the Arabs of his time, although his successors did not fully maintain his reforms. He called for equality and mutual responsibility among his followers, and for the abolition of class privilege and extremes of wealth. He is described as calling for social justice and sometimes even for socialism.

Muhammad is often criticized by non-Muslims for his wars and violence and such criticism commonly contrasts him, implicitly or explicitly, with the non-violent image of Jesus. Modernists respond that Muhammad's violence was dictated by the anarchic and violent society in which he lived. Jesus and the early Christians lived in societies with a significant measure of law and order, so that non-violence did not lead to their immediate destruction, as it would have for Muhammad. In fact, his violence was always in response to attack or serious threat. One of the most difficult cases is that of his expulsion of two Jewish tribes from Medina and the slaughter of the third. The reason given in the first two cases is that they were a serious threat and in the third case that they were guilty of high treason when Medina was under attack and that their treatment was no harsher than the standard practice of the time. Finally, Muhammad completed his mission and set up a political community, which could not be done without violence, but at least the violence was controlled by divine guidance. Jesus preached non-violence but provided little guidance for the ordering of society. When society did adopt Christianity three centuries later it drew its laws largely from human and sometimes barbarian sources. This is why Western history has been so violent.

Muhammad is also criticized for his attitude toward sex and women. Modernists point out that far from being oversexed, a long-standing Christian criticism, Muhammad lived most of his life celibate or with one wife, who was fifteen years older than he. The many wives he had later were to cement political alliances or to provide for women who otherwise would have had no support. His marriages involved responsibility more than sexual pleasure. In fact, Islam improved the condition of women in Arabia and elsewhere, especially by abolishing female infanticide and giving women property rights of a sort that English women obtained only in the nineteenth century. It permitted polygyny (multiple wives) out of necessity but it set monogamy as the ideal. The Qur'anic passage that permits four wives says one must be equitable among all of them (4:3) but another passage says this is impossible (4:129). Some say that the second verse effectively prohibits polygyny (cf. chapter 21, p. 347). Others say that polygyny is allowed in extreme circumstances, such as when there is a shortage of men after a major war.

Such views have been presented in innumerable writings for more than a century, and include a number of biographies or biographical treatments. The two most popular and influential have been *The Spirit of Islam* by Ameer Ali (1849–1928), an Indian Muslim community leader, and *The Life of Muhammad* by Muhammad Husayn Haykal (1888–1956), an Egyptian journalist and politician. Both present the sorts of views described earlier.

Several writings by major Egyptian literary figures take slightly different approaches. Taha Hussein, the greatest of these figures, tells us that the goal of his book, *On the Margin of the Sira* (three volumes, 1933–46), is to inspire the readers and encourage them to take an interest in the Arab heritage but that he is not overly concerned with historical accuracy. Muhammad here seems to be as much a cultural hero as divinely inspired prophet. Najib Mahfouz (the Nobel Prize winner) presents a symbolic and fictionalized version of Muhammad (under the name of "Qasim") in *Children of Our Alley* (serialized 1959, published 1967, see References for translations).

Here the humanity of Muhammad is brought strongly to the fore and social justice is the entire content of his message and mission. In 'Abd al-Rahman al-Sharqawi's *Muhammad the Messenger of Freedom* (1962) attention is specifically directed to Muhammad as a man rather than a prophet, in part to make him accessible to non-Muslims. His message is presented in explicitly socialist terms.

In all of these Muhammad is mainly a human hero. This idea had been presented much earlier by Thomas Carlyle in *On Heroes and Hero Worship* (1841 [1910]), where Muhammad is "The Hero as Prophet". Abbas Mahmud al-'Aqqad refers explicitly to Carlyle in the introduction to his biography, *The Genius of Muhammad* (1941), and goes on to say that his book:

> ... is an evaluation of the "genius of Muhammad" to the extent that it can be affirmed by every man and not only by the Muslim, and by virtue of the love of him diffused in the heart of every man and not of the Muslim only. Muhammad is great because his virtues and exploits are a model that any sincere person would want all people to emulate.
>
> ('Aqqad, n.d., 7)

Hero seems to be a distinctively modern category for Muhammad. Like a prophet, a hero is great and is a model, but divine revelation is not essential to this role and the hero is not protected from moral flaws. This category is both secular and potentially ecumenical.

Few if any of these biographies recognize any significant flaws in Muhammad. Mahfouz does in passing suggest that "Qasim" was "crazy about women" and drank alcohol and smoked hashish socially, but mostly he is presented as a paragon of honesty, gentleness, fairness and strength. By contrast, *Twenty-three Years* by the Iranian writer, Ali Dashti (1896–1991), presents Muhammad as a man with very human strengths and weaknesses, a flawed hero. Dashti is particularly critical of the supernatural events that people associate with Muhammad and he criticizes Muhammad's use of force and consequent restriction of religious and intellectual freedom.

An even greater exception is the famous, or infamous, novel, *The Satanic Verses*, by Salman Rushdie. Muhammad here becomes almost an anti-hero and is handled in a "deliberately transgressive" way. He is given the name Mahound, an insulting Medieval Christian label, and, among other things, he wrestles indecorously with the angel of revelation and forces the angel to say what he wants him to. But Rushdie does recognize the power of Muhammad's uncompromising "idea" (i.e. Islam), which is clearly fanatical but changes the world and has a place for mercy after victory. This book caused an enormous controversy and earned the author a death sentence (not carried out) from the Iranian leader, Ayatollah Khomeini.

The number of Muslims who share the ideas of either Ali Dashti or Salman Rushdie, or even Najib Mahfouz, is undoubtedly small but probably not insignificant.

For most Muslims, though, the words of one of Rushdie's critics apply: "Say what you will about God, but be careful with Muhammad" (Akhtar, 1989, 1). While God and the Qur'an have a higher status, it is Muhammad who, par excellence, is the human face of Islam. The point is made by a modern writer in the following words, with which we can appropriately close this chapter,

> It is often asked why love for the Holy Prophet has been made the test of a man's faith. The answer is quite simple. It is in his august personality that we can know the will of the Lord, His love for humanity, and His view how man should live in this world. In him all those values which our Lord wanted us to uphold took flesh and blood without compromise and without alloy. He has been, therefore, made for us the focus of loyalty because it is through him that we have learnt the true concept of God, the real implication of Tauhid, the role of man, his accountability in the Hereafter – in fact the whole of the religion.
>
> (Muslim, 31, footnote)

Key points

- Muhammad is a human figure, but more than an ordinary human.
- Muhammad's *Sunna* (words and deeds) is a pattern for human life.
- Muhammad's *Sunna* is contained in the *hadiths*, whose authenticity has been investigated by Muslims and Westerners.
- Most Muslims feel a strong love for Muhammad.
- Muhammad is viewed as an intercessor by most Muslims.
- Some modern people see Muhammad as a hero.

Discussion questions

1. What seem to you to be the main characteristics of Muhammad as presented in this chapter (and earlier ones)?
2. Do you think that to view Muhammad as "hero" could be a point of agreement between Muslims and non-Muslims?
3. Why is love of Muhammad the test of faith?
4. How does the description of Muhammad in the parts quoted here of the *Mevlid-i Sherif* fit with the insistence that Muhammad is purely human?
5. "Say what you will about God, but be careful with Muhammad!" Comment.
6. Some claim that in practice the *hadiths* are more important for Muslim thought and practice than the Qur'an. Would you agree, on the basis of what you have learned so far?

Critical thinking box 6.1

Compare and evaluate the assessments of Muhammad found in the *hadiths* quoted in this chapter and on the website, the statement at the end of this chapter and the assessments by al-'Aqqad, Mawdudi, Watt and Rodinson found on the website.

Companion website

The additional information features more *hadiths* and quotes from al-Aqqad, Taha Hussein, Mawdudi, W. M. Watt and Maxime Rodinson. There are also a number of further readings and some useful weblinks.

Further reading

Brown, Jonathan A.C. (2009) *Hadith: Muhammad's Legacy in the Medieval and Modern World*. One World: Oxford. (Thorough and detailed study. First couple chapters give an excellent presentation of the role and importance of *Hadith*. The rest are for those who want more detail, especially good on the early modern and modern periods.)

Schimmel, Annemarie (1985) *And Muhammad is his Messenger: The Veneration of the Prophet in Islamic Piety*. Chapel Hill, NC: University of North Carolina Press. (Study of the veneration of the Prophet by an expert in Sufism.)

Muhammad Ali, (1978) *A Manual of Hadith*, reprint. London: Curzon Press. (A useful selection, organized topically.)

Williams, J.A. (ed.) (1963) *Islam*. New York: Washington Square Press. (Chapter 2 has a good selection. See also other anthologies under the Further Reading section at the end of the book, p. 405.)

Ameer Ali, Syed (1965) *The Spirit of Islam: A History of the Evolution and Ideals of Islam, with a Life of the Prophet*, reprint. London: Methuen. (Described in the chapter.)

Ibn Ishaq (1955) *The Life of Muhammad (Sirat Rasul Allah)*, trans. A. Guillaume. London: Oxford University Press. (Most important early biography, mentioned in the chapter.)

Chelebi, Suleyman (1943) *The Mevlid-i Sherif*, trans. F.L. MacCullum. London: John Murray. (Described in the chapter.)

Dashti, Ali (1985) *Twenty-three Years: A study of the Prophetic Career of Mohammad*, trans. F.R.C. Bagley. London: G. Allen & Unwin. (Modern Iranian biography, described in the chapter.)

Haykal, M.H. (1976), *The Life of Muhammad*. Indianapolis, IN: North American Trust Publications. (Modern Egyptian biography, described in the chapter.)
Lings, Martin (1983) *Muhammad: His Life Based on the Earliest Sources*. New York: Inner Traditions International. (Sympathetic account by a Western Muslim with Sufi orientation.)

See also: Armstrong, *Muhammad* [3]; Cook, *Muhammad* [3]; Donner, *Muhammad and the Believers* [3]; Lapidus, *History of Islamic Societies* [F]; Knysh, *Islam in Historical Perspective* (Ch. 6) [F]; Watt, *Muhammad, Prophet and Statesman* [3]; Esposito, *The Oxford History of Islam* (Ch. 1) [F]; Renard, *Seven Doors to Islam* and *Windows on the House of Islam* (Ch. 1) [F].

Online resources (accessed 2 September 2013)

Hadith collections online (Center for Muslim–Jewish Engagement): http://www.usc.edu/org/cmje/religious-texts/hadith.
Searchable *Hadith* site (Effectively an online concordance; I have found it useful.): http://sunnah.com.

7 Rituals and ceremonies

> Perform the prayer (*salah*), and pay the alms (*zakah*), and obey the Messenger – that you may receive mercy.
>
> (Qur'an 24:56)

In this chapter we shall consider some of the main rituals and ceremonies in the lives of Muslims. Of these the five "Pillars" of Islam are the most important, but we shall also consider some of the "rites of passage" in the life cycle of individuals and the *mawlid* (birthday) of the Prophet, along with food regulations that impinge directly on Muslims' lives. One should be aware that there are many variations in these matters, based on varying legal (***fiqh***) interpretations, social and historical contexts and even personal preference, that cannot be covered here.

In this chapter

- Basic distinctions and concerns: *'ibadat* and *mu'amalat*; intention; purity
- The Pillars of Islam: *shahada, salah, zakah,* fasting in Ramadan, pilgrimage to Mecca
- Other pilgrimages
- The birthday (*mawlid*) of the Prophet Muhammad
- Life cycle rituals: birth, circumcision, marriage (and divorce), and death (and inheritance)
- The *sibha* or "rosary"
- *Halal* (permitted) food

Some basic distinctions and concerns

A fundamental distinction in human activities is made between *'ibādāt* and *mu'āmalāt*. Ritual actions, especially the Pillars and matters related to purification, are considered *'ibādāt*, "acts of worship". These are duties owed directly to God.

Their forms are more or less fixed and it is not thought that humans can discern the reasons for their details, although some of their benefits can be seen and will be mentioned later. They are sometimes compared to a medical treatment in which the patient benefits without understanding the reasons for the cure. The other category is *muʿāmalāt,* duties humans owe to each other. Generally laws relating to society fall in this category. Many Muslims today would argue that laws relating to society are no less "worship" than the ritual actions, since they too are prescribed by God. But the distinction still stands in Islamic law (*fiqh*).

Intention (*niyya*)

Essential to all human activity is proper intention. For ritual acts, particularly, one must state consciously and, if possible audibly, one's intention to carry out a particular act and must keep this intention in mind throughout. The Prophet said, "Deeds [are judged] by intentions and every person will receive according to their intention" (Bukhari).

Ritual purity

Also essential prior to performing many ritual acts is purification. This is related to physical cleanliness but is primarily a matter of sanctity. There are several kinds of impurity. *Najāsa* is caused by coming in contact with forbidden or unclean things such as urine, faeces or blood, pigs or dogs, or alcoholic beverages. For purification the affected parts must be washed. *Ḥadath* may be major or minor. Minor *ḥadath* is caused by such things as sleeping, going to the toilet, intoxication and touching a member of the opposite sex to whom one is not closely related. Major *hadath* is caused by such things as seminal emission, sexual intercourse, and menstruation. Minor *hadath* is purified by ablutions called *wuḍū',* which involves cleansing the hands, mouth, nostrils, face, arms, head, including ears and neck, and feet with water in specified ways (there is some variation in the details among different groups). In certain situations this may be replaced by cleansing with clean earth, called *tayammum.* Major *hadath* is purified by a complete bath, called *ghusl.* These laws of purity may seem strange to many outsiders, though not, presumably, to Orthodox Jews or Hindus. They do not imply that there is anything inherently evil about the body but they do stand as a reminder that sanctity relates to the physical as well as the mental and spiritual aspects of life.

The Pillars

These are the most important obligations for Muslims and include the *shahāda, ṣalāh* (prayer), *zakāh* (alms), fasting in Ramadan, and the *Ḥajj* or pilgrimage to Mecca.

The fact that the obligatory parts of the Pillars are virtually identical for all Muslims makes them one of the most important unifying factors for the *umma*. The Pillars are all mentioned and commanded in the Qur'an but their full forms are found only in the *Hadith* and details are worked out by the scholars of *fiqh* (law).

Shahāda

The first of the Pillars is the *shahāda*, or formula of witness, which consists of the following words:

> I testify that there is no god but God; I testify that Muhammad is the Messenger of God.

This is the basis of everything else in Islam. If a person converts to Islam, they do so publicly by saying these words in front of Muslim witnesses. Those born Muslim will not make this statement in this way but will have many occasions to utter and to hear the words. In fact, they will usually be whispered into the baby's ears just after birth (see below). Like the other Pillars, this one has a personal and a public dimension. It is personal in the belief it expresses but public in the act of witnessing, without which one is not a member of the *umma*. The precise form of the *shahada* does not appear in the Qur'an but its two elements appear separately (e.g. 47:19; 48:29). It does appear in the *Hadith*. Shi'is add to the two phrases a third, "'Ali is the *walī* of God (the guardian appointed by God)".

Ṣalāh

The term *Ṣalāh* (often written *salat*; *namaz* in Persian and Urdu) in its main usage refers to a highly structured form of worship, consisting of specified bodily movements, recitations and prayers that most Muslims are required to perform five times during the day, as well as on some other occasions. *Salah* is prescribed in the Qur'an (e.g. 11:114) but the precise five times are not specified there. It is said that these were given by God during the Prophet's *mi'raj* (ascension). Exact details of performance vary slightly among schools of *fiqh*. Other forms of prayer are called *du'ā'*. These may be spontaneous prayers but are more often set prayers for various purposes and are also quite important, but in a different way.

The beginning of the periods for *salah* are as follows:

- *Fajr* or *ṣubḥ*, dawn
- *Ẓuhr*, noon time
- *Aṣr*, mid-afternoon, half way between noon and sunset
- *Maghrib*, just after sunset
- *'Isha*, evening, when the glow of the sun disappears

Times for Salah in Christchurch, New Zealand

	Jan 1, 2012 (Winter, Standard Time)	July 1, 2012 (Summer Time)
Fajr	3:53 a.m.	6:32 a.m.
Zuhr	1:33 p.m.	12:33 p.m.
Asr	5:39 p.m.	2:45 p.m.
Maghreb	9:14 p.m.	5:03 p.m.
Isha	10:59 p.m.	6:29 p.m.

Source: Federation of Islamic Associations of New Zealand, http://www.fianz.net/salat/fianz_salat_any.php (accessed 15 March 2013)

Each *salah* may be offered from the beginning of its period until the beginning of the period for the next *salah* (except that *fajr* or *subh* must be offered from the first light of dawn but before sunrise), but it should be offered as early as possible. Times according to the clock vary with date and place. Times for summer and winter in Christchurch, New Zealand appear in the box. In the Muslim world the times for a particular day and locality are published in newspapers and other media. They are also published on websites. Under certain circumstances, e.g. when traveling, two *salahs* may be joined together or a *salah* may be made up later. Shi'is perform the *zuhr* and *'asr salahs* together, and also the *maghrib* and *'isha*. *Salah* is also performed on various other occasions, as we shall see. *Salah* may not be offered precisely at sunrise, noon or sunset. This is to avoid any idea that the sun is being worshipped.

As noted, those doing *salah* must be in a state of purity, and mosques normally have facilities for *wudu'*. A person does not have to repeat *wudu'* if they are in a state of purity from the previous *wudu'*, but it is considered advisable to do so to be certain. *Salah* is obligatory for all except those who are insane or suffering serious illness, women who are menstruating or have recently given birth (as these involve impurity that cannot be removed immediately), and children who have not reached the age of puberty, but children may and should be encouraged to start doing *salah* from about the age of 7.

Salah may be performed alone or in a group and it may be performed anywhere that is ritually clean, but it is preferable that it be performed in a group and in a mosque. It is obligatory for men to pray the Friday noon *salah*, called *ṣalāt al-jum'a*, in congregation in a mosque, and recommended for women. In fact, until recent decades in most places only men went to the mosque but in recent decades more women have been going to the mosques. When they do go, they usually do *salah* in a separate room or behind the men. In general Muslims believe that mixing the sexes in worship would be too distracting, as do Orthodox Jews and some Christian groups.

Figure 7.1 Men prostrating in *salah* (*tarawih*, see below, under Ramadan) at the Istiqlal mosque in Jakarta, the largest in Southeast Asia. Courtesy of iStockphoto

While *salah* in a mosque is always preferable, apart from *jum'a* it is usually performed for practical reasons at home or in the work place, either alone or in a small group. Prayer rugs are one way of assuring that an area is clean, but these are not usually necessary. When performing *salah* in public it is usual to place a small object a few feet in front of the person or people praying; it is a serious breach of etiquette for anyone to walk between this object and those praying. Whenever there is more than one person performing *salah*, one of them must act as prayer leader, or *imam*. This should be the oldest or most knowledgeable person (see chapter 9). Wherever there is a group, the worshippers will place themselves in straight rows and coordinate their actions by following the *imam*. The *imam* will be male unless the praying group is made up entirely of women (but see discussion on Amina Wadud in chapter 21). Shortly before the time of *salah* the *adhān* or "call to prayer" is recited in a loud voice by the muezzin (*mu'adhdhin*), ideally from the minaret but possibly from the roof or steps of the mosque or elsewhere. Today *adhan* is often recited on television, interrupting briefly the regular programming. Just before the *salah* starts the *iqāma* (entrance into *salah*) is said, similar in wording but in a lower voice.

The words of the *adhan* are as follows:

- *Allāhu akbar* (God is most great): four times
- *Ashhadu an lā ilāha illā allāh* (I witness that there is no god but God): twice

- *Ashhadu anna Muḥammadan rasul allāh* (I witness that Muhammad is the Messenger of God): twice
  - Shi'is may add here: *ashhadu anna 'Aliyan walī allāh* (I witness that 'Ali is the guardian appointed by God): twice
- *Hayya 'ala al-ṣalāh* (Come to *salah*): twice
- *Hayya 'ala al-falāḥ* (Come to success): twice
  - *Al-Ṣalat khayr min al-nawm* (Prayer is better than sleep): twice, only before *fajr salah* (Shi'is do not include this)
  - (Shi'is say instead) *Hayya 'ala khayr al-'amal* (come to the best deeds): twice before all *salahs*
- *Allāhu akbar* (God is most great): twice
- *Lā ilāha illā allāh* (There is no god but God): Sunnis once, Shi'is twice

(Website has links to *adhan*.)

When performing *salah* one must face the *qibla*, the direction of Mecca. Mosques have a niche, or *miḥrāb*, to indicate this. Other buildings or rooms that are used for *salah* may have a mark indicating the *qibla*. This includes many hotel rooms today. There are now compasses available to determine the *qibla*. Otherwise, this must be done the best one can; the *salah* will be accepted if a serious effort has been made.

The actual performance of *salah* consists of one or more *rak'as*. A *rak'a* goes as follows: standing and facing the *qibla* the worshipper raises his hands beside his head, states his intention, and says *Allahu akbar* (God is most great, called the *takbīr*). He then lowers his hands and says further words of praise to God and recites the *Fatiha* (opening *sura* of the Qur'an) and another short passage of his choice. He then bows and repeats the *takbir* and other formulae of prayer, and then stands again and says, "God hears the one who praises Him; our Lord, to You be praise." He then prostrates with his forehead on the ground, praises God, repeats the *takbir*, assuming a sitting position, and then prostrates a second time saying the same things as the first time. This ends the *rak'a*. He then stands for the second *rak'a*, which proceeds the same way except that the *niyya* is not repeated. At the end of the last *rak'a* the worshipper recites the *tashahhud*, a set of greetings to God and his Messenger and the *shahada* in a slightly longer form, and then turns to the right and then the left saying, "Peace be upon you and the mercy of God". These are traditionally seen as directed to the person's guardian angels, but also to one's fellow worshippers and all Muslims. These details will vary somewhat, but not much, depending on particular circumstances and also on the *madhhab* (school of *fiqh*, see chapter 10) one follows. Shi'is usually place a piece of clay from Karbala' on the ground and touch their foreheads on it in prostration. The precise number of *rak'as* varies with the times of day; generally there are between two and four obligatory *rak'as* and between two and five *sunna* (recommended, but generally done) *rak'as*.

The noon *salah* on Friday, called *salat al-jum'a* (or congregational *salah*), includes the *khutba*, a kind of a sermon. The *khutba* is delivered from the *minbar* (a kind of pulpit in the mosque) and has two parts, with the preacher briefly sitting down between them. The *khutba* may deal with a range of religious and moral topics, and political issues as well, but a considerable part of it is devoted to quotations from the Qur'an, praises to God and *du'a'* for the Prophet and the *umma*. Traditionally prayers for the ruler or the state have been included, and this has been an important symbolic recognition of the ruler's authority. Shi'is have given less emphasis to *salat al-jum'a* and sometimes refused to hold it because they so often question the legitimacy of the existing government. In 1979 the revolutionary government in Iran resumed *salat al-jum'a* and gave it particular emphasis, thus underlining its claim to legitimacy. It may be noted that Friday is not a Sabbath, i.e. a day of rest. The Qur'an tells people to go about their usual business after *jum'a* (62:10). There has, nevertheless, been some tendency to attach characteristics of the Sabbath to it, and today it is usually part of the "weekend" (often along with Thursday) in Muslim countries.

The philosopher Ibn Sina has suggested that the actions of *salah* are based on those traditionally followed when in the presence of a human king. It has also been suggested that one should face the *qibla* as facing the throne of God. Certainly at its most intense *salah* involves a strong and awesome sense of being in the presence of God. Even at a less intense level it is a regular reminder of one's faith and one's moral obligations. *Salah*, like the *shahada*, effectively integrates the individual and the social dimension. It is an activity done by the individual and brings the individual

Figure 7.2 Ornate *mihrab* and *minbar* at the Madrasa of Sultan Hasan (completed in 1362 CE) in Cairo. Courtesy of the author

face to face with God. But it is normally done along with others in a manner that emphasizes group solidarity. Even if one is praying alone, the whole *umma* is present by virtue of the fact that one is doing the same things as others at roughly the same time and facing toward the same center.

How many actually perform *salah* regularly as described here? The evidence is that there are, and always have been, a considerable number who do not pray regularly or do not pray at all. There are also those who drift away from it for a time and then return to it. The same appears to be true in a sense for societies. Since about 1970 there has been an increased practice of *salah* and other Pillars. Even those that do not practice, however, generally recognize that it is an obligation. This is important because, while failure to perform *salah* is a sin, it is only refusal to recognize its obligatory nature that puts one beyond the pale of Islam. This is also true of the Pillars that follow, and generally of the prescriptions of the Shari'a.

Zakāh

Zakah (sometimes written *zakat*) is a portion of one's wealth to be paid each year, in money or kind, as a kind of a tax or charity. The word *zakah* means purity and part of the meaning is that by paying over part of one's wealth one purifies the rest of it. All adult Muslims who have a stated minimum of wealth (*niṣāb*) must pay; on most forms of wealth it is figured at 2.5 percent of one's total possessions above the *nisab*. The recipients of the *zakah* are stated in the Qur'an (9:60) and include the poor and needy (i.e. whose income is under the *nisab*), new converts, prisoners of war to be ransomed, debtors, those who collect the *zakah*, travelers, and those laboring "in the path of God", interpreted especially as those studying and propagating Islam. Sometimes the *zakah* is collected and distributed by governments and sometimes it is given by the donors directly to the recipients or to mosques or appropriate charitable organizations to distribute. *Zakah* is not considered a "donation" but rather something that already belongs by right to the recipients. Voluntary donations are called *ṣadaqa* and are separate from *zakah*. Taxes to governments (apart from *zakah* where they collect it) are also separate from *zakah*.

Fasting (Ramadan)

During Ramadan, the ninth month of the Muslim year, Muslims are obliged to fast from just before the breaking of dawn to just after sunset, abstaining completely from food, drink, smoking and sexual intercourse. Exempted partially or completely from this are children, the elderly, those whose health will be adversely affected, travelers under certain circumstances, expectant and nursing mothers, and women during menstruation (who must not fast). In many cases the person should make up the fast by fasting a day for each day missed or providing a meal for a needy person (or its

Ramadan riddles

These days television programming in the Muslim world is geared to Ramadan, when families tend to be at home in the evening, but the programming itself is not necessarily religious. It includes plenty of the usual advertising and Ramadan serials, which may include spy programs and the like. In Cairo in the 1980s and 1990s it included programs featuring riddles, of which the most popular one was called "Ramadan Riddles" and featured a luxuriantly dressed female performer who each night would present a riddle to a new contestant, act it out and perform in other ways. In 2012 a popular but controversial thirty-session blockbuster about the Caliph 'Umar was aired in many countries. These and other developments suggest that Ramadan is being commercialized somewhat as Christmas has been in the West.

monetary equivalent). This also applies to people who miss one or more days for any other reason. Those who are not fasting should not, as a matter of consideration, eat in the presence of those who are (this should also apply to non-Muslim tourists or scholars!). The last meal before fasting, in the early hours of the morning, is called *suḥūr*. The breaking of the fast, *ifṭār*, occurs just before the *maghrib salah* as people take a small amount of food, such as a few dates or fruit juice, and then after *salah* have a large meal. In some places cannons are fired to mark the beginning and end of fasting. Today one may hear the cannon on the radio or television.

Ramadan nights are joyous and even noisy times with feasting, visiting and entertainment. Today there is also special programming on television including religious lessons but also quite secular entertainment. The coffee houses are open and the streets full of people long past the usual hours. There is a tendency for people to overeat at night, though this is hardly approved, and the less pious often miss the fasting but not the feasting.

Still, it is also a time of heightened spiritual awareness. Special *salahs*, called *tarāwīḥ* and consisting of eight or twenty *rak'as*, are performed after the *'isha salah* by Sunnis. Some people spend several days and nights in the mosques (some spend the last ten of the month), engaging in study, prayers and other spiritual exercises. It is also common for both mosques and families to arrange a *khātima*, a recitation of the whole Qur'an by Qur'an reciters, in which one of the thirty parts of the Qur'an is recited each night. Ramadan is said to be the month when the Qur'an was first revealed and also the month of the Battle of Badr. It has also been held that the *jinn* are confined in prison during Ramadan, thus allowing humans to celebrate more freely. Most important is the Night of Power, when the first verses of the Qur'an were revealed. It is described in the Qur'an in the following words:

> Behold, We sent it down on the Night of Power. And what shall teach you what is the Night of Power? The Night of Power is better than a thousand months; in it angels and the Spirit descend, by the leave of their Lord, with all decrees. Peace it is, till the rising of the dawn.
>
> (97)

The exact date of the Night of Power is uncertain; it could be any odd-numbered night from the twenty-first to the twenty-ninth of Ramadan, but is usually taken to be the twenty-seventh. On this night the heavens are especially open to convey blessings and answer prayers.

Ramadan reinforces the sense of solidarity of the *umma*. Those who are well off experience the hunger that the poor experience more regularly and thus have an increased sympathy for them. A certain fellow feeling also arises when you are hungry and looking forward to the *iftar* and you know that those in the street around you feel the same way. It is sometimes said that fasting makes people grumpy toward the end of the day but my experience does not back that up. More important, I think, is the sense of victory over one's lower impulses. By denying the lower self its usual due for a period of time, one demonstrates that the higher self is in control and one strengthens this control. Because of this, along with the fact that fasting is an adult thing, children usually do not need to be compelled to fast but want to before they

Figure 7.3 *Iftar* is served during Ramadan at the London Muslim Centre. Courtesy of iStockphoto

Estimated dates of Ramadan on the Western calendar 2013–20

2013: 9 July to 7 August
2014: 28 June to 27 July
2015: 18 June to 17 July
2016: 6 June to 5 July
2017: 27 May to 25 June
2018: 16 May to 14 June
2019: 6 May to 4 June
2020: 24 April to 23 June

Online: http://www.when-is.com/ramadan.asp
(accessed 17 August 2013)

can be permitted to. It is fair to say, though proof is lacking, that more Muslims fast Ramadan fully than regularly perform *salah*.

During Ramadan the rhythm of society changes and slows down as people's schedules, including work schedules, are revised. The Muslim year is about eleven days shorter than the solar year and so all of the festivals come earlier each year in relation to the seasons. When Ramadan falls in the summer the period of fasting each day is longer than in the winter, and the heat of summer makes it an even greater trial. Muslims living in non-Muslim countries face additional problems since society does not adjust to Ramadan and the days are often longer in the summer. These are not insurmountable problems, however. In modern times modernizers have complained that Ramadan reduces production. In 1960 the president of Tunisia, Habib Bourguiba, declared that economic development was a form of *jihad* and that the practice of Ramadan should therefore be suspended. Though he was a popular leader, he did not convince people of this.

The day (or three days in some places) following Ramadan is a festival day known as *'Īd al-Fiṭr* (the festival of the breaking of the fast) or the lesser *'Id*. It is one of two such festivals during the year, the other being *'Īd al-Aḍḥā*, described below. There is a special *salah* for the *'Id* in the morning, followed by visits to cemeteries, and then parties with gifts for children and the like. It is a national holiday in some countries. There is also the obligatory *Zakat al-fitr*, in which each person who can gives the value of one meal as charity. Most Muslims do not accept astronomical calculations for their festivals, so the new moon must actually be sighted for Ramadan to end and the *'Id* to begin, although this is a point of debate for some. As a result it may be celebrated on different days in different places, since the new moon is often visible in one place and not another.

Fasting at other times than Ramadan is recommended, but not obligatory. These times include a few days in the two months before Ramadan, the six days following

'Id al-Fitr, and Ashura (tenth of Muharram). One should not fast, however, on Fridays or *'Ids*.

The pilgrimage to Mecca, or *Ḥajj*

Every Muslim who is physically and financially able must make the pilgrimage to Mecca at least once in their lifetime. For most this is the high point of their life. Poorer people often save for a whole lifetime to be able to do it. After completing it they are entitled to call themselves *Ḥājj* or *Ḥajjī*, a title of considerable prestige (though involving no financial remuneration).

The *Hajj* was performed in pre-Islamic times and its rituals are believed to go back to Ibrahim and Isma'il, who erected the *Ka'ba* (or according to some rebuilt it after it had been built by Adam and destroyed in Nuh's flood). There is a black stone set in one corner of the *Ka'ba* that is traditionally believed to have come from heaven. Muhammad reformed the rites, purging them of idolatry, and in his "Farewell Pilgrimage" set the pattern for them for the future. Since then non-Muslims are not allowed in the sacred area, *ḥaram*, around Mecca. Mecca is sacred space par excellence for Muslims and is traditionally believed to be the center of the universe and the place most in touch with heaven. Here, in particular, one is in the presence of the King of the universe, though one prays to Him everywhere.

Before leaving home the pilgrims must pay their debts, make arrangements for any dependants and otherwise settle their affairs. Before the modern period the

Figure 7.4 *Hajjis* praying at the *Ka'ba* in Mecca during *Hajj*. Courtesy of iStockphoto

journey was both difficult and dangerous and could take months for those living far from Mecca. Many died on the way or during the *Hajj*, but it is understood that one who dies in the performance of the *Hajj* is guaranteed paradise. Because of modern transportation the numbers making the *Hajj* have increased considerably. Between 1800 and 1940 from 20,000 to 300,000 made the pilgrimage each year from outside Arabia. In 2006 this figure was more than 1,200,000. It may well be that today more people make the *Hajj* than completely fulfill the obligations of *salah* or Ramadan.

Before or upon arrival at the border of the *haram* male pilgrims don a special garb, called *iḥrām*, consisting of two pieces of white cloth. This symbolizes the equality of all believers before God, whatever their worldly status. Women wear modest garb, often ethnic garb, and do not cover their faces. It has been suggested that the male garb symbolizes the unity of *umma* and the female garb its diversity. From this point they are subject to certain prohibitions, including sexual intercourse, shedding blood or uprooting plants. Both before and during the pilgrimage the pilgrims regularly recite the *talbiya*, usually in Arabic:

> Here I am, O God, here I am.
> Here I am, You have no associate.
> Here I am. Praise belongs to you, and blessing and power.
> You have no associate. Here I am.

When recited loudly by a large number this is most impressive.

There are actually two pilgrimages, the *umra* or lesser pilgrimage, which may be performed at any time of the year, and the *Hajj* proper, which must be performed on the appointed days during the last month of the Muslim year, Dhu al-Hijja. Those who do the *Hajj* usually do the *umra* before it during the same visit.

The *umra* includes the *ṭawāf*, circumambulating the *Ka'ba* seven times, touching the black stone if possible. One performs *salah* at the Station of Ibrahim, from which Ibrahim supervised the building of the *Ka'ba*, and one runs between two hills called Safa and Marwa, recalling Hagar's frantic search for water for her baby, Isma'il (cf. Bible, Genesis 21:14–21). Near the Station of Ibrahim is the well of Zamzam, which burst forth from where Isma'il kicked his heel into the ground. For the *Hajj* proper the pilgrims travel on the eighth or ninth of Dhu al-Hijja to Mina, a town about four miles from Mecca, and then to the hill called Arafat or the Mount of Mercy, where they stand from noon till sundown, listening to *khutbas* and engaging in devotions, including the *talbiya*.

This "standing at Arafat" is absolutely essential; without it one has not performed the *Hajj*. It looks back to the time when Muhammad preached his farewell sermon here, and forward to the Last Day, when all humanity will stand before God, in whose presence the pilgrims are already standing. The pilgrims then rush to a place called Muzdalifa, where they spend the night, and then return to Mina on the tenth of Dhu al-Hijja where they stone three Pillars symbolizing the devil and then

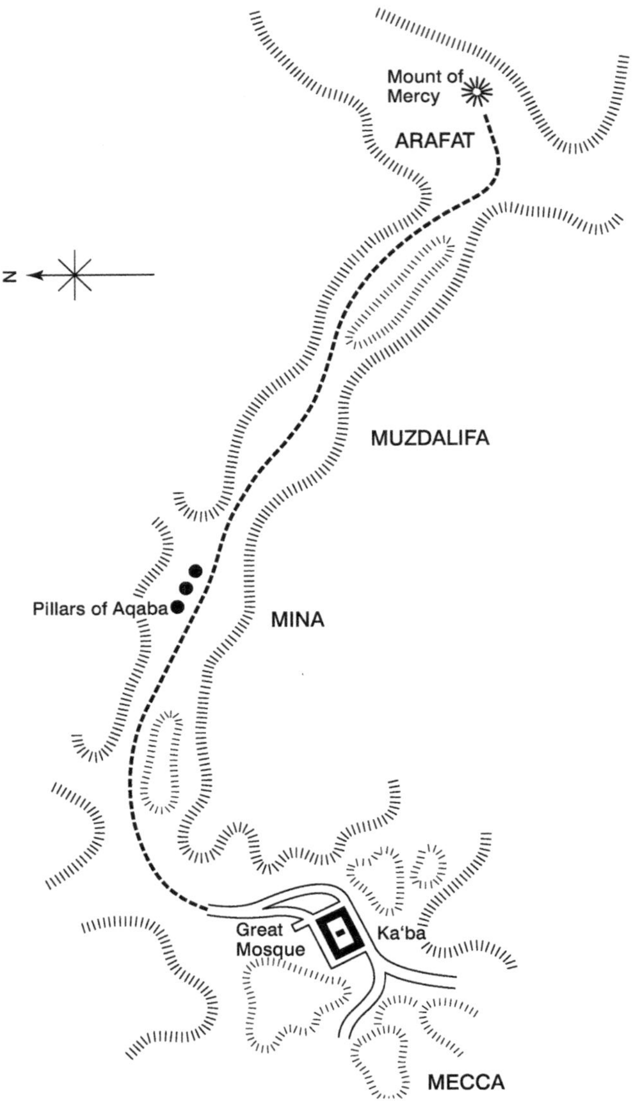

Map 5 Road between Mecca and Arafat

sacrifice an animal commemorating the fact that when God commanded Ibrahim to sacrifice his son, Isma'il, He substituted an animal at the last minute.

The pilgrims then cut their hair and may remove their *ihram* garb. They perform another *tawaf* of the *Ka'ba* and sleep at Mina from the tenth to the thirteenth of Dhu al-Hijja and stone the Pillars again on these days. They return to Mecca before sundown on the thirteenth, which marks the end of the *Hajj*, and they perform the *tawaf* again before leaving Mecca. Most pilgrims then go to Medina to visit the tomb of the Prophet, although this is not required.

It would be difficult to overemphasize the importance of the *Hajj*. Besides the spiritual dimension, which is central, there are important social and political effects. The *Hajj* not only symbolizes the unity of the *umma* but also helps to effect it. Here people from all parts of the Muslim world meet and, particularly in pre-modern times, this speeded up the exchange of ideas and information. Some have stayed on in Mecca to study before returning as scholars to their homes. The *Hajj* gives prestige to the government that hosts it, currently Saudi Arabia. In recent decades the Saudi government has expended considerable money and effort to improve the facilities and organization of the *Hajj* and some years ago the Saudi King took on the title of "Guardian of the Two Sanctuaries (Mecca and Medina)". In 1987 there were serious riots when Iranian pilgrims used the *Hajj* to propagandize their revolution and criticize the Saudis. Muslim governments today generally control the number of people going on *Hajj* and have some system for deciding who goes. Of particular interest is the Tabung Hajji in Malaysia, which since 1963 has helped people save up for the *Hajj* and then made the arrangements for them.

Other pilgrimages

Pilgrimages are made to other places than Mecca, but these, including the visit to Muhammad's tomb in Medina, are called *ziyāra* (visit) rather than *Hajj*. Jerusalem is considered the third sanctuary after Mecca and has been visited by pilgrims since early times, often on the way to Mecca. A *hadith* says: "A prayer in Mecca equals ten thousand ordinary prayers, a prayer in Medina equals a thousand, a prayer in Jerusalem equals five hundred." Visits are also made by Shi'is to the tombs of their *Imams* and by Sufis to the tombs of their saints (*walis*). (See chapters 8 and 12.)

The birthday of the Prophet Muhammad (Mawlid al-Nabi)

The birthday of the Prophet is commemorated by Sunnis on the twelfth of Rabi' al-Awwal, the third month of the Muslim year, although the festivities sometimes begin some days earlier. So far as is known, it was first celebrated during the Fatimid Dynasty during the eleventh century and involved only the caliph and his retinue. In the latter half of the twelfth century it was celebrated by Sunnis in Syria, Iraq, and in Mecca, involving the populace as well as the rulers. From these places it spread through the whole Muslim world. The actual ceremonies and festivities have varied, but generally they include the recitation of the Qur'an and poetry in praise of the Prophet, such as the *Mevlid-i Sherif* (see chapter 6), as well as feasts, processions, fairs and public *dhikrs* by Sufis. Because it began more than four centuries after Muhammad, it is clearly a *bid'a* (innovation) and has always been opposed by some. This opposition continues today, especially among those influenced by the Wahhabi thinking of Saudi Arabia (see chapter 15). Excesses of revelry that sometimes occur have also attracted criticism. Others argue that it is a "good *bid'a*" and for most Muslims it is an extremely popular and joyous festival. It is a public holiday in a number of countries. Shi'is celebrate it on the seventeenth of Rabi' al-Awwal, but it is not so important for them.

Life cycle rituals

The rituals and ceremonies that mark major stages in the individual's life do not have the status of Pillars and vary more from time to time and place to place but many are obligatory and all are extremely important to those involved. Here we shall focus mainly on those that involve all Muslims.

At birth the *adhan* is whispered into the baby's right ear and the *iqama* into the left ear, although precise practice varies. Both of these include the *shahada*, as mentioned earlier. The child is publicly named, usually on the seventh day, and it is recommended that a ceremony known as *'aqīqa* be performed in which two lambs for a boy or one for a girl are sacrificed. The mother is in confinement and ritually impure for forty days from the birth; after this she purifies herself with a *ghusl* and resumes her full activity.

Circumcision (*khitān*) is performed on males between the ages of seven days and 13 years, depending on local customs. It is often accompanied by considerable ceremony and the child is expected to show bravery in the face of the pain. Although some authorities consider it to be recommended rather than obligatory, it is in the minds of most Muslims extremely important, probably more so than some of the Pillars. Female "circumcision" (*khafḍ*), which may vary from a symbolic cut in the clitoris to a full labial removal, is practiced in some parts of the Muslim world, such as the Nilotic region. It is more rooted in custom than religion since non-Muslims in the same areas usually do it too and it is very weakly attested in the *Hadith*, while neither form of circumcision is mentioned in the Qur'an. Those who practice it, however, see it as commanded by religion also as a means of guaranteeing the girl's chastity. They defend it very forcefully, while reformers and most Westerners abhor it with equal or greater force. Here, as much as with terrorism, we need to seek the empathetic understanding discussed in the introduction *before* we criticize, however justified the criticism is.

Marriage is expected of Muslims and there are few who do not marry. Muslim spokespeople often contrast the importance of marriage in Islam with the ideal of monasticism among many Christian groups. Traditionally marriages have usually been arranged and have tended to be between related partners, with a certain preference for marriage between first cousins. The bride and groom may not have met before the marriage or may have had limited contact, but this is changing in modern times. Customs and ceremonies vary but usually involve considerable festivity. The core ceremony is the signing of the marriage contract by the groom and the bride's *walī* (guardian, if this is the bride's first marriage) and the payment of the *mahr*, a sum paid to the bride or her *wali* by the groom. Usually half the sum is paid at the time of the wedding and half on divorce or the death of the husband. The properties of the husband and wife remain separate but the husband is fully responsible for the maintenance of the family. A man may have as many as four wives at one time if he can support them and, when slavery existed, an unspecified number of slave concubines. This is the basis of the large "harems" among the wealthy and powerful of which we read. Financial considerations among other things have always made **polygyny** impossible for many. According to some interpretations a clause may be included in the marriage contract preventing the husband from taking a second wife.

In terms of the rules developed by *fiqh*, divorce is technically quite easy for the husband, since he needs only to pronounce the formula, "You are divorced", once or three times depending on the circumstances. There are several variants of this and there are also other forms of divorce. The wife may initiate a form of divorce called *khul'*, in which she compensates the husband, often by foregoing the part of the *mahr* still due her. If a woman is divorced she must wait for three menstrual periods before remarriage, to ensure that she is not pregnant from the previous marriage. There are, of course, many legal details surrounding divorce, some of which will be mentioned in chapter 10. The traditional rules have been subject to considerable criticism by modern reformers and many Muslim states have modified them. While legally easy, both polygyny and divorce have in practice been subject to significant constraints, not least from the families of the wives involved.

When death approaches the dying person's face should be turned toward Mecca and the first part of the *shahada* recited (otherwise, recited into the ear before burial). *Sura Ya Sin* of the Qur'an (36) should also be recited. After death the body must be washed (except in the case of a martyr, whose body is considered already pure) and wrapped in a shroud. A special *salah*, called *ṣalāt al-janāza* is performed, either in a mosque or elsewhere. Unlike other *salahs* this one is done standing and includes *du'a* for the deceased. The body is then carried in procession to the place of burial, where it is buried on its side in the grave with the head facing toward Mecca. These procedures are accompanied by recitations from the Qur'an and prayers (*du'ā'*). They take place as soon after death as possible. It is widely believed that two fearsome angels, Munkir and Nakir, question the deceased in the grave about his faith. Mourning customs vary; generally the full period is forty days but the most intense period is during the first few days. There is often loud mourning connected with death but the strictest do not approve of this.

Inheritance laws are among the most complex of the Shari'a. A person may leave up to one-third of his or her estate as a bequest, and the rest goes by a very complicated formula to specified heirs (who cannot receive any of the bequest). In many situations women receive half the share of men. Muslims often justify this on the grounds that men have the full responsibility of supporting the family. There have been some changes in inheritance laws under modern governments.

Figure 7.5 *Sibha.* Courtesy of Shutterstock

Sibha

A *sibḥa* (also pronounced *subḥa*) or *misbāḥa* is a kind of rosary, usually with thirty-three beads, but sometimes with eleven or ninety-nine, which is used to count the recitations of various prayer formulae, such as *subḥān allāh* (praise be to God) or the ninety-nine names of God. It is also often used in a more secular way to keep one's fingers occupied.

Halal *food*

There are rules concerning what meat may be eaten (comparable to Jewish kosher rules, but less extensive and strict) that are quite important. These are discussed in a number of passages in the Qur'an as well as in the *Hadith* and by scholars later. The following passage from the Qur'an gives the main points:

> So eat of the *ḥalāl* and good food God has provided for you, if it is indeed Him whom you serve. He has forbidden to you only carrion, blood, the flesh of pigs and that which has been offered to something other than God. But if one is compelled against one's will and without transgressing, God is forgiving and merciful.
>
> (16:114)

This gives the main categories of forbidden food (*ḥarām*). The *Hadith* adds beasts of prey and other specific animals have been added by later scholars. Alcohol is also *ḥarām*. Animals that are permitted, i.e. *halal*, must be slaughtered in a specified way, also called *halal*. For larger animals this includes cutting the throat quickly with a sharp knife so that the animal suffers minimally and as much blood comes out of the body as possible, saying, "In the name of God, the Merciful, the Compassionate", as the animal is killed, and pointing the animal's head toward Mecca. The issue of *halal* arises with any food (e.g. biscuits, cakes) that may include meat derivatives (e.g. lard) or alcohol. Since the Qur'an says that Muslims may eat the food of the People of the Book (5:5) some would say that Kosher food is suitable. Muslims generally believe that what is not *halal* is bad for our health and that this is the reason that God forbids it.

The importance of *halal* food is such that many otherwise non-practicing Muslims, in my experience, will go to great lengths to make sure that their food is *halal*. Some who live far from centers of Muslim population may have difficulty finding *halal* meat and become effectively vegetarian as a result. In this age of technology and international trade *halal* food has become a major industry and *halal* practice can have an effect on the food industry in general. In recent years a major point of debate has been whether *halal* meat can be purchased in a supermarket, where it may be contaminated by contact with non-*halal* meat, or only from *halal* butcher shops. In New Zealand, for example, meat export to Muslim countries is sufficiently important so that almost all beef and sheep abbatoirs follow *halal* practice (since non-Muslim countries will accept *halal* meat they do not produce non-*halal* meat). Here and elsewhere various technological issues have arisen, for example, over whether it is acceptable for the animals to be stunned before they are slaughtered in the *halal* manner.

Key points

- A basic distinction is made between *'ibadat*, "acts of worship" and *mu'amalat*, duties to other people.
- The body is brought into the ritual life in a major way at several points, e.g. purification, fasting, circumcision.
- Each of the Pillars has an individual and a social dimension.
- Life cycle rituals are extremely important to people but are less standardized than the Pillars.
- Rules around food (*halal*) are extremely important in practice.
- The two main holidays, or *'Ids*, are *'Id al-Fitr* and *'Id al-Adha*.

Discussion questions

1. How do the Pillars serve to unify the *umma*?
2. Which of the Pillars seems to you the most demanding or difficult to perform?

3. How might Muslims determine the times for *salah* and fasting if they are in the Arctic or Antarctic when it is always daytime or nighttime? What if they are in outer space?
4. Are there any Pillars that should never be performed by some individuals?
5. What might be the economic effects of the *halal* rules or rules for wills and bequests?
6. How would our conception of such holidays as Christmas, Thanksgiving and Independence Day (or comparable holidays in other countries) be different if they moved in relation to the seasons as the Muslim festivals do?

Critical thinking box 7.1

List the general purposes and meanings of ritual that you can think of and apply these to one major Muslim ritual or festival and one non-Muslim ritual or festival.

Companion website

Features mainly websites for YouTube links and recordings relating to the Adhan, Ramadan, Hajj and recitations of the Qur'an.

Further reading

Abdalati, Hammuda (1975) *Islam in Focus*. Indianapolis, IN: American Trust Publications. (A "standard" work by a leading Sunni scholar, focuses on ritual, personal and family life.)

Von Grunebaum, Gustave E. (1951) *Muhammadan Festivals*. London: Curzon Press. (Older study by a well-known scholar, somewhat dated but still useful.)

Al-Ghazali, Abu Hamid (1983) *Inner Dimensions of Islamic Worship*, trans. Muhtar Holland. Leicester: Islamic Foundation. (Part of al-Ghazali's *Iḥyā*, see chapter 13.)

Kamal, Ahmad (1964) *The Sacred Journey*. London: Allen & Unwin. (Reverent presentation of the details of the *Ḥajj*.)

Long, David E. (1979) *The Hajj Today*. Albany, NY: State University of New York Press. (Considerable detail and statistics.)

Bianchi, Robert R. (2004) *Guests of God: Pilgrimage and Politics in the Islamic World*. New York: Oxford University Press.

Kaptein, N.J.G. (1993) *Muhammad's Birthday Festival: Early History in the Central Muslim Lands and Development in the Muslim West until the 10th/16th Century*.

Leiden: Brill. (Detailed study, focusing especially on the origins of the festival as well as reactions to it.)

Fakhouri, Hani (1972) *Kafr el-Elow: An Egyptian Village in Transition*. New York: Holt, Rinehart and Winston (especially chapters 3–6). (Anthropological study.)

Fernea, Elizabeth (1969) *Guests of the Sheik*. Garden City, NY: Doubleday. (Well-regarded study of women in a southern Iraqi village.)

Padwick, Constance (1961) *Muslim Devotions: A Study of Prayer-manuals in Common Use*. London: SPCK. (An excellent source for *du'a*.)

See also: Knysh, *Islam in Historical Perspective* (Ch. 17) [F]; Jeffery, *Islam: Muhammad and his Religion* (Chs 5, 6) [F]; Renard, *Seven Doors to Islam* and *Windows on the House of Islam* (Ch. 2) [F]; Denny, *An Introduction to Islam* [F]; Rippin and Knappert, *Textual Sources for the Study of Islam* (Ch. 3) [F]; Esposito, *The Oxford History of Islam* (Ch. 2) [F].

Online resources (accessed 2 September 2013)

A recording of the Sunni version of the *adhan*: http://www.youtube.com/watch?v=UlLaUCAQlQQ

A recording of the Shi'i version of the *adhan*: http://www.youtube.com/watch?v=krHFI0kEh-k&NR=1

A recitation of *Surah Ya Sin* may be accessed at this website: http://www.youtube.com/watch?v=d1rOuS8ytx4

Guide to *salah* for beginners (takes one through the steps): http://www.youtube.com/watch?v=l1oF8DG4BDg&feature=related

8 *Divisions in the* umma

Sects and political theory

> O you who believe, obey God, and obey the Messenger and those of you who are in authority.
>
> (Qur'an 4:59)

> You will be ruled after me by rulers who are righteous and rulers who are depraved. Listen to them and obey them in all that is right. If they do good, it will tell for you and for them. If they do evil, it will tell for you and against them.
>
> (*Hadith*, quoted by al-Mawardi in *The Ordinances of Government*)

The major "sectarian" divisions of Islam began in the context of the early political struggles within the *umma*, and provide an illustration of the importance of politics to Islam. These divisions were never "merely" political but were about the proper guidance of the *umma*, that is, the way in which God's guidance should be mediated to it. They were also responses to the fact that social realities did not live up to the religious vision. Thus they were religious and political at the same time. This chapter will focus primarily on three different visions of how this guidance should take place, presented by three divisions of Islam, Khārijīs, Shīʿīs and Sunnīs, of which the last two are generally considered the major divisions, while the first represents a distinctive and significant option.

In this chapter

- The Khariji movments
- The Shiʿis
- The Zaydis or "Fiver" Shiʿis
- The Ismaʿilis or "Sevener" Shiʿis
- The *Imamis* or Twelver Shiʿis
- Shiʿi-related groups: ʿAlawis, Alevis and Druze
- The Sunnis: political development and theory
- Persian and Greek contributions

As the reader will be aware from chapters 3 and 4, the political history of the ***umma*** in the early centuries was marked by considerable political conflict and much of this involved groups with radically different views of how God's guidance is received and acted on. These conflicts were one of the main stimulants for the development of political theory. The main groups presented here, the Kharijis, three groups of Shi'is, and the Sunnis, are presented roughly in the historical order in which their distinctive doctrines came to light and challenged the rest of the *umma*. As a result these groups appear in the reverse of their importance and number of adherents today. (There is something of a parallel with the history of Christian doctrine, in which "orthodoxy" came into existence by defining itself against a series of "heresies", most of which did not prosper later.)

Kharijis

The word *khariji* may be translated "seceder" or "rebel". The Kharijis included those who broke with **'Ali** when, during the battle against **Mu'awiya** at Siffin, he accepted arbitration on the question of whether the killing of **'Uthman** had been justified. They held that 'Uthman had clearly violated the Qur'an and thus the matter should not be arbitrated by humans; 'Ali had committed a serious sin by accepting this. Their slogan was "judgment belongs only to Allah". 'Ali soon defeated them but movements based on their ideas mounted serious opposition to the existing governments for about two centuries.

They accepted the validity of the caliphates of **Abu Bakr** and **'Umar**, and part of 'Uthman's caliphate, but not that of 'Ali or of the **Umayyads** or **Abbasids**. They held that the *imām* (the leader of the *umma*) should be the most pious and capable free person in the *umma*, whatever his ancestry or family connections, and should be chosen by the believers and receive their unqualified obedience. If he commits a major sin (as 'Ali was thought to have done), however, he should be deposed. Most Khariji groups separated themselves from the rest of the community and believed they were the only true Muslims. The strictest of them, the Azraqis, held that people who did not make ***hijra*** to them (i.e. join them) were ***kafirs*** and should be fought and killed. Their attacks have been described as terrorism. A bit more moderate were the Najdis, who ruled part of Arabia for a time in the late seventh century and viewed outsiders as hypocrites, but not to be killed. There were also some who lived among non-Kharijis and practiced *taqiya* (i.e. hid their identity, see below). Some believed that there might be more than one *imam* in different places, while others held that an *imam* was not absolutely necessary. A still more moderate group, the 'Ibadis, continue to this day in Oman, where they are the majority of the population. Small groups are also found in Tunisia, Algeria and Tanzania. Perhaps the main importance of the Kharijis in the long run is that their positions on a number of political and theological issues forced the rest of the *umma* to define its own position(s) over against them.

Since they were extremely disruptive in the early centuries the word *khariji* came to be a term of abuse, suggesting fanaticism and violence. Apart from the survivals of the early movement, there is a continuing tendency that can be labeled Khariji with some justification though it does not so label itself. Movements such as the Wahhabis in Arabia in the eighteenth century and many of the violent movements of the later twentieth century might be included. In fact, the latter are often labeled Khariji by their critics. One such movement in Egypt was popularly labeled *Takfīr* (judging someone to be a *kafir*) and *Hijra*, both terms evoking features of the Khariji movement (see chapter 17).

Shi'is

The name Shi'i derives from the term *shī'at 'Alī*, the party of 'Ali. There are three main groups, the Zaydis or "Fivers", the Isma'ilis or "Seveners" and the "Twelvers" or Imamis, each with its own response to the issue of guidance.

In contrast to the common view that Muhammad did not appoint a successor, Shi'is believe that he did in fact appoint 'Ali as his successor a few months before his death at a place called Ghadir Khumm. His leadership was justified also by his character and the fact that he was the Prophet's nearest male relative. When 'Ali was passed over first for Abu Bakr and then for 'Umar and 'Uthman, he remained silent for the sake of the unity of the *umma*. In the view of most Shi'is they were, however, usurpers and under them the *umma* declined morally, whatever its material success. 'Ali, in his brief caliphate, was not able to stem the tide. 'Ali designated his eldest son, Hasan, as his successor, but, in the face of Mu'awiya's greater power, Hasan decided to stand aside so as to avoid useless bloodshed. After his death in 669 his brother, Husayn, succeeded him as rightful *Imam*. The actions of Mu'awiya's son and successor, Yazīd, prompted him to set out from Mecca, where he was living, with a band of seventy-two followers, to help the people of Kufa, in Iraq. They were intercepted at a place called Karbalā' by a large army sent by Yazid and were completely annihilated. This event, which took place in 680, has echoed down the centuries for Shi'is (and for others to some extent). Husayn has been viewed as sacrificing himself for his people and making a stand against oppression. The few survivors included his sister Zaynab, who along with 'Ali's wife, Fatima, is viewed as a model of female courage and devotion in the face of adversity, and Husayn's young son, 'Ali Zayn al-'Ābidīn (or al-Sajjād), who became the fourth *Imam* and who led a life of pious seclusion. According to most Shi'is an *Imam* is a son of the preceding *Imam*, except in the case of al-Husayn, and must be designated (*naṣṣ*) by him.

Zaydis or "Fivers"

At this point the lines of Shi'i *Imams* diverge, as different groups recognize different successions. In 740 Zayd, one of the sons of 'Ali Zayn al-'Abidin was killed in one of the many revolts against the Umayyads, but his movement continued and in 913 one of his successors established a state in the Caspian area that lasted for over a century, while another state was established in Yemen from about 897 and lasted with interruptions until 1962. Zaydis consider Zayd the fifth *Imam* but after him no specific lineage or designation is required for an *Imam* beyond being a descendant of 'Ali and Fatima, nor is there a continuous line of *Imams*. An *Imam* gains his position by demonstrating knowledge in religious matters and by his ability to lead a revolt against unjust (i.e. non-Shi'i) authorities, and Zaydis are obligated to follow him when he appears.

Isma'ilis or "Seveners"

Most Shi'is recognize a different fifth *Imam*, Muhammad al-Baqir (d. c. 732–43) and recognize Ja'far al-Sadiq (d. 765) as sixth *Imam*. Both were known as scholars and Ja'far was the founder of the Twelver Shi'i school of ***fiqh*** (see chapter 10). Isma'ilis consider Ja'far's son, Isma'il, to be the seventh *Imam* and a line of *Imams* continues from him to present time, though there is some question (in the minds of non-Isma'ilis) about the succession at certain points. These *Imams* have sometimes been in concealment (*satr*), including Isma'il's immediate successors, and sometimes visible. When concealed there has been a visible spokesman, called *ḥujja* (proof), and under him *dāʿīs* (propagators, missionaries), who have led the movement in particular areas. Isma'ilis led several violent revolutionary movements between the tenth and thirteenth centuries, including the Qarmati movement in Bahrain, the Fatimid movement in Tunisia and then Egypt, and the Nizārī movement, so-called "Assassins", in Syria, Iraq and Iran, which arose from a split in the Fatimid movement. The Nizaris, known to their opponents as Batinis (esoterics), went through several major doctrinal transformations – one *Imam* proclaimed a spiritual resurrection and the end of the Shari'a but this was reversed by a later one – before the basis of their power was destroyed by the Mongols in 1256 and their numbers decimated. The main group that has survived is the Khojas, whose leader, the Aga Khan, shifted to Bombay in 1845. Today they are a prosperous and peaceful community in India and Pakistan and spread worldwide. Also deriving from a split in the Fatimid movement are several groups of Bohras, who were established in Yemen for some time and then shifted to India, where they have traditionally been traders.

For Isma'ilis the truth is mediated by the *Imam*, who provides an esoteric interpretation of the scripture that yields an elaborate cyclical doctrine of the cosmos and of human history. This teaching is given most fully to those at the highest level, who are able to receive it, while others receive a more exoteric teaching. In practice Isma'ilism stimulated intellectual speculation and Isma'ilis developed doctrines considerably influenced by Hellenistic philosophy and other pre-Islamic traditions, through which they saw themselves as sharing in the secrets of the universe. They practiced *taqiya*, prudent dissimulation. For Twelvers this means the obligation to hide their identity as Shi'is or aspects of their belief when these would put their community in danger of persecution, but for Isma'ilis it also means that the initiate is not to reveal the teachings to outsiders or even to other Isma'ilis who are at a lower level of initiation.

Imāmīs or "Twelvers"

The Twelvers were the last major group of Shi'is to develop a clear identity, but they are by far the largest group today. They recognize a different son of Ja'far, Mūsā al-Kāẓim (d. 799), as the seventh *Imam* and his son, 'Alī al-Riḍā (d. 818), as the eighth. The latter was actually designated by the Abbasid caliph, al-Ma'mūn, as his successor, but he died before al-Ma'mun. His sister, Fāṭima Ma'ṣūma, is revered in her own right and her shrine in Qom is the most important one in that city. The next three *Imams* were Muhammad al-Taqī (d. 835), Muhammad al-Hādī, or al-Nāqī (d. 868), and Ḥasan al-Askarī (d. 872). All of these suffered persecution and all of them, indeed all eleven *Imams* according to Twelvers, were murdered by the ruling powers. According to the Twelvers Hasan al-Askari left a young son, Muhammad, who immediately went into hiding, called the Minor Occultation (*ghayba*) and communicated with his followers only through four successive deputies. In 939 this communication ended and it was announced that he had entered into the Major Occultation and would no longer communicate with humanity until he reappears as the *mahdī*, when he "will fill the earth with equity and justice as it was filled with oppression and tyranny" (Tabataba'i, 1977, 211). Meanwhile, he continues to be the *Imam* of This Age and the rightful ruler and teacher of humankind. Thus, apart from 'Ali none of the twelve *Imams* actually ruled, although they were the rightful rulers of the *umma*. They did teach their followers, however, and these teachings are authoritative, indeed are at the same level as the Prophet's teaching, since they were protected from error (*ma'ṣūm*). The *Imams*, along with Muhammad and Fatima the wife of 'Ali, are called the fourteen *ma'sums*. They also have a high cosmic status and have access to esoteric knowledge, though esotericism is not carried as far as with the Isma'ilis.

Implicit in their story is a pessimistic view of history and a quietist attitude toward politics. The *umma* went seriously astray as soon as the Prophet died and then from bad to worse after that, finally reaching the point where the world was no longer a fit place for the pure *Imam*. It is left for the true believers to worship God, cultivate devotion to the *Imams*, elaborate theological and legal doctrines and wait expectantly for the *mahdi*, practicing *taqiya* when necessary. In compensation they know that by following the *Imam* of the Age they are the true believers. It has also been a practice to curse the first three caliphs as usurpers, though this seems less common today.

In the absence of the *Imam's* leadership there would seem little scope for political action. In practice, though, it has not quite been this way. Only a few years after the Major Occultation the Shi'i Buyids took charge in Baghdad and remained in charge for about a century. Though they did not remove the Sunni caliph, they did support Shi'i interests and patronize Shi'i devotion and scholarship. There were other Shi'i dynasties in Syria and Iraq from 944 until about 1100 that were either Twelvers or sympathetic to Twelvers, such as the Hamdanids. The tenth and eleventh centuries also saw a flourishing of Shi'i scholarship. Many of the Mongols and their successors were sympathetic to Shi'ism, and one became Shi'i (Oljeitu, r. 1304–17). Twelver Shi'i populations have continued in the Arab world down to the present time, with Shi'i majorities in Iraq and Bahrain and substantial minorities in Lebanon and eastern Saudi Arabia.

With the rise of the Safavid Dynasty in Iran in the sixteenth century Twelver Shi'ism became the official creed of a major state. The first Safavid shah claimed descent from the seventh *Imam* and also the status of the "perfect master" and a divine manifestation, claims inconsistent with Twelver doctrine, but his successors made the lesser claim of being deputies of the Hidden *Imam*, who thus became the legitimating symbol of the regime. Thus Twelver Shi'ism found a formula for effective guidance in politics without the presence of the *Imam*, though one that could be contested. In fact, the *'ulama'* also came to claim the status of deputy of the *Imam*, thus putting them in potential, and eventually actual, competition with the shah. Also, as deputies of the *Imam* they receive half of *khums*, an annual tax of one-fifth of one's net income paid by Shi'is. This is used for charitable and educational purposes and also provides a measure of economic independence. *Khums* is based on Qur'an 8:41 (concerning the Prophet's share of booty); Sunnis interpret this passage differently and do not pay *khums*.

Twelvers have a number of distinctive rituals and celebrations. For example, they recognize not only the birthday of Muhammad but also those of all twelve *Imams*, Fatima and others. They make pilgrimages particularly to the shrines of 'Ali at Najaf, Husayn at Karbala', the *Imams* Musa al-Kazim and Muhammad al-Taqi at Kazamayn, *Imam* Rida at Mashhad and *Imam* Rida's sister, Fatima, at Qom, the first three places being in Iraq and the last two in Iran.

Most important are the extremely emotional activities commemorating the martyrdom of *Imam* Husayn that go collectively under the name of *ta'ziya* (consolation). These include dramatic recitations of Husayn's story, called *rawḍas*, and eulogies, which may be done at any time of the year. There are *dastas*, processions of young men who flagellate themselves to demonstrate their sorrow for Husayn's suffering and repentence at not helping his cause sufficiently. Best known is the

Figure 8.1 Shi'is participating in the *ta'ziya* in Baghdad in December 2010. Courtesy of AHMAD AL-RUBAYE/AFP/Getty Images

"passion play", called *ta'ziya or shabīh*, that re-enacts the events of Karbala' with such effect that people often virtually feel as if they are witnessing the actual event. (Those who play the villains have sometimes been in danger of their lives!) The processions of *dastas* and the *shabihs* are carried out during the first ten days of Muharram, the first month of the Muslim year, reaching a crescendo on the tenth, 'Ashura, the day of Husayn's death. The first recorded commemorations of Husayn's death were under the Buyids, beginning in 963. Commemorations also took place under the Safavids. The first recorded performance of the *shabih* took place in 1787 and the *shabihs* flourished under the Qajars in the nineteenth century. The *'ulama'* have been cautious about the *shabih* because it involves depicting human beings. In fact, it may have encouraged the depiction of religious figures in popular "coffee house" paintings in Iran. Husayn was to play a major role in the Islamic revolution of 1978–79 as we shall see in chapter 18.

Shi'i-related groups: Alawis, Alevis and Druze

There is not enough space to deal with these groups in detail but a brief mention is necessary since they all play a significant role in parts of the Middle East. They all derive from extreme forms of Shi'ism. 'Alawīs (or Nuṣayrīs) in Syria and the Alevis in Turkey are quite distinct groups, though their names are different forms of the same word, meaning "follower of 'Ali". Both recognize 'Ali as the highest manifestation of the divine.

The 'Alawis follow the teachings of Ibn Nusayr (ninth century) and believe in the transmigration of souls. Often persecuted in past centuries, they have dominated the Syrian government under the aegis of an Arab nationalist ideology, Baathism, since 1970 but are currently (2013) being challenged in a bitter civil war by predominantly Sunni opposition groups.

The Alevis derive from the Shi'i Safavid movement in the sixteenth century and are closely connected to the Bektashi Sufi Order. They have suffered considerable persecution at the hands of the Sunnis but are currently undergoing a significant revival. (See chapter 16.)

The Druze believe that the Fatimid ruler of Egypt, al-Hakim, who died or disappeared in 1021, was the final earthly manifestation of God. They also believe that human souls transmigrate. They live primarily in Lebanon, where they have played a major political role. All of these follow an esoteric interpretation of the Qur'an and in general their full doctrine is known only to a spiritual elite. All three groups differ in their ritual practices from other Muslims, many of whom do not consider them to be Muslims.

Sunnis

It must be pointed out at the beginning of this section that we conventionally use the word "caliph (*khalīfa*)" when discussing Sunni usage, but the sources actually use both *khalīfa* and *imām* with more or less the same meaning, and I will do this here.

The Sunnis are known in Arabic as *ahl al-sunna wa-l-jamā'a* (people of the *Sunna* and the main-line community) and comprise 85 to 90 percent of the whole *umma* today. They go back to those who sided with 'Uthman's supporters against 'Ali or stayed aloof from the quarrel and who accepted the rule of the Umayyads, whether willingly or with reservations. In time they came to accept that Abu Bakr, 'Umar, 'Uthman and 'Ali were all legitimate caliphs and were to be called the Rightly Guided Caliphs (*Rāshidūn*). In what later became the standard view, the Umayyads were politically capable but religiously and morally very suspect, oppressing people and governing arbitrarily or by pre-Islamic tribal standards, rather than by the Qur'an and the *Sunna* of the Prophet. This assessment is probably unfair and reflects the anti-Umayyad propaganda put forth by the Abbasids. They undoubtedly made many decisions on their own, especially since they had a very high view of their position, taking such titles as *khalīfat allāh* (deputy of God). But they also would have taken into account the *sunna* of the community as it was then understood, given that later ideas about the *Sunna* of the Prophet had not yet developed (see chapter 10).

There were many who disliked their actions, including some who openly criticized them, but refrained from rebelling against them. This was in part because of their power, in part because of the disruption caused by revolt, and in part because they at least maintained the political and military strength of the *umma*. This attitude toward unjust rule was to become typical of the Sunni position (see below). A good example of this attitude was Hasan al-Baṣrī (642–728), a well-known ascetic, popular preacher, sometime *qadi* and fighter in *jihad*, who was a forerunner of developments in both theology and Sufism. He and his followers openly criticized actions of the Umayyad caliphs but did not actively oppose them. They did encourage a spirit of opposition to them, reflected in *hadiths* such as "A religious man who goes to see a ruler loses his religion" (Zilfi, 1988, 28). Some important scholars did cooperate with the Umayyads, however, such as Sufyān al-Thawrī (d. 778) and Abd al-Raḥmān al-Awzāʿī (d. 774), both leading figures in *fiqh*.

When the Abbasids came to power they made a show of respecting and following the Shariʿa and consulting the *ʿulama*ʾ. They appointed *qāḍīs* who were to make decisions according to the Shariʿa. Their actions, however, were not so different from those of the Umayyads. Their lifestyle was more luxurious and the symbols of their authority more exalted. The title "shadow of God on earth" was used for them and many later rulers. Some claimed the right to define doctrine or law and all expected favorable interpretations of the Shariʿa from the *ʿulama*ʾ. While most *ʿulama*ʾ cooperated with them there were those who refused to. Abu Hanifa, one of the great scholars of all time, would not accept an appointment from them but his disciples did. While the *qadis* judged by the Shariʿa, the caliphs appointed and dismissed them and determined their areas of jurisdiction. The caliphs carved out a separate legal territory for themselves by establishing Courts of Complaints (*maẓālim*), designed to hear complaints about *qadis*' decisions and branching out beyond this. This is an example of what came to be known as *siyāsa* (a word that now means "politics" but in this context means "policy"), the right of the ruler to make fairly free decisions in many areas within the wide bounds of the Shariʿa. They were not willing (or able), however, to implement the recommendation of one of their Persian bureaucrats, Ibn Muqaffaʿ (who also made major contributions to literature, see chapter 14), that the caliph codify the existing laws, formulating on each question the view to which God would guide him.

Beginning in 833 the caliphs instituted an "inquisition" (*miḥna*) in an effort to force the *ʿulama*ʾ to accept the **Muʿtazili** doctrine that the Qur'an is created (see chapter 11). The traditionalists resisted this, led by Ahmad ibn Hanbal, who spent many years in prison for his opposition, and the government finally reversed itself about 848. This was a victory for the relative independence of the *ʿulama*ʾ, as it became clear that the caliph's role was not to determine law or doctrine but to administer it, though with some rights of interpretation, particularly in the areas designated *siyasa*.

When actual power passed from the hands of the caliph to military leaders, *amīrs* or sulṭāns, political theory had to allow for this while still asserting the importance of the caliph. An example of this can be found in *The Ordinances of Government* (*Al-aḥkām al-sulṭāniyya*) by al-Mawardi (d. 1058), which is usually seen as the classic statement of Sunni theory on the caliphate. It was written to support the Abbasid caliph at a time when actual power was wielded by Shiʿi Buyid *amirs* but it also justifies the existing situation. It makes the following points, among others: The obligation to have an *imam* to lead the community and guarantee its political existence is known by divine revelation, not by reason (against the Mu'tazilis and the philosophers) since the authority of the *imam* comes from God. The *imam* must have high moral qualities and sufficient knowledge to make independent decisions, soundness of body, prudence, courage and he must be descended from the Quraysh, but he does not have to be the best person available (against the Kharijis). His duties are executive and do not include interpreting the Shari'a. He must be chosen by qualified electors, but one may be enough. He may be designated by his predecessor (but it is not clear whether a father may designate his son). There cannot be two *imams* at the same time (against the Fatimids and the Spanish Umayyads who also claimed the imamate at that time). The *imam* should not be designated *khalifat allah* (as the Umayyads were). If the *imam* becomes unjust he should resign, but no means is specified for compelling this. If he is under the control of one of his officials (the actual situation at the time), this is acceptable for the sake of the public good if that person acts according to the dictates of religion and justice. If someone seizes control of a province but recognizes the authority of the caliph (the case of the Ghaznavids at the time) and governs according to the Shari'a, this also is acceptable, on the grounds of necessity.

Al-Mawardi's acceptance of the actual situation is carried somewhat further by another scholar, al-Ghazali (see chapter 13 for more on him), who lived two generations later under the Sunni Saljuk sultans. Ideally, he says, the *imam* should have practical competence, sufficient learning to interpret the Shari'a (al-Mawardi is less clear on this), piety and descent from the Quraysh. If he lacks the first three but is willing to take advice from the *'ulama'*, he should be accepted since the effort to overthrow him would cause social disruption and since without an *imam* all public activities are invalid. He may be chosen by the previous *imam* or by someone with actual power, such as a military leader. What this meant in practice was that the Saljuk sultan ruled and chose or at least confirmed the *imam* while the *imam* in turn legitimated the sultan's rule as well as social life in general. Both al-Mawardi and al-Ghazali rely on the juristic principle that "necessity makes forbidden things permissible", though al-Ghazali emphasizes it more and seems more comfortable with the situation.

In 1256 the Mongols captured Baghdad and effectively ended the Abbasid caliphate, although an Abbasid line continued in the court of the Mamlukes in Cairo and was recognized by some. Its authority was supposedly passed on to the Ottomans when they took over from the Mamlukes, but few people knew of or accepted all of this until the Ottomans began to make something of it in the nineteenth century (see chapter 16). Also, some rulers took the title *amīr al-mu'minīn* (commander of the faithful), traditionally associated with the caliphate, to emphasize their commitment to the Shari'a. Typical of the position to which many Sunnis came in this situation was that taken by Ibn Taymiyya in his book *Siyāsa Shar'iyya* (Shari'a-based Governance).

He makes no reference at all to an ongoing caliphate but he insists very strongly that the actual rulers should follow the Shari'a. For him the only true caliphs are the first four, a view held by others also over the years. Here the Shari'a is sovereign and the rulers are meant to be its servants. While criticizing rulers, Ibn Taymiyya does not advocate rebellion against them (see chapter 13).

Thus the Sunni position came to be that a ruler, caliph or otherwise, is legitimated by seeing that the Shari'a is implemented, though this implementation was never complete. *Siyasa* should be subordinated to the Shari'a but often has not been. He is also legitimated by his success in gaining power, since it is assumed that this success is granted by God. The manner of choosing the ruler is therefore less important and, in fact, often has happened by force, though the desirability of a Qurayshi *imam* was usually maintained in theory. If the rulers are unjust but at least remain outwardly Muslims and protect society and its institutions, one should be very slow to rebel against them. The Prophet is quoted as saying, "Thirty years of tyranny are better than one day of anarchy." With the occultation of the Twelfth *Imam* the Twelver Shi'i position came to be almost the same for practical purposes, although with more potentiality to delegitimate the ruler.

While the Sunnis have been the majority of the *umma* throughout history (or, more precisely for the earlier centuries, the majority of the *umma*, who rejected the Khariji and Shi'i positions, are now labeled Sunni) their distinctive political and theological doctrines came to maturity only with figures such as al-Mawardi and al-Ghazali and, especially, with the development of Sunni ***madrasas***, the mutual recognition of the four Sunni schools of *fiqh* (***madhhabs***) (see chapters 9, 10 and 13).

Persian and Greek contributions

From the later Umayyad period onward both Iranian and Greek thinking influenced Muslim ideas about government. The *mazalim* courts, mentioned earlier, were derived from the **Sasanian** administrative tradition. The well-known saying, "The sultan (authority; later, the one who exercises it) is the shadow of God on earth" is ascribed to the Prophet but is certainly Iranian in origin. The "shadow of God" may be connected with the Iranian idea of a divine effulgence (*khvarr* or *farr*) granted by God to the one He chooses to be king. The Iranian courtiers believed that this power had passed from the Sasanians to the Muslims in the time of 'Umar and Muhammad took pride in the fact that he had been born during the time of Khusraw Nushirvan, one of the greatest of the Sasasian kings. There is a genre of literature known as "mirrors for princes" that provides moral and practical advice for rulers. In this literature pre-Islamic Iranian kings regularly appear as examples of just rule. Muslim and Greek rulers and philosophers also appear. It is said that the Iranian kings ruled for many centuries, though they were unbelievers, because they were just, and the conclusion is drawn that a realm can survive unbelief but not injustice.

One such book is ascribed to the Saljuk *wazir,* Nizam al-Mulk and another to al-Ghazali. Both have been translated into English.

Greek ideas, such as that of the philosopher king in Plato's *Republic,* mediated through the later Hellenistic traditions, were taken up and Islamicized by philosophers such as al-Farabi and **Ibn Sina**. Al-Farabi, in his book entitled *The Opinions of the Dwellers in the Virtuous City,* says that a ruler should be to the polity as the mind is to the body or God is to the world. He argues that the best polity is one ruled by a prophet or a philosopher whose intellect is fully developed and in direct contact with the Active Intellect (the supramundane source of knowledge, see chapter 13). Failing these the polity should be ruled by a philosopher or philosophers of lower stature who follow the laws established by the earlier rulers. A polity not ruled by a philosopher will not long retain its excellence. Both the Greek and Iranian visions emphasize strong leadership and have a hierarchical view of society.

A thinker who drew on the philosophical tradition and on the tradition of historiography that had developed among Muslims, but added a distinctive approach of his own, was Ibn Khaldūn (1332–1406). In the *Introduction* (*Muqaddima*) to his massive universal history he seeks to show the pattern underlying political and social events. A state or dynasty is based on the *'aṣabiyya,* group feeling or solidarity, of the ruling group. A group with strong *'asabiyya* will establish a state but then, in a process that includes the absolutism of the ruler and the enjoyment of luxury by the ruling class, its *'asabiyya* decreases and it is eventually defeated and replaced by another group. This is the "natural" pattern. If a state is based on a *shari'a* bought by a prophet it will be stronger – this is the best kind of state – but it still needs *'asabiyya* and is still subject to its laws. This theory provides a largely "secular" explanation of the course of history and thus Ibn Khaldun has been considered by many to be one of the founders of modern social science. Ibn Khaldun, of course, considered God to be in control of "secular" history.

Key points

- The main divisions in Islam began and to some extent continue to be over "political" issues, but these are also religious issues since they concern the manner in which God guides the *umma*. They illustrate the close relation between religion and politics in Islam.
- All groups have had to find a balance between the desire for an ideal ruler and the actual situations in which they lived.
- Kharijis have mostly insisted that the actual ruler be ideal. Their movement has not prospered numerically but a "Khariji" tendency has always been present.

- Twelver Shi'is have located the ideal *Imam* outside the worldly domain and have tended to be pessimistic about worldly politics, although they have often seen the ruler as the representative of the *Imam*.
- Sunnis came to recognize three bases for a ruler's authority: his actual power, however acquired, because he would not have it if God had not willed it; his maintenance of order in society; his recognition of the Shari'a and implementation of at least part of it.
- Sunnis have seen the period of Muhammad and the first four caliphs as enshrining the ideal of government. Some have believed that the true caliphate ended with them. Others hold that it continued in less perfect form until the Mongol capture of Baghdad. Others believe that it continued until the end of the Ottoman period.
- Persian and Greek contributions have generally strengthened the ideal of an autocratic and divinely guided ruler.
- Ibn Khaldun developed a relatively secular theory of political development based on the idea of *'aṣabiyya*.

Discussion questions

1. Some Muslims today want to restore the caliphate. In view of the history of the caliphate given in this chapter how important do you think this is?
2. What elements of democracy can you see in the political ideas presented here?
3. How have various groups handled the gap between the ideal and the real? How do the Muslim groups compare with other groups or states that you know about?
4. Was the period of the Rightly Guided Caliphs a "golden age"?
5. It is sometimes suggested that Sunnis find authority primarily in texts and Shi'is primarily in persons. Do you agree?

Critical thinking box 8.1

Rewrite the "introductory overview of Islam" in chapter 1 from a Twelver Shi'i point of view.

Critical thinking box 8.2

Suppose Ali had not been assassinated when he was, would the history of Islam have been radically different? If so, how might it have been?

Companion website

Includes additional information on the Shi'i *Imams*; a long passage from al-Ghazali on the caliphate; information about Iranian ideals relating to kingship; and websites for Shi'i material, including *ta'ziya*, and one for Al-Farabi.

Further reading

Black, Anthony (2001) *The History of Islamic Political Thought from the Prophet to the Present*. Edinburgh: Edinburgh University Press. (Covers the main thinkers and theories.)

Crone, Patricia (2004) *God's Rule: Government and Islam: Six Centuries of Medieval Political Thought*. New York: Columbia University Press. (A very interesting and perceptive study of political theory and practice to the end of the Abbasid caliphate, covering the main Sunni and Shi'i views of government as well as Persian and Greek contributions.)

Lambton, Ann K.S. (1981) *State and Government in Medieval Islam*. New York: Oxford University Press. (Covers in some detail the groups and theorists discussed in this chapter, along with others.)

Momen, Moojan (1985) *An Introduction to Shi'i Islam*. New Haven and London: Yale University Press. (A detailed study, widely used.)

Richard, Yann (1991/5) *Shi'ite Islam*, trans. A. Nevill. Oxford: Blackwell. (Lively, strong sense of the emotional, mythic and relevance of the historic to the present.)

Halm, Heinz (1994) *Shiism*. Edinburgh: Edinburgh University Press. (Detailed, academic in style, topically organized. More than half is devoted to the modern period.)

Malekpour, Jamshid (2004) *The Islamic Drama-Ta'ziya*. London: Frank Cass. (Traces the history of the *ta'ziya* in Iran from the eighteenth century.)

Tabataba'i, A.S.M.H. (1977) *Shi'ite Islam*, 2nd ed. Albany, NY: State University of New York Press. (Survey by a leading modern Shi'i scholar.)

Al-Mawardī (1996) *The Ordinances of Government*, trans. Wafaa H. Wahba. London: Garnet Publishing. (Probably the best known classical Islamic study of government.)

Nizam al-Mulk (1960) *The Book of Government or Rules for Kings*, 2nd ed., trans. Hubert Darke. London: Routledge and Kegan Paul. (Practical advice by the best known of the Saljuk viziers, "mirror for princes" genre.)

See also: Knysh, *Islam in Historical Perspective* (Chs 7, 11–12) [F]; Rippin and Knappert, *Textual Sources for the Study of Islam* (Ch. 7) [F]; Williams, *Islam* [F].

9 *Those who know*

Scholars and learning

The scholars (*'ulamā'*) are the heirs of the prophets.
(Bukhari)

It is frequently said that there are no clergy in Islam. This statement is true in some respects but is probably more misleading than helpful. To be sure, there is no group ordained to a sacramental function in the manner of Christian clergy but there is a class of people who have a status and functions similar to clergy, though they are more like Orthodox Jewish rabbis than Christian clergy. They are also similar to lawyers in many respects. These are the *'ulamā'*. In this chapter we will consider some of their various roles and activities, especially in relation to worship and education.

In this chapter

- Who are the *'ulama'* ?
- Their role in the mosque
- Education and learning
- *'Ulama'* and government

Who are the 'ulama'*?*

The Arabic word *'ulamā'* means "those who know" and the singular is *'ālim*. The usual English translations are "scholars" or "the learned". Another term for members of this group is *mullah*, especially in Iran and in South Asia. The most important functions of the *'ulama'* relate to interpreting **Islamic law** and will be discussed in the next chapter. Other functions have included theology (*kalam*), teaching, leading *salah* (as *imams*) and preaching in mosques, serving as government officials, supervising trusts and acting as guardians, notaries and scribes. In this chapter we will consider some of their roles related to the mosque and then discuss at greater length their education and their relation to government, the latter having been dealt with to some extent in the previous chapter.

We will be dealing with institutions and practices that have changed and developed over a period of about a thousand years and have also varied from place to place, but change was comparatively slow until modern times. While this chapter cannot take account of all of the variations it can generalize about many things without being too misleading. Modern times have seen considerable change, however, and some of this is described at the end of the chapter.

The mosque

The central role for *'ulama'* in the mosque is that of *imam*, the leader of ***salah***, particularly the Friday noon *salah*. This role may be carried out by any Muslim but preferably by a trained scholar. Mosques will usually have a designated *imam* and where possible he will be salaried, either by the government or by an association. Other functions connected with worship are that of the *khaṭīb*, who gives the Friday *khuṭba* or sermon, the *wā'iẓ*, who gives sermons and teaches on other occasions, the *qāri'*, who recites the Qur'an, not only in the mosque but elsewhere, and the muezzin (*mu'adhdhan*), who gives the *adhan*, the call to *salah*. In most mosques one or two people would carry out these functions. Only in the largest mosques would there be separate individuals for each. The *imam* will usually carry out teaching activities for the people who attend the mosque and also ritual functions such as those connected with marriages and funerals.

Note that the word *imam* has at least four distinct usages: the one given here; its use for the twelve *Imams* recognized by Shi'is as the rightful leaders of the *umma*; its use by Sunnis as a synonym for caliph; its use as honorific for great scholars, such as *Imam* al-Ghazali, *Imam* Ibn Taymiyya and others.

Education and learning

Primary level education through most of Islamic history was carried out by schools known as *kuttābs* or *maktabs*. In Western writings they are often called Qur'an schools. They began before the end of the first century *Hijri* and in form may have been developed from pre-Islamic teaching arrangements among the Arabs or Byzantine schools but their content was purely Islamic. The *kuttab* might be located in a room connected to a mosque or in some other place. There was a teacher (***shaykh***), one or two assistants and usually a small group of students aged from 4 to around 10. The students were usually boys but sometimes girls also studied. The main activity was the recitation and memorization of the Qur'an, along with reading and writing and possibly some arithmetic or other subjects. Typically, each student would have a slate on which the passage to be learned would be written and he would recite and memorize it. When he had finished, the old passage would be wiped off the slate and a new passage written on it. Each student would proceed at his own pace and

Figure 9.1 Ibn Batuta as a boy studying (modern rendition). Ibn Batuta (1304–c.1377) became an *'alim* and wrote a book about his travels throughout the Muslim world. Courtesy Norman MacDonald/Saudi Aramco World/ SAWDIA

recite what he had memorized to the *shaykh* or assistant. When the student had memorized a certain amount there would be some sort of recognition and/or reward, but there was no diploma or formal graduation. Students would stay at a *kuttab* for as long or as short a time as interest and circumstances dictated. Only a few would go on to become *'ulama'* and there was no organic connection between this level of education and the next.

The *shaykh* was supported by fees or donations from the parents and these would often vary with the parents' circumstances. In general, teaching in a *kuttab* was a low status activity and many of the *shaykhs* were poorly qualified. The stress on memorization follows from the nature of the Qur'an as a sacred text meant to be recited. The student would benefit from the ***baraka*** of the Qur'an even if he did not understand its meaning, and in any case it was considered pedagogically appropriate first to memorize a text, to implant it in the heart, and then to learn its meaning. This emphasis on memorization, the prominence given to oral recitation assisted by writing and the relatively unstructured and individualistic approach to teaching also characterized the traditional higher level institutions, though to a lesser degree.

Modern reformers have been very hard on the *kuttabs*, depicting them as dirty, ill-resourced, ill-taught, disorganized and backward in method. Over the last century *kuttabs* in many places have been replaced by Western-style elementary schools, which include the teaching of religion but stress secular subjects. For over a millennium, however, they met the needs of Muslim peoples.

The sciences and higher level teaching

The "religious sciences" are Qur'anic interpretation, ***Hadith***, ***fiqh*** and ***uṣūl al-fiqh***, and somewhat later and problematically, theology (*kalām* or *'ilm al-tawḥīd*). Various language-related subjects such as grammar and rhetoric and some literature, especially poetry, were seen as necessary for these. The study and teaching of these began with informal circles in mosques or in homes, as almost an inevitable concomitant of piety. They became institutionalized later on but never completely so.

Interpretation of the Qur'an began with the Prophet himself and his immediate followers, as teachers were sent to teach the Qur'an to particular groups or tribes. The *Hadith* movement began at the same time according to most Muslims but perhaps a century later according to most non-Muslim scholars. As mentioned in chapter 6, scholars often traveled considerable distances to hear *hadiths* from those who knew them. Teaching circles were formed dealing with Qur'anic interpretation and *Hadith*, and soon also with *fiqh*, language and other subjects. The teachers were sometimes popular preachers known as *quṣṣās* (story tellers) or were ***qāḍis***.

In about the tenth century *khāns*, hostels for students studying in a mosque, were built and the mosque–*khan* complexes became major centers of learning. The next stage was the *madrasa*, which brought together the teaching and residential functions. In modern Arabic the word *madrasa* refers to any school, but prior to the modern period it referred specifically to the kind of school described here. The first *madrasas* were probably established also during the tenth century but began to flourish in a major way in the following century. While the mosque was primarily for worship and used, secondarily, for teaching, the *madrasas* were primarily for teaching, though they might have a mosque attached. Teaching in the mosques might focus on any of a number of subjects but *madrasas* focused on *fiqh*. The other subjects (those mentioned earlier and sometimes others) were treated as ancillary. Both mosques and *madrasas* were funded by *awqāf* (singular: *waqf*), a kind of trust under the Shari'a in which property is set aside by the donor and its income used for various pious, charitable and public purposes. Whereas revenues for mosques came under the control of the caliph or other ruler, the *awqaf* for *madrasas* gave much more control to their founders. If these founders were politically powerful the *madrasas* could be a means of gaining patronage. Particularly famous, and forming a model for others, was the Nizamiyya *madrasa*, opened in Baghdad in 1067 under the sponsorship of the Saljuk *wazīr*, Nizam al-Mulk, who also built others in other cities. Within two or three centuries *madrasas* spread throughout the Muslim world from Spain to India. One of the most prolific builders of *madrasas* was **Salah al-Din.**

These *madrasas* taught the Sunni form of Islam and were, in fact, part of the effort to spread and establish Sunni Islam against the various forms of Shiʿism that were active at the time. Individual *madrasas* usually taught only one *madhhab* (school of *fiqh*, see next chapter) but in time *madrasa* buildings were built that accommodated up to four *madhhabs*. While the founders of the *awqaf* that provided for these *madrasas* were frequently rulers or high government officials, the *madrasas* were not government institutions. Those who founded them did so in their capacity as private individuals and the *awqaf* came under the rules of the Shariʿa, interpreted by the *ʿulama'*. In fact, the administrators of the *awqaf* were usually *ʿulama'*. There is also another kind of *waqf* known as *waqf ahlī*, in which the beneficiaries are the family of the donor and the purpose is to save the family estate from confiscation or division through inheritance.

Initially each *madrasa* had one professor and about twenty students, although later there were often more of both. Courses usually taught a particular book. The professor would read aloud the text of the book and make comments along the way and the students would take down the text and make notes of the comments. Later, copies of the texts became available but the text was still read out and students took notes. Students sought to memorize the basic texts and also to understand them, though they did not memorize the professor's comments. Professors would also lecture on their own material. When the student mastered one book he would then move on to another. At a higher level students were often expected to produce compilations based on their notes from their teacher's lectures and also to engage in disputation on set topics. Students still proceeded to some extent at their own pace although the program was more prescribed than in the *kuttabs*. When a student had mastered certain texts, the professor would give him an *ijāza*, i.e. permission to teach that text to others. In some cases the *ijaza* would permit the student to teach all the subjects the professor taught. Students would seek to accumulate *ijazas* on various texts and from various professors, and in this way qualify themselves to become professors. The personal relationship between the student and his teacher usually became very close though also respectful. (This has been illustrated in recent years by the fact that many of the leaders of the Islamic Republic in Iran have been Khomeini's students.) The *ijaza* is the closest this system came to offering a degree or diploma. Under this system the line between students and teachers was not always completely clear since a person might be teaching one book and learning another.

In spite of the relatively structured program in the *madrasas* and the close relations between student and teacher, students still moved around a fair bit, seeking new *ijazas* in other places and from other teachers and seeking to study under the best and most famous teachers.

It is to be noted that memorization and recitation still hold pride of place in this system although understanding is also demanded and writing holds a necessary place at least as an aid to memory. The tendency is still to see memorization of material as a prelude to understanding it. The scarcity and cost of written texts, which had to be copied by hand, is one justification for the emphasis on memory. (One might almost suggest that these students acquired books by memorizing them where we, today, acquire them by purchasing them.) Another is that an *'alim*, when functioning as a judge, will not have to refer to a written manual if he has the manual by heart. Beyond this there seems to be a sense that one has not really mastered a text if he has not memorized it. A scholar has advised: "When you read a book make every effort to learn it by heart and master its meaning. Imagine the book to have disappeared and then you can dispense with it, unaffected by its loss" (Makdisi, 1981, 89).

Private teaching circles and the mosques continued alongside the *madrasa* and institutions specifically for teaching the Qur'an and *Hadith* also existed. There were Sufi institutions that also taught *fiqh* and other religious sciences, variously called *ribāṭs*, *zāwiyas*, *khanqahs* and *tekkes*. Philosophy was viewed as heterodox by many and was generally taught privately, but there were some teaching institutions for it, known as *dar al-'ilm*, until about the twelfth century. Some aspects of philosophy were taught to some extent in the *madrasas*, such as logic and astronomy. Medicine was generally taught separately although it sometimes appears in *madrasa* curriculums. Libraries established by rulers or wealthy men were sometimes made available to scholars. Higher education was almost entirely a male venture. We hear occasionally of female students and of female teachers, though probably not often located in

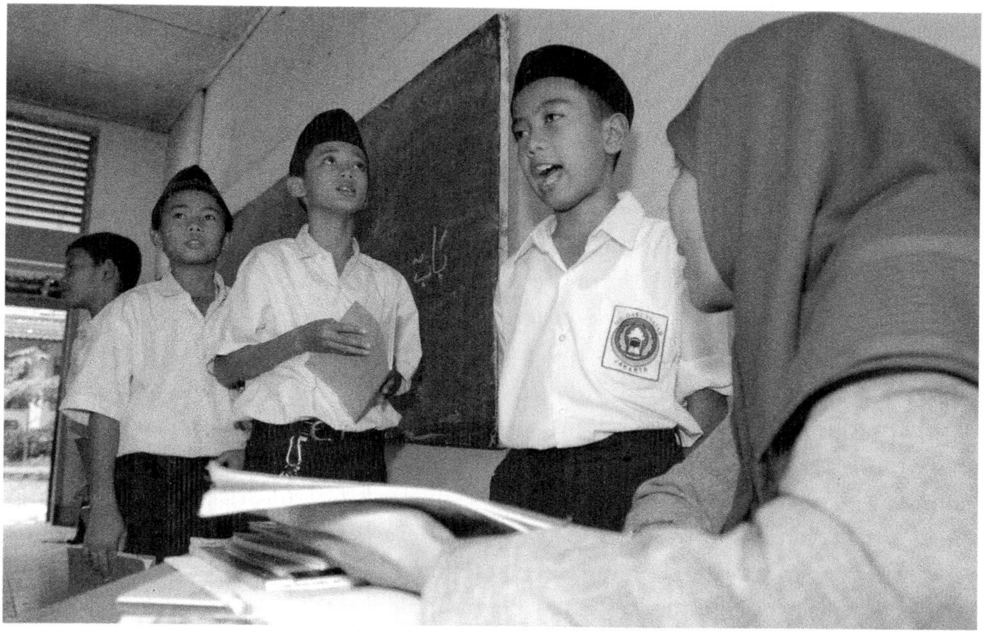

Figure 9.2 A student recites a memorized prayer in front of his teacher in a *pesantren* school in Jakarta, Indonesia (2002). Courtesy of Dimas Ardian/Getty Images

madrasas. Ibn Arabi and Ibn Taymiyya had female teachers. We also hear of women endowing *madrasas*.

In Java, and in other parts of what is now Indonesia and Malaysia, *madrasas* were commonly connected with communal boarding schools known as *pesantrens*. These were usually located in rural areas and served their communities. They gave consideration to Sufism and their leaders, known as *kiais*, were spiritual guides as well as teachers, and were highly respected. Generally a *pesantren* was founded by a *kiai* and was not supported by the government or wealthy patrons.

Among the Isma'ilis schools were established to propagate their version of Islam and these included philosophical subjects. The most famous of these was al-Azhar, in Cairo, which later became a Sunni *madrasa* and, indeed, the most highly esteemed in the Muslim world as a whole after the Mongol invasion set learning back in so many places.

Learning among the Twelver Shi'is began with the *Imams*, who taught their followers, and this teaching function continued among the *'ulama'*, mostly teaching privately. There may have been a Shi'i *madrasa* in Najaf shortly after the founding of the Nizamiyya in Baghdad but significant building of *madrasas* began in Iran under the Safavids as part of their program to impose Twelver Shi'ism on the populace. The teaching methods and programs have been similar to the Sunni *madrasas* except that they teach Twelver Shi'ism and also have more of a place for philosophy. They also have a source of income not available to the Sunnis in the ***khums*** tax, distinctive to Shi'ism, which has given them greater independence from the state than Sunni institutions usually have.

Like the *kuttabs*, though somewhat less so, the *madrasas* have suffered in the last century or so from the competition of Western-style high schools and universities. Mostly they have survived with considerable change but they no longer serve the majority of the students in most countries. Often the state has taken control of their endowments, sometimes using the money for other purposes, starving them of resources, as well as exercising considerable control. This happened to the Azhar in Egypt in the nineteenth century, and it underwent state-sponsored reforms in the early 1960s, but it has by no means lost its influence. In Turkey the secular government closed the *madrasas* in the 1920s and eventually replaced them with theological faculties somewhat on the Western model. In Iran the *madrasas* were largely marginalized under the Pahlavis but kept their independence and played a major role in the Islamic revolution of 1979. In India the most influential conservative *madrasa*, Deoband, was founded in 1867 in reaction to British influence and continues to be quite important. In Pakistan there were only a few *madrasas* at the time of independence in 1947 but their number has grown to thousands although their quality is problematic (some may be more like *kuttabs*) and some are said to be training schools for terrorists. In Indonesia *pesantrens* continue to be strong and have modernized to some degree. They also in some cases now admit women. They form the basis for the largest social movement in Indonesia today, the Nahdlatul 'Ulama'. In recent years a few have provided a base for terrorists. The state institutes for religious teaching (IAIN, National Islamic Religious Institute) seem not so much to compete with *pensantrens* as to provide further training for their students.

'Ulama' *and government*

As mentioned in chapter 8, many of the early *'ulama'* criticized or tried to avoid contact with rulers. There are a number of *hadiths* supporting this stance, one mentioned in the previous chapter. Two others are "He who accepts the office of *qadi* is like someone who is slaughtered without a knife" (Messick, 1993, 143) and "Of three *qadis* two are in hell" (*ibid.*). On the other hand there were good reasons for both the *'ulama'* and the rulers to seek good relations with each other. The rulers had the power to provide both material and political support to the *'ulama'* and their institutions and some of the positions that the *'ulama'* might fill, such as *qadis*, were under the control of the rulers. Moreover, while the *'ulama'* could interpret the law based on the Shari'a, only the ruler could enforce it on society and the *'ulama'* were concerned that the law be put into practice. From the rulers' point of view the *'ulama'* could provide guidance when he sought it and legitimate his actions in the eyes of the people and urge them to obey the ruler. On the other hand, the *'ulama'* often acted to bring the concerns of the people before the ruler. The *'ulama'* rarely had anything more than moral power to bring to bear on the rulers but this could be quite effective at times. As mentioned in chapter 8, the result of the ***miḥna*** led to at least a minimum degree of independence for the *'ulama'*.

An interesting combination of the ideals of non-involvement and involvement is found in the following statement ascribed to Sufyan al-Thawri, one who did cooperate with the Umayyads, "The best of rulers is he who keeps company with *'ulama'*, and the worst of the *'ulama'* is he who seeks the society of the king" (Zilfi, 1988, 227). A particularly high statement of the *'ulama'* claims ascribed to 'Ali among others is that, "Kings are rulers over the people and the *'ulama'* are rulers over the kings". In brief, the principle was that the *'ulama'* should advise the rulers and serve as intermediaries between the rulers and the people. Often enough the rulers refused to heed the *'ulama'* and the *'ulama'* allowed themselves to be corrupted by privilege, though if they got too close to the rulers they could lose the trust of the people. In any case the ideal still stood and provided a benchmark for criticism or reform.

The call for abstinence always had an appeal and there were always some who followed it but most *'ulama'* accepted the necessity and even the desirability of dealing with rulers. Al-Ghazali, for example, quotes in his writings the strictures against dealing with rulers but in fact considered himself divinely commanded to serve them when called to. Ibn Taymiyya's views regularly got him into trouble with the ruler and into prison several times, but it was not distance from the ruler that he sought but rather the ruler's acceptance of his unwelcome advice. In fact, as we have seen, the *'ulama'* of the late Abbasid period were willing to accept, though not approve, considerable laxness on the part of the rulers so long as they kept order and adhered minimally to Sunni belief and practice. This has been largely true of the Sunni *'ulama'* since then.

Although the *'ulama'* were recognized as a distinct professional group in society they have usually had little in the way of formal hierarchy. Some degree of hierarchy was involved in the government offices held by the *'ulama'*, as suggested by a title like Chief Qadi. Some *'ulama'* would hold positions considered more prestigious than others but these did not constitute a hierarchy. Some would be highly respected for their piety and learning and the greatest would come to be called *imam*, such as al-Ghazali, but none of this resulted from formal decisions by anyone.

The main exception to this was the Ottoman Empire. The Ottomans very strongly viewed themselves as defenders of the Sunni faith and included the higher levels of the *'ulama'* into the governing elite, as a distinct corps known as the *ilmiye*, with distinct duties and privileges. At the top of the hierarchy was the Shaykh al-Islam, who was appointed by the sultan and was the only one who could confirm the deposition of a sultan (this happened in 1807), followed by the chief judges of the major provinces and the professors in the major schools and *madrasas*. Below this was a subhierarchy of teachers, preachers and judges with less training who were not given the official title of *'ulama'*, with its perquisites, though they can be considered *'ulama'* under the more general definition. The *ilmiye* gained considerable political influence and power within the Ottoman government although it stood a continuing risk of suffering corruption. Under the republican government from the 1920s the *'ulama'* lost their political power but remained under government control and still with a degree of hierarchy.

Twelver Shi'i *'ulama'* for some time remained distant from government partly because their doctrine tended to consider all government in the absence of the Twelfth *Imam* illegitimate and partly because the governments under which they lived were mostly opposed to Twelvers. Even though the Buyids gave them support, the situation was ambiguous since the formal ruler, the caliph, was Sunni. Under the Safavids, however, there was a close relationship from the beginning since the Safavids needed the *'ulama'* to propagate Shi'ism and the *'ulama'*, being outsiders initially, depended heavily on the rulers, whom they recognized as deputies of the Twelfth *Imam*. A post called *sadr* was created and put in charge of the propagation of Shi'ism, administering *awqaf* and supervising some of the judges; later the position of *mulla-bashi*, head of the *mullahs*, was created. With the collapse of Safavid authority in the eighteenth century, however, the *'ulama'* of Iran learned to flourish independently of government connections. They came to serve as important figures of authority at the local level and began to assert themselves vis-à-vis the ruler and this competition continued into the twentieth century, effectively a competition for the role of deputy of the Twelfth *Imam*. At mid-century the *'ulama'* were considerably weakened but maintained a greater independence of the state than Sunni *'ulama'* elsewhere. This resulted partly from their system of jurisprudence, to be discussed in the next chapter. In the revolution of 1979 this competition ended with victory for the *'ulama'*. The issue of *'ulama'* relations with the state continues, but on different terms.

In spite of popular criticism and even cynicism about the *'ulama'*, as a group they have generally been held in high respect. In the words of a leading scholar of Salah al-Din's time, "Know that learning leaves a trail and a scent proclaiming its possessor ... the learned man is esteemed in whatever place or condition he may be, always meeting people who are favourably disposed to him, who draw near to him and seek his company, gratified in being close to him" (Makdisi, 1981, 91).

The incomparable Mulla Nasreddin

While the role of the *'ulamā'* is highly respected, not all scholars have lived up to it and popular imagination can produce interesting variations. Undoubtedly the best known of these is Molla Nasreddin (variously spelled), a kind of "wise fool" whose stories have been popular in Iranian and Turkish cultural areas since about the tenth century CE. Here is a short anecdote.

> A neighbour asked Mulla Nasrudin to stand by him in a case of disputed possession of some grain.
>
> "Did you see the transaction?" the judge asked him.
>
> "Yes, I distinctly saw the sacks of barley change hands."
>
> "But this case is concerned with sacks of wheat, not barley!"
>
> "That is irrelevant. I am here to say that my friend is right. As a false witness surely I can say anything without it being held against me."
>
> (Shah, 1968, 139)

For a good scholarly article on Molla Nasreddin in the Encyclopaedia Iranica see: http://www.iranicaonline.org/articles/molla-nasreddin-i-the-person (accessed 17 August 2013).

Key points

- The *'ulama'* are the learned, who to some extent function as a clergy but have other roles too.
- The main teaching and preaching positions in mosques are held by *'ulama'*.
- For nearly 1,000 years before modern times the main teaching institutions were the *kuttab*, which focused on memorizing the Qur'an, and the *madrasa*, which focused on *fiqh*.
- Memorization played a large role in the educational institutions of the *'ulama'*; there were various reasons for this.
- The *'ulama's* relation to government was complex; sometimes they stood aloof and sometimes they dealt with rulers in different ways. Ideally they wanted to advise them.
- Although they have often fallen short of the ideal, they have been and are highly respected by the Muslim community.

Discussion questions

1. "The scholars (*'ulama'*) are the heirs of the prophets." To what extent and in what way has this been true?
2. What is the point of the statement, "He who accepts the office of *qadi* is like someone who is slaughtered without a knife"?
3. Why do you think Salah al-Din might have been so interested in founding *madrasas*?
4. To what extent could one say that religious institutions and leaders were separate from political institutions and leaders?
5. Shi'is when speaking or writing English are more likely to speak of *'ulama'* as "clergy" than are Sunnis. Why might this be?
6. What effects do you think the internet and other forms of electronic communication may have/are having on Islamic education?

Critical thinking box 9.1

Make a case for the value of traditional Islamic education as described in this chapter against modern Western forms of education. Then, if you wish, rebut the case you have made. (Note: this is a "debating" type of presentation: in the first part at least you do not have to believe the point you are making; cf. the discussion of empathy on pp. 4–5.)

Critical thinking box 9.2

Read some modern accounts of *kuttabs*. Do you think they give a fair judgment? (See, e.g. autobiographies of Taha Husayn, Ahmad Amin and Sayyid Qutb, listed on the website.)

Companion website

Further reading lists the biographies of the modern critics of *kuttabs* mentioned above.

Further reading

Dodge, Bayard (1961) *Al-Azhar: A Millennium of Muslim Learning*. Washington, DC: Middle East Institute. (A straightforward, not very critical account.)

Messick, Brinkley (1993) *The Calligraphic State: Textual Domination and History in a Muslim Society*. Berkeley, CA: University of California Press. (Focuses on the actual role of the Sharia and scholarship in Zaidi Yemen and discusses modern changes.)

Zilfi, Madeline C. (1988) *The Politics of Piety: the Ottoman Ulema in the Postclassical Age (1600–1800)*. Minneapolis, MN: Bibliotheca Islamica. (Studies the hierarchical character of the Ottoman *'ulama'* and the nature and extent of their political influence.)

Makdisi, George (1981) *The Rise of Colleges: Institutions of Learning in Islam and the West*. Edinburgh: Edinburgh University Press. (By one of the leading authorities on this subject.)

Makdisi, George (1981) "Hanbalite Islam" in Merlin L. Swartz, ed. *Studies on Islam*. New York and Oxford: OUP. (Includes details on the Nizamiyya, including its political role.)

See also: Robinson, *The Cambridge Illustrated History of the Islamic World* (Ch. 7) [F]; Knysh, *Islam in Historical Perspective* (Ch. 16) [F].

10 *To know God's will*

Islamic law

In this chapter we consider what is the central concern of Islam next to God Himself, that is God's law, the Shari'a. We will consider the nature of the divine law and the ways in which Muslims have sought to discover it, but we will not attempt a systematic overview of the content of this law. Aspects of this content appear in most of the chapters of this book.

In this chapter

- Law: Shari'a and *fiqh*
- The five Shari'a valuations or categories
- *Usul al-fiqh* (the sources of legal thinking or jurisprudence), the Sunni form
- Sunni "schools" of jurisprudence, *madhhabs*
- *Usul al-fiqh*, the Shi'i form
- *Muftis* and *fatwas* (interpreters and interpretations of the law)
- Brief history of *fiqh*, Sunni and Shi'i
- The Shari'a and popular appropriation

Law: Shari'a and fiqh

It is common in religious studies to describe Judaism and Islam as "religions of law" and Christianity as a "religion of creed". This means that while Christians have devoted considerable energy to elaborating creedal statements and the major divisions have been over such creeds (as has been seen in chapter 2) in the Jewish and Muslim cases comparable attention has been given to elaborating details of ritual, ethical and legal practice, often called "religious law", and their major debates and divisions have been over these matters. Among modern Jews, for example, the main difference between Orthodox, Conservative and Reform or Progressive Judaism is the degree to which they observe traditional practices (e.g. keep *kosher*). While for Muslims the

Sunni–Shi'i "sectarian" division is rooted in politics, within these divisions the main "denominational" differences have related to details of practice. While Muslims have had a significant theological tradition, to be discussed in the next chapter, the "legal" matters discussed in this chapter have been far more important.

When we speak of "Islamic law" we are in fact speaking of what Muslims call "Shari'a" and "*fiqh*", neither of which terms quite corresponds to the Western concept of "law". The word Shari'a originally means a path leading to water. The symbolism, especially in an arid land such as Arabia, is clear: it is the path God has laid out for us to walk in our lives to reach the waters of true life. The Shari'a is understood to cover all areas of human life that involve moral choice, since God is concerned with all of these areas. It therefore covers many things, such as worship and personal habits, that Westerners would not include under the heading of law. In brief, it represents the will of God for human life as a whole.

The word *fiqh* means understanding, and soon came to mean the practical understanding of the Qur'an and the *Sunna* that allowed one to apply them to actual situations in life and actual cases that came before courts. From this understanding a body of law was gradually developed and the term *fiqh* came to refer both to this body of law and to the process by which it was developed. This process is seen less as creating law than as discovering the law, i.e. the Shari'a, that God has created. The experts in *fiqh* are called *fuqahā'* (singular: *faqīh*); they are *'ulamā'* who specialize in *fiqh*. The words *fiqh* and *faqih* are often translated "jurisprudence" and "jurisprudent" respectively.

Put concisely, Shari'a is what God ordains and *fiqh* is what humans understand of it. In practice, however, the body of *fiqh* law is often called Shari'a and this usage reflects the confidence that the *faqihs* have been largely successful in discovering God's law, so that *fiqh* is indeed the Shari'a as it is available to humans. Many modern reformers, however, insist on the difference between *fiqh* and Shari'a since they do not consider that traditional *fiqh* represents God's will for the present time.

I will sometimes use the English terms "law", "Islamic law" and "Shari'a law" (i.e. law based on the Shari'a), where both Shari'a and *fiqh* are involved and where the meaning is clear.

The five Shari'a valuations

If the Shari'a differs from Western law codes in being more comprehensive than them, it also differs in that it is not so much a set of "dos" and "don'ts" as a moral classification of actions. In principle all possible human actions can be placed in one of five categories (*aḥkām*, singular: *ḥukm*, valuations or qualifications):

1. Obligatory (*wājib* or *farḍ*). These must be done and God rewards one for doing them and punishes for omitting them. Examples include *salah*, fasting in

Ramadan, *zakah*, and *Hajj*, with qualifications in some cases. The obligatory category is divided into two subcategories: individual obligations (*farḍ 'ayn*), such as those just mentioned, and communal obligations (*fard kifaya*, obligation of a sufficient number). These latter are obligatory for everyone in a community until a sufficient number have undertaken them, and then the rest are no longer obliged, e.g. performing the funeral *salah* and becoming a doctor or a teacher.

2. Recommended (*sunna, mandūb, mustahabb*). Highly desirable but not required. One is rewarded by God for these actions but not punished for omitting them. For example, Friday noon *salah* in congregation is obligatory for men but recommended for women.
3. Permissable, neutral (*mubāḥ*). These are actions to which God assigns a neutral value, neither rewarding the doing of them nor punishing the omission. The means by which I travel between home and work, for example, would normally come into this category. In fact, the majority of actions probably come into this category. Political and administrative matters have often been placed in this category.
4. Reprehensible (*makrūh*, literally "hated"). Undesirable actions that are not, however, forbidden. One is rewarded by God for omitting these actions but not punished for doing them. Divorce is the classic example, since the Prophet said, "Of permitted actions divorce is the most hated by God."
5. Forbidden (*harām*). Absolutely forbidden. One is punished by God for committing them and rewarded for avoiding them. Among the best known examples are the consumption of wine or pork and the committing of murder, robbery and fornication.

One also often speaks of the permitted (*ḥalāl*) and the forbidden (*ḥarām*). Here the permitted include the first four valuations in the preceding list and the forbidden classification includes the last.

The worldly legal effect of an action is sometimes distinct from its Shari'a valuation. For example, the most acceptable form of divorce by a man is when he says to his wife, "You are divorced" and waits for three *'iddas* (periods of purity between the woman's menstruation), at which time the divorce takes effect. Another form, in which the man says "You are divorced" three times in the same *'idda*, is forbidden by the Shari'a but if the man does it the divorce takes effect immediately.

Penalties fall into a different classification. (1) The penalties to be imposed by God in the afterlife, the most important in this system. (2) Discretionary punishments (*ta'zīr*), to be decided by the judge or ruler. The majority of worldly penalties fall into this category. (3) A small number of *ḥadd* penalties, specifically imposed by God in the Qur'an or *Sunna*. These can apply to fornication (*zinā*, which includes adultery), false accusation of fornication, wine drinking, theft and highway robbery. The punishments are most often whipping but may be cutting off of the hand of a thief or stoning those guilty of fornications, depending on conditions, such as a minimum amount stolen and whether those guilty of fornication are married. Although Westerners tend to focus on these, they are applied relatively rarely. A number of conditions must be met and they are not to be applied where there is doubt about the case. Authorities are reticent to apply them, as was the Prophet Muhammad himself.

The system of five valuations is more flexible than may appear from the presentation so far. Which valuation an action is given can depend on a number of factors. For example, consumption of wine and pork is forbidden, but if in some situation these are the only foods available and are necessary to sustain life, then their consumption becomes obligatory. Performance of the *Hajj* is obligatory but only if one has the means and the health. Otherwise it would be forbidden. Al-Ghazali in his discussion of music finds that it may have any valuation except obligatory depending on the circumstances (see chapter 13).

Usul al-fiqh, *the roots of jurisprudence: the Sunni form*

How does a *faqih* determine which valuation an action receives? The answer is suggested by a well-known *hadith*:

> The Prophet asked Mu'adh ibn Jabal, when he sent him to Yemen as governor, "How will you decide matters that come up?"
>
> Mu'adh answered, "According to the Book of God."
>
> The Prophet asked, "What if you do not find there what you need?"
>
> Mu'adh replied, "Then according to the *Sunna* of the Prophet of God."
>
> The Prophet asked, "What if you do not find there what you need?"
>
> Mu'adh answered, "Then I will exert effort (*ijtihād*) to form my own judgment (*ra'y*)."
>
> The Prophet then said, "Thank God for guiding the Prophet's deputy to that which the Prophet approves."

This *hadith* mentions three of the four *usul al-fiqh*, i.e. the roots or sources of understanding/jurisprudence. The four are the Qur'an, the ***Sunna*** of the Prophet, ***ijtihād*** and *ijmā'* (consensus).

1. Qur'an. The Qur'an is the Book of God, and wherever it speaks on a matter of practice it must be followed. Only a small proportion of its verses, however, variously estimated from 80 to 500, deal with matters related to *fiqh*. Quite often it is in need of interpretation. The *faqih* dealing with the Qur'an needs a number of the disciplines learned as an *'alim*, such as the Arabic language, pre-Islamic poetry (for certain rare words), Qur'anic commentary and especially *asbāb*

al-nuzūl (occasions of revelation) in the case of the abrogation of an earlier verse by a later one, as mentioned in chapter 5.

2. *Sunna*. The *Sunna* of the Prophet, contained in the *Hadith*, is the second "root". As mentioned in chapter 6, the Qur'an commands Muslims to obey the Prophet and this is not taken to be limited to his lifetime. Since he is considered *ma'sum* (protected from error), sound *hadiths* are virtually on the level of the Qur'an for *fiqh* purposes. Both are considered *naṣṣ*, authoritative text. The *Sunna* both elucidates the Qur'an and deals with matters not covered in it. For example, the Qur'an commands *salah* but it is the *Sunna* that gives the details of how to do it. The *faqih* will need to have knowledge of which *hadiths* are considered "sound" and which are not, although in practice weaker *hadiths* are often used. The words and deeds of the Companions of the Prophet are also important, though they do not have the same level of authority.
3. *Ijtihād*. This word means "effort" and has been technically defined as the *faqih* putting forth all of the effort he is capable of in order to solve a case. The person qualified to do *ijtihad* is called a *mujtahid* and among his qualifications are learning (*'ilm*) and righteousness (*'adāla*). Learning includes a very high level of accomplishment in the various scholarly disciplines of the *'ulama'*. Faced with a novel situation for which the Qur'an and *Sunna* do not have a complete and clear answer, the *faqih* uses various methods (see below) to determine the Shari'a classification of an action. The purpose of *ijtihad* is not to make law but to discover God's law, but the *mujtahid* is not protected from error. A *hadith* says: "The *mujtahid* who errs gets one reward; the *mujtahid* who gets it right gets a double reward." One who does not have the qualifications of a *mujtahid* is called *muqallid* and practices *taqlīd*, literally "imitation" or "emulation", following the guidance of past or present *mujtahids*.
4. *Ijma'* or consensus. *Ijma'* is said to occur when all of the leading *mujtahids* of a particular time come to the same view on a particular issue. This may occur because of the prestige of a particular *faqih* or for other reasons. *Ijma'* does not happen in the context of a council or formal meeting but is recognized after the fact. Over time a particular position on a given issue comes to be recognized as agreed on. *Ijma'* is often justified by the *hadith*, "My community will not agree on an error". It is therefore believed to provide certain knowledge of the Shari'a, unlike the decisions of individual *mujtahids*. In Sunni theory the caliphate, for example, is understood to be based on *ijma'*. There have been some who accept only the *ijma'* of the Companions of the Prophet but most also accept later *ijma'* (see below).
5. Continuing *ijtihad*. Where there is an *ijma'*, *ijtihad* is no longer necessary or possible, but elsewhere it is still needed (some have questioned this; see below on the history of *fiqh*). Reformers often see existing *ijma'* as no longer adequate

because of the changed circumstances of modern times. There are a variety of methods, some more acceptable than others, that may be used by the *mujtahid*.

a. *Qiyas* or analogy. This is the favored method, involving a strict form of logical reasoning. An illustration of the most common form comes from the prohibition of wine in the Qur'an. Is whisky then prohibited? The answer is that wine is prohibited because of the effects it has on human behavior (this is called the *'illa*, or cause). Whisky has the same effect or more so (the same *'illa*), so it is also prohibited. What about hashish? According to the *fuqaha'* it too has the same *'illa*, and so is prohibited (although many ordinary people have not agreed). What about coffee? Some effort was made to forbid coffee when it first came into the Muslim world in the fifteenth century, but the consensus was for permitting it. The same was true of tobacco in the sixteenth century, though today there is a diversity of opinion due to health issues.
b. The welfare of the Muslim community, *maṣlaḥa* (or *istiṣlāḥ*). Where the other approaches give more than one result, the one that is in the best interests of the community should be chosen. In a variant called *istiḥsān* (preference), if the strictest analogy gives a result that is clearly not in the interests of the community a less strict approach is chosen, though this method has less general approval. In practice many accept a form of *maslaha* that is unrestricted, i.e. the interest of the community should be followed even when not supported by the other sources. A wide view of *maslaha* has been increasingly common in modern times, especially with adoption of modern technology. The problem with *maslaha* is that the judgment is more or less subjective and different *faqihs* are likely to see the community welfare differently.
c. Necessity (*ḍarūra*). There is a principle that "necessity makes forbidden things permitted". Thus, eating carrion is forbidden, but if the alternative is starvation, then it becomes permitted. Likewise, as we have seen, later political theory justified allegiance to rulers who were not qualified by Shari'a standards on the grounds that the disruption caused by trying to remove them would destroy the community.
d. The Aims of the Sharī'a (*maqāṣid al-sharī'a*). Many hold that the general goals of the Sharī'a can be known and judgments made in the light of them. The most important goals are usually said to be protection of religious faith, of life, of progeny, of property and of the mind. This approach allows considerable flexibility in judgments and has become more popular in modern times among Islamic modernists and Islamists.

6. Four problematic sources:
   e. *Ra'y*, the considered opinion of the *faqih*, not based on a formal procedure of reasoning but on his understanding of the situation and his sense of justice.

This was the most common approach in the early days but was later rejected as being too arbitrary and subjective. Nevertheless, it has been followed in practice, though not admittedly so.

f. Devices or "legal fictions" (*ḥiyal*). Basically, ways of getting around the law. For example, interest on loans is forbidden, but the "debtor" might sell an item to the "creditor" for a given price and immediately buy it back at a higher price to be paid later. This kind of procedure was rejected by many but also in practice used by many.

g. Custom, *'āda* (or *adat*) or *'urf*, the existing, usually pre-Islamic, custom of an area. In practice this is usually followed insofar as it does not clearly violate the Qur'an and *Sunna* (and sometimes when it does). It is not usually recognized as a formal source of *fiqh* but is very important in practice. Custom may be brought under the umbrella of the Shari'a by being declared consistent with it, possibly put in the *mubah* category. In some cases, however, it is perceived as separate from the Shari'a, so that people see some aspects of their lives as coming under the Shari'a and some as coming under customary law. An example of this comes from Aceh, a strongly Muslim part of Indonesia but one where customary law governs much of life. Among other things women receive houses and often land from their family that are exempt from the inheritance rules of Shari'a law. The term *'urf* is sometimes used for the law and the courts controlled directly by the ruler rather than the *'ulama'*, as was the case in Iran for some time. Practices based on custom are particularly open to criticism by modern *salafī* reformers, of both a liberal and a conservative tendency (see chapter 15).

h. *Siyāsa*, governance or policy (see also chapter 8). Generally the practical activities of government that are not subject to the rules of the Shari'a in practice. Often it has been seen as separate from the Shari'a but, like *'ada*, the effort may be made to bring it under the Shari'a. In the Ottoman Empire this was called *qanun* and was claimed to be consistent with the Shari'a. Ibn Taymiyyah wanted to bring the activities known as *siyasa* under the actual control of the Shari'a, as would Islamist reformers today.

An alternative way of listing the *Usul al-fiqh*

The Sunni *usul al-fiqh* are listed in the previous section as the Qur'an, the Sunna of the Prophet, *ijtihad and ijma'* (consensus). This way of listing may be said to be diachronic, providing a somewhat simplified and idealized account of how the *usul* have functioned over time to develop the corpus of *fiqh*.

An alternative way of listing the *usul* that you will find in many books is: Qur'an, Sunna, *ijma'*, *qiyas*. This way may be said to be synchronic, providing a simplified and idealized account of how a *faqih* will approach any question at a particular point in time. Here the *ijma'* is more or less fixed at that time and one is not too concerned about how it came to be. The existing *ijma'* thus becomes the third "root" and the *faqih's ijtihad,* when appropriate, becomes the fourth, except that it is called *qiyas* since *qiyas* is the preferred form of *ijtihad*.

I think the first way of listing the *usul* will be more congenial to modernists, who want to question the existing *ijma'*, and the second to traditionalists (see chapters 15–21).

Sunni "schools" of jurisprudence, madhhabs

While *ijma'* is often discussed as if there were one consensus covering the whole Muslim world, this is not so. In fact there have been several different "schools" or traditions of *fiqh* among Sunnis, each having its own *ijma'*, so to speak. These are called *madhhabs* ("road to follow" or "opinion") and named after those who are considered their founders. Four have survived to the present:

- Ḥanafī, named after Abū Ḥanīfa (d. 767)
- Mālikī, named after Mālik ibn Anas (d. 795)
- Shāfi'ī, named after Muḥammad ibn Idrīs al-Shāfi'ī (d. 819)
- Ḥanbalī, named after Aḥmad ibn Ḥanbal (d. 855)

These generally recognize each other today as equally valid (somewhat like many Protestant denominations) though this was not always so in the past. The Prophet is reported to have said, "Differences of opinion among scholars are a mercy from God." In principle every Sunni Muslim should be an adherent of one, and only one, of these *madhhabs* and should follow its rulings. There have always been some, however, who would select rulings from different *madhhabs* where this seemed appropriate and this has been a common procedure of modern reformers. Adherence to a *madhhab* is in practice usually determined by one's membership in some group, such as a family, village, tribe or subjects of a common ruler. Different *madhhabs* generally predominate in different areas, such as the Hanafis in much of the Middle East and South Asia, the Malikis in much of Africa, the Shafi'is in part of Egypt, Southern Arabia, Malaysia and Indonesia, and the Hanbalis in North and Central Arabia.

Differences between *madhhabs* in their rulings are usually minor but can be significant. At the beginning of *salah*, for example, Hanafis fold their hands below the navel, Shafi'is fold them over the breast, while for Malikis it is not specified where to fold them. On the question of whether the parent or guardian has to give consent for the marriage of an adult woman (i.e. past puberty), the Hanafis say no but the others say yes. On whether a marriage contract that forbids the husband from taking additional wives is valid, the Hanbalis say yes but the others say no. The Shafi'is hold that the circumcision of a male is obligatory, while others hold it is recommended.

Usul al-fiqh: *the Twelver Shi'i form*

Twelver Shi'i *fiqh* is often called the Ja'fari *madhhab* after the sixth *Imam*, Ja'far al-Sadiq, who is considered its founder. There are two versions of it. The most important today is that of the Uṣūlīs, the other is that of the Akhbārīs, who were stronger in the past. The Usulis recognize four "roots": Qur'an, *Sunna, ijma'* and Reason.

1. Qur'an. This is the same as for the Sunnis, but the Shi'is are more inclined to esoteric interpretations and to find references to 'Ali in the text.
2. *Sunna*. The *Sunna* includes not only the words and deeds of Muhammad but also of the twelve *Imams*, so that there is a considerably larger and more varied body of material. In politics, for example, one might follow the second *Imam*, al-Hasan, who did not resist the tyrant's power or one might follow the third *Imam*, al-Husayn, who did resist. Only the *Imams* know fully the esoteric interpretation of the Qur'an, so that it may be more important to follow them than to follow the apparent meaning of the Qur'an.
3. *Ijma'* is seen as evidence of the *Imams'* views. If during the period of the *Imams* there was a consensus of Shi'i scholars on some issue but no direct evidence of the *Imam*'s view, that consensus may be taken as evidence of the *Imam*'s view, since it is inconceivable that the Shi'i scholars would have come to a consensus differing from the *Imam*'s view.
4. Reason. Human reason is viewed as a reliable guide on ethical matters as it is believed that the Shari'a and reason cannot contradict each other and that human reason can discern right and wrong. In this they were influenced, more than the Sunnis, by the rationalism of the Mu'tazilis and the philosophers, to be discussed in the next chapter.

Qiyas, as done by the Sunnis, is too open to error. For example, Sunnis derive the prohibition of hashish by analogy with the prohibition of wine. Shi'is, by contrast, use reason to derive the same prohibition directly from the harm the drug causes. The substantive difference between the two lines of argument does not seem very great, but the Shi'is think their approach gives more certainty.

Ijtihad is not considered *one* of the "roots" of *fiqh* but refers to the *whole* process by which judgments are drawn from them. In recent years *mujtahids* have commonly been given the title Ayatollah ("sign of God"). Every Shi'i believer who is not qualified to be a *mujtahid* should choose a living *mujtahid* and follow his judgments. This is the Shi'i form of *taqlid*. In the past century or two it has been usual for a small number of Ayatollahs to acquire a considerable following of *muqallids* and become known as *marja'-i taqlid* ("source of emulation"). These are given the title of Grand Ayatollah. This system gives the Ayatollahs more authority than Sunni *'ulama'* have and in recent years they have been able to turn it into significant political power. To this is added the economic power derived from *khums* (the one-fifth tax), also distinctive to Shi'ism.

The other group, the Akhbārīs, are found only in a few places today, such as Bahrain. They recognize only two roots of *fiqh*, the Qur'an and the reports, *akhbār*, of the Prophet and the *Imams*. Some, in fact, have recognized only the *akhbar*, on the grounds that only the Prophet and the *Imams* could interpret the Qur'an and therefore it should be received only through them. Where these roots are silent the *faqihs* should not presume to exercise *ijtihad*. In practice this means that large areas of life have been left to more secular agencies, such as the *siyasa* of the Safavid shahs and their *'urf* courts.

Just as the differences between the rulings of Sunni *madhhabs* are usually minor but can be significant, so also are the differences between Sunnis and Shi'is. One well-known difference is that Shi'is permit *mut'a* marriage, that is, a marriage for a specified period of time and with other conditions. This is understood to be permitted by a Qur'anic passage (4:24) but was forbidden by 'Umar. Shi'is do not recognize 'Umar's decision. Shi'i *fiqh* gives a larger share of an inheritance to women in most situations than does Sunni *fiqh*. This reflects the fact that Sunni *fiqh* presumes that pre-Islamic customs were meant to continue unless the Qur'an or the Prophet specifically changed them, so that certain customs favoring male heirs continued, but Shi'is see the Qur'an and Prophet as instituting a radically new system.

Muftis *and* fatwas

A *muftī*, among both Shi'is and Sunnis, is a scholar who gives an opinion on specific issues of *fiqh*. This opinion is called a *fatwa*. It is strictly advisory and it is up to the person who requests it to implement it or not. *Fatwas* are often requested by judges, especially in complex cases, and also by rulers to confirm whether their proposed actions are permitted by the Shari'a. They are also commonly requested by private individuals for a wide range of personal concerns, including questions of ritual. In the earliest centuries *muftis* were private individuals but in time many came to be attached to the courts and the rulers and today most Muslim states have an official *mufti*. In modern times *fatwas* are also given by boards or committees of *'ulama'*. *Fatwas* are also regularly given today in newspapers and popular magazines and, more recently, on the internet.

The following example is taken from a Saudi source online (edited slightly):

> *Question:*
> Is there anything wrong with using mobile phones which play tunes, because these tunes are a kind of music, or not?
>
> *Answer:*
> Praise be to Allah. The Prophet (peace and blessings of Allah be upon him) stated that musical instruments are *haram* when he said: "There will be among my

Figure 10.1 Egypt's grand *mufti* Shawki Ibrahim Abdel-Karim (R) with his predecessor Ali Gomaa (L), during a meeting at al-Azhar in Cairo, March 2013. The grand *mufti* is the leading interpreter of the Shari'a in Egypt. He is elected by the leading *'ulama'* of al-Azhar and confirmed by the president of the republic. The position was created in 1895 and held by the famous reformer, Muhammad 'Abduh from 1899 to 1905 (see chapter 17). © epa european pressphoto agency b.v./Alamy

umma people who will regard as permissible adultery, silk, alcohol and musical instruments." (Narrated by al-Bukhari, 5590)

This *hadith* indicates that musical instruments are *haram* in two ways. First, the Prophet (PBUH) said "they will regard as permissible," which clearly indicates that the things mentioned – including musical instruments – are forbidden in Shari'a but those people will regard them as permissible. Second, musical instruments are mentioned alongside things which are definitively forbidden, namely adultery and alcohol. If they were not *haram*, they would not be mentioned alongside these things. (*al-Silsilah al-Sahihah* by al-Albani, 1/140–41)

Shaykh al-Islam Ibn Taymiyah (may Allah have mercy on him) said: This *hadith* indicates that musical instruments are *haram*. (*Majmu' al-Fatawa*, 11/535).

It is not permissible to use musical tunes for telephones or any other devices, because listening to musical instruments is *haram*, as is indicated by the evidence of Shari'a. It is possible to do without them by using the ordinary ringing tone. And Allah is the Source of strength.

http://www.islam-qa.com/en/ref/47407 (accessed 18 November 2008)

A brief history of fiqh

So far *fiqh* has been presented largely from a theoretical point of view. Now we briefly consider its development as critical historians see it (but perforce skipping over a number of differences among these historians).

Sunni *fiqh*

During Muhammad's career law was largely a continuation of pre-Islamic traditions as modified by the Qur'an and by decisions of Muhammad as leader of the community. Under the "Rightly Guided" caliphs and the Umayyads law continued to be based on decisions of the caliph, along with his governors and administrators, and of the ***qadis***, after they began to be appointed. Local custom in various conquered territories also contributed to the content of the law, as did Byzantine and Sasanian administrative and legal practice. The Qur'an and the *Sunna* of the Prophet also played some role though the latter would not have been as detailed and specific as it was to become. At this time the concept of *sunna* often referred to the normative practice of the *umma* or groups within it, although there were also *sunnas* of well-known individuals. During the later part of the Umayyad period the *'ulama'* movement began, as we have seen, largely apart from government. This included the beginning of *fiqh*, often as an implicit or explicit critique of the ruler's actions, as well as the quest for *hadith*.

The leading scholars, such as al-Awza'i (d. 774), relied mainly on the *sunna* of the *umma*, and might advise or criticize the existing ruler. Many early *faqihs* relied heavily on their own considered opinion, *ra'y*, but as the *hadith* movement grew its partisans sought to base their judgments on the *Sunna* of the Prophet, as providing greater certainty. This would also give the *'ulama'* more authority vis-à-vis the rulers, since they were masters of the *Hadith*. What happened in practice, according to critical scholars, was that rules originally based on custom or rulers' decisions were reprocessed into *Hadith*. The first two "founders" of *madhhabs*, made little use of *Hadith*. Malik ibn Anas set forth the doctrines of the scholars of Medina and Abu Hanifa used very few *hadith* and depended more on *ra'y*. Abu Yusuf and al-Shaybani (d. 805), Abu Hanifa's colleagues, made greater use of *Hadith*. The victory of the *Hadith* position was enshrined in the work of al-Shafi'i (d. 819), who developed the Sunni theory of *usul al-fiqh* in its basic form, although it took about a century for it to be recognized and refinements were made later on.

Al-Shafi'i is counted as the founder of the third *madhhab*. The fourth *madhhab* is associated with Ahmad ibn Hanbal (d. 855), the key figure in the ***mihna***, and has tended to stress a fairly literal reading of the Qur'an and *Hadith* over *qiyas*. The Ẓāhirī *madhhab*, founded by Dawud ibn Khalaf (d. 884), emphasized a very literal interpretation of the Qur'an and *Hadith* and counted some important figures among its adherents, such as the great mystic **Ibn 'Arabi**, but it has not survived, as was the case with a couple of others. The four that have survived struggled with each other for some time but by 1300 had come to recognize each other as valid. The **Mamlukes** in Egypt, for example, appointed a chief *qadi* for each of them. By this time the rulers had recognized the right of the *'ulama'* to determine the content of the law but retained the right to implement it as well as to act in matters considered *siyasa*, as we have seen.

The concept of *maslaha* appeared about 900 and aspects of Greek logic were introduced by **al-Ghazali** (d. 1111). The use of the "Aims of the Shari'a" was developed particularly by al-Shāṭibī (d. 1388). About 1200, some scholars began to claim that *ijtihad* was no longer possible, i.e. that "the gate of *ijtihad* was closed" and this idea came to be widely accepted. By this was meant "absolute *ijtihad*", i.e. going directly to the Qur'an and the *Sunna* to derive rules without being bound by previous scholarship. There never was a complete consensus on this, however. The Hanbalis in particular insisted on the possibility of *ijtihad* and some, such as the reformer Ibn Taymiyya (see chapter 13), claimed the right to do it.

Others performed a more limited *ijtihad* within the guidelines of their *madhhab* and in most times and places there seem to have been at least a few *mujtahids* of this type. In other cases *ijtihad* seems to have been performed in practice without necessarily being called such. To be sure, it was understood that most *faqihs* would practice *taqlid*, but this was not necessarily the rigid imitation it is sometimes made out to be. A *mufti* might be *muqallid* but he would still confront new situations and would have to adapt the principles of his *madhhab* to them. It was mainly through the activities of such *muftis* that *fiqh* continued to develop. If the pace of development slowed down in later centuries, it was probably because the legal system had reached a certain maturity, that is to say, a large degree of consensus had been achieved. It never ceased to develop, however, in response to new situations. Still, even if the "gate of *ijtihad*" was not actually closed the idea that it was closed had considerable influence and reopening it has been one of the main slogans of modern reformers.

Twelver Shi'i *fiqh*

While the sixth *Imam*, Ja'far al-Sadiq is considered the founder of Shi'i *fiqh*, developments in *usul al-fiqh* began in a significant way only with the Greater Occultation, since before that time the *Imam* could give an authoritative answer to questions. At this point there appear to have been two tendencies, one emphasizing the *akhbār* (reports) of the *Imams*, which were being collected at this time, and the other emphasizing *ijtihad* and a more rationalist approach. From the thirteenth to the fifteenth centuries a number of scholars developed this latter approach. In the seventeenth century the other tendency crystallized as the Akhbari school, stimulated by the writings of Mulla Astarabadi (d. 1623), and this was predominant until well into the eighteenth century. Toward the end of that century the more rationalist position, now known as Usuli, was successfully reasserted under the leadership of Vahid Behbahani (d. 1792) and has predominated since then. For them the "gate of *ijtihad*" has never been closed. The system of Ayatollahs, Grand Ayatollahs and *marja's* developed during the nineteenth and twentieth centuries.

The Shari'a and popular appropriation

Given human nature, it is not surprising that Shari'a law is quite diversely appropriated in practice. We have already seen that parts of Shari'a law can be superseded in practice or very broadly interpreted. But there are other things to notice. The relative importance given by people in practice to particular prescriptions may be different from what the texts say. For example, the Pillars are all equally obligatory, but one will find many people who do not perform *salah* regularly but do fast during Ramadan and go on *Hajj*. Circumcision of males is recommended rather than obligatory in three of the four Sunni *madhhabs* but is often treated in practice as if it were one of the most important obligations. Female "circumcision" is generally understood to be a matter of custom rather than Shari'a and in most places is not practiced at all, but those who do practice it see it as dictated by the Shari'a. Wine and pork are both forbidden, but popular attitudes to them are quite different. Pork is viewed as disgusting and one will find few Muslims, even among those who are otherwise non-practicing, who will knowingly eat it. Wine, by contrast, is viewed as inherently desirable and has been consumed, especially at the higher levels of society, since the beginning of Islam. It is also used as a symbol in both secular and sacred poetry. A reporter in contemporary England describes customers who are at pains to make sure a restaurant is *halal* and then the first thing they ask for is beer. People often make their own judgment about things. For example, the *faqihs* declare hashish forbidden, on analogy with wine, but it has been widely used in Middle Eastern societies for centuries. Najib Mahfouz has a character in one of his novels, *Midaq Alley*, say of the Egyptian government in the 1940s, "It has legalized wine, which God forbade, and has forbidden hashish, which God allowed" (Mahfouz, 1975, 39). While in some societies custom and Shari'a are consciously distinguished from each other, in most societies much that is strictly speaking custom is put on the same level as Shari'a, and even above some Shari'a provisions, with many members of the society being unaware of the difference.

Despite these various sorts of disjunction between the Shari'a and social reality, the Shari'a has been one of the major defining symbols and foci of loyalty for Muslims for centuries and continues to be so. Religious commands do not lose their validity simply because they are not obeyed. In fact, the legal devices mentioned earlier may be seen as a means of protecting the sanctity of the Shari'a even though violating its substance. It is worth noting that the definition of apostasy is often given as "permitting the forbidden and forbidding the permitted". What is serious here is not doing what is forbidden but refusing to recognize that it is forbidden. It is by no means surprising that the Shari'a is very much at the center of the current "resurgence" of Islam, both in the Islamic world and among Muslims in the West, as we shall see.

Key points

- Though often translated "Islamic law", the Shari'a differs from Western law in three ways: (1) It comes from God, (2) it covers many more areas of life than Western law does (e.g. ritual) and (3) it is more like a moral evaluation of actions (from commanded to forbidden).
- *Fiqh*, often translated "law" or "jurisprudence", is the human effort to understand the divine Shari'a and the results of this effort. It involves discovering the law, not creating it and is done by scholars, not by rulers or governments.
- *Usul al-fiqh*, the sources of this understanding: the Qur'an, the *Sunna* of the Prophet, the effort (*ijtihad*) of the scholars and the consensus (*ijma'*) of the scholars. Shi'is and Sunnis differ somewhat on this.
- Sunni *madhhabs* represent four traditions of *fiqh* that differ in details but generally recognize each other. Twelver Shi'is are often seen as a fifth *madhhab*.
- *Muftis*, often translated "jurisconsults", are the ones who give opinions based on *fiqh* in specific cases. They are not judges and their opinions are advisory.
- At the popular level the Shari'a has been followed or not followed in complex ways.

Discussion questions

1. In what ways does Islamic law differ from Western law?
2. To what extent has the Shari'a actually guided all areas of human life over the course of Muslim history?
3. Do you think that the procedures of the *faqihs* are more like those of Western legislators or of Western scientists?
4. If you were a *mufti* asked to answer the question whether tobacco is permitted, how would you proceed?
5. Why might some have considered the "gate of *ijtihad*" to have been closed?

Critical thinking box 10.1

Analyze the *fatwa* on ring tones presented in this chapter and construct an alternative one.

Critical thinking box 10.2

A person is fined for speeding and appeals the fine on the grounds that he or she was taking someone to the hospital. How would one decide this using the methods of *fiqh*?

Do you think *fiqh* could lead to a different judgment than the law of your state or country? (You may substitute an alternative case, such as neighbours arguing over who should mow a common strip of lawn.)

Companion website

Features further reading and weblinks relating to debates on coffee and smoking, and on women in Indonesia. The website includes weblinks for the Fatwas listed in the online resources below.

Further reading

Hallaq, Wael (1997) *A History of Islamic Legal Theories: An Introduction to Sunni Usul al-Fiqh*. Cambridge, UK and New York: Cambridge University Press. (Thorough treatment by one of the leading contemporary scholars of the subject. Other books by him are also useful.)

Schacht, J. (1965) *An Introduction to Islamic Law*, 2nd impression. Oxford: Clarendon Press. (A good summary of the author's critical views on the history of *fiqh* and a presentation of the content of Hanafi *fiqh*.)

Zubaida, Sami (2003) *Law and Power in the Islamic World*. London and New York: I.B. Tauris. (Detailed study of the history of *fiqh* and related topics in the pre-modern period.)

Dien, Mawil Izzi (2004) *Islamic Law: From Historical Foundations to Contemporary Practice*. Notre Dame, IN: University of Notre Dame Press. (Detailed survey covering in greater depth many of the same topics as this chapter; stresses the centrality of *maslaha*.)

Coulson, Noel J. (1969) *Conflicts and Tensions in Islamic Jurisprudence*. Chicago, IL: University of Chicago Press. (Accessible presentation of a number of issues.)

Mutahhari, M. (n.d.) *Jurisprudence and Its Principles*. Elmhurst, NY: Tahrike Tarsile Qur'an (Shi'i *usul al-fiqh*). (Short accessible book by a leading Iranian ayatollah.)

Al-Qaradawi, Yusuf (n.d.) *The Lawful and the Prohibited in Islam*. Indianapolis, IN: American Trust Publications. (Widely read book by a leading Islamist scholar.)

Pearl, David (1979) *A Textbook on Muslim Law*. London: Croom Helm. (Details of family law with attention to the British situation.)

Esposito, J. (1982) *Women in Muslim Family Law*. Syracuse, NY: Syracuse University Press. (Good, basic explanation of *usul al-fiqh*, followed by discussion of legal status of women's issues in some modern countries.)

Powers, David S. (2002) *Law, Society, and Culture in the Maghrib, 1300–1500*. Cambridge: Cambridge University Press. (Studies especially *muftis* and *fatwas* of this period and place.)

See also: Esposito, *The Oxford History of Islam* (Chs 2–3) [F]; Knysh, *Islam in Historical Perspective* (Chs 9–10) [F].

Online resources for *fatwas* (accessed 23 August 2013)

http://www.islam-qa.com/en. (The source of the *fatwa* quoted in this chapter; deals with a wide range of topics; interpretations appear to be conservative (***salafi***).)

http://qa.sunnipath.com. (Focuses on worship and personal relations; appears traditionalist.)

http://www.fatwa-online.com. (Appears to be Saudi and *salafi*.)

http://darulifta-deoband.org. (From the Deoband school in India; appears more traditionalist than *salafi*.)

11 *Theology and philosophy*

"God talk", Muslim style

> Thus God makes clear to you the signs; perhaps you will reflect.
>
> (Qur'an 2:266)

The previous chapter dealt with the will of God for human behavior, the Shari'a, and how it can be discovered. This has always been the main concern. But Islam has also had both a theological movement and a philosophical movement, which have been of less importance but still significant. These are discussed in this chapter.

In this chapter

- Theology (*kalam, usul al-din*) and its main schools
- Theological issues: unity of God (*tawhid*), justice, etc.
- Philosophy
- Main teachings of the philosophers

Theology (kalam, usul al-din)

There were several stimuli to theological speculation and debate. There were apparent contradictions in the Qur'an and ***Sunna*** that needed to be resolved. Political conflicts during the first century, particularly those involving the **Kharijis**, raised issues that had theological implications. Debates with Christians, Jews, Zoroastrians and others in the newly opened lands also raised theological issues. When the tradition of philosophy deriving from ancient Greece became known to the Muslims, it offered challenges to belief and also tools for argumentation. It contributed to theology and also gave rise to the distinct tradition of philosophy that will be discussed in the latter part of this chapter.

The term for an important form of theology among Muslims that appeared in the second century *hijri* is *'ilm al-kalām* (or *kalām*, for short), literally the science of words, i.e. discussion or debate, reflecting the manner in which theology was conducted. It is sometimes called "dialectical theology" in English and was primarily concerned with defending the truth of religion against erroneous views. Other names for theology in Arabic are *'ilm uṣūl al-dīn* (the science of the roots of religion) and *'ilm al-tawḥīd* (literally: the science of the affirmation of [God's] unity).

While the activities of the Kharijis raised theological issues about the nature of faith and groups such as the Murji'is and the Qadaris discussed theological issues (see below), the Mu'tazilis were the first proper school (*madhhab*) of *kalam* and largely set the agenda for the movement. Their methods and views were strongly rejected by the **Traditionalists** (*ahl al-ḥadīth* or ***Hanbalis***), while the **Ash'aris** and **Maturidis** used their methods but rejected many of their views.

The Mu'tazili movement is said to have begun in the circles around Hasan al-Basri (d. 728) though current critical scholarship puts its beginning closer to 800. It was at its greatest political strength from 833 to about 850 during the *miḥna* (inquisition), when the caliphs attempted to impose its doctrine about the Qur'an on the *'ulama'*. It continued strong intellectually for two or three centuries among Sunnis and has been the main theological *madhhab* of Twelver and Fiver Shi'is. The Mu'tazilis called themselves the "people of *tawhid* and justice". *Tawhid* and justice are the first two of their five fundamental principles, the others being "promise and threat", "the intermediate position", and "commanding the good and prohibiting evil". They were influenced both by debates with non-Muslims and by Greek philosophy and they used reason to interpret the Qur'an and *Hadith* and, indeed, often relied on reason alone.

The Traditionalists (*ahl al-ḥadīth*), initially under the leadership of **Ahmad ibn Hanbal** during the *mihna*, objected strongly to this use of human reason to explain (and in their view sometimes explain away) divine truths and commands. They provided a continuing, forceful and often sophisticated critique of all the schools of *kalam*. Their greatest later representative was Ibn Taymiyya (d. 1328), whose refutations of philosophy and *kalam* were acute and showed a considerable grasp of these subjects (see chapter 13)

Abu al-Hasan al-Ash'ari (d. 935) was a Mu'tazili who converted to Traditionalist views but sought to defend them with Mu'tazili methods. His successors in the Ash'ari *madhhab* adopted more philosophical methods and ideas than he did. **Al-Ghazali** (see chapter 13) introduced the Aristotelian syllogism into theology as he did into *fiqh* and Fakhr al-Din al-Razi (d. 1210) was particularly notable for his use of philosophical concepts. Another *madhhab*, beginning about the same time as the Ash'aris, derived from Abu Mansur al-Maturidi (d. 944), who lived in Central Asia. Its teachings differed from those of the Ash'aris in certain details. The creedal statement composed by the Maturidi, al-Nasafi (d. 1142), attracted commentaries by both Maturidis and Ash'aris.

Mu'tazilis and Maturidis were generally associated with the **Hanafi** *madhhab* of *fiqh*, the Ash'aris with the **Shafi'is** and the Traditionalists with the Hanbalis, but there were Traditionalists also in the other *madhhabs* of *fiqh*, so that Traditionalism has been more important than has often been recognized. Since the fourteenth century theological discussion has continued but produced relatively little that was new or creative before modern times. In modern times some reformers have sought to reappropriate some of the Mu'tazili theses (especially that of "justice"), sometimes accepting the label and sometimes not.

Theological issues

It will be convenient to discuss the main issues dealt with by the theologians using the five principles of the Mu'tazila as headings.

Tawḥīd

The Mu'tazila held that people are obligated to know God by reason since only in this way can one be sure that He exists and is truthful, and thus be justified in relying on the Qur'an and the *Sunna*. The later Ash'aris and the Maturidis also held that the existence of God can be known by reason.

The Mu'tazilis' strong concern for God's unity led them to insist that various divine attributes, such as knowledge, power, will, life, hearing, sight and speech, could not be faculties distinct from God's essence. Thus God knows by His essence, not by a distinguishable attribute called knowledge. Otherwise, God's pure unity would be compromised. They may possibly have been reacting against Christian theologians of the time who explained the Trinity in terms of divine attributes. The Traditionalists and al-Ash'aris stated that God has such attributes since the Qur'an and *Hadith* speak of them and that we are not to speculate about them but are to accept them, as they put it, *bilā kayf* ("without [asking] how"). Later Ash'aris and Maturidis also affirmed the attributes of God and said they are "not He and not other than He" (e.g. in Nasafi's creed).

The Qur'an sometimes speaks of God's face or hand or has Him sitting on the throne. The Mu'tazila argued that such "physical" statements had to be interpreted metaphorically (*ta'wīl*) since they were rationally impossible if taken literally. Thus God's hand could be seen as meaning His power and God's face as His essence. The Traditionalists and al-Ash'ari held that these, like other attributes, must be held *bilā kayf* as true. God knows better than human reason what terms should be applied to Him. Later Ash'aris, however, accept metaphorical interpretations of the "physical" attributes.

This issue becomes concrete and contentious in relation to the attribute of speech, since the Qur'an is God's speech. What is the relation between God and the Qur'an that we read and recite? The Mu'tazilis held that the Qur'an was created by God, since otherwise it would be identical with God. The Traditionalists led by Ibn

Hanbal, however, insisted that the Qur'an is the uncreated word of God. This was the issue on which the *miḥna* centered and on which the caliphs finally gave way, since Ibn Hanbal's view was clearly the popular view. The Ash'aris and Maturidis also held that the Qur'an is uncreated; like other attributes of God it is "not He and not other than He". This does not mean that the physical copies of the Qur'an and the spoken words of its recitation are eternal. In the words of Nasafi's creed, "The Qur'an is the uncreated speech of God and is written on our pages, preserved in our hearts, recited by our tongues and heard by our ears, but does not inhere in them" (Taftazani, 1980, 58, modified). There was, interestingly, a political "pay off" to all this. If the Qur'an were in the category of created things then it might be outranked by other created beings, such as a divinely guided ruler, which the early caliphs often claimed to be, or a Shi'i *Imam* protected from error. But if it was uncreated it clearly stood in a category of its own above everything else and elevated the status of its official interpreters, the *'ulama'*.

It also is worth noting that the Traditionalist position on the Qur'an parallels the orthodox Christian position on Christ as the uncreated Son and Word (Logos) of God and the Mu'tazili position parallels that of the Arians, who believed Christ to be the highest of creatures. In fact, the caliph al-Ma'mun, a supporter of the Mu'tazilis, complained of the Traditionalists, "They are, thus, like the Christians when they claim that 'Isa the son of Mary was not created because he was the word of God" (Grunebaum, 1966, 104–5). The view of the attributes as "not he and not other than he" is reminiscent of the Christian view of the relationship among the Persons of the Trinity. Likewise, the view of the relation between the uncreated Qur'an and the written and recited Qur'an seems reminiscent of the orthodox Christian view of the human and divine natures of Christ. There could be Christian influence here but it may also be that similar issues bring forth similar solutions. As suggested in chapter 5, the Qur'an occupies for Muslims a place similar to that which Christ occupies for Christians.

It is commonly believed that believers will see God in paradise. This also the Mu'tazilis interpreted metaphorically, since God cannot be seen. The Traditionalists and al-Ash'ari insisted that God will in fact be seen but "without [asking] how". Later Ash'aris and Maturidis also said that God will be seen but not in any physical manner.

Justice

The Mu'tazilis believed that God is perfectly just and thus incapable of evil. Therefore, He is bound to do what is best for His creatures. The others, however, argued that to say this is to put limits on God, and God has no limits since there is no one superior to Him who could impose limits on Him.

For the Mu'tazilis right and wrong inhere in actions themselves and therefore moral principles can be known by human reason apart from revelation, although some things, such as the ritual requirements, are known only by revelation. One corollary was that people who did not know of Islam or Muhammad were still obligated to obey God. For the Ash'aris what is right or wrong is so because God makes it so, not because it is inherently so. Therefore, if God declared murder or lying to be morally good, they would be good. (God himself does not lie, not because lying is bad but because He is incapable of lying. Thus, we can trust His promises.) Therefore moral principles and moral obligation come only with revelation. Most Maturidis allowed that some moral principles could be known by reason but their moral quality is given by God, not inherent in them.

A major issue under this heading was that of predestination (*qaḍā' wa-qadar*) versus free will. The Qur'an makes such statements as "Whoever God guides, he is rightly guided and whoever He leads astray, they are the losers" (7:178), but also makes statements such as "God does not change what is in a people until they change what is in themselves" (13:11). While the Qur'an and the *Hadith* have more statements tending toward predestination than toward free will, the very call to obey God would appear to presume the ability to choose. In the early decades of Islam the idea of predestination seems to have predominated, in part possibly because of a sense of the overwhelming power of God and its manifestation in the dramatic conquests. It also suited the political interests of the Umayyads, since their morally questionable actions could be ascribed to God's will.

In the latter part of the Umayyad period there appeared people known as Qadaris, who held that humans have the power of moral choice, and some of these were critical of the **Umayyads**. Al-Hasan al-Basri seems to have expressed this view and it was taken up by the Mu'tazila, who said that humans create their actions in the moral realm. They argued that God would be unjust if He punished people for actions He had created. Their opponents argued that this would involve creators beside God and thus be *shirk* and a form of "dualism" (a polemical term used against Manicheans and others). Moreover, as indicated above, God is not bound to do what is best for his creatures. Al-Ash'ari, however, proffered a doctrine known as "acquisition", according to which God creates actions but humans "acquire" them. Al-Ash'ari's account involves a special human power for each "voluntary" action and this power is created by God, so that it is hard to see in what way humans are free. Later Ash'aris and Maturidis came up with various formulations, most of which seem to amount to the same thing, although some Maturidis spoke of "choice" rather than "acquisition" and appear to have held that God responds, in some sense, to human choice. This doctrine of *kasb* became a by-word for complexity and obscurity and further details are beyond the scope of this book. Traditionalists hold that God determines all human actions and punishes and rewards for them, without being unjust in so doing. They do not seek to reconcile these points rationally. Nor do many ordinary Muslims, who believe practically in free will and responsibility before they act and in the predestination of the results afterward. Belief in predestination in this way, it is claimed, helps one face the calamities that occur in life without inhibiting action.

Promise and threat

The Mu'tazila held that God must of necessity send the one guilty of serious sins to eternal punishment, since this threat is made clear in the Qur'an. They either rejected the idea of intercession by the Prophet or held that it will not benefit such people. The Ash'aris and Maturidis however, hold that Muslims who commit great sins may be punished in the Fire but will eventually come out of it and enter Paradise and Traditionalists hold a similar position.

Faith

The issue of the nature of faith (i.e. that which makes one a Muslim or a Believer and thus within the pale of the *umma*) was raised very early in Islamic history, since the Kharijis claimed that those guilty of serious sins were *kafirs*, and for the extreme Kharijis this applied to everyone except themselves. At the opposite extreme were those who are known as Murji'a, "postponers", who argued that serious sinners were still believers and part of the *umma* so long as they professed faith, the final decision on them being postponed until God makes it. This appears to have developed out of a political desire to be neutral between 'Uthman and 'Ali, i.e. to "postpone" the judgment between them. The Mu'tazila argued that such people were in an intermediate position, neither believers nor *kafirs* but *fāsiq*, corrupt. They are to be treated as members of the *umma* in this world, but will be punished in the afterlife for their sins. The Ash'aris and Maturidis took a position similar to that of the Murji'a although they did not accept this label.

By most theologians faith was analyzed into three parts: affirmation in the heart, confession by the tongue and action by the limbs. According to the Traditionalists, Mu'tazila and al-Ash'ari, all three were part of faith and therefore faith could increase or decrease in terms of actions performed. Others held that faith proper consisted only of affirmation or affirmation and confession and does not increase or decrease with deeds.

Commanding the good and forbidding iniquity

Commanding the good and forbidding iniquity is a command from the Qur'an (9:71; 22:41 and elsewhere) commonly referred to by Muslims, Mu'tazili and non-Mu'tazili, past and present. It is the obligation to work for a just and moral society in accordance with the power one has, as the Prophet has said: "If you see any wrongful act, you must first correct it with your hand, failing to do so with your speech, failing to do so with your hearts and that is the lowest state of faith." For most authorities this has not included the right of rebellion against an unjust ruler, as mentioned in chapter 8.

The theologians also discuss the need for a leader (*imam*), specifying that he does not have to be protected from error (*Ma'ṣūm*). They also discuss the merits of the Companions of Muhammad and the relative merits of the first four caliphs, though the Mu'tazili, 'Abd al-Jabbar (d. 1024) treats them as equal. Sunnis generally see Abu Bakr as the most meritorious, then 'Umar, then 'Ali. Shi'is, of course see 'Ali as the first *Imam* and specify that the *imams* must be protected from error.

Philosophy

If theology uses reason to explicate revelation and rebut error, the philosophers sought to build a positive system strictly on reason. Philosophy was often called *falsafa* in Arabic, a word that signals its non-Islamic origin, but was also called *ḥikma*, wisdom, a good Arabic word with a wide range of uses (*hekmat* in Persian). Islamic philosophy was a continuation of the tradition going back to the pre-Socratics in Greece and continuing modified but unbroken into the Greek and Syriac world of late antiquity. From here it passed to the Muslims and a few centuries later was taken up by the Western Christian world. Although claiming to base themselves on reason alone, the philosophers gave considerable authority to the great Greek philosophers, particularly Aristotle. In fact, however, the philosophy they received did not clearly distinguish Aristotelianism from neo-Platonism and included a summary of Plotinus that went under the title of "The Theology of Aristotle".

Philosophy at this time comprised a much wider range of disciplines than it does today. It included most of what we would put under the heading of "science", such as cosmology, astronomy (and astrology), physics, chemistry (and alchemy), biology and psychology. It was also closely associated with medicine and several of the well-known philosophers were also physicians. This was one reason they were popular with rulers. Philosophy was the "science" of its time and claimed a status and prestige akin to that which we give to science today, although with much less success.

Like science today, philosophy was very ecumenical. Muslims, Jews, Christians and others participated on a largely equal basis, debated with each other and read each others' works. The early Muslim philosophers had non-Muslims for teachers and read translations done by scholars such as Hunayn ibn Ishaq, a Nestorian Christian. Between the tenth and thirteenth centuries **Andalus** was the site of an impressive "trialogue" of Muslims, Jews and Christians and it was mainly there that Muslim philosophy was translated into Latin by Jews to be read by Christians such as Thomas Aquinas.

The most important philosophers were al-Kindi (801–66), who was Mu'tazili in theology, al-Farabi (c. 870–950), Ibn Sina (Avicenna, 980–1037), probably the

Figure 11.1 Al-Farabi (c. 870–950) on a banknote from Kazakhstan. Courtesy of iStockphoto

greatest of the philosophers, and Ibn Rushd (Averroes, 1126–98), who distinguished Aristotelian from Neo-Platonic teachings and whose work was particularly influential in the West. Ibn Sina will be discussed in chapter 13.

Main teachings of the philosophers

The philosophers sought to coordinate their teachings with Islamic religious doctrine in an interesting way. Philosophy, they claimed, represents the pure truth that can be discovered by reason but only by an elite with the intelligence and the leisure to pursue it. For the rest religion provides a series of concrete symbols and prescriptions that point indirectly to the same truths. Ibn Rushd's *On the Harmony of Religion and Philosophy* provides an accessible example of this. Hence philosophy by its own understanding as well as in fact was a highly elitist and esoteric movement that could never appeal to a large number. They could, though, hope to be a kind of leaven in the loaf of society and in particular an influence on its rulers. Al-Farabi's description of the ideal polity has been mentioned in chapter 8. On the other hand, Ibn Tufayl (d. 1186) wrote a long allegory, *Ḥayy ibn Yaqẓān* (*Alive the Son of Awake*) in which the protagonist grows up on an uninhabited island and works out the truths of philosophy by himself. Eventually someone who has been raised in a traditional religion comes to his island and they work out that the traditional religion is the same as Hayy's philosophy. They then return to the inhabited island and try to teach the people philosophy, but they fail and finally return to Hayy's island to devote themselves to contemplation.

The philosophers' views of God, creation and the afterlife illustrate their approach. The God of the philosophers tends to be rather abstract, a combination of Aristotle's "unmoved mover" and **Plotinus'** "One" from whom the universe emanates (see chapter 2). Most people cannot grasp or appreciate this, so the Qur'an presents a God with very concrete attributes that people can relate to. The philosophers believed that the universe is dependent on God but has always existed in largely the same form (the "eternity of the world"). The Qur'an teaches that God created the universe apparently at some point in time. Thus the essential point, that the universe depends on God, is made in a way that all people can appreciate. The philosophers believe that the soul survives the body and receives the consequences of its earthly action while the Qur'an makes the point of reward and punishment by teaching the more concrete doctrine of the resurrection of the body.

Reason, in the philosophers' usage, generally has a mystical dimension, unlike the usual view today. Discursive reasoning at some point in one's spiritual journey is transformed into a mystical vision of the highest realities, as with Plato and Plotinus. The vision that the philosophers achieve at the highest level is essentially the same as what the prophets have, except that the prophets have a strong imaginative faculty that allows them to create the concrete symbols of religion. As this was presented by al-Farabi it seemed to put the prophets at a lower level than the philosophers, but Ibn Sina reinterpreted it to assure the superiority of the prophets. Most Muslims still have felt that the philosophers do not recognize adequately the distinctiveness of prophecy. A further presentation of some of these doctrines in Ibn Sina's writings will be given in chapter 13.

The philosophers also introduced Greek ethical ideas into Muslim thinking, both the analysis of virtues and vices and the means of inculcating them. These were asserted to be consistent with the Shari'a. The most important of these philosophers was Ibn Miskawayh (c. 940–1030), whose work gave rise to a continuing tradition of writing on ethics in Persian,

There was a small number of "free thinkers" who rejected essential Islamic doctrines. Both the eminent physician Abu Bakr al-Razi (d. 923 or 932) and the ex-theologian Ibn al-Rawandi (d. 910) rejected the need for prophecy and argued that reason and philosophy were sufficient for spiritual needs. Al-Razi also believed in four eternal principles in addition to the Creator (time, space, matter and soul).

Philosophy ceased to be a distinct movement in the Sunni world after about 1200, but elements of it, including both metaphysics and ethics, were absorbed into later thinking. Theological treatises and creeds came to have an introductory section dealing with philosophical ideas such as substance and accidents and philosophical concepts and terms were used by the speculative Sufis. In the Iranian Shi'i world the philosophical tradition continued and its mystical side developed into a full-fledged mystical philosophy known as *irfan*. *Irfan* and speculative Sufi thinking are called "wisdom" (*hikma/hekmat*) in Arabic and Persian and often "theosophy" in English ("divine wisdom", no connection with the Theosophy of Annie Besant). More will be said of these in chapter 12.

In modern times some Muslim scholars have studied and interpretered philosophers such as Ibn Sina and Ibn Rushd as part of their heritage, availing themselves of Western as well as Muslim scholarship for this purpose.

Key points

- Theology represents a response to certain political events, to apparent contradictions in the Qur'an and *Sunna*, to debates with non-Muslims and to Greek philosophy.
- The first school of theology was the Mu'tazila, who called themselves the People of *Tawhid* and Justice, after their two main theses.
- These theses led to such issues as the nature of the Qur'an, the metaphorical interpretation of Qur'anic statements, the relation of ethics to God's will, and predestination.
- The other main schools are the Ash'aris and the Maturidis. The Traditionalists represent another option, the rejection of the *kalam* approach.
- Philosophy represents a continuation, in Islamic terms, of the ancient tradition of Greek philosophy.
- Philosophy saw itself as conveying in a purer form the basic truths of religion.
- Its teachings included a rather abstract view of God, the "eternity of the world" and the survival of the soul.
- Philosophy as a distinct movement died out in the Sunni world but survived in a mystical form in the Iranian Shi'i world.

Discussion questions

1. How did Islamic philosophy and theology differ from each other and from their namesakes in the West today?
2. Are things good because God commands them or does He command them because they are good? Which Islamic theologians speak of this and what do they say? Can you compare this to discussions of this question outside Islam?
3. Can the issue between God's power and human free will be resolved?
4. Does God cause evil?
5. What was the view of the Murji'a and why did they hold it?
6. Do you think it is feasible to have one view for the elite and another for the common people?
7. Why was theology less important than *fiqh*?

Critical thinking box 11.1

Compare a Mu'tazili/Shi'i creed with a non-Mu'tazili Sunni creed (e.g. the creed of al-Hilli with that of al-Nasafi in Watt's *Islamic Creeds: A Selection*). Where are they similar and where different? What is the significance of these similarities and differences?

Companion website

Includes further information and reading on *qadar* and other issues, and weblinks particularly on philosophy.

Further reading

Watt, W. Montgomery (1985) *Islamic Philosophy and Theology: An Extended Survey*, 2nd ed. Edinburgh: Edinburgh University Press. (One of the standard treatments.)

Watt, W. Montgomery (1994) *Islamic Creeds: A Selection*. Edinburgh: Edinburgh University Press. (Creeds from various schools of theology, including one Shi'i, with brief introductions.)

Netton, Ian Richard (1989) *Allah Transcendent: Studies in the Structure and Semiotics of Islamic Philosophy, Theology, and Cosmology*. London and New York: Routledge. (Surveys mainly philosophers, also attention to Sufism, Irfan and Traditionalism.)

Nasr, Sayyed Hossein and Leaman, Oliver (eds.) (1996) *History of Islamic Philosophy*, Part I. London and New York: Routledge. (Articles by different authors on a large number of topics and philosophers.)

Fakhry, M.A. (1970) *History of Islamic Philosophy*. New York and London: Columbia University Press. (Surveys main philosophers, also attention to Sufism, Irfan and Traditionalism, may be dated at points.)

Martin, Richard, Woodward, Mark and Atmaja, Dwi S. (eds.) (1997) *Defenders of Reason in Islam*. Oxford: One World Publications. (Part I deals in some detail with the Mu'tazila and Part II deals with modernism in Indonesia.)

Al-Taftazani, Mas'ud ibn 'Umar (1980) *A Commentary on the Creed of Islam*, trans. Earl Edgar Elder. New York: Books for Libraries. (Creed of al-Nasafi with commentary by an Ash'ari theologian.)

Ibn Tufayl (1972) *Hayy Ibn Yaqzan*, trans. L. E. Goodman. New York: Twayne. (In addition to what is mentioned earlier, this provides a very nice introduction to Islamic philosophical thinking.)

McCarthy, Richard J. (1953) *The Theology of al-Ash'ari: The Arabic Texts of al-Ash'ari's Kitab al-Luma' and Risalat Istihsan al-Khawd fi 'ilm al-Kalam, with Briefly Annotated Translations*. Beirut: Imprimerie Catholique. (Translation of important works, is reasonably accessible.)

See also: Esposito, *The Oxford History of Islam* (Chs 4, 6) [F]; Knysh, *Islam in Historical Perspective* (Ch. 15) [F].

Online resources

Islamic Philosophy on Line (Has material on a number of Islamic Philosophers, some of which appears in links in the text, and much else.): http://www.muslimphilosophy.com (accessed 23 August 2013).

12 *The Sufi path to God*

Spiritual dimensions of Islam

O you who believe, be ever mindful (*dhikr*) of God.

(Qur'an 33:41)

All who are on the earth are perishing (*fanā'*), but the Face of your Lord abides (baqā'), with majesty and honor.

(Qur'an 55:26–27)

Surely the friends (*walīs*) of God's shall know no fear nor sorrow.

(Qur'an 10:62/63)

We are traveling to see the king. As we cross the border of his realm we are informed of its laws and learn to obey them. As we come closer to the palace we talk with people who have been told a lot about the king but have not met him. When after some effort and preparation we enter the palace we meet people who have met the king and some who know him well. Finally we meet the king himself and our lives are transformed. This is a parable of the Sufi approach to God, the king of the universe, in comparison to that of *fiqh* and *kalam*. This chapter presents a general overview of the Sufi approach and sketches the history of the Sufi movement and its expression in poetry and "theosophy".

In this chapter

- Knowledge, love and remembrance of God
- *Tariqa*, the path
- The goal: *fana'* and *baqa'*
- *Walis* (saints)
- Sufism and Shari'a-mindedness
- Historical outline of Sufism
- Sufi poetry and theosophy
- Some recent developments

Knowledge, love and remembrance of God

The word Ṣūfī is derived from the Arabic word *ṣūf*, wool, because the early Sufis wore rough woolen garments, a form of asceticism also practiced by some Christian ascetics at the time. Roughly synonymous words are *faqīr* and *darwish* or *dervish*, which mean "poor" (i.e. poor in spirit) in Arabic and Persian respectively.

Knowledge of the **Shari'a** and obedience to it is central to Islam, but the Sufis wish to go further. They distinguish between two kinds of knowledge, *'ilm* and *ma'rifa*. *'Ilm* is the sort of knowledge we get by reading or hearing about something or someone and drawing conclusions from that. The ***'ulama'*** have this sort of knowledge of God's will and attributes. *Ma'rifa* is the direct and intimate knowledge we have when we have become acquainted with a person. It is this sort of knowledge that Sufis seek of God.

Corresponding to these two kinds of knowledge are two sets of attitudes and relationships. Corresponding to *'ilm* is the obedience that a servant or slave (*'abd*) gives to a master. Corresponding to *ma'rifa* is the love a lover has for his or her beloved, and love is the central theme of Sufi expression.

How does one achieve this knowledge and love of God? The Sufis speak of *dhikr*, which is commonly translated "remembrance" but in this context is probably better translated "having in mind" or "being fully aware of". This word appears in the Qur'an in varying forms around 300 times; an example is quoted above (Qur'an 33:41. A common literal translation is: "O you who believe, Remember God with much remembrance"). Since all humans have the *fiṭra*, the God-given nature that orients them to Him, the point is to clear away distractions and "remember" or become aware of the reality to which this *fitra* directs us.

Dhikr is also the name of the techniques used to stimulate this awareness, usually involving the recitation of certain names of God, often accompanied by bodily motions and controlled breathing. In one version seven names of God are recited and these are believed to purify seven levels of the soul. Sometimes individuals recite the names of God or other phrases, such as "Praise be to God" and "God is most great" (*subḥān allāh, al-ḥamdu li-llāh, allāhu akbar*) with the aid of a *sibḥa* (rosary). *Dhikr* may also involve forms of singing and dancing (known as *samā'* or *sema*) and may be accompanied by singers called *munshidūn* or *qawwals*. The dance of the so-called Whirling Dervishes is a form of *dhikr*. Similar practices are, of course, known in other religions. One thinks of the Jesus prayer in Orthodox Christianity, the recitations of the name of Amitabha Buddha in Pure Land Buddhism or the names of Krishna recited by the Krishna Consciousness devotees.

Some Sufis will also spend time in retreat (*khalwa*), engaging in these practices in isolation. Forty days is a typical period for this. One may also engage in fasting in addition to that of Ramadan. In general a Sufi should lead a lifestyle in accordance with the dictates of the Shari'a, but go further.

Tariqa, *the path*

By doing these things the Sufi proceeds along the *tariqa*, or path, toward God, which is marked by a series of stations (*maqamāt*) and states (*aḥwāl*), various lists of which have been given by different Sufi writers. The stations usually begin with repentance, that is, turning away from ordinary life to the Sufi path. Other stations include humility, sincerity, renunciation (of physical pleasures and whatever distracts one from God, even if allowed by the Shari'a), complete reliance on God, poverty, patience, gratitude, fear and hope. States include expansion and contraction of the soul (*basṭ* and *qabḍ*, enthusiastic joy and something like depression), intoxication and sobriety (see below), love, *ma'rifa*, intimacy with God, nearness to God, longing (*shawq*), annihilation or passing away in God (*fanā'*) and continuance in God (*baqā'*, see below). In general, stations are achieved at least in part by human effort and may be permanent once achieved. States, by contrast, are gifts of God's grace over which the human being has no control and are usually temporary. They are commonly described as forms of ecstasy. Within this framework there is considerable emphasis on moral virtues as preparatory for and part of spiritual achievement.

One does not travel this path on one's own, as it would be far too dangerous spiritually and psychologically, and even physically. One must have a spiritual guide, variously called a *shaykh*, *pir* or *murshid* (comparable to a guru in other traditions and in some respects to a psychological counsellor in the West). The disciple is called a *murīd* (one who seeks). Ideally the relationship between *murid* and *shaykh* is extremely close. The *shaykh* should be able to discern the spiritual state of the *murīd* so as to be able to advise him and act as a moral guide. It has been claimed that a *shaykh* could do this at a distance telepathically. The *murid* should obey the *shaykh's* advice implicitly. It is said that the *murid* should be to his *shaykh* as a corpse in the hand of its washer and also that a person who has no *shaykh* has Satan for a *shaykh*. Often the *murid* is expected to learn and practice a number of rules for proper behavior and practical and ethical advice that go under the label of *adab* (roughly "good manners", "ethics"; see chapter 14 for more on this term). The relationship to a *shaykh* normally begins with a formal initiation and pledge of allegiance called a *bay'a* (the same term as that used in the political context for the pledge of allegiance the representatives of the *umma* give to the incoming caliph).

In rare cases a Sufi may not have a human *shaykh* or formal initiation, but be initiated by the spirit of a great Sufi or prophetic figure of the past. This initiation is called *uwaysi* or *veiysi*.

How does one choose a *shaykh*? Often the choice is determined by a long-standing relation between a particular *shaykh* and a particular family, village or other group. A person may be directed to a *shaykh* by a friend or acquaintance who is already a *murid* of that *shaykh*. A *murid* may seek out a *shaykh* on the basis of personal attraction or affinity. It is possible that a dream or a vision may direct the *murid* to the *shaykh* or the *shaykh* to the *murid*. *Shaykhs* also have "credentials" in the form of a *silsila* ("chain" of discipleship), which gives the name of his *shaykh*, and his *shaykh's shaykh*, and so back to Muhammad, usually via 'Ali. At least in recent times this will be contained in a written document given to him by his *shaykh* when the latter gives him authority to guide others. Thus the *silsila* attests his competence and his spiritual connection. The *silsila* has a parallel in the *sanad*, the chain of authorities that guarantee a ***hadith***. The *silsila* also has its parallels in mystical and disciplic traditions outside Islam. It may be observed that the way one chooses a Sufi *shaykh* is not totally different from the way Westerners choose a doctor or comparable professionals. Westerners may have a family doctor with whom they have dealt for years. They may go on the advice of friends who are "satisfied customers". If appropriate, they may want to know the doctor's credentials, "*silsila*", so to speak, which will usually be evident in the form of diplomas on his or her office walls. Admittedly they are not likely to be directed by a dream or vision in this.

The *shaykh–murid* relationship is fundamental to the structure of Sufism. From about the twelfth century CE Sufism developed into large-scale movements commonly called *tariqas*, the same word as used above for the "path" but here referring to specific different groups following specific "paths" leading to the goal. In English these are usually called "Sufi orders", but this term perhaps puts more emphasis on the organizational aspect than is appropriate. *Tariqas* are, in the first place, spiritual lineages. The members of a *tariqa* all trace their *silsila* back to (or, more precisely, through) a great *shaykh* of the past, for whom the *tariqa* is usually named. The oldest *tariqa*, for example, is the Qadiriyya, which traces its lineage back to 'Abd al-Qadir al-Jilani (d. 1166). 'Abd al-Qadir is generally considered the "founder" although it is probably his descendants that developed it into a *tariqa*, and this is true in the case of other *tariqas*.

Tariqas did in fact develop organizational aspects. Usually there would be a center for instruction and the performance of *dhikr*, and perhaps the residence of the *shaykh* and others, cells for retreat, guest quarters and a tomb of the founder of the *tariqa*. This is called a *khanqah* or a *tekke*, or sometimes a *zāwiya* or *ribāṭ*. There will usually be an inner circle of *murids* who devote considerable time and energy to the activities of the *tariqa* and may reside at the center, and an outer circle of people who are more loosely involved. The *shaykh* will often appoint *khalīfas*, deputies, to carry out some of his functions, such as leading *dhikr*, when he is not present. The *shaykh* will normally choose his successor from among his own sons and/or disciples. This does not preclude the possibility of quarrels over the succession, leading possibly to a split in the *tariqa*.

Tariqas can subdivide for other reasons. For example, one of the most popular *tariqas* in Egypt is the Ahmadiyya, founded by Ahmad al-Badawi (1199–1278). In the eighteenth century, one of its *shaykhs*, 'Ali al-Bayyumi, was a well-known ecstatic and attracted such a following that they became known as the Bayyumiyya. The

Ahmadiyya *silsila* up to 'Ali al-Bayyumi is retained, however, and the *tariqa* may be called Bayyumiyya Ahmadiyya.

Different *tariqas* have distinctive characteristics. This includes distinctive forms of *dhikr* (such as that of the "Whirling Dervishes", mentioned earlier), use or not of dancing and music, distinctive doctrinal emphases, distinctive garb, and distinctive forms of accepted behavior (*adab*). Some *tariqas* are related to particular social groupings or classes; some have been close to craft guilds. Some are interested in politics and influencing rulers; others eschew this. Some *tariqas* are limited to one area or one country while others, such as the Qadiriyya, are spread worldwide. It is not unusual for an individual to be initiated into more than one *tariqa*, although some demand exclusive allegiance. A *tariqa* usually celebrates a *mawlid* (or *mulid*), a commemoration of the birthday of its founder (see below).

The goal: fana' *and* baqa'

The goal of the Sufi path is commonly called *fanā'*, "passing away" or "annihilation", viz. in God, along with *baqā'*, "continuance" in God. This can be related to the Qur'anic verse quoted earlier, "All who are upon the earth are perishing (*fana'*), but the Face of your Lord abides (*baqa'*), with majesty and honor" (55:26–27). There is a ***hadith qudsi*** that says, "My servant continues to draw near to Me with devotions beyond what is obligatory until I love him; and when I love him, I am his hearing with which he hears, and his sight with which he sees, and his hand with which he smites, and his foot with which he walks" (Bukhari).

One of the early Sufis, Bayazid Bistami (d. 874), describes his experience in these words, "Behold, now I say that God is the mirror of myself, for with my tongue He speaks and I have passed away (*fana'*)" (Smith, 1972, 27). Elsewhere he says,

> Then I began to melt away, as lead melts in the heat of the fire. Then He gave me to drink from the fountain of Grace in the cup of fellowship and changed me into a state beyond description and brought me near unto Him, and so near did He bring me that I became nearer to Him than the spirit to the body. I continued thus until I became even as the souls of men had been in that state before existence was and God abode in solitude apart, without created existence or space or direction or mode of being – may His glory be exalted and His Name sanctified.
>
> (*Ibid.*, 29)

Mansur al-Hallaj (850–922), another famous Sufi, said, "If you do not recognize God, at least recognize His signs. I am that sign, I am the Truth (*al-ḥaqq*, also a name of God), because through the Truth I am a truth eternally" (Arberry, 1970, 60). The phrase, *Ana al-ḥaqq* (I am the Truth), became famous and has been much commented on and alluded to by al-Hallaj's defenders and detractors.

Statements such as these have attracted much criticism from those concerned for obedience to the Shari'a, since they appear to constitute an extreme form of *shirk*, identifying the speaker with God. Sufis, however, deny the charge. Far from identifying the human self with God, the consciousness of the self is obliterated and there is consciousness only of God. In effect, it is God saying, "I am the Truth". Jalal al-Din Rumi writes,

> This is what is signified by the words "Ana al-Haqq". People imagine that they are a presumptuous claim, whereas it is really a presumptuous claim to say "I am the servant (i.e. human being)". The one who says, "I am the servant" affirms two existences, his own and God's, but he that says "I am the Truth" has made himself non-existent and has given himself up and says "I am God," i.e. "I am naught, He is all: there is no being but God's". This is the extreme of humility and self-abasement.
>
> (Nicholson, 1950, 184).

Here the accusation of *shirk* is turned back on the accuser. *Shirk* consists not of identifying oneself with God but of claiming, like God, to have (independent) existence. It is not a question of a human becoming divine but of experiencing God's unity, ***tawhid***, in its fullness.

Another approach to this question is that of Abu al-Qasim al-Junayd (d. 910), who was for a time al-Hallaj's teacher. He held that the goal of the path is to return to the primordial state of humans, described in the following words of the Qur'an: "When your Lord took from thee children of Adam from their loins, their seed, and made them testify touching themselves, 'Am I not your Lord?' They said, 'Yes, we testify'" (7:172). At that time humans existed only in God's mind. This seems implicit also in the quote above from Bayazid Bistami.

Sufis distinguish between the states of "drunkenness", when one is in ecstasy and unable to control one's words and actions, and "sobriety", when one is in control. Statements such as "I am the Truth" are understood to be uttered in a state of "drunkenness" and are given a special name, *shaṭḥ*. Bayazid in a state of ecstasy said, "Praise be to me, how great is my majesty!" (Attar, 1979, 115) but disowned these words when he returned to a normal state. Al-Junayd, well known as a sober Sufi, and many others have held that the *shaths* ought not to be uttered publicly since most people would misinterpret them and they might attract persecution. For al-Junayd and probably most Sufis the state of sobriety that comes after the state of drunkenness is higher than the state of drunkenness. The highest state is to continue with the consciousness of God in a sober state.

Nevertheless, the *shaths* were uttered publicly and much discussed, and drunkenness was much praised by the Sufi poets. Thus for example, Rumi:

Figure 12.1 The tombs of Jalal al-Rumi and his son in Rumi's mausoleum at Konya, Turkey. Courtesy of iStockphoto

I am intoxicated with Love's cup, and two worlds have passed out of my ken;
I have no business save carouse and revelry.
If once in my life I spent a moment without thee,
From that time and from that hour I repent of my life.
If once in this world I win a moment with thee,
I will trample on both worlds, I will dance in triumph for ever.
O Shams-i Tabriz, I am so drunken in this world,
That except for drunkenness and revelry I have no tale to tell.
(McNeill and Waldman, 1973, 243)

Along with drunkenness, as we see here, is love. Love here is *'ishq*, a particularly passionate form of love. This is the term usually used by Sufis at least from the time of al-Hallaj. Others, such as Rabi'a (see below) have used *ḥubb* or *maḥabba*, the more usual and less intense terms for love. These themes are drawn from secular poetry, which sings much of love and wine going back to pre-Islamic times. Much of the force of Sufi poetry comes from the often ambiguous relationship it has with secular poetry (see also chapter 14).

Some Sufis are said to be *majdhūb*, permanently "intoxicated", so to speak. Their odd mental state and often bizarre behavior would lead most Westerners and many Muslims to call them mentally ill, but others believe they have been overpowered by God and have considerable ***baraka***. Perhaps they provide support for the argument that mental illness is culturally constructed.

Walis *(saints)*

Those who reach the goal come to be known as *walis*, close friends of God. In English they are commonly called "saints". The Qur'anic passage: "Surely God's friends, no fear shall be upon them, neither shall they sorrow" (10:63) is thought to refer to them. The founders of the *tariqas*, along with other great Sufis of the past, are understood to be *walis*, but there are also *walis* living in the present who may not be recognized as such by those around them. By virtue of their closeness to God *walis* have considerable *baraka* and through them God performs wonders called *karamāt* (acts of nobility or generosity). These include physical miracles, supernormal knowledge and acts of outstanding judgment. Some, however, have questioned the value of physical miracles. One *wali* said, "It is better to restore one dead heart to eternal life than to restore to life a thousand dead bodies" (Schimmel, 1975, 213). A distinction is made

The following account indicates the kinds of benefits people may hope to receive from *walis*

Once two friends and I were visiting Tanta during the big mulid of Sayyid al-Badawi. Each of us had a problem. I was suffering from a pain in my lower back. One of my friends, a professor of law at Ain Shams University, was worried that his son would fail his college examinations. And the other, a physician, was bothered by debts which he could not pay. After we visited the shrine of Sayyid al-Badawi, each of us found that his problem had been resolved. I had a dream in which two doctors took me into the operating room, and when I woke up the pain in my back was gone. And it has not bothered me since. The law professor learned that his son would receive passing marks on his examination, even before they took place. And the doctor received an inheritance that allowed him to pay his debts.

(Quoted in Reeves, 1990, 66)

between *karamat*, the wonders performed by *walis*, and *muʿjizāt*, the miracles that testify to a prophet. One also distinguishes between the "inspiration" (*ilhām*, *kashf*) that comes to a *wali* and the "revelation" (*waḥy*) received by a prophet.

Many believe that there is an invisible cosmic hierarchy of *walis*, headed by the *quṭb* (axis or pole), who is assisted according to one version by three *naqībs* (substitutes), four *awtād* (pillars), seven *abrār* (pious), forty *abdāl* (substitutes), 300 *akhyār* (good) and 4,000 hidden *walis*. Upon them the well-being of the world depends.

People visit the tombs of *walis* to seek benefits from them such as a cure for an ailment, success in an examination or a business deal, help for marital problems and other things. These visits are known as *ziyāra* (literally, visit), as distinct from the *Hajj*, the pilgrimage to Mecca. *Walis* may appear to people in dreams. **Ahmad al-Badawi** is reported to have appeared in a dream to berate one of his later followers for failing to visit him, i.e. his tomb. All of these things are extremely important for popular Islam and, indeed, in some times and places they have been the primary manifestation of Muslim religion. In fact, in some times and places to deny the existence of *walis* would have been seen as tantamount to ***kufr***.

The *mawlid* or "birthday" of the *wali* is celebrated once or more a year, not necessarily on his actual birthday. These can be very lively and popular events attended by large numbers of people beyond the actual members of the *tariqa*. One of the most popular is that of Ahmad al-Badawi, celebrated in October each year in Tanta, in northern

Figure 12.2 Procession in honor of the *khalifa* of the Badawiyya during *mawlid* of Ahmad al-Badawi. Courtesy of the author

Egypt. It is a carnival, commercial fair and religious event more or less rolled into one. It lasts for a week with the greatest activity at night. Most visitors camp out on the streets. People visit the tomb of Ahmad al-Badawi, circumambulating it and touching the *maqsura* (wooden protecting screen) for *baraka*, which seems almost physical here. There are amusements and stalls and stores for all sorts of things, especially chickpeas, which are symbolic of the *mawlid* and said to especially convey its *baraka*. Sufis perform *dhikrs*. *Tariqas* and other groups erect tents in a large field to provide hospitality. The government participates, as it is politically wise to be seen to support this event. It is considered a good occasion to have children circumcised. During the last twenty-four hours there are two processions, the first commemorating an event that happened just after the death of Ahmad al-Badawi and the other honoring the current *khalifa* of the Ahmadiyya.

Sufism and Shari'a-mindedness

There is a definite tension between the Sufi orientation and the attitude of those primarily concerned with Shar'a and *fiqh*, called "Shari'a-mindedness" by Marshall Hodgson. In terms of moral and ritual activities, Sufis sometimes go to extremes of practice, as they practice extra fasts or take extra precautions about ritual cleanliness. By contrast, some claim that once *ma'rifa* is attained external rituals are not necessary. Groups like the Qalandaris and Malamatiyya openly flout the Shari'a, at least in public (they may be ascetic in private but concerned that demonstrating their asceticism publicly might amount to hypocrisy). The use of music and dance by some Sufis is frowned on by some of the Shari'a-minded, as is the use of love poetry and some theosophical ideas, to be mentioned later. So also extreme actions such as eating glass or putting skewers through parts of one's body to demonstrate one's *baraka* or that of one's *shaykh*.

Some have given more importance to Sufi practices such as *dhikr* and *ziyāra* than to corresponding Shari'a practices such as ***salah*** and ***Hajj***. Abu Sa'id ibn Abi al-Khayr (d. 1049) said that the true *Hajj* is the spiritual pilgrimage within oneself and that the heavenly *Ka'ba* comes and circumambulates the *wali*. He encouraged people to visit the tomb of his *shaykh*. More often preference has been given to Sufi practices in practice but not in theory, e.g. some who show great devotion at a *wali's* tomb may say that *salah* is necessary but perform it with less fervor. Likewise, the authority of the *walis* may be more lively for many than that of the prophets. The veneration of *walis* is viewed by some as *kufr* or at least *bid'a* (see Ibn Taymiyya in the next chapter) and this view has become common among modern reformers, especially those known as ***salafis*** (see chapter 15).

These tendencies have made Sufis often willing to adopt and adapt the ideas and practices of the non-Muslims around them, ideas and practices that have often been

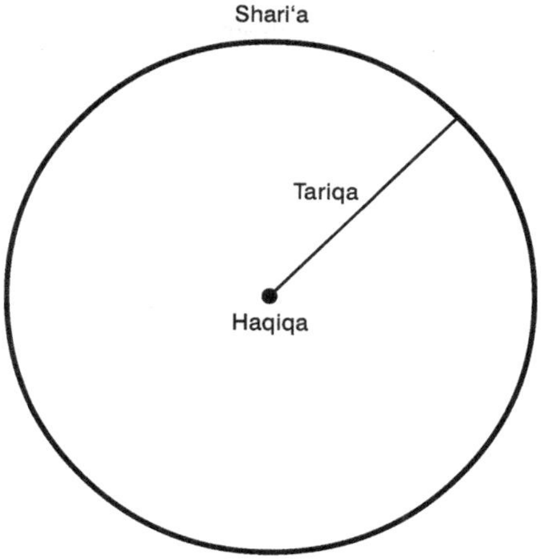

Figure 12.3 Diagram of the relationship between the Shari'a and the *tariqa*

considered "superstitions" and ***bid'a*** by other Muslims. This, however, has helped to make them good missionaries for Islam in much of the world.

Sufism, like Shari'a-mindedness, has been largely male-oriented, but has had a bit more scope for female expression. One of the greatest of the early Sufis was Rabi'a al-Adawiya (d. 801), a former slave girl, and there have been women in the *tariqas* and women *shaykhs*. Two of Ibn 'Arabi's (see below) Sufi teachers were women. Women are quite active in visiting the tombs of *walis* and participating in the *mawlids*. There is an ironic twist to Rabi'a's case. One of her biographers writes, "If it is proper to derive two-thirds of our religion from 'A'isha (i.e. from the *hadiths* she transmitted), surely it is permissible to take religious instruction from a handmaid of 'A'isha. When a woman becomes a 'man' in the path of God, she is a man and one cannot any more call her a woman" (Attar, 1979, 40).

For most Sufis these tensions can be and are reconciled. This can be illustrated by the diagram of a circle, radius and center (Figure 12.3). The circumference of the circle is the Shari'a, which must be accepted and lived by before going further. The radius is the path, *tariqa*, leading toward the center, the *ḥaqīqa* or the divine. Another illustration is drawn from the walnut. Its hard shell, which protects the kernel, is like the Shari'a, which protects the *tariqa*. In fact, many of the *'ulama'* have also been members of Sufi *tariqas*.

Historical outline

The Sufi movement had its roots among the independent scholars and other pious people of the late Umayyad period, as did *fiqh* and theology. Some of these engaged in extreme asceticism, denying themselves the goods and the glory of this world. The most famous of these was al-Hasan al-Basri (see chapter 8), important also for the beginnings of theology, who wrote, "Beware of this world with all wariness, for it is like to a snake, smooth to the touch, but its venom is deadly ... as I am told, God has created nothing more hateful to him than this world" (Arberry, 1970, 33–34). To this was soon added the concern for the love and direct experience, probably first by Rabi'a al-Adawiya. She sang to God:

> I love you with two kinds of love, a "selfish" love
> And a love that is truly appropriate to you.
> As for my "selfish" love,
> It is that thought of you turns me from all else.
> As for that truly appropriate love,
> It is that you lift the veil and I see you.
> No praise to me for either kind,
> To you the praise for both.
>
> (Arberry, 1970, 43, modified)

Rabi'a called for a totally disinterested love of God. She is said to have gone about the streets of Basra with a pail of water in one hand and a torch in the other. When asked about this, she said that the pail of water was to put out the fires of hell and the torch was to burn up heaven, so that people would worship God for His own sake.

She was followed by other outstanding individuals. For example, Harith al-Muhasibi (781–837) wrote especially about self-discipline. Dhu al-Nun the Egyptian (d. 861) is said to have been the first to formulate a theory of *ma'rifa*, to have expressed passionate love for God and developed ideas related to *fana'* and *baqa'*. Bayazid Bistami (d. 875) is considered the first of the "intoxicated" Sufis and developed more fully the idea of *fana'*. He was the first, also, to take the prophet's *mi'rāj* as a model for his experience. Al-Junayd, the well-known "sober" Sufi, followed the line of al-Muhasibi and was probably the most important Sufi leader of this time. He provided the classic Sufi definition of *tawhid*, "separating the Eternal from what is created and temporal". For him separation from God and union with God were both essential aspects of the Sufi experience. Abu al-Husayn al-Nuri (d. 907) was one of the first to speak of *'ishq* (passionate love) and died when in a state of ecstasy he ran through a field of cut reeds and slashed his feet but did not feel the pain. *Al-Hallaj* (d. 922) was undoubtedly the most famous Sufi of this period and was executed in part for statements such as "I am the Truth", but probably more because he was overly popular and perceived as a political threat in powerful circles and because of his own desire for martyrdom. He sang, "Kill me, my friends, for in my death is my life."

After the death of al-Hallaj, the Sufi movement went through a period of consolidation and reflection. A number of writers compiled books recounting the lives of Sufis, explaining their teachings and seeking to show that Sufism is consistent with the Shari'a. These include Abu Nasr al-Sarraj (d. 988), al-Kalabadhi (d. 990),

Abu Talib al-Makki (d. 996), Sulami (d. 1021), Abu Nu'aym al-Isfahani (d. 1037), Hujwiri (d. 1071, the first to write this sort of work in Persian) and Abu al-Qasim al-Qushayri (d. 1074). Al-Ghazali (d. 1111, see chapter 13) is often said to have reconciled the Sufi and Shari'a traditions, but he stood very much on the shoulders of his predecessors, nor did the tension totally disappear after his time.

The early Sufis had circles of followers, but from about the thirteenth century the *tariqas* began to be formed and to draw in large numbers of followers. This coincides roughly with the end of **Shi'i** ascendency in many places and also to some extent with the end of mass conversion from the older religions, and it would appear that Sufism met spiritual needs that had earlier been met by these. Like Shi'ism it allowed for considerable devotion to the Prophet's family and the *walis* have a somewhat similar cosmic role to the Shi'i ***Imams***. Nevertheless, there are Shi'i *tariqas* though Sufism is not as strong in the Shi'i as the Sunni world. From probably the fourteenth century to the nineteenth century the *tariqas* were to be the most popular expressions of Islam in most places. It is possible to mention only a few of the more important here. The first of the *tariqas*, as mentioned earlier, was the Qadiriyya. Also early was the Suhrawardiya, founded by Abu Hafs al-Suhrawardi (1145–1234), which has been more willing than most to deal with political rulers. Both of these have spread widely and are strong in South Asia. The Shadhiliyya was founded in Tunisia by 'Abdallah al-Shadhili (1196–1258) and spread to Egypt and elsewhere in the Arab world. The Rifa'iyya, founded by Ahmad ibn 'Ali al-Rifa'i (1106–82), became known as "the howling dervishes" and engaged in dramatic behavior such as walking on coals, eating snakes and cutting themselves with knives. The Mevlevi (or Mawlawi) *tariqa*, founded by Jalai al-Din Rumi (1207–73) was strong in the **Ottoman** lands and is best known for its "whirling" dance, which is in fact a controlled and highly symbolic movement. The Naqshbandiyya, named after Baha' al-Din Naqshband (d. 1390), is noted for its "silent" *dhikr* and the fact its *shaykhs* trace their *silsila* to Abu Bakr. They insist on following the Shari'a and seek political influence. Other Sufi *tariqas* that have been mentioned earlier are the Ahmadiyya and Bayumiyya in Egypt. The Bektashis in Turkey were close to the ruling classes in the Ottoman Empire, though their doctrines and practices are quite unorthodox by usual standards. From around 1300 to 1900 the majority of Muslims probably had some connection with a *tariqa*.

Poetry and theosophy

One of the major expressions of Sufism has been in poetry, not only in Arabic but in all of the major Islamic languages and especially in Persian. The greatest of the Persian poets is generally agreed to be Jalal al-Din Rumi, whose poetry arises out of a spirituality that was most strongly experienced in the context of an intense personal relationship with another Sufi, Shams-i Din-i Tabrizi. A few lines of his poetry have already been quoted. The following refers to the reed flute used in the Mevlevi *dhikr*, and evokes the longing both for God and his companion.

> Hearken to this reed forlorn,
> Breathing, even since 'twas torn,
> From its rushy bed a strain
> Of impassioned love and pain.
> "The secret of my song, though near,
> none can see and none can hear.
> Oh, for a friend to know the sign,
> And mingle all his soul with mine!
> 'Tis the flame of love that fired me,
> 'Tis the wine of love inspired me.
> Wouldst thou learn how lovers bleed,
> Hearken, hearken to the reed!"
>
> (Nicholson, 1950, 31)

A well-known poem that deals both with a journey along the Sufi path and the final union with God is "The Conference of the Birds" by Farid al-Din 'Attar (d. 1220). Here thirty birds set out to find the mythical *simurgh* (something like the phoenix in Western legend), suffering greatly along the way. When they are finally admitted into the *simurgh*'s presence they find (a reflection of) themselves, for *si murgh* in Persian means "thirty birds".

Sufis have developed speculative theories about God, humans and the universe that we may call "theosophy". These have been especially elaborated by thinkers such as Shihab al-Din al-Suhrawardi and Ibn 'Arabi. Suhrawardi (1153–91), who was killed for his views, taught a philosophy of "illumination" focused on light as the true nature of all existence. The human soul seeks to return to the angelic realm of light from which it came. He was influenced by the mystical side of **Ibn Sina** and claimed to draw on ancient wisdom transmitted through the Greeks and the Persians.

The greatest of the theosophers was Muhyi al-Din ibn 'Arabi (1166–1240), known to his followers down to the present as *al-shaykh al-akbar*, the greatest master. Drawing on a wide range of previous thought, pre-Islamic and Islamic, he developed an extraordinarily complex system. He often used the language of philosophy to express what for him was based on mystical intuition rather than reason. At the heart of it is the idea of *waḥdat al-wujūd*, the unity of existence (or being). The existence of the creation is not other than the existence of God, though creation is not identical with God. "You are no other than God ... though you do not become He nor He you ... ". Being at its highest level is unmanifest and indescribable but at another level it is Allah, Lord and the various names ascribed to God in the Muslim tradition, and these in turn are correlated with and interdependent on things in the world. Everything in the world (even evil things) is connected with one or more names of God. In effect, the world is the means by which God knows and expresses himself, "It is for this that the Reality created me, I give content to His knowledge and manifest him" (Ibn al-'Arabi, 1980, 95). This is an interpretion of the *hadith qudsi*: "I was a hidden treasure and longed to be known, so I created the world." It is also reflected in the following oft-quoted lines of Ibn 'Arabi's poetry:

> My heart has become capable of every form: it is a pasture of gazelles and a convent for Christian monks.
> And a temple for idols and the pilgrims' *Ka'ba* and the tables of the Torah and the book of the Qur'an.
> I follow the religion of Love: whatever way Love's camels take, that is my religion and my faith.
>
> (Ibn al-'Arabi, 1911, 67)

This expresses tolerance in that God is manifested in all of these forms, but it also implies the author's claim to high spiritual status, since he can perceive the divine in all of them, while most people would be limited to one. The Essence of Muhammad (*ḥaqīqa muḥammadiyya*, see chapter 6) corresponds to the totality of the divine names and plays an important role in this system. In these and his many other teachings, his followers say that he was not so much innovating as expressing more fully and openly what his predecessors had believed. Ibn 'Arabi seems to have seen himself as the "seal of the *walis*", i.e. the completer of the cycle of esoteric teaching that followed Muhammad's mission.

While reviled by many, Ibn 'Arabi was followed by many more and he massively influenced both his detractors and his followers. Ahmad Sirhindi (1564–1624) was both a follower and a critic of Ibn 'Arabi. He taught the "unity of appearance" (*waḥdat al-shuhūd*), according to which the ecstatic perceives only God but later moves to a state where he recognizes the existence of other things, as one may recognize that stars exist even though they are hidden by the sun. He also developed complex ideas about the cosmic hierarchy that seem to have involved a high status for himself.

Iran saw the development of *'irfan*, a mystical but strongly intellectual tradition that is not considered part of Sufism. Its greatest exponent was Mullah Sadra (d. 1640), who developed the ideas of Ibn Sina, Suhrawardi and Ibn 'Arabi. He takes his departure from the pure experience of existence (as distinct from the idea of existence or qualities in the mind), which is transcendent but different on every occasion. God is existence in its purest form. The tradition of *'irfan* continues to this day among the Iranian *'ulama'* and Ayatollah Khomeini was one of its practitioners.

Some recent developments

Since the late nineteenth century the *tariqas* have been under considerable pressure from reformers, both modernist and **Islamist**, accused of superstition, un-Islamic activity and lack of relevance to modern society. While they do not have the dominance they once had, they have adapted and retained considerable influence. Under communism they were often better able to maintain themselves than the *'ulama'* because of their more flexible organization. In recent decades Sufism has attracted considerable attention in the West and gained Western converts (some of whom think of Sufism as separate from Islam). Some *tariqas* give considerable attention to this aspect of their mission, publishing books in Western languages, giving cultural performances (e.g. the Mevlevis) and maintaining websites and e-mail lists (e.g. Naqshbandi-Haqqani, who even allow for initiation online).

Sufi theosophy has also attracted some attention from Western intellectuals, some of whom constitute a movement often called "perennialism" or "traditionalism". Its proponents include René Guenon and Frithjof Schuon and many of them have been initiated into Sufi *tariqas*. They teach a "perennial philosophy" that underlies all religious forms, according to which ultimate reality transcends the personal God and can be intuited by the intellect, but only by an elite. The major religions in their traditional or orthodox forms provide partial symbols through which ordinary people may be guided and are seen as essentially equal. The "perennialists" reject modern rationalism as a step away from, not toward, the primordial truth. They may be said to be modern heirs of Ibn 'Arabi, but with their own distinctive approach.

Sufism has offered its benefits at several levels. A few claim to reach the highest level of God-consciousness. Many more experience an improvement in their moral and spiritual life. Many focus on the concrete benefits of the *karamat*. The *tariqas* also fulfil a number of social needs, for individuals and society. For some Westerners it is an attractive counterbalance to modern rationalism and materialism.

Key points

- Sufism seeks an intimate knowledge of God and stresses love in addition to obedience (and sometimes more than or instead of obedience).
- *Tariqa*, the path, refers both to the Sufi disciplines and to the large-scale groups or movements often called "orders" in English.
- The relationship between master and disciple (*shaykh* and *murid*) is a very close one and is central to the structure of Sufism.
- The final goal for the elite is often called *fana'*, or *baqa'* after *fana'*, and is described in diverse and often unconventional ways.

- Distinctive Sufi practices are in addition to and sometimes instead of *fiqh* prescriptions but most Sufis see *fiqh* prescriptions as a prerequisite to Sufi practices.
- Poetry and music are major forms of Sufi expression.

Discussion questions

1. Some see Sufism as the essence of Islam. Others consider Sufism un-Islamic. Still others see Sufism as the essence of all religions. What do you think?
2. What is the idea and role of love in Sufism?
3. How do Sufis use unconventional ideas and practices to further spiritual goals?
4. What appear to be the goals of Sufism? Are they the same for all Sufis?
5. How has Sufism related to society in general?
6. To what extent does Sufism encourage tolerance and freedom in its followers?
7. What do you think Farid al-Din al-Attar meant when he described Rabi'a as a "man"?

Critical thinking box 12.1

Various writers, Sufis and others, have given short definitions of Sufism. Here are a few:

> Sufism is freedom and generosity and absence of self constraint.
>
> (al-Sarraj)
>
> Sufism is polytheism (*shirk*), because it is the guarding of the heart from the "other" and the other does not exist.
>
> (Shibli)
>
> Islamic mysticism is the attempt to reach individual salvation through attaining the true *tawhid*.
>
> (Hans Heinrich Schraeder)
>
> The Sufi is he who persists in purity with Allah and good character with creation.
>
> (al-Suyuti)*

Analyze these definitions. What do they tell you about Sufism? What do they leave out? Do they tell you anything about the author of the definition? Produce your own short definition of Sufism and analyze it.

*These definitions are found in Schimmel, 1975, 15, 16, 23 and Haeri, 2004, 12. Other definitions will be found in these places.

Critical thinking box 12.2

Sufism has proven attractive to some Westerners. Why do you think this is so? What aspects of Sufism might be unattractive to (some) Westerners? In what way might Sufism be modified or changed by Western adherents?

Companion website

Includes considerable information related to al-Hallaj, Rumi, the Bayyumis and the Ahmadiyya, with picures from the *mulid* of Ahmad al-Badawi, and additional reading and weblinks on various topics, including *qawwals*.

Further reading

Arberry, A.J. (1950) *Sufism, An Account of the Mystics of Islam*. London: George Allen & Unwin. (Short and readable, by one of the major Western scholars; somewhat dated but still an excellent place to start.)

Ernst, Carl W. (1997) *Sufism*. Boston, MA: Shambala. (Empathetic topical approach to the main features and concepts, including the *tariqas*, poetry, music and the modernist critique.)

Schimmel, Annemarie (1975) *Mystical Dimensions of Islam*. Chapel Hill, NC: University of North Carolina Press. (Could be considered the "classic" work by a Western scholar who knew the Sufi tradition intimately. Not always easy reading.)

Trimingham, J.S. (1971) *The Sufi Orders in Islam*. Oxford: Clarendon Press. (Dependable, somewhat "external" survey of the *tariqas*.)

Haeri, Shaykh Fadhalla (2004) *The Thoughtful Guide to Sufism*. New York: O Books. Earlier pusblished as *The Elements of Sufism*. (Very attractive presentation for the modern reader by a contemporary master.)

Nurbakhsh, Javad (1982) *Sufism*, trans. W.C. Chittick. New York: Khaniqahi-Nimatullahi Publications. (Selections from Sufi masters relating to the Sufi stations and states and many other works of his.)

Smith, Margaret (1928) *Rabi'a the Mystic and Her Fellow Saints in Islam*. Cambridge: Cambridge University Press. (The main secondary source on Rabi'a, still much in use.)

As-Sulamī, Abū 'Abd ar-Raḥmān (1999) *Early Sufi Women*, ed. and trans. Rkia E. Cornell. Louisville, KY: Fons Vitae. (Biographical notes on Sufi women by eleventh century CE Sufi writer. Extensive introduction by editor.)

Biegman, Nicolas H. and Schwartz, Gary (1990) *Egypt, Moulids, Saints, Sufis*. The Hague: SDU Publishers. (Attractively written and illustrated, and very informative.)

Hoffman, Valerie J. (1995), *Sufism, Mystics and Saints in Modern Egypt*. Columbia, SC: University of South Carolina Press. (Detailed, sensitive and attractive treatment.)

Al-Attar, Farid al-Din (1966) *Muslim Saints and Mystics*, trans. A.J. Arberry. London: Routledge & Kegan Paul. (Translation of one of the most important traditional hagiographies of early Sufis, such as Rabi'a, al-Hallaj, and others.)

Rumi (1950) *Rumi, Poet and Mystic: Selections from His Writings*, trans. R.A. Nicholson. London: Allen and Unwin. (Excellently translated selections by a leading Western scholar.)

See also: Nasr, *Three Muslim Sages: Avicenna, Suhrawardi, Ibn Arabi* [13]; Renard, *Seven Doors to Islam* and *Windows on the House of Islam* (Chs 3, 6–7) [F]; Ernst, *Following Muhammad* (Ch. 5) [1].

Online resources (accessed 23 August 2013)

Sufi.Soul, Documentary. 49 minutes. (Excellent footage and music from Turkey, Pakistan and Morocco, Sufism presented as peaceful and tolerant in contrast with Islamism.): http://documentarystorm.com/sufi-soul-the-mystic-music-of-islam.

Threshold Society (in the lineage of Mevlana Rumi): https://sufism.org/lineage/threshold.

Website of the Naqshbandi Haqqani order: http://naqshbandi.org.

Website of the Nimatullahi Sufi order: http://www.nimatullahi.org.

13 *A philosopher, a scholar-mystic and a reformer*

This chapter will help us get a better understanding of the movements and ideas presented in the previous chapters by considering in more detail the lives and teachings of three major figures who represent three different tendencies within classical Islamic thought. Ibn Sina is generally considered the greatest of the classical Muslim philosophers. Al-Ghazali perhaps did the most to integrate the various strands of Muslim thinking, philosophy, theology, *fiqh* and Sufism. Ibn Taymiyya was a fearless reformer who challenged many of the trends of his time and who inspires both reformers and radicals among Sunnis today. All three have remained important and are still studied today.

In this chapter

- Ibn Sina, his life and teachings
- Al-Ghazali, his life and teachings
- Ibn Taymiyya, his life and teachings

Ibn Sina

Abu 'Ali ibn Sina (980–1037) took the definitive steps in Islamizing the Greek philosophical tradition, although he has been at least as much appreciated among Westerners as among Muslims. He was no "ivory tower" philosopher, however, but like some others was also a physician and an active politician. Information about his life is mainly based on a biography begun by him and finished by his disciple. Ibn Sina's father was an official in the **Samanid** court in Bukhara and had some sympathy with the **Isma'ilis**. From family talk Ibn Sina learned something about their doctrines as well as something of philosophy. Based on his own account Ibn Sina was a child prodigy (probably true, given his later accomplishments). By the age of 10 he had memorized the Qur'an and many literary works and by 18 he had studied ***fiqh*** and mastered medicine and philosophy largely by studying on his own.

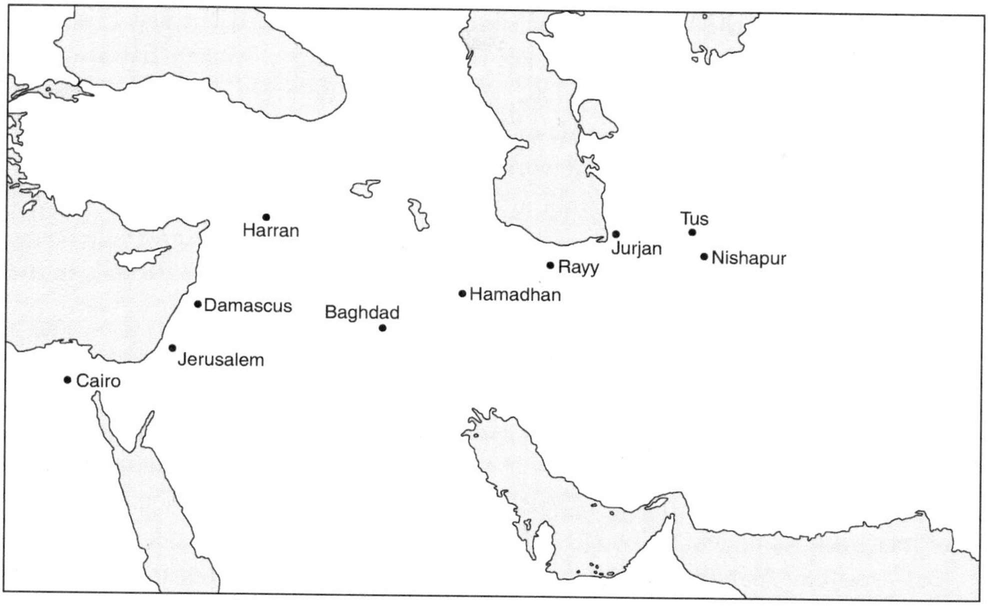

Map 6 Middle East in the early thirteenth century and cities mentioned in this chapter

This was facilitated when the ruler opened his library to him after he had helped treat him for an illness.

When he was 22 his father died and he took an administrative position under the ruler, but soon had to flee when the Qarakhanid Turks took control of Bukhara about this time. He kept moving from court to court, spending time in Jurjan, Rayy and Hamadhan. His moves were dictated in part by his desire not to be taken to the court of Mahmud of Ghazna, who was extending his empire into Iran. Mahmud was a patron of scholars but a militant opponent of Shiʿism and Muʿtazilism. Though Ibn Sina did not admit to either of these positions he preferred the patronage of the **Buyids** or their allies. Finally, in 1024, he made his way to Isfahan, where he spent the rest of his life enjoying the favor of the ruler, ʿAlaʾ al-Dawla ibn Kakuya, who patronized scholars and whom Ibn Sina often accompanied on campaigns. Life was not secure even here, however, as ʿAlaʾ al-Dawla was very much under pressure from the Ghaznavids. Ibn Sina died in Hamadhan when he insisted on joining ʿAlaʾ al-Dawla there although he was quite sick. On more than one occasion his medical ability helped gain him favor with a ruler. He became a ***wazīr*** several times but was also almost killed in a mutiny and later imprisoned in Hamadhan.

Through all of this activity he wrote a large number of works on philosophy, medicine and other topics. Much of this writing was done at night after an active day's work. He regularly took wine to assist him in his thinking and writing, arguing that the prohibition on wine is not absolute for those who can benefit from it and do not abuse it. His *Qānūn fī al-Ṭibb* (Canon of Medicine) was to be the main authority on medicine even in the West until the sixteenth or seventeenth century. His most important compendia of philosophy are *Shifā'* ("Healing"), *Najāt* ("Salvation", a summary of *Shifa'*), *Ishārāt wa-Tanbīhāt* ("Hints and Pointers", more mystical in orientation) and *Danishnameh-yi 'Ala'i* ("Book of Knowledge" dedicated to 'Ala' al-Dawla, the first major philosophical work written in Persian).

Building on the work of al-Farabi and his predecessors, Ibn Sina developed a "grand theory" of the universe impressive for its comprehensiveness and coherence, integrating science and religion in a manner we hardly imagine possible today. In the

The Lady

Muhammad is reported to have said that a kingdom ruled by a woman would not prosper, though the authenticity of this is questioned by many today. Still if one looks at the formal of lists of Muslim rulers one finds very few women. Two of these are 'Asma bint Shihab (d. 1087), who ruled together with her husband and Arwa bint Ahmad (d. 1138), who ruled almost 40 years in her own name. Both were of the Isma'ili Sulayhi dynasty. (See Fatima Mernissi, *The Forgotten Queens of Islam*, Cambridge: Polity Press, 1993.) Another example is Shajarat al-Durr, mentioned in chapter 4. In a number of cases women effectively ruled through their husbands or sons, but it is the latter whose names are found in the lists.

Ibn Sina lived in Rayy under one such woman, known as Sayyida (the Lady), who ruled from 997 to 1029 in the name of her son, Majd al-Dawla, whom she is said to have distracted with wine and the harem. When Mahmud of Ghazna was asked why he did not intervene there, since his ambitions were well known, he said that since the place was ruled by a woman, he had nothing to fear from that quarter. A different perspective, however, is afforded by a letter she is said to have written to him, in which she said,

> I said to myself, "Sultan Mahmud is a reasonable monarch; he knows that a ruler like himself ought not to make war against a woman like me." But should you come, God knows I will not run. For there can be but two outcomes, since one army must be beaten: If it is mine that carries the day, I shall write to the entire world that I have broken Sultan Mahmud, who broke a hundred kings. ... But if it is you who are the victor, what will you write? That you have broken the power of a woman?
>
> (Goodman, 1992, 27)

After her death Mahmud took over Rayy, but Ibn Sina had already left for Isfahan.

interests of brevity the following presentation omits many of Ibn Sina's proofs and many details and sacrifices some precision.

We may begin with his distinction between essence and existence. The essence of a thing is the characteristics it must have to be itself. Its existence is whether it actually exists or not. Something can have essence and not existence, e.g. a unicorn. Other things, such as my house, exist at one time but not another. These are possible or contingent. If one traces back the causes of any existing contingent thing one must come, finally, Ibn Sina argues, to something whose existence is not contingent but necessary, i.e. whose existence is included in its essence and therefore has to exist. According to Ibn Sina this necessary existent must be one, must know itself and this knowledge must be the cause of everything else. In religious terms, this is God. This proof was taken over by Thomas Aquinas and other Christian theologians.

Prior to Copernicus, Muslims, Christians and Jews believed that the earth was surrounded by nine concentric heavenly spheres, living beings with bodies and souls, in which the stars and planets were set. According to Ibn Sina these spheres were related to the necessary existent (aka God) in the following manner. By knowing itself the necessary existent emanates an intelligence (understood as a distinct substance). This in turn, by thinking of the necessary existent in one way and of itself in two different ways, emanates a second intelligence along with the soul and body of the outer sphere of the universe. The soul of this sphere longs for the intelligence that emanated it but cannot reach it; the result is the rotating motion of the sphere. The second intelligence emanates a third intelligence, and the soul and body of the next

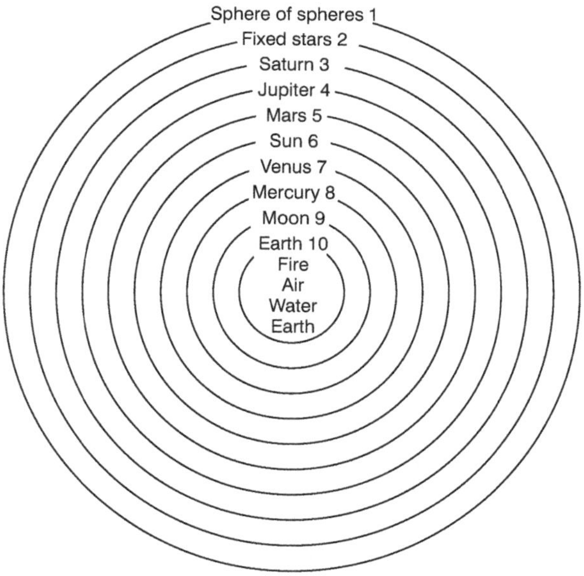

Figure 13.1 The cosmos as envisaged by scholars from Ptolemy (d. c. 168 CE) until Copernicus, including Ibn Sina

sphere, that of the fixed stars. This process continues through the spheres of Saturn, Jupiter, Mars, the Sun, Venus, Mercury and the Moon. This is not a temporal order, however, but an order of causal dependence. The universe has always existed and will always exist essentially as it is. The intelligences correspond to angels in religious terminology.

The tenth intelligence, also known as the Active Intelligence and the Angel Gabriel, is too far removed from the source of existence to emanate a single perfect and unified intelligence, soul and body. These are, rather, diffracted into a multitude of entities, thus creating the sublunar world of change and decay. At the lowest level is matter, which receives progressively souls that make it into things, plants and animals, each level with its appropriate faculties. Among the animal faculties are the five exterior senses (sight, hearing, etc.) and five interior senses, including imagination and memory. Humans have in addition to the animal soul a rational soul or intellect, emanated directly from the Active Intelligence. Because of this connection with the Active Intelligence this soul is capable of individual immortality. It has a practical intellect by which humans engage in arts and crafts and develop moral principles. It also has a theoretical intellect which puts it in contact with the Active Intelligence and which provides the ability to think abstractly. Beyond this, for some, there is the "acquired intellect". Here truths come from the Active Intelligence as a direct vision, either in a discursive or fully intuitive way. This is the level of the philosophers and the prophets. The prophets are at a higher level than the philosophers because, in addition to receiving the truths they perceive, they are able, with the aid of the imaginative faculty, to clothe them in symbols for ordinary people.

The "acquired intellect" seems to be a form of mystical experience. Mysticism here does not contradict reason but represents its full flowering. Ibn Sina may have gone further. In three allegorical stories, *Hayy ibn Yaqzan*, *The Epistle of the Bird* (*Risālat al-Ṭayr*) and *Salman and Absal*, he may have pointed toward a symbolism and a mysticism that is less rational and worldly, possibly moving in the direction of al-**Suhrawardi**'s thinking (see chapter 12, p. 188), but this is a matter of debate among scholars.

Religion depends on the symbols produced by the prophets. For example, common people are thought to be unable to understand or appreciate the eternity of the universe or the survival of the soul without a body, so the prophet speaks of creation *ex nihilo* and the resurrection of bodies. The truth behind the first is that the world is totally dependent on God, even if it is eternal. As for the second, those whose intelligences are not adequately developed will miss the highest bliss after death, which comes from contemplating the spiritual realms, but their imaginations will create for them a quasi-physical realm in accordance with their moral character, i.e. a heaven or a hell that will be subjectively quite real.

This whole system is driven by **'ishq**, passionate love, as each element yearns for what is above it. (Love makes the world go round!) But it is also quite logical and

Figure 13.2 Ibn Sina lecturing, from a Persian manuscript, seventeenth century. © Bettmann/CORBIS

apparently quite deterministic. Things happen almost by logical necessity and no beings, even God, seem to exercise any real choice. This contrasts with the main line of Sunni theology, which wants to preserve absolute freedom for God. Whatever we may say about it scientifically or theologically today, it is one of the most elegant worldviews developed by humans and a major intellectual ancestor of contemporary Western and Muslim thought.

Al-Ghazali

Abū Ḥāmid al-Ghazālī (1058–1111) has been called by some the greatest Muslim since Muhammad and has been roundly criticized by others. He made significant contributions to most of the religious sciences and contributed, perhaps more than any other one person, to the reconciliation of the Shari'a-minded and Sufi approaches to the faith.

Al-Ghazali was born in Tus, in Khurasan, and began his studies there. In 1074 he went to Nishapur to study under the prominent **Ash'ari** theologian, al-Juwayni, known as the *Imam* of the Two Sanctuaries because he had spent time in Mecca and Medina. Al-Ghazali stayed there until al-Juwayni's death in 1085. He may have also had some Sufi instruction during this period. He then went to the headquarters of Nizam al-Mulk, the *wazir* of the Saljuk Turkish ***amirs***, who had taken control in Baghdad in 1055 and were at the height of their power. Nizam al-Mulk was both a gifted administrator and a patron of scholarship and he became al-Ghazali's patron. In 1091 he appointed al-Ghazali professor at the Nizamiyya ***madrasa*** in Baghdad, the most important of the *madrasas* currently being built. There he taught *fiqh*, along with other subjects. He was recognized as a brilliant, up and coming young man and for about four years was one of the most prominent figures in Baghdad. During this period he also studied philosophy on his own and wrote a refutation of it. He also wrote a forceful defense of the caliph against the Nizari **Isma'ilis** (*Batinis*), whose campaign of proselytizing and assassination had recently begun. In July 1095, however, he suffered an emotional breakdown that prevented him from teaching and led him to leave Baghdad. He later gave as the reason for this a feeling that he was working for worldly honor rather than for God and the afterlife and that he was in grave spiritual danger. One thinks that the stress of an extremely heavy work load may have contributed and also political factors. In 1092 Nizam al-Mulk had been killed by the Isma'ilis and al-Ghazali may have feared the same fate. Also, the political situation in Baghdad had become less stable after Nizam al-Mulk's death.

From Baghdad he went to Damascus and spent his time in ascetic and spiritual exercises. He also visited Jerusalem and made the ***Hajj*** (1096). Family and financial concerns led him to return briefly to Baghdad and then to go to Tus, about 1099, where he continued his spiritual practices and did some teaching. During this period he wrote his major work, *The Revival of the Religious Sciences* (*Iḥyā' 'Ulūm al-Dīn*), a major compendium of religious theory and practice. During this period and soon afterward he also wrote two important works on *fiqh*. In 1106 he was prevailed on by the current *wazir*, the son of Nizam al-Mulk, to teach in the Nizamiyya *madrasa* in Nishapur, and did so for four or five years. He then retired to Tus, where he had a *madrasa* and a *zawiya*, and where he died a few years later.

Near the end of his life he wrote a short, schematic autobiography called *The Deliverer from Error* (*Al-Munqidh min al-Ḍalāl*), in which he uses his life experience to guide spiritual seekers. It will be convenient to follow the structure of this book in presenting his thinking. He tells us that as a young man he was briefly a complete skeptic, doubting not only religious propositions but also the truth of sense experience and the validity of the basic axioms of reason. God, he says cured him of doubt about sense perceptions and the axioms of reason, but he was left to seek certainty in religious matters.

He first considers theology, but concludes that since it usually argues from the premises provided by its opponents and does not go back to first principles, it is useful only for answering certain objections. For people who do not have those particular objections it will probably be harmful, like the wrong medicine for an illness. He did in fact write a major work of Ash'ari ***kalam*** and made two major contributions to it, introducing syllogistic reasoning and calling attention to certain issues raised by philosophy. He also, however, wrote a work urging that ordinary people be kept away from theology. Next he deals with philosophy, which does claim to start from first principles. Al-Ghazali accepts much of philosophy, including logic, mathematics and most of natural science, but rejects much of their metaphysics. He first wrote a book, *The Intentions of the Philosophers* (*Maqāṣid al-Falāsifa*), in which he presented Ibn Sina's views, and then another book, *The Refutation of the Philosophers* (*Tahāfut al-Falāsifa*), in which he criticized them on twenty points. Of these, three, he says, involve *kufr* (unbelief), the eternity of the world, the survival of souls without their bodies, and the claim that God knows universals but not particulars (possibly a misunderstanding of Ibn Sina's view). On the second of these points, however, there are indications in other writings that Ghazali may have accepted the philosophers' view. Third, he deals with the Batinis or Isma'ilis. He rejects their claim that certainty can be found with a living infallible ***Imam***. There is an infallible *Imam*, to be sure, but he is the Prophet Muhammad, and ***ijtihad*** provides a valid link to his ***Sunna***. In this connection he wrote a book deriving the rules of logic, on which *ijtihad* depends, from the Qur'an.

Finally, he deals with the Sufis and it is among them that Ghazali finds what he is seeking. The Sufi experience (***dhawq***) goes beyond intellect just as intellect goes beyond sense experience. While it falls far short of prophecy, it is analogous to it and can provide a glimpse of the nature of prophecy and a reason for faith in it. Indeed, simply associating with Sufis without having their experience is enough and, failing this, dreams are also analogous to prophecy and are experienced by all. Along with this, knowledge about Muhammad and his activities will be sufficient to convince one that Muhammad was a prophet.

He affirms the experience of ***fana'*** but denies it involves union with God. In a more advanced work on spirituality, *The Niche for Lights*, he says that those who in a "drunken" state say such things as "I am the Real" perceive only God in that state but on return to sobriety they realize that there was not a real union, for this contradicts reason and reason is "God's balance-scale on earth". Therefore these ***shaṭḥs*** should not be stated publicly. In this same work, however, he ignores the difference between intellect and mystical experience (*dhawq*) that he draws in the *Deliverer* and presents a psychology and cosmology that is very neo-Platonic, a point noted by his critic, **Ibn Rushd**, and also by some contemporary scholars. Moreover, he states that only God has true existence and all other existence is derivative from Him. This is a neo-Platonic position but is stated in a way that could be seen as pointing toward Suhrawardi's illumination or **Ibn 'Arabi**'s unity of existence. Al-Ghazali more than once indicates that there are Sufi teachings that cannot be written down, so it is impossible to know his final position on some things.

Sufism is also important to al-Ghazali as a moral force, both for producing moral character and for deepening the understanding of the Shari'a. For example, in discussing fasting in the *Ihya'* he distinguishes three levels: the fast of the common people, which involves abstinence at the physical level; the fast of the elite, which involves abstinence from sinful thoughts, speech, etc.; and the fast of the elite of the elite, which is to abstain from thinking about anything but God and the Last Day. Much of the *Ihya'* is devoted to moral concerns and the development of character and draws on philosophers such as al-Miskawayh as well the Sufi traditions of moral training. It was to be a mainstay of ethical thinking after his time.

His approach to those Sufi practices criticized by the strict Shari'a-minded is illustrated by his discussion of music in the *Ihya'*. He analyzes the nature and effect of music at some length and concludes that it is not forbidden in and of itself but its actual valuation depends on the listeners. It is forbidden for most people because it will stir up their lusts and blameworthy qualities and also where the lyrics involve something forbidden or instruments associated with drinking are used. It is reprehensible when these are not the case since it encourages the listener in vain activities. It is permissible for the one who uses it only for wholesome pleasure or where it encourages people to engage in permissible activities, such as permitted love and permitted expressions of joy and sorrow. It is recommended where it encourages recommended or obligatory actions, such as going on *Hajj* or fighting in a legitimate war. It is also recommended for properly prepared Sufis, in whom it will stir up the love of God that is already in their hearts. For them, even poetry in praise of wine or forbidden love will be taken as referring to God or spiritual things and thus be permissible.

Al-Ghazali saw himself as a spiritual physician, tailoring his treatment to different needs. For most people it is enough to follow tradition. For their guidance he wrote on *fiqh*. For those inclined to question, theology and refutation of philosophical errors may be sufficient. For those with the need and ability, Sufism properly practiced is the way. This involves an esotericism in which there is often one teaching for the common people and others for elite. In this lies the key to his "reconciliation" of Shari'a-mindedness and Sufism, and of his integration of other aspects of the Islamic tradition as it was in his time. Different things are appropriate to different people and if this is recognized the different currents of Islam can live in harmony.

Al-Ghazali's views have been criticized by many, including Ibn Rushd, who wrote a refutation of them, *The Refutation of The Refutation* (*Tahāfut al-Tahāfut*), and his books have even been burned. On the whole, however, he has been extremely influential and is still much studied today, by both Muslim and non-Muslim scholars. His personal inner struggle and his effort to reconcile diverse religious currents echo positively for many today.

Ibn Taymiyya

If Ibn Sina was the greatest of the philosophers and al-Ghazali according to some the greatest of the Muslims generally, Taqi al-Din ibn Taymiyya (1263–1328) was perhaps the greatest of the mavericks. He was convinced that many of the religious leaders and people of his time had deviated seriously from the teachings of the Qur'an and the Prophet's *Sunna*, and he called for a society that was truly obedient to the Shari'a. For him Ibn Sina was one of several major dangers to the *umma*'s faith and al-Ghazali represented a kind of compromise that was almost as dangerous. He was a pious, learned and courageous man, but also outspoken, defiant and not afraid to make enemies. His greatest enemies were among the leading ***'ulama'*** and Sufi ***shaykhs***, while the rulers often protected him.

The political world in which he lived was dominated by the **Mamlukes** and the Mongols. The Mamlukes had taken control of Egypt and Syria in 1250. In 1258 the Mongols had sacked Baghdad but in 1260 the Mamlukes had stopped their advance at Ain Jalut, south of Damascus. Conflict between the Mamlukes and the Mongols continued, however, even after the Mongol leaders converted to Islam in 1295, and the Mongols threatened Damascus more than once.

The Mamlukes, under whom Ibn Taymiyya lived, were slaves, mostly of Turkish origin, who had been purchased as children and trained to be soldiers. The leading commanders (*amirs*) formed an oligarchy from among whom the **sultan** was chosen, often by violent methods. While the Mamlukes were often brutal they patronized the religious and charitable institutions, building monumental mosques, *madrasas*, hospitals and ***khanqahs***, often connected with tombs for themselves. While they could be harsh with religious leaders, they also often listened to them since they were influential with the people. The sultan during much of Ibn Taymiyya's career, al-Nasir Muhammad ibn Qalaun (r. 1293–1340), was twice deposed and restored to power. He was generally favorable to Ibn Taymiyya.

Ibn Taymiyya was born in 1263 in Harran, in northern Syria (now southern Turkey), into a family of Hanbali scholars. In 1268 the family moved to Damascus to escape the Mongols and there he studied the various religious sciences with his father and others, including one woman teacher, Zaynab bint Makki. He also studied philosophy and theology on his own. He was evidently initiated into the Qadiri ***tariqa*** by his father and an uncle. After his father died, in 1282, he took his position as professor of Hanbali *fiqh* and came to have a considerable following in Syria. In 1292 he performed the *Hajj*, later complaining of some innovations (*bid'a*) he had witnessed. In 1294 he was involved in a protest against a Christian scribe who was accused of insulting the Prophet Muhammad. About five years later he produced a statement of belief criticizing the Ash'ari view of divine attributes, and refused to recognize the *qadi's* authority to question him. When the Mongols threatened Damascus in 1300 he was one of the leaders of the party calling for ***jihad*** in resistance against them and in 1303 he was present as a preacher at the Mongol defeat at Shaqqab and issued a ***fatwa*** saying those fighting do not have to fast. He was also present at a battle in northern Syria against Isma'ilis.

Soon afterward he was again questioned by the authorities about his view of the divine attributes, first, apparently, in Damascus and then in Cairo, and then was put in prison for a year-and-a-half. There, according to some, he undertook to teach his fellow prisoners and virtually turned the prison into a *madrasa*.

During this period he demonstrated his opposition to various actions and ideas of the Sufis, writing a letter to one of the leading Sufis in Cairo denouncing Ibn 'Arabi's doctrines. Later a popular demonstration against him by Sufis led to his imprisonment for a few months. At a time when Sultan al-Nasir Muhammad had been deposed by a coup, Ibn Taymiyya was again arrested and held for seven months, but released when the sultan returned to power. He was sometimes consulted by the sultan but it is said that he refused to give the sultan a *fatwa* that would have allowed him to take revenge on his enemies.

In 1313 he returned to Damascus and resumed his teaching position. In 1318 he was forbidden to give *fatwas* on certain matters relating to divorce. He disobeyed this order and was imprisoned for some months. In 1326 he was imprisoned for a *fatwa* he had written earlier against the visitation of tombs and remained there until his death in 1328. During this imprisonment he wrote a lot but then was deprived of books, paper and ink, after a complaint by one of his enemies whom he had abused in something he wrote. It is said that as many as 200,000 men and 15,000 women attended his funeral. Some, it is also said, sought pieces of his clothing and other relics, something he would have certainly disapproved of. He was buried in a Sufi cemetery.

Ibn Taymiyya's basic demand was for a strict, though not necessarily rigid, obedience to the Qur'an and *Sunna* with minimal admixture of human speculation, partiality or popular practice. He emphasized the limits of reason in theology and rejected the syllogism, which Al-Ghazali had introduced into theology, as overly formalized and not giving the certainty claimed for it, though he used other forms of reasoning. He also criticized both the philosophers and al-Ghazali on the grounds that their goal was knowledge of God, whereas the proper goal is service (*'ibāda*) to God.

This concern for *'ibāda* is reflected in his view of *qadar*. From the divine point of view all actions are determined but from the human point of view there is freedom. Qadar should be accepted as a reason for bearing up in adversity but not as an excuse for sinning or for tyranny.

His views on the "physical" attributes of God got him into trouble and attracted charges of "anthropomorphism". He held that since the Qur'an says that God sits on his throne we must affirm this *bila kayf* ("without [asking] how"), as Ibn Hanbal had put it, but we must also affirm the Qur'an's statement, "There is nothing like him" (42:11). Therefore, any attribute of God will not be the same as an attribute of the same name in humans. It is thus presumptuous to "interpret" (*ta'wil*) the Qur'anic terms metaphorically, as if reason could improve on what God has given us. We may, however, and should, study the divinely given terms linguistically. We may also use reason where it supports revelation, for example, to demonstrate God's perfection and then derive the various divine attributes from this perfection. The important thing about the attributes is that they show that God, and God alone, is worthy of worship, and thus to encourage *'ibada*.

While Ibn Taymiyya approved of a moderate Sufism that would help people to obey God, he vigorously opposed Ibn 'Arabi's unity of existence (***wahdat al-wujud***), "God, praises be to Him, is not His own creature, and not a part of His creation or an attribute of it" (Williams, 1963, 195). To say that we share "existence" with God is misleading, because this shared "existence" is only in our minds, not something "out there". More seriously, this doctrine appears to destroy the difference between good and evil. The proper goal is not unity of existence but unity of will, where the believer desires and does only what God desires. Likewise, true *fana'* is complete worship and obedience to God.

Ibn Taymiyya likewise opposed aspects of popular religion such as the veneration of relics and visits to the tombs of holy men, and dramatic activities such as eating of glass, walking on fire, handling serpents, which the Rifa'i Sufis engaged in at the time. His *fatwa* on this particularly got him into trouble.

As we have seen in chapter 8, Ibn Taymiyya rejected the division between *siyasa* (government policy) and Shari'a made by some. Government in particular should be carried out according to the Shari'a and the ruler's legitimacy was derived precisely from doing this, not from divine choice (in the Shi'i sense) nor from election by the *umma* (as in earlier Sunni theory). This was the basis of his *fatwa* against the Mongols. They now claimed to be Muslims but were still governing according to the pre-Islamic Mongol law. Thus they were still ***kafirs***. This *fatwa* was to be claimed as a precedent by the assassins of the Egyptian president in 1981.

Interpretation of the Shari'a must rigorously follow the Qur'an, the *Sunna* and the *ijma'* of the earliest generations of Muslims (***salaf***), but beyond this it must not be bound by any existing ***ijma'***, since circumstances are constantly changing. One must, rather, apply the revealed texts directly to the existing situation with attention to the welfare of the Muslims (***maslaha***). *Ilham* (Sufi-style inspiration) was an acceptable source of guidance, and indeed preferable to a weak analogy or weak *hadith*, but was fallible like all *ijtihad*. Ibn Taymiyya considered himself a *mujtahid* and had no idea that the gate of *ijtihad* was supposed closed, as some were then claiming. His strictness is illustrated in his position on the divorce spoken three times in the same *'idda* (see chapter 10). It is considered by most to be valid in terms of effect but morally a violation of the Shari'a. Ibn Taymiyya denied its validity as well as its morality.

Ibn Taymiyya was controversial in his lifetime and had limited influence in the immediately following centuries. In modern times, however, he has inspired many Sunni reformers, both modernist and **Islamist**, precisely on the points on which he was controversial.

All three people discussed in this chapter appeal to people in modern times, though for different reasons. Secular intellectuals can find in Ibn Sina an example of the adaptation of "foreign" thinking that can help justify their own efforts at adapting Western thinking. People of more traditional inclination, including many *'ulamā'*, find al-Ghazali's synthesizing efforts appealing, as they seek a synthesis of various elements while remaining true to their faith. Ibn Taymiyya, with his forceful rejection of *bid'a*, has inspired the modern ***salafi*** movement in its various forms.

Key points

- Ibn Sina was the greatest of the Islamic philosophers and also led an active political life.
- He produced a comprehensive theory of the universe that influenced much later thinking, both Muslim and Western.
- He understood religion to be a popularization of philosophical truths in symbolic terms.
- Ghazali's emotional breakdown led him to commit himself to the Sufi way, according to his account.
- Ghazali sought to integrate the various currents of Muslim thinking and practice on a Sufi basis.
- Ibn Taymiyya struggled to get the community to follow the Qur'an and *Sunna* and to reject the various practices that he considered *bid'a*.
- He believed that the Shari'a should be applied in all areas of life.
- He often got into trouble for his insistence on these things.

Discussion questions

1. Why would rulers want to patronize and/or protect Ibn Sina, al-Ghazali and Ibn Taymiyya?
2. What criticisms did Ibn Sina, Ghazali and Ibn Taymiyya make of each other, or what might they have made?
3. What were the attitudes of Ibn Sina, al-Ghazali and Ibn Taymiyya to the common people?
4. Was Ibn Taymiyya a revolutionary?
5. How were Ibn Sina, al-Ghazali and Ibn Taymiyya related to Sufism?
6. If a fourth person were to be added to this chapter, who should it be, of those you have read about so far?

Critical thinking box 13.1

Read the autobiographies of Ibn Sina (*The Life of Ibn Sina*) and al-Ghazali (*The Faith and Practice of Al-Ghazali* to p. 68) and consider the similarities and differences between the life experiences and thinking of the two men.

Companion website

Features more on Ibn Sina's view of the cosmos, an outline of al-Ghazali's *Ihya'*; further readings and links for all three figures.

Further reading

Ibn Sina

Corbin, Henri P. (1960) *Avicenna and the Visionary Recital*, trans. Willard R. Trask. New York: Pantheon Books. (Includes translation of one of the visionary recitals.)

Goodman, L.E. (1992) *Avicenna*. London and New York: Routledge. (A major monograph.)

Ibn Sina (1974) *The Life of Ibn Sina*, ed. and trans. William E. Gohlman. Albany, NY: SUNY Press. (Ibn Sina's autobiography, short and easy to read.)

Nasr, S.H. (1964) *Three Muslim Sages: Avicenna, Suhrawardi, Ibn Arabi*. Cambridge, MA: Harvard University Press. (Teachings of these figures by a well-known contemporary Muslim scholar sympathetic to perennialism.)

Lerner, Ralph and Mahdi, Muhsin (eds.) (1963) *Medieval Political Philosophy: A Sourcebook*. New York: Free Press of Glencoe. (Passages from Ibn Sina are found in chapters 5 to 8.)

Al-Ghazali

Al-Ghazali (1953) *The Faith and Practice of Al-Ghazali*, trans. W. M. Watt. London: Allen & Unwin. (Al-Ghazali's autobiography, the most readable translation.)

Al-Ghazali (1980) *Freedom and Fulfillment*, trans. R. J. McCarthy. Boston, MA: Twayne Publishers. (Translates several works, including the autobiography; translation is more literal than Watt's.)

Al-Ghazali (1998) *The Niche of Lights*, trans. David Buchman. Provo, UT: Brigham Young University Press. (Most recent and accurate translation, rather literal; has English and Arabic on facing pages. Has a good biography of Al-Ghazali.)

Al-Ghazali (1924) *Al-Ghazzal's Mishkat al-Anwar (The Niche for Lights)* trans. W. H. T. Gairdner. London: Royal Asiatic Society. (Older, less accurate but usable; probably more available than Buchman.)

Watt, W. Montgomery (1963) *Muslim Intellectual: A Study of al-Ghazali*. Edinburgh: Edinburgh University Press. (Not up-to-date but still of value.)

Ibn Taymiyya

Ibn Taymiyya (1984) *A Muslim Theologian's Response to Christianity: Ibn Taymiyya's Al-Jawab al-Sahih*, trans. T. Michel. Delmar, NY: Caravan Books. (Introduction to the translation is a very good introduction to Ibn Taymiyya as a whole.)

Memon, M.A. (1976) *Ibn Taymiyya's Struggle against Popular Religion*. The Hague: Mouton. (Includes translation of another major work.)

See also: Esposito, *The Oxford History of Islam* (Ch. 6) [F]; Watt, *Islamic Philosophy and Theology* [11]; Netton, *Allah Transcendent* [11]; Nasr and Leaman, *History of Islamic Philosophy*, Part I [11]; Fakhry, *History of Islamic Philosophy* [11].

14 *Culture and counter-culture*

> God is beautiful and loves beauty
>
> (Hadith)

Islamic religion has been conditioned by the Islamic civilization that it helped to create and cannot be fully understood apart from it. This chapter will give a very selective overview of the art, architecture, literature and music of that civilization as they relate to religion.

In this chapter

- Visual art: arabesque, calligraphy
- Visual art: pictures
- Architecture, especially mosques
- Literature: poetry, prose
- Music

In the case of art and architecture the main attention will be on how it reflects Islamic religion or spirituality. In the case of literature there will be more focus on the anti-religious, or anti-pious, forms, since much religious literature has already been dealt with. Music has held an ambiguous position. In Islam, as in other civilizations, the religious has stood in some degree of tension with aggressively worldly elements. Nevertheless, the line between the secular and the religious is often not very clear.

Visual art

Arabesque

One of the most distinctive Islamic art forms is the arabesque, which includes both floral and geometrical ornamental designs (although the term is sometimes limited to the floral form). These may be found on almost any surface, such as the wall of a building, the page of book, a carpet or the surface of an implement or utensil. Historically they derive from the ornamental geometric and vegetal designs of the ancient world, but they become much more important and less naturalistic in Muslim art.

The floral arabesques involve flowers, leaves and stems in stylized, repetitive and usually interweaving form. Often there is no central focus and the elements may be seen as growing out of each other. Thus the eye is encouraged to move from one part to another, but not in a particular direction. They do not reproduce nature as it is but rather abstract from it something more regular and harmonious, though still quite complex. Much the same can be said of the geometrical form, except that it carries the abstraction from nature much further and presents perhaps "purer" forms.

These are often said to express the divine unity underlying the world of diversity and the harmony it imparts to this world. They may be interpreted as the Platonic forms underlying the physical world or, in Islamic esoteric terms, the world of images intermediate between the mundane world and God. They are sometimes described as a visual expression of what one experiences in contemplation. Also, they reject individualism as an ideal. Arabesques applied to massive walls give them a much lighter and ethereal aspect. We might say that they speak of the ephemeral nature of the physical world, of the beauty and harmony of the spiritual world behind the physical, and of the unity of the source of all of this. Isma'il Faruqi, a leading twentieth-century Muslim academic, has argued that the arabesque provides an intuition of infinity and a realization that it cannot be achieved in this world. Since it is repetitive it has no built-in limit but is cut off by an arbitrary boundary (e.g. the end of the wall or page, the frame of the picture). The eye wants to continue on past the limit to infinity if it were possible, but it isn't. I do not think this holds in every case, but it does in some. Faruqi argues that the main purpose of Islamic art is not to depict the divine, which is impossible, but to depict the fact that the divine cannot be depicted.

Calligraphy

Calligraphy (beautiful writing) using the Arabic script arose very naturally as an "art" form in the Islamic context since God has spoken to humans in words and words are put into visual form as writing. Writing has been described as "a distant shadow of the divine act" (Burckhardt, 1976, 51). The words of God in the Qur'an are the fullest expression of God in the material world and it is appropriate that they should be put into the most beautiful form possible. Just as an icon of Christ or a saint is a material window on the spiritual world for the Orthodox Christian, so the physical words of the Qur'an are in some sense the eternal word of God for a Muslim (see the debate about the uncreated Qur'an in chapter 11). The appropriateness of this comparison

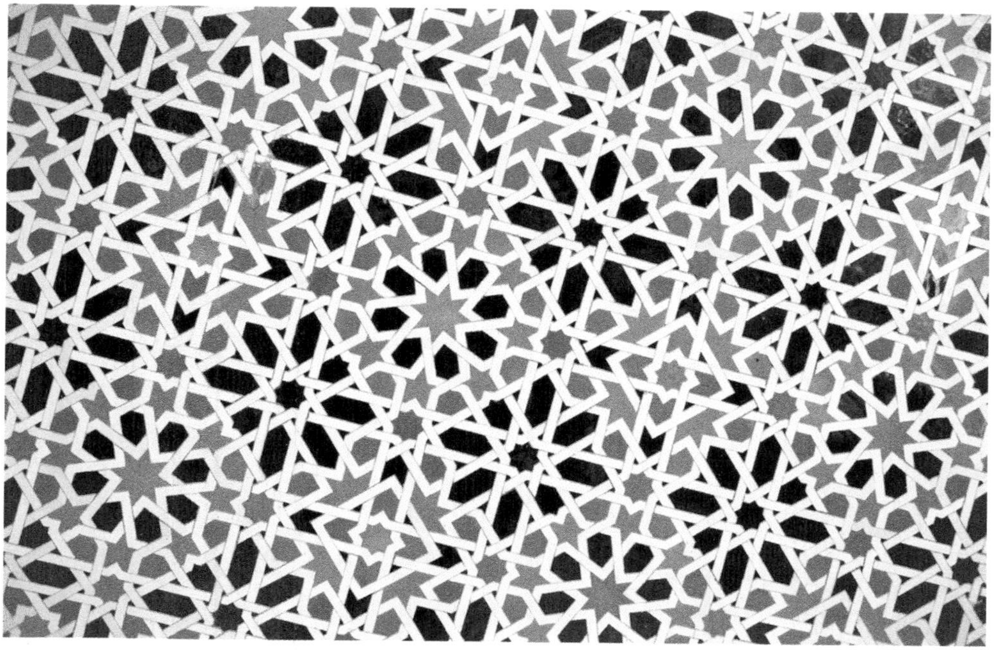

Figure 14.1 Geometrical arabesque: wall tiles, Reales Alcázares de Sevilla, Spain. Courtesy of Shutterstock

Figure 14.2 Floral arabesque: wall tiles, mosque in Tehran, Iran. Courtesy of Shutterstock

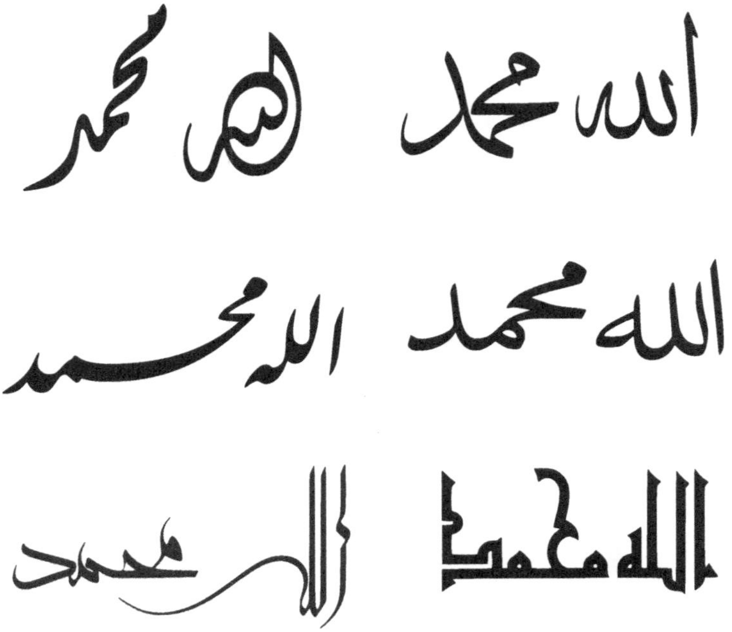

Figure 14.3 "Allah" and "Muhammad" in various calligraphic styles (right to left and top to bottom): *thuluth, diwani, naskh, nasta'liq, kufic, mu'alla*. Courtesy of Shutterstock

is illustrated, perhaps, by the fact that when the Ottomans converted the cathedral of the Hagia Sophia to a mosque they covered over the *Christos Pantokrator* in the dome and replaced it with a passage from the Qur'an.

The earliest form of the Arabic script under Islam was the angular Kufic script, said to have been developed by 'Ali, and the earliest Qur'ans were written in this script. By about 900 a number of more rounded scripts had been developed, including *naskh, thuluth* and *diwani*, and rules were made for their writing. Later *nasta'liq* was developed in Iran and used in India and by the Ottomans.

The flexibility and grace of the rounded forms make them especially suitable for calligraphy. It is claimed that calligraphy combines the greatest geometrical strictness with the most melodious rhythms. Calligraphy is not limited to the Qur'an but is used for many kinds of writing. Verses of Persian poetry, for example, are immensely enhanced when written in flowing *nasta'liq* script. Sometimes the letters are made so as to form animals or objects. The *tughra* was the highly stylized signature of the Ottoman sultan, found on *Ottoman coins* for example, but the same form is used elsewhere. In many cases of calligraphy the letters are superimposed on each other in a manner that makes them almost impossible to read unless one already knows what they say (as one often does). A line between "utility" and "art" is particularly hard to draw in the case of calligraphy. The tradition of calligraphy is very much alive today and some very interesting work is being done.

Pictures

It is commonly claimed that Islam forbids making representations of humans and animals, but the actual situation is more complex. From the Umayyad period onward palaces and other secular buildings have had human figures, but this has been disapproved of by the strictest and avoided for religious buildings such as mosques. The closest the Qur'an comes to the subject is a prohibition of "wine, games of chance, idols (or statues) and divining arrows" (5:92). In a *hadith*, however, it is stated that on the Day of Judgment painters will be commanded to breathe life into the forms that they have fashioned and, failing to do so, will be sent to hell. On the other hand, the Prophet is said to have protected a painting of Jesus and the Virgin Mary in the *Ka'ba* from erasure (it was destroyed during fighting in 683). Other evidence from the earliest period is inconsistent. The ban, nevertheless, became established and the thirteenth-century *faqih*, al-Nawawi, stated, "the painting of a picture of any living thing [plants are not included] is strictly prohibited and is one of the great sins ... because it implies a likeness to the creative activity of God" (Arnold, 1965, 9). Nevertheless, pictures continued to appear in secular contexts and eventually in religious contexts, more often Sufi and Shi'i than Shari'a-minded Sunni.

From the late twelfth century there was an increase in human and animal imagery on ceramics, carpets, drinking vessels and other small items. Of particular interest is the illustration of books, including the finely detailed "miniatures" to be found in volumes produced for the wealthy and powerful, especially in Iran and later the Ottoman Empire and India (see Figures 4.2 and 13.2 for examples). Perhaps the best known examples are those in several volumes of the ***Shahnameh***, depicting scenes from pre-Islamic Iranian history. Generally the miniatures are somewhat stylized and do not convey distance perspective. It has been suggested that the best ones seek to convey the immutable essences of things rather than their mundane reality. From the Mongol period they show Chinese influence, especially in the backgrounds.

Illustrations of humans are mostly found in secular books and involve secular subjects, but some pictures of Muhammad, his companions and earlier prophets, as well as religious teaching and Sufi activities are also found, particularly in books of history and poetry. The earliest pictures of Muhammad are found in the universal history written by Rashid al-Din (1247–1318), ***wazir*** to the Mongol rulers. These pictures are more naturalistic than most and show the Prophet's face. Later it became standard to cover the faces of all the prophets and place fiery nimbuses reminiscent of Buddhist iconography about their heads, thus indicating their sanctity. The *mi'raj*, with Muhammad riding on Buraq, is one scene often depicted. In fact, one could illustrate most of the major events in Muhammad's life with pictures produced by Muslims. In spite of their artistic importance, however, such pictures are rare and, given the sorts of books in which they appeared, were presumably not often seen by most people. They never appear in copies of the Qur'an or *Hadith*. The *'ulama'* have generally condemned them and probably most other Muslims, too. Shi'is have generally been more willing than Sunnis to produce pictures of prophets and other sacred figures. In their case 'Ali and the other *Imams* have their faces covered and have fiery nimbuses. Under the influence of the *ta'ziya*, pictures of Husayn and figures in the Karbala' epic have become more popular among Shi'is since the nineteenth century. They are not found in mosques, however.

In spite of initial resistance, human pictures in secular contexts have become quite common in the Muslim world in modern times but resistance to depicting prophets continues strong. When a Hollywood-style film, *The Message*, was made about Muhammad in 1976, Muhammad himself was neither seen nor heard on screen. When a Danish newspaper published cartoons of Muhammad in 2006 much of the ensuing outcry was articulated in terms of the general prohibition against depicting a prophet, although it was certainly driven more by the offensive nature of some of the cartoons. In the context of this controversy attention was called to a picture supposedly of Muhammad as a boy and said to be a favorite of Ayatollah Khomeini. The point was made, however, that this was of Muhammad before he became a prophet.

Architecture

Architecture is considered by many to be the finest artistic achievement of Islamic civilization. For reasons of space, most of our attention will be given to mosques.

The word for mosque in Arabic, *masjid*, literally means a place for prostration in prayer, thus indicating its primary but not its only purpose. In the earliest days of Islam the mosques were very much political and communal centers, with Friday congregational **salah** led by the ruler or his representative and important political announcements made. It also has been a site for teaching activity and has provided shelter for travelers. Mosques range in size and importance from the small *muṣallā* ("place for *salah*", not usually used for Friday congregational *salah*) to the often monumental *jāmi'* ("that which brings people together"), often called a Friday or congregational mosque, where all the people from a town or district are supposed to come for the congregational *salah*.

The first mosque was connected with Muhammad's residence in Medina. It consisted of a courtyard with rooms for the Prophet and his family along the east wall and with columns of palm trunks supporting palm branches on the north and south sides, the south being the *qibla* (direction to Mecca), which may have been marked in some way. The Prophet probably stood on a sort of stool to give his sermons. There was no minaret. This mosque provided the very basic pattern for the later ones. The *miḥrāb* (which marks the *qibla*), *minbar* (pulpit) and minaret developed from this or were introduced within the next century. The *mihrab* developed into a niche usually flanked by pillars and topped by an arch, with considerable embellishment in many cases (see Figure 7.2 on p. 105). Although basically a very utilitarian item, it has been seen also as symbolizing the gate to paradise. The *minbar* is a set of steps with a railing leading to a seat at the top. It has been suggested that the seat is symbolically a throne, suggesting both secular and religious power. The preacher stands on one of the steps below the seat, thus possibly disclaiming the highest human authority, which belongs to the Prophet. The minaret is the tower from which the muezzin gives the *adhān* (today, sadly for lovers of tradition, often by loudspeaker). Its form may derive from the square towers used by Christian hermits in Syria or from church towers. Practically, it allows the *adhan* to be heard most widely. Symbolically, it indicates the importance of Islamic faith, since it would have been the highest structure in traditional towns and cities. While having the same basic function minarets vary in their specific forms. Square minarets are typical of North Africa, for example, while pencil-shaped minarets are typical of Ottoman mosques.

As the Muslim world rapidly expanded, impressive mosques were built partly out of need to accommodate large numbers of worshippers and partly as symbols of the power and significance of the ***umma*** and its rulers. These include the Umayyad mosque in Damascus (built 706–14), constructed on the site of a Christian church and, before that, of a pagan temple. It still holds the relics of St. John the Baptist that had been in the church. The great mosque of Samarra, the Abbasid capital from 836 to 870, was the largest of all mosques, with a spiral minaret slightly reminiscent of a Babylonia *ziqqurat* (though no historical connection has been established).

Other early large mosques include that of Ibn Tulun in Cairo (879, see Figure 4.1 on p. 51), the Great Mosque of Qayrawan in Tunisia (670–875) and the Mosque of Cordoba (begun 784?) in Spain. In these and many other mosques the palm trunks of the Prophet's mosque have become impressive colonnades.

Domes appeared early above the *mihrab* area and the Ottomans, influenced by Byzantine churches and presumably climate, placed domes over what would have been the courtyard of the mosques. Iranian mosques typically have one or more *iwans*, lofty semi-circular vaults possibly derived from Sasanian royal architecture, containing an entrance from the courtyard to the *mihrab* area or other part of the mosque. Other cultural areas also have distinctive features to their mosques (see those from Mali in this chapter and Indonesia in chapter 19, Figure 19.1, p. 312). Mosques are also included in larger complexes that may include the tomb of the patron (usually a ruler), a ***madrasa*** and possibly a hospital or a ***khanqah***. The *madrasa* of Sultan Hasan in Cairo, for example, contains the Sultan's tomb and four *iwans* off the courtyard for teaching each of the four Sunni ***madhhabs***, as well as mosque space. Some modern mosques are built in contemporary architectural styles, but probably more of them hold to older patterns. Many newer mosques in Cairo, for example, are built in the Mamluke style.

The mosque is sacred space, as indicated by the requirement to remove one's shoes before entering, but as such has its own character. Perhaps the predominant impression is that of spaciousness and light, especially where the courtyard is open to the sky.

Figure 14.4 Mosque of Muhammad Ali in the Citadel, Cairo. The style is Ottoman, with the dome and pencil-like minarets. Courtesy of the author

This space is relatively undifferentiated in character. Unlike most Western Christian churches, whose architectural plan directs the eye to the altar or communion table, the plan of the mosque does not usually direct the eye toward the *mihrab* (which may not be visible from everywhere) or any other feature. Rather, the mosque layout suggests that God is equally present everywhere. If there is a focus to the mosque it is outside the mosque itself, the *Ka'ba* in Mecca, to which the *mihrab* points.

There is space to say only a few words about other forms of architecture. The most notable of these is the earliest surviving Islamic monument, the Dome of the Rock. This is not a mosque, but a place for circumambulation, and is the only one of its type. Built by the Umayyad caliph Abd al-Malik between 688 and 692 on the site of the Jewish Temple and the place where Muhammad was believed to have ascended into heaven, its structure and symbolism stress the victory of Islam and its role as successor to previous religions and regimes (it has a number of Qur'anic quotations relating to Christ). At the time when it was built Mecca was in the hands of the anti-Umayyad, Ibn Zubayr, and some say it was meant to offer an alternative destination for pilgrims.

There are mausoleums, particularly of rulers and Sufi *walis*. Undoubtedly the best known and possibly the best architecturally is the Taj Mahal, built by the Mughal emperor, Shah Jahan (r. 1627–58), for his wife, Mumtaz Mahal, and in which he too is buried. Palaces and especially the gardens associated with them usually, at some level, symbolize paradise, the "gardens under which rivers flow" (Qur'an 2:25

Figure 14.5 Great Mosque at Djenne in Mali – the largest mud building in the world. Courtesy of iStockphoto

and elsewhere). This is true also when they appear in pictures. Here, in a sense, the secular becomes sacred, a reminder of the indefinite boundary between them. Other kinds of buildings that may be architecturally significant include *madrasas*, *khanqahs*, *ribats* (initially, fortified bases for *ghazis*, frontier warriors) *caravansarais*, public fountains and public baths.

Literature

As indicated earlier, we will focus here on secular literature, especially some that questions traditional religious values. In fact, the religious and the non-religious elements in Islamic culture, as in other cultures, have influenced and to some extent defined each other.

What we call Arabic or Islamic literature is usually called *adab* in Arabic. *Adab* in general refers to proper behaviour, and in this sense there is an *adab* for various groups, such as Sufis, *muftis* and others. In the present context it refers both to a cultivated lifestyle that developed among the administrators and bureaucrats of the Abbasid Empire and was imitated by others and to the elegant style of speaking and writing based on a broad general knowledge that was its main expression. In this *adab* piety was respected but was not necessarily the highest of values. There was also a popular literature but it is not so well known since less of it was recorded and space does not permit us to give it much attention here.

Poetry

Pride of place in Islamic literature goes to poetry, which was more commonly recited or sung in public than read in the privacy of one's home or study. Poetry was the only form of literature in pre-Islamic Arabia and this poetry set the standard for some time. Its standard form was the *qasīda* (ode), a long poem that begins by describing the traces of an old encampment in the desert and the love affair the poet had there, and then an arduous camel ride through the desert, and then the topic of the poem, which may be boasting (usually of prowess in love or battle), panegyric, satire or lament. The most famous *qaṣīdas* were seven *mu'allaqāt* that were supposedly hung in the *Ka'ba* after a competition. The greatest of the pre-Islamic poets was considered to be Imru al-Qays (see chapter 3).

This style of poetry continued into the Umayyad and Abbasid periods although it became a standard more to be admired than effectively imitated and although it provoked, for a time, a movement called *shu'ūbiyya* that championed the traditions of non-Arab peoples, especially the Persians. The place of the pre-Islamic ode was strengthened, paradoxically, by the fact that it was viewed by the *'ulama'* as a source for understanding obscure words in the Qur'an.

New forms of poetry soon developed, the first, during the Umayyad period, being the *ghazal*, used for love poetry. The best known example is the tragic love story of Majnun and Layla. Majnun means "crazy" and reflects the extremes to which Layla's lover went, unsuccessfully, to reach her. It was reproduced in Persian and Turkish literature and the theme was taken up by the Sufis. Two forms of poetry were developed in Andalus, the *muwashsha* and the *zajal*, which were probably influenced by the Romance language.

The themes of love, wine, panegyric and satire continued to be important throughout Islamic literature. Praise of a ruler or satire of his enemies was an important form of propaganda and could be highly rewarded. The best known praiser of the libertine life was Abu Nuwas (d. c. 815), but he was also a reformer and genius in poetic style and a boon companion of the caliph Harun al-Rashid. He criticizes bondage to the pre-Islamic ode in the following terms:

> The lovelorn wretch stopped at a desert camping ground to question it,
> And I stopped to inquire after the local tavern.
>
> (Kritzek, 1964, 84)

Of wine he sings:

> Come Sulaiman, sing to me,
> And the wine, quick, bring to me.
> Lo, already Dawn is here
> In a golden mantle clear,
> Whilst the flask goes twinkling round,
> Pour me a cup that leaves me drowned.

With oblivion, ne'er so nigh
Let the shrill muezzin cry!

(*Ibid.*, 87)

Perhaps the greatest master of the panegyric and satire, as well as of the classical form of Arabic poetry, was al-Mutanabbi (915–65). Described as "gifted with an almost peerless talent and an almost demonic pride" (*ibid.*, 107), he traveled about seeking to live by his panegyrics and could be devastating when he found the reception inadequate. For example:

I went there as a guest of liars, who
Would neither entertain nor let me go,
Liar for whose putrid frames death would not function
Unless equipped with a disinfecting staff.

(*Ibid.*, 107, wording modified)

In a different mode, but hardly pious, is the gently skeptical and pessimistic Abu al-'Ala' al-Ma'arri (d. 1057). Here are some of his verses:

Now this religion happens to prevail
Until by that one it is overthrown, –
Because men dare not live with men alone,
But always with another fairy tale.
A church, a temple, or a Kaaba Stone,
Koran or Bible or a martyr's bone –
All these and more my heart can tolerate
Since my religion now is love alone.

(*Ibid.*, 126, 128)

It would be a mistake to imagine that these sentiments were very common at the time, but the fact that they were preserved indicates that they had some resonance in the culture.

Persian poetry in Islamic times is marked by no less greatness than Arabic poetry. It used the *qasida* and the *ghazal* forms and added to them the *mathawi*, rhyming couplets, and the *ruba'i*, quatrains. The first major poet in this tradition was Firdowsi, whose long epic poem, the *Shahnameh* (Book of Kings) tells the story of Iran from creation to the Muslim conquest. It is considered by many the greatest work of Persian literature. For many Iranians it is virtually sacred literature.

Undoubtedly the best known Persian poet in the English-speaking world is Omar Khayyam (1048–1131), though he was known in his own time and for years afterward mainly as a mathematician and scientist. Only with Edward Fitzgerald's free translations of his skeptical quatrains, which spoke to the condition of Victorian skeptics, did his poetry become famous. He praises the quiet life and articulates a hedonistic skepticism. Here are three of his quatrains, the first in both Fitzgerald's translation and a more literal one and then two others in the more literal translation.

> A book of verses underneath the Bough,
> A jug of wine, a Loaf of Bread – and Thou
> Beside me singing in the wilderness –
> Oh, Wilderness were Paradise enow!
>
> (Kritzek, 1964, 167)

> I need a jug of wine and a book of poetry,
> Half a loaf for a bite to eat,
> Then you and I, seated in a desert spot,
> Will have more wealth than a Sultan's realm.
>
> (Khayyam, 1979, 71)

> If the heart could grasp the meaning of life,
> In death it would know the mystery of God;
> Today when you are in possession of yourself, you know nothing.
> Tomorrow, when you leave yourself behind, what will you know?
>
> (*Ibid.*, 5)

> From that wine jug, which has no harm in it,
> Fill a bowl, boy, drink and pass it to me,
> Before, by some wayside,
> A potter uses your clay and mine for just such a jug.
>
> (*Ibid.*, 68)

Other poets blended the sacred and the secular in enticing ways, praising drunkenness, Sufi or otherwise, and proffering worldly advice. Rumi, the greatest of the Sufi poets, we have met in chapter 12. More on the borderline of the sacred and the secular are the three great Persian poets, Nizami (d. 1209), Saadi (d. 1292) and Hafez (c. 1320–90), the most beloved of all. Hafez illustrates the ambiguous mixture of wine and mysticism in the following:

> The rose has flushed red, the bud has burst,
> And drunk with joy is the nightingale –
> Hail, Sufis! Lovers of wine all hail,
> For wine is proclaimed to a world athirst!
>
> (Robinson, 1996, 264)

Is the wine a metaphor? Or perhaps the Sufis are metaphorical. Persian poetry, according to Roy Mottahedeh, is "the emotional home in which the ambiguity that was at the heart of Iranian culture lived most freely and openly ... In Persian poetry of any worth nothing was merely something else ... " (Mottahedeh, 1987, 164). The images had become quite conventional and were yet open to diverse interpretation, so that the black tresses of the beloved might (or might not) symbolize the darkness of unbelief and a bright cheek might (or might not) symbolize the light of faith. A temple of idolatry might (or might not) symbolize true inward faith in contrast to hypocritical formalism. Here are some lines from a twentieth-century admirer of Hafez:

> The city preacher's moralizing irritated me,
> I sought help from the breast of the besotted drunkard
> Permit me to recall the temple of idols
> I was awakened by the hand of the idol of the wine house.
>
> (Fischer and Abedi, 1990, 452)

The author is Ayatollah Khomeini, the greatest "preacher" of all.

Prose

Adab prose has been described as "highly mannered, anecdotal, reservedly didactic and vastly entertaining" (Kritzek, 1964, 72). The oldest of such works is *Kalilah and Dimna*, a collection of animal fables translated from a Persian version of the Sanskrit *Pancatantra* by Ibn al-Muqaffa'. The style of *adab* was raised to a high artistic level by al-Jahiz (d. 869), a writer of tracts and essays and philological works and also a Mu'tazili theologian.

Important types of prose literature have included the "mirrors for princes" (see chapter 8), accounts of travels, of which the most famous is that of Ibn Battuta, who traveled through much of the Islamic world between 1325 and 1354, and universal histories, of which al-Tabari's is the best known. Another such history is that of Ibn Khaldun, the introduction to which presents the theory of the rise and fall of dynasties mentioned in chapter 8. Undoubtedly the work best known in the West is the *Thousand and One Nights* (or *Arabian Nights*), though it is not so highly regarded in the Muslim world. It is a collection of popular stories from many cultures and times. Also close to popular literature in content are the *Maqāmāt* (*Assemblies*) of which that of al-Hariri (1054–1122) is considered the greatest. It features the adventures of a witty and somewhat unscrupulous vagabond named Abu Zayd. In one account, an eloquent mosque preacher turns out to be Abu Zayd, who preaches by day and drinks wine by night. Similar are figures of Jiha (Goha in Egyptian pronunciation) a comical figure known for centuries in the Arab world and elsewhere and Mulla Nasrudin, an unconventional *'alim* known mainly in the Turkish and Iranian worlds (see text box in chapter 9).

Jiha

Stories of the peasant Jiha (variously spelled; pronounced Goha in Egyptian dialect) have been popular in the Middle East since about the eighth century CE as a "wise fool" or "trickster" figure; for Egyptians he is the prototypical *fallāḥ* (peasant). He may be identified with the later figure of Mulla Nasreddin, who superseded him in the Turkish and Iranian culture areas.

> Jiha had a bull which he was fattening up to sell in the market. He took great pride in making a great show of it in the village, boasting about the money he would get from the bull. Everyone asked Jiha to say, when he used to boast about his future wealth, that he would get it "if God wills". On each occasion Jiha replied: "There is no need to add this phrase, because the bull is mine, and God has nothing to do with all this; I shall sell the bull and get the money, whether God wills or not."
>
> On market day Jiha was eagerly looking forward to selling his bull and declared ostentatiously that from now on he would become a rich man. People again advised him to say "if God wills", but he refused to comply. He sold his bull at last, putting the money in his pocket. A thief had been watching him, and deftly stole the money.
>
> Jiha went off to buy some new clothes, swaggering and puffed up with conceit. When he put his hand in his pocket to pay the merchant he found that his money was gone. Then people came to ask Jiha about his money, and his reply was, "If God wills, I have lost it."
>
> (Ammar, 1973, 180)

Music

We may begin by noting that the recitation of the Qur'an does not come under the heading of music in Islamic cultures, although it is claimed that its recitation has influenced music. Music itself was generally rejected as morally dangerous by the *'ulama'*, but it of course existed at both the popular and courtly levels and there was a wide range of opinion as to which music was acceptable (cf. Al-Ghazali, p. 202). Lois al-Faruqi claims that the more acceptable music has an abstract and repetitive quality that suggests infinite continuity, as does the arabesque. Sufis used music, as we have seen, and increasingly so in Ottoman times. Sufi singers called *munshidin* are active to the present time as are the *qawwals*, musicians connected with the Chishtiyya *tariqa* in South Asia, and there are other forms of popular religious music. Sufi music has been appropriated by modern culture in various ways. For example, in Egypt the songs of the *munshidin* are being remixed into very popular youth-oriented dance music. Music is also used in connection with the rituals for Husayn, especially the *shabihs*. A number of popular singers began their careers singing religious songs, of whom the Egyptian, Umm Kulthum (d. 1975), is undoubtedly the best known. Such contemporary forms as rock, rap, hip-hop and heavy metal are generally condemned by religious spokesmen but are played, sometimes with Islamic themes infused, and listened to by the young. They may express the same alienation that leads others to more violent action. Rap and hip-hop have been important for the "Black Muslims" in America and played a role during the "Arab spring", especially in Libya and Tunisia (see chapters 15 and 20).

As we can see, the artistic culture sometimes directly expresses religion, sometimes reacts against it or flouts it and sometimes does both. Rarely if ever in pre-modern times did it ignore religion.

Key points

- Islamic art, architecture, literature and music illustrate the varied ways religion has related to the material and secular world in which it is set.
- Abstract patterns are particularly characteristic of Islamic art and may enshrine an intuition of infinity and of an ideal realm behind the mundane world.
- Calligraphy is particularly important since it can put the divine word into visual form.
- It is simplistic to say that Islam forbids pictures of living beings. Such pictures exist but their place is problematic and is usually in more secular contexts.
- Architecture is another major form of Islamic artistic expression.
- Mosques are sacred space but also suggest the presence of God everywhere.
- The word *adab* refers to a kind of refined, courtly culture and to the literature produced within it.
- Of the various forms of secular literature, poetry is the most important not only in Arabic but in Persian and other Islamic languages.
- Much secular literature has an anti-pious character but the Sufis have turned this kind of poetry to a religious use. This leads to interesting ambiguity in Persian poetry.
- The recitation of the Qur'an is not considered "music".
- Though often forbidden, music is present in Islamic cultures and often used for religious purposes.

Discussion questions

1. In what sense can Omar Khayyam be said to be an Islamic poet?
2. Why is calligraphy so important?
3. How is a mosque like a church or a synagogue? How is it not?
4. What do you suppose Khomeini meant by his verses?
5. Writing has been described as "a distant shadow of the divine act". What might this mean? Do you agree?
6. Why is wine so important in Islamic poetry?

Critical thinking box 14.1

Try your hand at writing a few verses along the lines of Hafez (e.g. reflecting his kind of ambiguity and/or his poetic style as it appears in English translations). (You should check Mottahedeh's comments in *The Mantle of the Prophet*, pp. 163–64, partly quoted above. You may want to look at some of the poems of Hafez. One source is *Hafez: Dance of Life* [trans. Michael Boylan et al. Washington D.C.: Mage Publishers, 1988], others will be placed on the website.)

Critical thinking box 14.2

Is it true that Islam forbids making images of human beings? If not, could one say that it devalues them in relation to other artistic forms? If either of these is true, what do you think are the reasons? (It is up to you to determine what you mean by "Islam" here.)

Companion website

Features a reflection on the concept of art, information and reading on Omar Khayyam, readings and links relating to hip-hop and other music, links for calligraphy and pictures, and for the Mu'allaqa of Imru al Qays, Layla and Majnun, and a summary of the *Shahnameh*.

Further reading

Al-Faruqi, Isma'il R. (1968) "Islam and Art", *Studia Islamica*, 37: 81–1009. (See reference to al-Faruqi in the chapter.)

Burckhardt, Titus (1976) *Art of Islam: Language and Meaning*. Westerham: World of Islam Festival Publishing Company. (Wide ranging and beautifully illustrated spiritual interpretation of Islamic art by a leading proponent of "**perennialism**".)

Denny, Walter (1984) "Contradiction and Consistency in Islamic Art", and al-Faruqi, Lois Ibsen, "Unity and Variety in the Music of Islamic Culture" in Yvonne Yazbeck Haddad, Brian Haines, and Ellison Findlay (eds.) (1984) *The Islamic Impact*. Syracuse, NY: Syracuse University Press. (Denny explores a variety of issues and interpretations; Faruqi's ideas are mentioned in this chapter.)

Ettinghausen, Richard, Grabar, Oleg and Jenkins-Madina, Marilyn (2001) *Islamic Art and Architecture, 650–1250*, 2nd ed. New Haven, CT: Yale University Press. (Well-illustrated and detailed historical study of all the forms of art.)

Grabar, Oleg (1990) *The Great Mosque of Isfahan*. New York: New York University Press. (Presents the social setting and tours the building; black and white photographs.)

Grabar, Oleg (1996) *The Dome of the Rock*. London: Thames and Hudson. (Large format with excellent color photographs, covers the architecture, art and some historical sources.)

Khayyam, O. (1968) *Rubaiyyat of Omar Khayyam*, trans. Robert Avery and John Heath-Stubbs. London: Cassell. (To my knowledge the best work on Khayyam by Western scholars.)

Kritzek, J. (ed.) (1964) *Anthology of Islamic Literature*. New York: New American Library. (Contains a wide sampling of pre-modern Islamic poetry and prose, usually a good introduction to the author's excerpts.)

Nasr, Sayyid Hossein (1987) *Islamic Art and Spirituality*. Albany, NY: State University of New York Press. (By a well-known and prolific writer on Islamic spirituality, inclined toward "perennialism".)

Schimmel, Annemarie (1992) *Islamic Calligraphy*. New York: Metropolitan Museum of Art. (By a leading expert on Sufism; well illustrated.)

Vernoit, Stephen (1996) "Artistic Expressions of Muslim Societies", chapter 8 in Francis Robinson, ed., *The Cambridge Illustrated History of the Islamic World*. Cambridge: Cambridge University Press. (Covers a very wide range of topics, including the modern period.)

Herrera, Linda and Bayat, Asef (eds.) (2010) *Being Young and Muslim: New Cultural Politics in the Global South and North*. New York: Oxford University Press. (Chapters 18–20 deal with hip-hop, rap and heavy metal.)

See also: Esposito, *The Oxford History of Islam* (Ch. 5) [F]; Renard, *Seven Doors to Islam* and *Windows on the House of Islam* (Chs 3–5) [F]; Knysh, *Islam in Historical Perspective* (Ch. 18) [F].

Part III

Modern developments

15 *Modern challenges*

Western imperialism and Muslim response

> The fundamental malaise of modern Islam is a sense that something has gone wrong with Islamic history. The fundamental problem of modern Muslims is how to rehabilitate that history: to set it going again in full vigour, so that Islamic society may once again flourish as a divinely-guided society should and must.
>
> (Smith, 1957, 47)

What we call "modernity" has come to the Muslim world largely as part of Western colonialism and imperialism and the response has been a profoundly ambivalent one of rejection and acceptance. At the religious level the question is posed whether and in what way Muslim society can truly be a divinely guided society. This chapter will survey the main features of Western imperialism and the main kinds of Muslim response to the challenge it poses.

In this chapter

- European imperialism and colonialism
- Modernization, Westernization, secularization
- The challenge to Islam: "the great reversal"
- Pre-modern reform
- Responses to the challenge: traditionalism, Islamic modernism, secularism, Islamism
- Resurgence of Islam
- The special case of Israel and Palestine
- The "Arab spring"
- Post-Islamism?

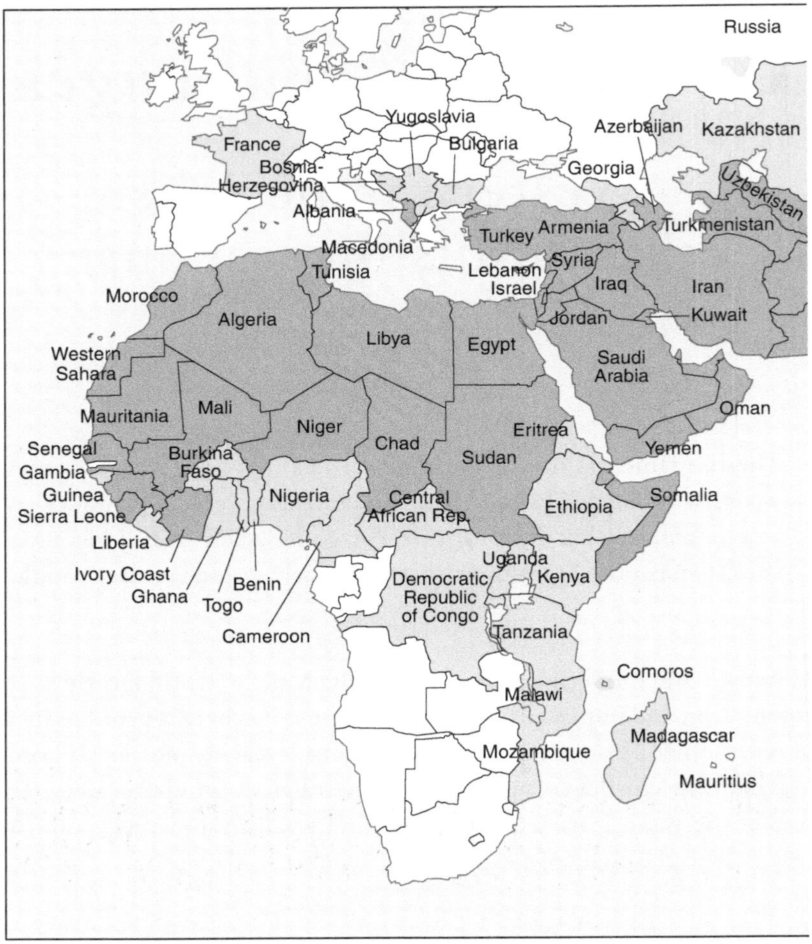

Map 7 Modern Islamic World

European imperialism and colonialism

In 1798 a French military expedition under the command of Napoleon Bonaparte invaded Egypt, primarily in order to cut off the British route to their new colonies in India. He quickly took control of the country, defeating its Mamluke rulers and quelling popular revolts. At the same time he proclaimed to the people that he had come to liberate them from Mamluke tyranny, grant them liberty and equality, and respect the true values of Islam. He brought with him a number of scientists and scholars, whose investigations in Egypt did much to forward the fledgling discipline of Orientalism (European study of the "orient") and whose activities also attracted the interest of some Egyptian scholars. He formed a council of *'ulama'* but the people would not accept being ruled by non-Muslims. They revolted and were put down forcefully. It was rather the British, assisted by disease, who forced the French to

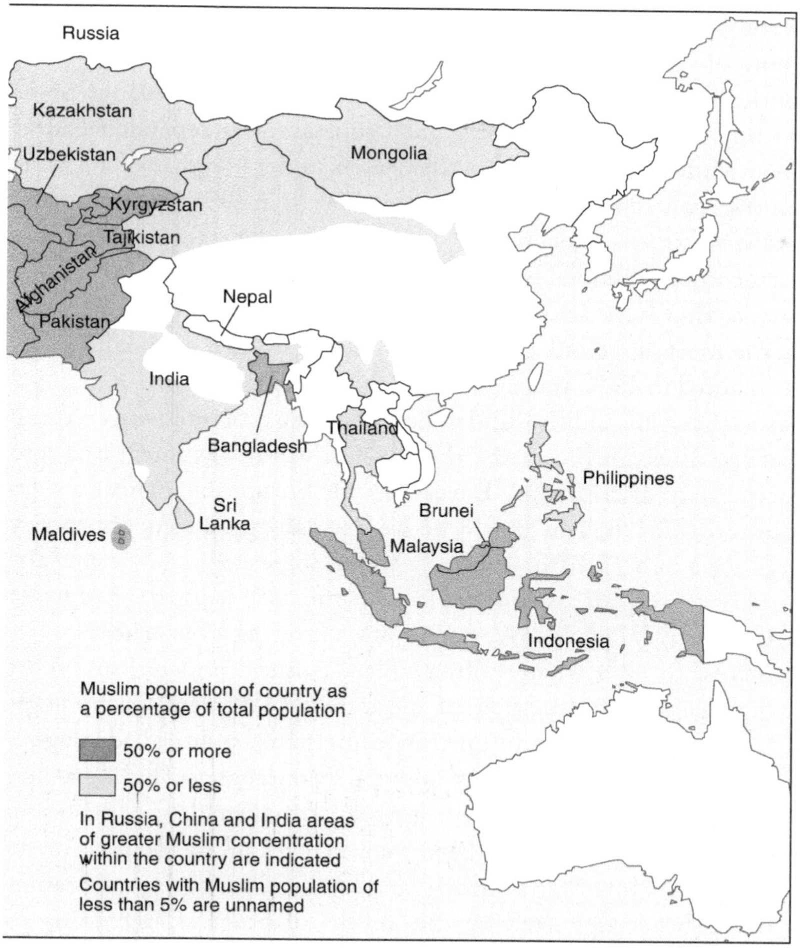

leave in 1801. The longer-term results of this expedition for Egypt will be discussed in chapter 17. It is mentioned here because it is commonly treated as the beginning of the modern period in the Middle East, although there had been important developments earlier. Also, it illustrates many of the kinds of actions that were to mark the European imperialism and the reaction to it in the following century.

From this point European power spread until, by about 1920, almost all of the Muslim world was under the political sway of European countries. Some were ruled directly as colonies; some were protectorates or "native states"; some were nominally independent but subject to restrictions and effective pressure. Only central Arabia and Afghanistan retained genuine independence. Muslim responses had sometimes been military or popular resistance, unsuccessful in the long run, and sometimes more or less reluctant cooperation with the Europeans, complicated by the fact that some elements in the Muslim populations found cooperation to be in their interest while others did not.

After 1920 political and military imperialism retreated, though unevenly. Some countries, such as Egypt, Turkey and Iran, gained substantial independence after the First World War while other areas found themselves under mandates for a time. Most Muslim countries gained independence before 1970, or in 1991 with the end of the Soviet Union. Even this was not complete, however. If the Western armies were no longer center stage, they remained in the wings prepared to return to the stage if it was felt necessary, as they have done in Iraq and Afghanistan. Moreover, what for many Muslims is the most egregious example of imperialism and colonialism, the state of Israel, was planted in 1948 and shows no sign of leaving.

Imperialism has not been just political and military but also economic and cultural. Over the course of the nineteenth century, the Muslim world was integrated into a worldwide economic system created by Europeans for Europeans, almost always on disadvantageous terms for the Muslims, who were usually producers of primary products that were then processed in Europe. Today some countries, especially the oil producers, have carved out a stronger place for themselves in the worldwide economic system, but it is still largely a Western system favoring Westerners.

Of particular interest to us is what is often called "cultural imperialism". This included such things as the introduction of modern, i.e. Western, technology, medicine, public health, education, administrative methods, political ideologies, newspapers and other mass media, clothes and entertainment (including plays, operas, novels). New professions were created, such as journalism, law, engineering and (modern) medicine. All of this has been viewed by Europe as part of its "civilizing mission" or "the White Man's burden" and has been seen as a justification for imperialism. It has been supported by the "myth" of progress, according to which human history is the story of continual progress led, currently, by the West. This myth is probably unique to modern Western civilization since the eighteenth century, since other civilizations, including the Muslim and earlier Christian ones, have usually seen the long course of history as cyclical or declining. Whatever else the myth of progress is, it has been extremely effective cultural propaganda. The modern Christian missionary movement has been closely, if ambiguously, related to imperialism. The missionaries have had little success in converting Muslims to Christianity but they have established schools and hospitals that have been much appreciated and used by many and thus have been effective purveyors of Western ideas and practices.

Although we label it "imperialism", cultural imperialism has been driven as much by the desire of Muslims for Western cultural goods as by the Western effort to spread them. From the beginning the Muslim elites wanted to learn the "secrets" of Western success and for a time many accepted that they needed a period of European tutelage. Today they feel that the need for such tutelage has long passed, if it ever really existed, but cultural imperialism continues with almost unabated force, witness the largely one-way flow of new technology, ideology and fashion. From the latest advances in military and medical technology to tee-shirts and Barbie dolls (now renamed "Fulla" and wearing Islamic garb), the Muslim world still largely looks West.

Modernization, Westernization, secularization

Western imperialism set in train profound changes in Muslim societies, which are variously labeled "modernization", "development", "Westernization" and "secularization". These words refer to substantially the same processes, but are conceptually distinct. "Modernization" and "development" refer in the first instance to the technology that increases human control over the physical environment and then, by extension, to changes in such areas as education and politics. It also includes certain attitudes, such as openness to change and innovation. The myth of progress encourages the belief that change will be for the better. "Westernization" underlines the fact that virtually all of these things come from the West, so that to modernize has almost always meant to Westernize. "Secularization" means in particular to shift interest from the spiritual world or the future life to this world, to draw one's values and beliefs primarily from human rather than divine sources, and to limit the influence of religious institutions on society, often by separating them from other institutions, but not necessarily seeking to destroy them. While Muslims are generally in favor of modernization and development, many of them reject the identification of these with Westernization and secularization, and this tendency has increased notably in recent years.

A major effect of these changes has been to strengthen enormously the power of the state (as it has done in the West and elsewhere) by giving it the technological means to extend its power and to accomplish certain social goals. Another effect has been a decrease in mortality rates and a dramatic rise in populations due to the introduction of Western medicine and public health. Education and new professions created a new class in many places, often called "*effendi*", a Westernized elite, wearing Western-style clothes, sending their children to Western-style schools and living a largely Western lifestyle. Thus society came to be divided into "modern" and "traditional" sectors. In 1900 the numbers of the modern elite were still very small, though their influence was considerable, but they increased rapidly in the following decades and often took control of the state.

The challenge to Islam: "the great reversal"

All of this has been a spiritual as well as a cultural and physical challenge to Muslims and to Islam. The Qur'an says of the Muslims, "You are the best *umma* ever brought forth to humankind, enjoining right conduct, forbidding indecency and having faith in God" (3:110) and also, "Power and glory belong to God and to His Messenger and to the believers" (63:8). These were taken to mean that the Muslim *umma*, because it properly worshipped God, would be stronger both physically and culturally than other communities. Even when the Muslims did not live up to the high standards of Islam, they at least recognized the truth and came closer to living by it than the ***kafir*** nations. As indicated at the end of chapter 4, as of the year 1600 Muslims could feel that their history on the whole fulfilled these promises. They could with some justification feel superior to the other civilizations of which they knew. Admittedly the *umma* had suffered setbacks, but it had rebounded from these. The Mongols had been the greatest challenge and within half a century the Mongols had accepted Islam. The loss of **Andalus** had been a blow, but God compensated it with the advance of the Ottomans. In any case, they had taken the measure of the uncivilized "Franks" during the Crusades; at their best the Franks were eager students of the sciences and philosophy of the Muslims.

With apparent suddenness, this situation was reversed. Now the "Franks" were defeating the Muslims and demonstrating their superiority in science, statecraft and a range of other cultural accomplishments, but without ceasing to be *kafirs*. To some it seemed that the Crusades had been revived in a much more virulent form. What could they make of this "great reversal"? Why had God permitted this to happen?

Many thought God was punishing His people for their sins or testing their faith. For others it was simply that God's will is inscrutable. But as European success continued and deepened, these answers became inadequate for more and more people. It seemed as if the historical process ordained by God had somehow gone off its track, as suggested by the quotation at the head of this chapter. How to understand this? What to do about it?

Pre-modern reform

Before discussing the responses to these questions, we must consider developments in the Islamic world on the eve of European imperialism. At this time as at all times, the Islamic tradition was not monolithic and static but diverse and in constant change, although the pace of change was slow by modern standards. The central lands had been going through a period of political decline in the eighteenth century and there was a certain sense of malaise, but there were also reform movements, as had been the case in such circumstances in the past. The two most important were the Wahhabi movement in central Arabia and the movements connected with Shah Waliullah of Delhi in India.

The Wahhabi movement was founded by Muhammad ibn 'Abd al-Wahhab (1703–92), an admirer of **Ibn Taymiyya**, who preached a strict interpretation of the Qur'an and ***Sunna*** and rejected rigid ***taqlid*** to later interpretations. He rejected popular

Sufi practices as ***bid'a*** and, indeed, ***shirk***, and his movement destroyed the tombs of *walis* and also of Shi'i *Imams* when it raided the shrine cities in southern Iraq. It took control of Mecca in 1803 and was defeated in 1818, but it had considerable influence on other reform movements. It survived out of the limelight during the rest of the nineteenth century and resurfaced in the twentieth to become the official doctrine of Saudi Arabia. Wahhabis do not call themselves Wahhabis but simply *muwaḥḥidūn*, people of ***tawḥīd***. Their doctrinal position is commonly labeled *salafī*, referring to their strict adherence to the Qur'an, the Sunna and the teachings of the *salaf*, i.e. the earliest generations of righteous Muslims. Salafism in various forms, both conservative and liberal, was to characterize many of the reform movements of the later centuries.

Shah Waliullah of Delhi (1701–62) was a **Naqshbandi** Sufi in the line of Ahmad **Sirhindi** and opposed what he considered the compromises with non-Islamic practices by both rulers and Sufis. He also stressed *ijtihad* over unquestioning *taqlid*. He called for economic reforms and was concerned to heal divisions within the community. He undertook to reconcile Sirhindi's *wahdat al-shuhud* with Ibn Arabi's *wahdat al-wujud*. He had considerable influence on later thinkers in India of various persuasions. His son issued a *fatwa* in 1803 declaring India to be ***dār al-ḥarb*** because of British rule, while one of his successors later led a ***jihad*** against the Sikhs and others still later fought against the British.

Responses to the challenge

Neither the Wahhabis nor Shah Waliullah were responding to the Western challenge, but they provided resources and precedents for many who later did respond. These responses may be grouped into four broad categories: traditionalism, Islamic modernism, secularism and Islamism. These categories overlap to some degree and each contains considerable diversity, but they are useful for analysis. In each we can consider only a sampling of the many people and ideas involved.

Traditionalism

Traditionalists have emphasized continuity with the past. Some became rigid in the face of the challenge from outside, but most continued making gradual changes in the recognized ways. For them the situation they faced was part of the oft-repeated cycle of flourishing and decline described by Ibn Khaldun and others, and the view that God was punishing Muslims for their sins or testing them was adequate explanation. They did not perceive that the Western challenge was deeper than this. When and to the extent that they did perceive it they ceased to be traditionalists.

Probably the vast majority of Muslims in the nineteenth century, including the lower classes and most of the ***'ulama'*** and Sufis, can be considered traditionalist.

Their attitudes and actions toward the imperialists varied from open resistance, which rarely succeeded, to reluctant cooperation. Mostly the *'ulama'* went along with practices and rules they disliked, dragging their feet or subverting where possible, following their time-honored practice of supporting rulers and seeking to advise them. Modernization, however, strengthened the rulers' position vis-à-vis them, with stronger administrative resources, greater control over the law (usually in the name of reform) and, in the twentieth century, the establishment of state-run schools that often displaced the ***kuttabs*** of the *'ulama'*.

With the spread of modernization and Westernization pure traditionalism became impossible to sustain, but we can speak of neo-traditionalism, which is strongly concerned for continuity with the past but also appreciates the depth of the Western challenge and selectively adopts Western ideas and practices. The Sufi movement, which maintained its strength through the nineteenth century and remains strong to the present, though not so all-pervasive as before, has generally become neo-traditionalist. To a considerable extent its more dramatic practices have been curtailed by reform. Several reformist ***tariqas*** were founded in the nineteenth century, such as the Tijaniyya and the Sanusiyya, stressing obedience to the Shari'a and criticizing local non-Islamic customs. These were founded without reference to European influence but eventually came into contact with it. The leader of the Sanusiyya led resistance to the Italians in Libya in the twentieth century and became king of Libya in 1951. Likewise, the movement of the Sudanese Mahdi began as a reform movement with local concerns and then defeated the Egyptians, already influenced by the West, in 1885 and were defeated by the British in 1899. The reformist Deobandi movement founded in India in 1867 established *madrasas* teaching both the traditional and rational disciplines. It combines these with a Sufi affiliation, while some of its organizational features show Western influence. It has been and still is very influential. Movements as diverse as the **Tablighi** and the **Taleban** in Afghanistan (see chapter 20) are connected to it. It has faced major competition, however, from the more popular and more traditionalist Barelvi movement founded somewhat later, which accepts many traditional Sufi practices and stresses the suprahuman characteristics of the prophet Muhammad. These are rejected by the Deobandis. Both now have political parties connected with them.

During the last century different kinds of neo-traditionalism can also be seen in Ayatollah Khomeini and his colleagues in Iran (see chapter 18) and in the Nahdlatul Ulama in Indonesia (see chapter 19). The former proclaims its resistance to the West while in fact adopting a lot from it, while the latter cautiously cooperates with Westernizing forces while drawing on traditional resources. As of the early twenty-first century most *'ulama'* and Sufis could probably be considered neo-traditionalist.

The conservative forms of Salafism in recent years may be considered neo-traditionalist (the liberal forms are discussed later). They wish to follow the *salaf* as closely as possible under modern conditions and are quite strict in matters related to ritual, gender and family concerns as well as being highly critical of Shi'is and Sufis. Conservative Salafism has been particularly associated with Saudi Arabia, both because of the "Wahhabi" background and because oil wealth has allowed the Saudis to put considerable resources into propagating it. In fact, conservative Salafism is widespread and has become increasingly prominent since about the 1980s. We will consider Salafis in Egypt and Indonesia in later chapters. The ***Ahl-i Hadith*** in South Asia is considered Salafi. Salafis are strong in the diaspora and among the transnational "terrorists" (chapter 20). In most cases Salafi groups have some kind of connection with Saudi Arabia.

We may distinguish several types or tendencies among conservative Salafis. There are the "establishment" *'ulama'* who in Saudi Arabia support the long-standing alliance between the Saudi government and the descendants of Ibn 'Abd al-Wahhab and follow the Hanbali *madhhab*. There are those who insist on absolute *ijtihad* and refuse to follow a *madhhab*. There are those who criticize the government but do not openly or forcefully oppose it, a position common at all times and in many places. Nasir al-Din al-Albani (d. 1999, see chapter 6), perhaps the most highly respected Salafi scholar, represented both of these tendencies. Others call more forcefully for reform, such as the *saḥwa* movement in Saudi Arabia since the 1970s. Still others seek to impose morality on society (*ḥisba*), sometimes forcefully. From this tendency came those who took over the Grand Mosque in Mecca in 1980, believing that one of their number was the *mahdi*. There are those who have turned to violence and terror against the West or their own rulers and are commonly called *salafi jihadis* (see chapter 20). The more politically oriented Salafis are often strongly opposed by the non-political Salafi as compromising the purity of doctrine and practice.

Islamic modernism

Among the educated and ruling classes there were those who perceived the deeper nature of the Western challenge and recognized that neither responding in the old ways nor haphazard copying of Western ways was sufficient. If Islam was the truth from God and if it applied to all areas of life it had to be profoundly rethought to meet the Western challenge. If the West, having received science and wisdom from the Muslims, had then surpassed them, it was because the Muslims had closed the gate of *ijtihad* and been satisfied with *taqlid*, thus stifling creative thinking, and because they had accepted un-Islamic superstitions and *bid'a*. (Modernists tend to use the terms *ijtihad* and *taqlid* in the sense of general creativity and rigidity, not just as *fiqh* terms.) Only the Qur'an and the true *Sunna* are completely authoritative though other sources are respected. The door of absolute *ijtihad* must be opened wide and the implications of the Qur'an rethought in the light of modern knowledge and practice. Modernists have also been more inclined than traditionalists to reject *hadith* that were weakly based.

They continue many of the concerns of the pre-modern reformers and many have been labeled *salafis* (especially the movement associated with al-Afghani and 'Abduh discussed later) but their intention is not only to remove corruption but also to open the way for modernization by limiting the range of past authority. *Bid'a* is to be replaced not by a strict following of the *salaf* but by ideas and practices appropriate to the modern age that represent what they see as the rational spirit of early Islam. They are sometimes called "liberal" or "progressive" *salafis*.

In practice modernist interpretation has often meant finding Islamic justification for Westernizing practices. One example is the interpretation of the Qur'anic passages on polygyny mentioned in chapter 6 (p. 94; also chapter 21, pp. 344–48) Also, it has been common to link Qur'anic concepts to Western ones. Thus ***shura*** (Qur'an 42:38), which traditionally has meant the obligation of the ruler to consult with others but not necessarily to follow them, is now often interpreted in terms of parliamentary government. Another approach has been to choose rulings from different ***madhhabs*** as appropriate to current needs, rather than being bound to follow one *madhhab*, as is the traditional expectation. The most thorough approach, as articulated by the twentieth-century modernist, Fazlur Rahman, is to reduce all the positive commands of the Qur'an (such as stoning for adultery or cutting off the hand of the thief) to underlying principles and then to apply these principles to the contemporary situation. This approach is not much applied in practice, so far as I know (but see chapter 20). Modernists do not ignore the scholarship of the past, but they are not bound by it and may try to use it in creative ways.

Modernist discourse usually looks in two directions. On one hand it seeks to persuade traditional Muslims to change their ways; on the other hand it seeks to convince Westerners and Westernizing Muslims that the things they criticize about Islam are not part of true Islam. Modernists also go on the offensive and criticize many aspects of Western life, not least its violence, its loose sexual mores, its racism, its use of alcohol, its extreme individualism and its rejection of legitimate authority. Other aspects of Western life, however, are appreciated, such as its order and discipline, its progressive mentality, its inventiveness, and its concern for the rights of the individual and good government. These will also characterize Muslims when Islam is properly understood and practiced. Islam once led the caravan of human progress. It has now fallen behind but with the needed reform it will take the lead again, adding to its own virtues the virtues of the West but avoiding the West's vices. One reason this is possible is that much of what is desirable in the West was originally learned from Muslim sources.

One of the first modernists was Sir Sayyid Ahmad Khan (1817–98), who was raised within the Mughul nobility and lived through the Bengal Mutiny (1857), which resulted in the official replacement of the Mughul Empire with direct British rule, and which left the Muslim community in India in disarray and on bad terms with the British. He was determined to improve the lot of his community. He argued that there was no call for *jihad* against the British since the Muslims had freedom to practice their religion and they had much to learn from the British. Among other things, in 1875 he established the Muhammedan Anglo-Oriental College in Aligarh, modelled on Cambridge University, which trained many of the next generation's leaders. One Englishman commented that he taught his people how to play English games and then how to beat them at their games. Sir Sayyid was a rationalist and believed that the Word of God (the Qur'an) could not contradict the work of God (nature). He gave naturalistic explanations of the miracles recounted in the Qur'an and claimed that angels are natural forces and the devil is a symbol of the unruly side of human nature. He believed that Shari'a law needed to be thoroughly reconsidered, using rational methods that took account of changes in society, while there were many areas, such as clothing, in which religious guidance was not needed or in which general ethical guidance was sufficient. For example, on the Qur'an's prohibition of usury (*riba*) he argued that this was to prevent poor people from being exploited, but there was no harm in charging interest to those who can pay and the community may benefit. Many other modernists share this view. Sir Sayyid worked for good relations among all the communities, Muslim and non-Muslim, in India but he discouraged Muslims from joining with Hindus in the Indian National Congress founded in 1885 as he did not consider it in their interest. By contrast, the Deobandi movement was to support the Indian National Congress in opposition to the British.

Two other important modernists in India were Ameer Ali (1849–1928), whose *The Spirit of Islam* has been mentioned in chapter 6, and Abdullah Yusuf Ali (1872–1953), whose translation of the Qur'an has been widely used among English-speaking Muslims. He included a modernist commentary but this is not always reprinted.

Another early modernist was Jamal al-Din "al-Afghani" (1838–97). He was an Iranian and known as "Asadabadi" in Iran, but in Sunni countries he claimed to be an Afghan to disguise his Shi'i background. He was a charismatic figure who inspired disciples but was far from a systematic thinker. The most consistent thread in his teaching was his opposition to European, especially British, imperialism. He, perhaps more than anyone else, taught Muslims to think of Europe as a danger. He was a critic of Ahmad Khan for this reason. He was constantly on the move, traveling in India, Afghanistan, Iran, Iraq, Istanbul, Cairo, Tehran and several European cities. Among his political activities were involvement in the Tobacco Protest in Iran (see chapter 18) and some implication in the assassination of the shah in 1896. He argued that religion was necessary for the well-being of society and Islam properly practiced would make its followers strong. He called on Muslims to adopt European science and technology and to reopen the gate of *ijtihad*, clear away the innovations that have weakened them and return to the early practices of Islam. It had made them strong then and would do so again. It is not clear, however, in what sense he thought Islam was true. In a letter to the French writer, Ernest Renan, he said that all religion is against science and that he was not defending Islam but the millions of Muslims. His political program, usually described as pan-Islam, seems to have been to find a strong Muslim ruler under whom the Muslims of the world could unite. The most likely candidate was the Ottoman sultan, who did make use of this idea but apparently not as Jamal al-Din would have wished. His utilitarian view of religion and his tendency to say different things to different people seem to reflect classical Islamic philosophy, which he would have studied in Iran. His most important disciple was Muhammad 'Abduh, who will be discussed in the chapter on Egypt.

Muhammad Iqbal (1876–1938) is generally considered the greatest Muslim philosopher of the twentieth century. Born in the Punjab, he was initiated into the Qadiri *tariqa* and later studied in England and Germany. He was active in the Muslim League (founded in 1906), which spearheaded the movement that led to the creation of Pakistan and is commonly called the spiritual father of Pakistan. His thinking and writing drew on Sufi ideas and themes, which he often transposed and reinterpreted. He was also influenced by European thinkers such as Nietszche, Bergson and Marx. His main philosophical work, *Six Lectures on the Reconstruction of Religious Thought in Islam*, was written in English and engages with a wide range of Islamic and Western thinkers. He was best known in India, however, for his poems in Urdu and Persian, which were written in the Sufi style. In two poems, entitled "Complaint" and "Answer to Complaint" (1911–12) he laments before God the lost greatness of the *umma* and receives the answer that this is the result of the *umma*'s own failings, especially its lack of activism and self-confidence. The main goal of his efforts was to restore these. His philosophy focuses on the self or ego and inverts the Sufi idea of ***fana'***. God is the supreme self in the universe and each human is a self, meant to affirm its individuality in a constantly evolving universe.

> If thou wouldst pass away (*fana'*), become free of Self: If thou wouldst live, become full of Self!
>
> (Iqbal, 1972, 99)

This self is to be characterized by love (***'ishq***), which is to be directed toward worldly goals as well as God. It is "the moving power of life which ... must be united with power".

Though greatly influenced by Europe he still saw Europe as a major hindrance to human ethical and spiritual advancement.

> The bottle of modern civilization is brimful with the wine of *la*
> Perhaps there is no cup of *illa* in the hands of the cupbearer.
>
> (Schimmel, 1963, 92)

The allusion is to the Sufi interpretation of the ***shahada*** according to which *La ilaha* means the destruction of all false gods and spiritual impediments and *illa Allah* is the affirmation of God.

Islamic law can and must evolve to meet present needs, without rejecting all of the past, and thus there is the need for absolute *ijtihad*, which he calls "the principle of movement in the structure of Islam" (Iqbal, 1971, 146), and it should be done now by Muslim legislative assemblies which include laypeople as well as *'ulama'*. In a letter to a colleague he stated, "For Islam the acceptance of social democracy in some suitable form and consistent with the legal principles of Islam is not a revolution but a return to the original purity of Islam" (Schimmel, 1963, 235).

Modernism became widespread in the twentieth century, primarily among "lay" thinkers and writers but also to some extent among the *'ulama'*. Specific forms of modernism vary with background, context and individual characteristics. They also vary with the form of Western practice or ideology to which they are attending, such as democracy, nationalism, socialism or even Marxism and in fact modernists may speak of "Islamic socialism" and "Islamic democracy". Two variants of modernism that do not have wide followings but represent interesting possibilities are those of Ghulam Ahmad Parwez (1903–85), in Pakistan, and Mahmud Muhammad Taha, in the Sudan. The former recognized only the Qur'an as binding and rejected interpretations based on *hadith*. The latter held that the Meccan part of the Qur'an, which contains general principles, is the permanent message of Islam, while the Medinan part of the Qur'an, which contains legal details and sometimes commands violence, was a concession to the social realities of Muhammad's time. It has now been superseded by the permanent message. This reverses the usual order of abrogation. Taha was executed for his views in 1985.

Although modernism has been widespread, it has rarely provided the official ideology for any nation-state. The main and possibly only example is the Pakistani constitution. Its preamble asserts that "sovereignty over the entire Universe belongs to Almighty Allah alone" and that the authority of the people is a "sacred trust" exercised "within the limits prescribed by Him" and that "the principles of democracy, freedom, equality, tolerance and social justice as enunciated by Islam shall be fully observed". Here, as often with modernism, it is hard to tell whether essentially Western ideas have been given an Islamic cover or whether there has been a genuine reinterpretation of Islam (and also, perhaps, of the Western ideas).

Secularism

Secularism in the Muslim world may be defined as the explicit withdrawal of some or all areas of public life from the guidance and tutelage of the Shari'a. Secularists wish to adopt modern ways without justifying them at the bar of the Shari'a. Usually they claim not to reject Islamic religion as such, but they do reject the proposition that Islam is a total way of life. In the political arena Islam is replaced with a secular ideology, usually nationalism, often in combination with liberalism or socialism. Secularism has commonly been justified as being required by "modern civilization", a vague but potent concept that means, in effect, the West. The West is supposed to have separated religion (here viewed as a conservative or reactionary force) from other areas of society in order to make progress possible. Only by doing likewise, secularists believe, can their nations become strong and fully independent in the modern world. Secularism also is seen as the appropriate solution when a society is divided by religion or sect. In fact, however, secularism in the Muslim world rarely if ever involves separation of religion and state; rather, the state almost always controls or tries to control the religious institutions and use them for its purposes. Most of the time certain areas of social life, designated "personal status" and including such matters as marriage, divorce and inheritance, are left under Shari'a law (which may be reinterpreted in a modernist way). Secularists may or may not be anti-religious. In fact, some are very pious in their personal lives. Though not wanting society to be run by Shari'a law as such they may want it to be guided by an Islamically informed ethics (where this concern is strong the line between modernism and secularism may not be clear). Secularists may also value the Islamic tradition as "heritage", often a very important part of the national heritage. For this reason they may engage in the same sort of apologetics in defense of that heritage as modernists do and they regularly take an interest in pan-Islamic concerns.

There was little open secularism before the twentieth century, although a few nineteenth-century figures, such as Chiragh Ali, an associate of Ahmad Khan's, did articulate a secularist position. More importantly, there were rulers who engaged in a practical secularism in that they often ignored Shari'a dictates, but this can be seen as continuation and perhaps intensification of what rulers often did in pre-modern times under the guise of *siyasa*. Secularism can, in fact, be seen as an intensification of *siyasa* with a new and more positive justification.

The most extreme forms of secularism were those practiced by communist governments, which were anti-religious and restricted religious practice as much as they could. Albania went the furthest, officially abolishing all religion from 1967 to 1989.

The classic example of secularism is Turkey, where reforms in the 1920s and 1930s located sovereignty in the Turkish nation, replaced Shari'a law with law codes derived from Europe, closed the *madrasas* and the Sufi *tekkes*, and took other measures that will be discussed in the next chapter. This was widely debated throughout the Muslim world and other countries adopted secular constitutions but did not go as far as Turkey. Sovereignty was located in the nation but Islam was usually the religion of state and Shari'a law was in force in some areas of public life. The cases of Egypt, Iran and Indonesia will be discussed in chapters 17 to 19.

The case of Pakistan is a distinctive one, since its first leaders were secularists but it was a nation based on Muslim identity and claiming to be an Islamic state. Muhammad Ali Jinnah, the leader of the movement for the partition of India when the British left and first president of Pakistan, had been an associate of Iqbal and was

Figure 15.1 Portraits of Jinnah (L) and Iqbal (R) are held during a rally in Lahore to mark Pakistan Day (March 2009). © RAHAT DAR/epa/Corbis

very Westernized in his personal life. He developed the theory, vaguely anticipated by Ahmad Khan and Muhammad Iqbal, that the Muslims and Hindus of India are two different nations and two different civilizations, with different religions, different social customs, different literatures, different and often incompatible heroes and historical stories, and cannot be yoked together in the same state. While he wanted a state for Muslims he did not want to institute Shari'a law in it. Religion would continue as personal faith but not as political identity. The opposition to this secularism has been considerable, however, and its history has been checkered, to say the least.

It should be mentioned that while modernists and secularists have accused traditionalists of *taqlid*, traditionalists have accused modernists and secularists of engaging in *taqlid* of the West.

Islamism

Islamism, sometimes referred to as "fundamentalism", appeared in the twentieth century as a reaction to secularism and modernism. For Islamists, the ideology of society must be Islam and the Shari'a must be applied in society. Secularism is attacked as an open replacement of God's laws with human laws and modernism as a veiled way of doing the same thing. For some Islamists nationalism is nation worship, thus *shirk*; for others it is acceptable if subordinate to a larger Islamic loyalty. Like modernists, Islamists hold that only the Qur'an and *Hadith* are fully authoritative and the gate of absolute *ijtihad* must be open. They insist, however, that *ijtihad* must be rigorously Islamic and not a cover for *taqlid* of the West. Also like the modernists, they wish to eliminate the *bid'a* and superstitions inherited from the past that traditionalists accept. On the other hand, they generally accept more of the tradition than do the modernists and Sunni Islamists particularly value the writings of people like Ibn Taymiyya. Their main concern, in any case, is with the *bid'a* coming today from the West and they are particularly inclined to anti-Western rhetoric. While some use violent methods, many limit themselves to education and propaganda (***da'wa***) while others involve themselves in politics. Sunni Islamists are often considered *salafis* although the conservative *salafis* often criticize them for not being strict enough and too inclined to make political compromises.

Islamism is definitely a modern phenomenon. Islamists more than others insist that it is possible to have modernization without secularization. It has especially appealed to people with a scientific or technical education and much less to peasants or workers. Its program would involve a more thorough application of the Shari'a, or a more thorough Islamization of society, as it is often put, than was the case in pre-modern times. For example, the call for an "Islamic state" is particularly characteristic of Islamism, but the state here is not the pre-modern state whose power usually did not go much beyond keeping order and collecting taxes, but the modern state, whose writ reaches every corner of the land and touches every individual. Such a state will Islamize society far more thoroughly than was possible before. Islamism would also Islamize the new activities and professions that have come into existence with modernity. As for non-Muslims in a Muslim society, Islamists usually call for *dhimmi* status rather than equality before the law, which is usually affirmed in principle by secularists and modernists.

Such phenomena as Islamic banking and Islamic economics can be considered aspects of Islamism. Where secularists would justify interest on loans as part of the modern world and modernists would reinterpret the basic sources to show that they are permitted, Islamists would retain the prohibition and revise the banking system to eliminate interest. There are those, also, who want to Islamize the social sciences, since in their present form they are based on secularist assumptions. There is also Islamic dress, primarily for women but also in some respects for men. Contemporary "Islamic garb" covers up as much as traditional garb, if not more, but is different in form and tailoring. It can be quite stylish and, in fact, a fashion industry for this garb has developed. The term "muhajababes" has been coined for the young women who are part of this scene. The appeal of things such as Islamic banking or Islamic garb is, however, broader than political Islamism and would include many who politically would be in other categories, even Muslim secularist. Islamic science seems to me to appeal to many who generally are modernist.

It should also be noted that in relation to politics the label Islamist is today often applied quite widely, to some who are more strictly speaking Islamic modernists (e.g.

Tendentious terms

The terms "Islamism" and "Islamist" are used here where many speak of "fundamentalism" and "fundamentalist". Since the latter terms are primarily used for Christian fundamentalism, many consider their use in the Islamic context misleading and unduly emotive. Islamist has therefore come into use as a more accurate and neutral substitute. Media usage in recent years, however, has tended to identify Islamism with violence, so that it is no longer as neutral as it was and some now reject the term as they earlier rejected "fundamentalism". Since it is not possible to keep ahead of the media's debasement of terms, I continue to use it for those who call for the application of the Shari'a in all areas of community life, especially government, in the modern context, whether they are violent or not. (As mentioned in chapter 1, Islamist must be distinguished from Islamicist, a scholar whose academic specialization is some aspect of Islam.)

The term "political Islam" is commonly used instead of "Islamism" but strictly speaking its meaning is both broader and narrower. It is broader in that virtually all forms of Islam have a political dimension; it is narrower, since Islamism includes more than politics. I prefer to keep the two terms distinct.

The term "secularist" is also tendentious for many Muslims, since it is commonly understood as anti-religious. This is probably even truer of the Turkish term, *laik*, which is usually translated as "secularist" and is associated with Atatürk's movement. Arabs who see themselves as secularist but not anti-religious often use the term *madanī*, which means civil or civilian. Islamists also sometimes use this term to mean a government that is Islamic but not run by the *'ulama'*. I am aware of no suitable alternative to "secularist" but stress that in this book it does not necessarily mean anti-religious.

Al-Nahda in Tunisia) or to neo-traditionalists who are highly critical of the West (e.g. Khomeini, many Salafis).

The best known Islamist organization is the Muslim Brothers, founded in Egypt in 1928 by Hasan al-Banna (1906–49). It became a mass organization within ten years and its program included a wide range of educational and social service activities, as well as a call for political reform. It spread to other Arab countries after the Second World War. It will be discussed in a later chapter, as will Islamist groups that have appeared in Iran and Indonesia and the Islamic Liberation Party, founded in 1952 by a Palestinian judge.

The Jama'at-i Islami was founded in India in 1941 by Abul 'Ala' Mawdudi (1903–79), a journalist who had been associated with Iqbal. Mawdudi favored the creation of Pakistan but opposed the secularism of Jinnah. After partition and

Figure 15.2 Cyclist rides past election posters and the party symbol of Jama'at-i Islami – Rawalpindi, Pakistan, May 2013. Courtesy of FAROOQ NAEEM/AFP/Getty Images

the establishment of Pakistan in 1947, Mawdudi and the Jama'at worked to make Pakistan a truly Islamic state. The Jama'at is a fairly elitist organization, unlike the Muslim Brothers, and has never done well in elections, but still has had considerable influence. Mawdudi's writings are clear and relatively consistent. They have been widely translated and disseminated and he has probably been the most influential Islamist writer.

He states that Islam is a "total scheme of life", distinct and not to be identified with some other system such as "democracy" or "communism", nor may people create "a new Islam to suit the values of their choice" (Mawdudi, 1981, 90). It is diametrically opposed to nationalism, including the "Muslim nationalism" of Jinnah. Islam is based on creed and morality and offers equal rights to all races and classes, while nationalism divides the human race on the basis of national interest and prejudice.

An Islamic state must recognize that God alone is sovereign and therefore must follow His law. Sovereignty of the people, in the sense of making law is excluded, but it is the people who are to run the state and elect the leaders who administer the divine law. Moreover, in many areas the Shari'a does not give specific guidance and here humans do legislate in accordance with the general principles of Islam. In other words, it is the people, not just the rulers, who exercise the ***khilafa*** that was first given to Adam. "The entire Muslim population runs the state in accordance with the Book of God and the practice of His Prophet." (Mawdudi, 1960, 132). He suggests the term "theo-democracy" for this. Women should have the vote but not be active in politics (in fact, though, he supported a woman for president of Pakistan in 1965). ***Dhimmis*** may participate in government but may not be head of state or occupy certain key government positions. ***Hadd*** penalties such as cutting off the hand of a thief apply only in a truly Islamic society characterized by economic justice and where the government guarantees the basic necessities of life to all. This position is taken by many Islamists.

Islamic law is not static but develops and evolves by *ijtihad*, which must be done by fully qualified *mujtahids* and must be a serious effort to understand the Shari'a and not an independent exercise of personal opinion, as some think. Islamic law in fact evolved over the centuries as long as it was applied, but for a century it has not been applied and a strenuous effort must be made to bridge that gap, so that its application and evolution can resume. Mawdudi accepts the idea of progress but it needs to follow the moral avenues laid out by Islam.

Resurgence of Islam

Since 1970 there has been a considerable increase in religious interest and expression across the Muslim world, often labeled a "resurgence" of Islam. One major reason appears to be a feeling that secularism has failed to deliver on its promises. Copying "modern civilization" has failed to close the gap between the Muslim world and the West materially or culturally. A prominent symbol of this was the disastrous defeat of Egypt and Syria by Israel in the Six Day War in 1967. There was a feeling that we have tried everything else, now let us try our own home grown ideology, Islam.

This "resurgence" has taken various forms. There has been increased attendance at the mosques, including a movement for women to become more involved, and increased participation in the fast of Ramadan and the *Hajj*. Sales of popular religious books have increased as has religious programming on radio and television. More than one preacher or religious teacher has become a media celebrity. Sufi groups have become more active. Islamic banking has taken hold and grown. Islamic dress has become one of the most prominent features of the resurgence.

In politics the "resurgence" has been marked by a striking growth and spread of Islamism. The most dramatic example, and probably the most significant, has been the Islamic revolution in Iran, to be discussed in chapter 18. Islamist activity resumed in Egypt after a period of repression, as we shall discuss in chapter 17. Also dramatic was the successful Afghan *jihad* against Russian occupation in the 1980s. In this struggle Islamists, secularists, modernists and traditionalists all participated, but then divided after the Russians were removed. (More will be said about Afghanistan in chapter 20.) Similar things have happened in other situations. An Islamist government also took power in the Sudan by military coup in 1990. In Pakistan Islamism was strongest under the military rule of Zia ul-Haq from 1979 to 1988, who introduced various "Islamic" laws and had the support of the Jama'at-i Islami for a time. Pakistan has supported Afghan Islamists for political reasons but at home Pakistan has been unable to decide between Islamism and a Muslim secularism. Saudi Arabia is a special case. It did not reach its strongly Islamic position in reaction to a previous colonial occupation or a previous secularism, as is usual with Islamism, but as a direct development from its Wahhabi origins. Thus it has made it easier to cooperate with the West to develop its oil resources while maintaining its Salafi character and using some of its wealth to support Islamist and Salafi movements elsewhere. At the same time, its rapid modernization from a very traditional base has led to severe social and moral tensions (that have produced people like Bin Laden, see chapter 20).

Many associate Islamism with violence and terrorism but this is simplistic and misleading. In fact, secularist groups also engage in violence and terrorism, such as groups connected with the Palestine Liberation Organization and some of the Kurdish groups. Violence, in fact, depends very much on the situation. For example, in Algeria the Islamic Salvation Front took part in the first stage of elections in 1991 and appeared set to win the second stage, but the secularist military government cancelled the second stage. As a result many of the Islamists turned violent and violence between them and the government continued for almost a decade, with atrocities on both sides.

The Shi'i Islamist group in Lebanon, Hizbollah, has gotten the most publicity for the success of its "suicide bombers" in getting American and French "peacekeepers" to leave in 1983 and its role in the withdrawal of the Israelis in 2000 and resisting them in 2006. But its greater strength lies in the social services it provides its followers and others. It also participates in elections and has become one of the major players in Lebanese politics.

In fact, Islamist groups sometimes cooperate with secularist governments, sometimes engage in the political process, sometimes engage in violence depending on the circumstances, as do other groups.

In spite of the resurgence of Islam, secularist governments still rule most of the Islamic world. As of 2010 only Iran and the Sudan had Islamist governments. Almost all secularist governments have become more Islamic, however, at least in appearance, since 1970. A clear example of this was Saddam Hussein in Iraq, who introduced various Islamic laws and symbols in the 1980s and put the phrase *Allahu akbar* on the Iraq flag.

While the failure of secularism is commonly given as a reason for "resurgence of Islam", another lies in the success of modernization. This has brought many traditional Muslims into the main steam of "modern" life but without divesting them of their religious beliefs. These people have felt uneasy with the Westernization and secularization that has accompanied modernization and many have transmuted their traditional faith into modernism or Islamism as a result, while others have found refuge in more modernized forms of Sufism or practicing more intensely the basics while accepting new popular forms, e.g. via the media. Even after four decades it is impossible to tell where this resurgence will lead and the "Arab spring" has not yet made it any clearer (see below).

The special case of Israel and Palestine

The words "Zionism" and "Israel" are among the most negative terms in the Muslim lexicon today, in part because the state of Israel (aka "occupied Palestine") is a particularly acute illustration of the basic problem of modern Islam, as described in the quote at the beginning of the chapter by Smith. Not only has land been taken away by force but it has been settled and is not likely to be returned. It was Western powers that made this possible and continue to support it and it was European Jews who created it. Israel is a European intrusion as much as were the medieval Crusades.

Moreover, traditional Muslim thinking puts Jews at a lower level than Christians. The Qur'an has both good and bad things to say about Christians, but it has only criticism for the Jews of Muhammad's time. Jews are viewed as disobedient to God (an attitude that can be found in the Bible also, though a bit more nuanced) and under His punishment. Also, for obvious reasons Jews were viewed as weaker than Christians, since there were no Jewish states. Moreover, Muslims in the past often welcomed Jews into their lands and allowed them to prosper. To have land taken by force by people who are perceived as weak, out of favor with God and ungrateful for past Muslim favors is triply galling. All of this is added to the fact that Jerusalem is the third holiest city for Islam and to the undeniable sufferings of the Palestinian people.

Zionism began in the late nineteenth century as a Jewish nationalist movement seeking a homeland for Jews, who were persecuted in much of Europe. Zionist settlement in the "land of Israel", then part of the Ottoman Empire and populated by Arab Muslims and Christians, began in the 1880s but increased considerably after the British took control in 1920 with a mandate to encourage it. It was stimulated by increasing anti-Semitism in Europe and by 1939 about a third of the population was Jewish. Arabs resisted, not very successfully, under the banners of nationalism (mainly Arab) and Islam. After the war violence increased as Zionists demanded increased Jewish immigration and independence, backed up by some terrorist actions, and Arabs resisted. United Nations efforts for partition failed and the British left in 1948. There followed the proclamation of the state of Israel and a war between it and the neighboring Arab states supporting the Palestinian Arabs. Israel won, occupying most of mandate Palestine, taking over much land owned by Arabs and displacing some 750,000 of them, who with their descendants remain displaced to this day. At the time much of the world saw Israel as a legitimate response to Jewish suffering, especially the Holocaust, and as an underdog vis-à-vis the more numerous Arabs, while Palestinian suffering got much less attention. After the "six day" war in 1967, Israel occupied the rest of Palestine and created more refugees, and ceased to be seen as the underdog.

Efforts to reverse this situation, whether by diplomacy or violence have failed. One response was the development of a Palestinian nationalism, largely secular, enshrined in the Palestine Liberation Organization (PLO), which until 1986 was committed to the termination of the state of Israel. The largest of its member organizations, Fatah, has a strongly Muslim constituency and ethos but a secular nationalist ideology. Other, smaller groups were Marxist in ideology and Christian in leadership and it was one of these that killed Israeli athletes in Munich in 1972. This and other armed actions by *fida'iyyin* (self-sacrificers) were seen as *jihad*, but of a secular sort. In the words of one person. "I'm proud to be a Muslim and it is important to me, but *jihad* to me means to fight strongly for something – it isn't part of religion to me ... " (Johnson, 1982, 76).

Palestinians shared in the general "resurgence" of Islam in the 1970s and 1980s, initially in peaceful ways. In December 1987, frustrated by both Israeli intransigence and Arab ineffectiveness, they mounted a popular uprising called the *intifada*, and two Islamist groups came to the fore, Hamas and Islamic Jihad, both with their roots in the Muslim Brothers, who had for some time been engaged in non-violent activities in Palestine. Islamic Jihad has limited itself to armed action while Hamas, the larger group, has had a considerable program of social and educational services, as well as engaging in armed action. According to its Charter, published in 1988, the Caliph 'Umar made Palestine into a permanent trust (*waqf*) for the Muslims and therefore *jihad* to regain all of it is a duty of every Muslim (***fard 'ayn***), while participating in peace conferences effectively makes *kafirs* arbiters over Muslims. It rejects the secularism of the PLO and sees itself as taking up the struggle for the whole of Palestine that the PLO has abandoned.

After the failure of a peace settlement in 2000 and a second *intifada*, Hamas turned to violent actions (terrorism in the view of much of the world) and was joined in this by a secularist group, al-Aqsa Brigades. In 2005 Israel withdrew its troops and settlers from Gaza, and the following year Hamas participated in elections to the Palestinian Legislative Council and was successful in Gaza. The following year it took control there by force, whereupon Israel virtually sealed off Gaza. This has led to considerable suffering for the Palestinians and continuing violence on both sides.

At present it is hard to see a resolution to this situaton, but many Palestinians and others take hope from Salah al-Din, viewed today as a great Muslim and nationalist hero. He threw the Crusaders out of most of Palestine about seventy years after they arrived and both the PLO and Hamas have been committed to repeating this history. I would guess, however, that the majority of Palestinians and Muslims worldwide would be reconciled to the existence of the state of Israel if a lasting peaceful arrangement could be made. Until that happens, Zionism and Israel will continue unfortunately to be prime symbols of evil and of their weakness for many Muslims.

The "Arab spring"

While Arab governments have proclaimed high ideals of Arab nationalism and Arab socialism, the reality has often been repressive dictatorships catering to a favored few, marked by corruption, presiding over stagnant economies and supported in varying degrees by Western powers. A growing youth population, while better educated than their parents, has suffered from lack of economic opportunities.

On 17 December 2010 a young unemployed Tunisian, university educated but unable to find any work but street vending and harassed in this by the authorities, suffered one too many humiliations and displayed his despair by publicly immolating himself. This triggered massive demonstrations by mostly young people venting their pent up rage at the existing regimes, first in Tunisia in December, and then in several other Arab countries in the following months. These demonstrations were apparently largely spontaneous and were coordinated via social media such as Facebook and Twitter.

In Tunisia the demonstrations soon forced President Ben Ali out and in October 2010 elections were held for a constitutional assembly in which a plurality of seats was won by Ennahda (al-Nahda), generally seen as "Islamist" although its leader, Rachid Ghannouchi, who returned from more than twenty years of exile in England, is better described as Islamic modernist (as defined earlier), holding that values such as justice, democracy and human rights are Qur'anic values. Ennahda formed a government with secularist allies and promised a constitution that would speak of democracy but not of Shari'a and has continued in power to the present (August 2013), though increasingly criticized by secularists who are suspicious of its longer-range goals and fear the influence of the Salafis, who call for a strict application of Shari'a law and are sometimes violent in their efforts. The assassination of two secularist politicians in 2013 has increased the pressure. The country has suffered economic stagnation and experienced continuing demonstrations. Nevertheless, there is still hope that the Tunisians will find their way to a stable and democratic government if the more moderate Islamists and secularists can work together and outmaneuver or outlast the more extreme elements.

Tunisia, in fact, represents the most hopeful continuation of the Arab spring to this date, except perhaps for Morocco, where the youth movement was somewhat defused when the king called early elections and allowed the winning Islamist party to form a government. Demonstrations began in Egypt in January 2011 and also soon led to the departure of the president. After some months of rule by a military council elections gave primary power to the party associated with the Muslim Brothers. An Islamist president was elected but later deposed, with a violent aftermath. More detail will be given in chapter 17. Likewise, mention will be made of the more recent developments in Turkey and Iran in chapters 16 and 18 respectively.

In Libya violent protests in February 2011 developed into an armed revolt that eventually defeated the government with the support of NATO air strikes and killed the leader, Mu'ammar Qaddafi. In elections in July 2012 a relatively liberal party did better than the party associated with the Muslim Brothers, but the government has had little success in controlling the various militias, who consider themselves the "revolutionaries", and the country has suffered continuing violence and disruption.

In Yemen demonstrations eventually forced the president, Ali Abdullah Salih, to hand over power to his vice-president, who was later elected president, but Salih remained in the picture as head of a political party. In Bahrain the demonstrations were met and eventually quelled by force. The government has held firm against further demonstrations. The majority of the population in Bahrain is Shi'i but the monarchy is Sunni. Although the demonstrations were billed as non-sectarian, most of the demonstrators were Shi'i, so that the government has been able to play on sectarian fears and fear of Iran to get Sunni support.

In Syria demonstrations calling for the end of the Baath regime were harshly repressed and in time developed into a bloody civil war between disunited rebels, some of whom are Islamists, and a determined and unrelenting government. Sectarianism exacerbates this conflict since the government is mainly **Alawi** (see chapter 8) and the population mainly Sunni; the sectarian character of the government makes it more united and its supporters more fearful of what might happen to them if they lose. At the time of writing the conflict is getting worse and may lead to military involvement by Western powers.

The Arab spring has been dramatic and undoubtedly significant. The youth who have spearheaded the movements were largely secularist and relatively well educated and concerned for such "Western" values as freedom, democracy and human rights. They demonstrated the ability of such a secularism to make its mark and even topple regimes, but they have also allowed Islamists to demonstrate their popular appeal though not an ability to govern successfully. For many the Arab "spring" has become an Arab "winter".

Post-Islamism?

As some of the larger Islamist groups have become more integrated into larger society (e.g. through successful social services) and as they have come closer to political power they have sometimes articulated a position that holds to Islamic values but does not seek to impose the Shari'a or establish an Islamic state.

Current examples include the dominant parties in Turkey and Tunisia. Many observers describe this as "post-Islamism", which might be defined as secularism or modernism that is colored by past Islamist convictions and activities and by many of the same moral concerns that originally led to Islamism. Some secularists believe that this is just a cover to gain power, after which they will revert to form. There is reason to believe that in many cases, at least, the change is sincere and represents a significant new ideological (or post-ideological?) departure. *Wa Allāhu a'lam* (And God knows best)!

Key points

- Probably the most important element in the Muslim experience of the last two centuries has been a sense that history has gone wrong, that Muslim societies have not prospered as they should.
- The main cause of this has been Western imperialism, although even before the impact of this there was a sense in some quarters that reform was needed.
- Zionism and Israel have posed the same issue in a particularly intense form.
- The responses have involved both acceptance and rejection of Western ways, in varying degrees.
- Traditionalists generally seek a minimum of change and change that is continuous with what went before.
- Modernists seek a significant reformulation of Islam in the light of the Western impact.
- Secularists want to create a social space not governed by Islam.
- Islamism wants to create a society whose governing ideology is Islam.
- Salafism forcefully rejects "innovations" (*bid'a*) not found among the early generations of Muslims, but takes both a "liberal" and a "conservative" form.
- Since about 1970 there has been a "resurgence" of Islam, which has involved many forms of Islamic expression.
- The "Arab spring" was sparked mainly by secular youth but has also given more scope to Islamists.

Discussion questions

1. "Modernization means Westernization." Do you agree?
2. It is stated at the beginning of the chapter that Napoleon's expedition to Egypt illustrates many of the characteristics of European imperialism. Can you mention some?
3. Is Islamism an attempt to return to the seventh century?

4. Is "resurgent" Islam a threat to the West?
5. Which thinker, movement or ideological position described here is most likely to "rehabilitate" Muslim history?
6. What was the "great reversal"? Were there any other "great reversals" in Muslim history?

Critical thinking box 15.1

Lord Cromer (British consul-general in Egypt from 1883 to 1907) is reported to have said, "Islam reformed is Islam no longer". To what extent has the last century proven this dictum true or false? Would any Muslims today agree with him?

Critical thinking box 15.2

Why have Salman Rushdie's book, *The Satanic Verses*, and the Danish cartoons of Muhammad caused so much debate and disturbance? (Material from chapters 5, 6 and 14 as well as this chapter are relevant. Some resources will be placed on the website.)

Companion website

Features examples of modernist and Islamist statements, further reading and weblinks on important figures.

Further reading

Voll, John Obert (1994) *Islam: Continuity and Change in the Modern World*, 2nd ed. Syracuse, NY: Syracuse University Press. (Probably the most thorough study.)

Smith, Wilfred Cantwell (1957) *Islam in Modern History*. Princeton, NJ: Princeton University Press. (A minor classic, less dated than the date of publication suggests.)

Rahmena, Ali (ed.) (1994) *Pioneers of Islamic Revival*. London: Zed. (Good introductory articles on the main figures, e.g. Abduh, Afghani, Iqbal, etc.)

Enayat, H. (1982) *Modern Islamic Political Thought*. London: Macmillan. (Well written, more attention to Shi'i thinking than most.)

Esposito, John (1992) *The Islamic Threat, Myth or Reality*. New York: Oxford University Press. (By a well-known scholar sympathetic to Islam.)

Ahmad, A. and von Grunebaum, G.E. (eds.) (1970) *Muslim Self-statement in India and Pakistan, 1857–1968*. Weisbaden: Harrassowitz (anthology). (Excellent selection of writings from various positions.)

Ali, Amir (1968) *Islam*. Lahore: Premier Book House. (Classic example of modernism in a short work.)

Al-Qaradawi, Yusuf (1981) *Islamic Awakening between Rejection & Extremism*. Herndon, VA: American Trust Publication and The International Institute of Islamic Thought. (By a leading contemporary "moderate" Islamist.)

Mawdudi, S.A.A. (1969) *Islamic Law and Constitution*, 2nd ed. Lahore: Islamic Publications. (Good example of his position on social and political issues.)

Ayoob, Mohammed (2008) *The Many Faces of Political Islam: Religion and Politics in the Muslim World*. Ann Arbor, MI: University of Michigan Press.

Khalifa, Abdul Hakim (1965) *Islamic Ideology: The Fundamental Beliefs and Principles of Islam and Their Application to Practical Life*, 3rd ed. Lahore: Institute of Islamic Culture. (Detailed presentation of a modernist position with socialist orientation.)

See also: Knysh, *Islam in Historical Perspective* (Chs 20, 22–23) [F]; Esposito, *The Oxford History of Islam* (Chs 12–13, 15) [F]; Robinson, *The Cambridge Illustrated History of the Islamic World* (Ch. 4) [F]; Lapidus, *A History of Islamic Societies*, Parts II & III (Ch. 4) [F]; Hourani, *Arabic Thought in the Liberal Age* [17]; Ernst, *Following Muhammad* (Ch. 4, Postscript) [1]; Kurzman, *Liberal Islam: A Sourcebook* [20].

16 *Ideology and politics in Turkey*

Secularist reform

> How happy is the one who says, "I am a Turk."
> (Atatürk)

In the middle of the sixteenth century the Ottoman Empire was possibly the most powerful state in the world (see chapter 4). By the nineteenth century it was "the sick man of Europe", although still the most powerful state in the Muslim world. This aptly illustrates at the political level the low state of the Muslim world at that time. In the twentieth century the Turkish subjects of that empire were to provide a dramatic response to that challenge at several levels, including the religious.

In this chapter

- Ottoman defeats and the reforms prompted by them
- The Ottoman "pan-Islamic" policy and claim to the caliphate
- "Turkism" among the Ottoman elite in the early twentieth century
- The nationalist and secularist Republic established by Atatürk
- The partial retreat from secularism since about 1950
- The Nurcu and Gülen movements
- Alevi revival since the 1980s
- The Turkish experience

Ottoman defeats and reforms

In 1683 the Ottomans besieged and almost took Vienna during a war with Austria and other European powers, but in 1699 at the end of that war they had for the first time to sign a peace treaty with Europeans as the defeated party. During the eighteenth century they had occasional successes but more defeats and lost more land to the Europeans. During the nineteenth century this decline accelerated and their Christian subjects in Greece and the Balkans developed nationalist aspirations

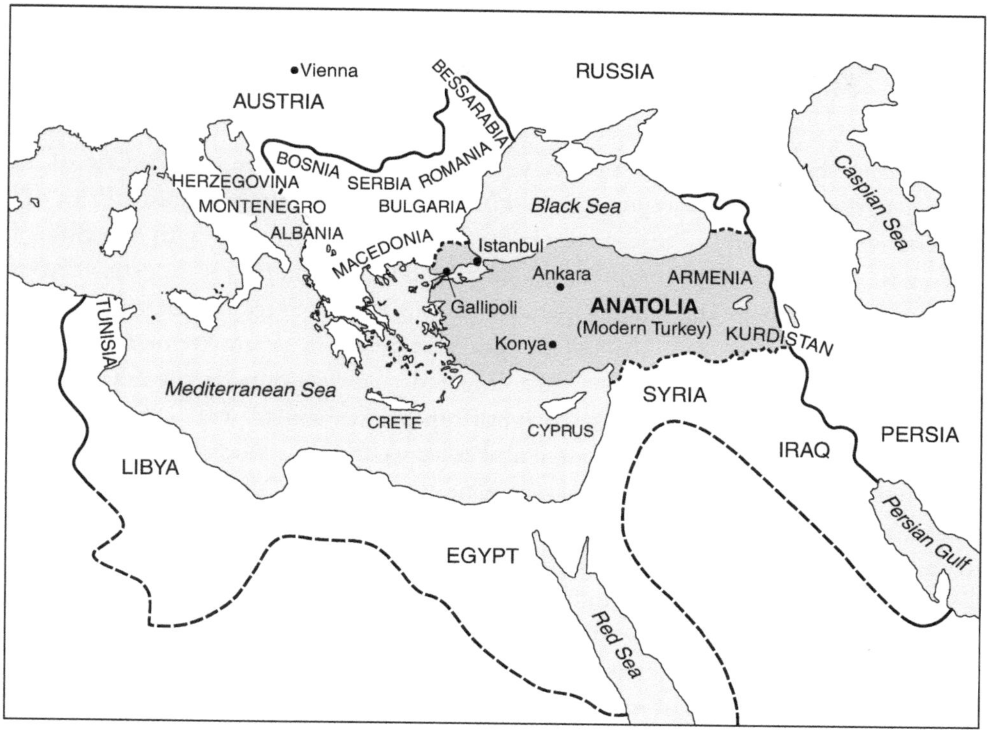

Map 8 Ottoman Empire and modern Turkey (shaded)

and were able to detach themselves from the empire with the help of the European powers. By the beginning of the twentieth century the empire had survived mainly because European rivalries allowed it to.

In the face of this situation efforts at administrative and military reform were made and there was a continuing tug of war between the Westernizers or "progressives", who saw the introduction of elements of Western technology and culture as both necessary to the survival of the empire and desirable in themselves, and the conservatives, usually acting in the name of Islam, who saw in these measures threats to their position and to the soul of their society.

The earliest reform efforts were successfully resisted by conservative forces, especially the Janissaries and the higher ***'ulama'*** (see chapters 4 and 9). In 1826, however, serious reforms were begun, after the Janissaries were brutally destroyed and the **Bektashi** Sufi order, closely associated with them, was suppressed. The earliest reforms included the creation of a new army with schools for the officers, some of whom were sent to study in Europe, a ministry of ***awqaf*** to give the government more control over these endowments, a postal service, and the opening of the empire to free trade, thus integrating it into the European economic system. Western garb began to be popular among the elite and the fez was introduced, a modified European hat with the brim removed so that the wearer could touch his forehead to the ground when doing ***salah***.

From 1839 to 1877 a more extensive series of reforms called Tanzimat (reorganizations) was undertaken. These began with an edict issued by the sultan recognizing the rights of life, property, honor and equality before the law of all religious groups, officially replacing the ***dhimmi*** system (though social realities did not change so quickly). These were claimed to be in accordance with the Shari'a although no ***fatwa*** was obtained. Later the death penalty for apostasy from Islam was abolished. The Shari'a penal and family laws were codified, and their administration taken from the *'ulama'* and put under a newly created Ministry of Justice. A commercial code was promulgated that was outside the Shari'a and based on French law. Civil courts, distinct from Shari'a courts, were established. A Ministry of Education was established and state secondary schools were developed. Thus both the legal and educational systems were divided into a state-run sector and an *'ulama'*-run sector. There was land reform, which gave full ownership of land to some, while others were reduced to the status of sharecroppers or hired labor. Technological developments included the telegraph and the beginnings of railroads. Newspapers also began during this period though the government tried to suppress some of them. One result of these efforts was government overspending that led to European administration of its debt.

Although there was talk of limiting the power of the **sultan** (in theory unlimited) and other liberal concerns, the main purpose of these reforms was to strengthen the central government, both vis-à-vis the provinces and vis-à-vis elements that might challenge it. Traditionally the role of the sultan had been to maintain a balance among the various elements in society. Now the government was to take charge and lead change.

An interesting, though short-lived, ideological group during this period was the Young Ottomans, who favored liberal reforms but sought to root them in a reformed Islam. They were among the first Islamic modernists. They were banned by the government in 1867.

Ottoman "pan-Islamic" policy and claim to the caliphate

In 1876 a constitution, based on that of Belgium, was promulgated, partly to impress Western powers. It was soon effectively suspended, however, by the new sultan, Abdul Hamid (r. 1876–1909), who then ruled as an autocrat. Reacting against the previous policy, which seemed not to have strengthened the empire against the West, he based his ideology on Islam, calling it *din u devlet* (religion and state). In general he favored a fairly traditional form of Islam and supported certain Sufi orders. But he and his supporters also propagated modernist arguments such as the claim that the West is materialistic but Islam properly balances materialism and spirituality, and that what is good in the West comes ultimately from Islam. In the 1890s he launched a pan-Islamic ideology, according to which he was caliph and thus the spiritual leader of all Muslims, and used it to seek support from Muslims outside the empire. This claim goes back to the Treaty of Küçük Kaynarca with Russia in 1774, when the Ottoman sultan claimed to be the protector of Muslims in Russian territory in response to Russia's demand to protect Orthodox Christians in Ottoman territory, but it began to be advanced seriously only about 1860. At the same time, the empire continued to modernize. Technological development continued. Schools spread as did newspapers, and popular literacy increased. In combining an assertive interpretation of Islam with an interest in modernization Abdul Hamid foreshadowed later Islamism. In reaction to his ideology at the time, however, many intellectuals opted for an uncritical pro-Westernism.

"Turkism" in the early twentieth century

By the first decade of the twentieth century, Ottoman reformers had three ideological options. One was to base the empire on a reformed and "purified", i.e. modernist, Islam. The second option was "Ottomanism", to create a multi-ethnic and multi-religious society in which all groups would be equal and would be loyal to the Ottoman state. This was the hope of most of the "progressives" at this time, but the defection of the Christian *millets* and the beginnings of Arab nationalism were soon to make it irrelevant. The third was "Turkism", to build society on a Turkish ethnic basis. This was hardly thought of in 1900 but was soon to become the effective if unstated policy of the government and was eventually to prevail.

In 1908 a successful revolution was mounted by the Committee of Union and Progress (CUP), which had begun as a secret organization in 1889 and was popularly known as the "Young Turks". Abdul Hamid was deposed in 1909. The CUP soon developed into a dictatorship and undertook a "Turkification" program among the minority groups. They took the empire into the First World War, calling for a *jihad* but receiving no response from other Muslim countries. They were responsible for the massacre of up to one million (Christian) Armenians, an event still much debated about and still a sore point for both groups; the Turks reject the claim of Armenians and others that this was genocide. Among the many factors were Christian–Muslim tensions (cf. Greeks, below) and fear that Armenians were helping the Russian enemy. They increased state control over religion by putting the Shari'a courts, *medreses*, and *awqaf* administration under secular ministries.

Nationalist and secularist republic established by Atatürk

The war saw the revolt of the Arabs, and defeat confirmed the dismembering of the empire. Moreover, in 1919 the Greeks invaded Western Anatolia seeking to recover what they considered their lost territories, in which there were still many Christians living. The sultan's government was powerless in the face of all this and, in 1920, signed the draconian Treaty of Sèvres, which confirmed the various territorial claims against the empire. At this point the Muslims of Anatolia took things into their own hands, under the leadership of Mustafa Kemal, the hero of Gallipoli and one of the few Ottoman war heroes, later to be known as Atatürk, "the father of the Turks". A Grand National Assembly was called together in Ankara. It declared the sultan's government deposed and mounted an army that defeated and drove out the Greeks. They were then able to negotiate the more favorable Treaty of Lausanne (1923) from the allies, establishing essentially the current boundaries of Turkey.

It is important to note that all of this was done in the name of Islam. Some 20 percent of the Grand National Assembly were *'ulama'* or leading Sufis and on the defeat of the Greeks Mustafa Kemal was given the title *ghazi*, an Islamic title traditionally given to those who fight the *kafirs* on the frontiers of Dar al-Islam. In 1924 there was a population exchange of Greeks from Anatolia and Turks from Greece, and whether one was Greek or Turk was determined by one's religion. The concept of a Turkish nation barely existed in 1918 among Turks. Among Westerners the word "Turk" had an ethnic meaning (earlier it had also meant Muslim) but in Turkish it meant a country bumpkin from Anatolia. The sense of Turkish national identity was created by these events and what followed. It is one measure of the extent of this accomplishment that a derogatory term such as "Turk" became a label of pride, summed up in the saying of Atatürk, "How happy is the one who says, 'I am a Turk.'"

Having driven out the Greeks in the name of Islam, Mustafa Kemal and his supporters undertook drastically secularizing reforms in the name of Turkish nationalism over the next decade and a half. His party, the Republican People's Party, ruled unchallenged until 1950. The reform measures included the following:

- The statement in the 1921 Constitution, "Sovereignty belongs unconditionally to the nation". Later constitutions have substantially the same provision. The sovereignty of the nation (or of the people) is a prime mark of a nationalist and secularist constitution.
- The provision making Islam the religion of state was deleted in 1928. Laicism (*Laiklik*) was explicitly written into the constitution in 1937.
- The abolition of the sultanate (secular power of the sultan) in 1922 and the caliphate (spiritual authority over the *umma*) in 1924. This officially terminated the Ottoman Empire and cut important symbolic ties to the rest of the Muslim world. The limitation of the caliphate to spiritual authority was already a major secularizing move.
- Separate Shari'a courts were abolished (1924) and Shari'a law was replaced with a civil code adapted from the Swiss code (1926).

- *Medreses* were closed (1924), replaced for a time by government schools for *imams* and a faculty of theology but these were closed by 1933. There was no religious instruction in state schools until 1949.
- The office of the Shaykh al-Islam was replaced with a government department controlling *awqaf* and paying the costs of mosques, etc. A figure with some degree of influence and independence is replaced by a department controlled by the government.
- Sufi ***tariqas*** were disbanded and ***tekkes*** closed after a Kurdish revolt in 1925 under the leadership of the Naqshbandi Shaykh Sa'id. Sufi orders were seen as hotbeds of superstition, but were also dangerous because they had the support of people and a tradition of independence of the government. On this Atatürk said: "The straightest, truest *tariqa* is the way (*tariqa*) of civilization. To be a man, it is enough to do what civilization requires" (Lewis, 1961, 405). (It should be noted that the Kurds, as Muslims, had supported the Turks against the Armenians, but then the government of the Turkish Republic refused to recognize the Kurds as a distinct ethnic group. This eventually led to a long-running Kurdish rebellion from 1984 to 1999. Only in the 1990s did the government recognize the Kurds as a distinct ethnic group. Thus nationalism divided two Muslim peoples.)
- The ***adhan*** was to be given in Turkish rather than Arabic (1932). This may have caused more resentment than anything else. It was reversed in 1950.
- People were expected to wear Western garb and the fez, in particular, was forbidden (1925). Veiling by women was discouraged. Note that in a century the fez had gone from being a Westernizing innovation to an intolerable symbol of tradition. Atatürk's statement on the subject speaks eloquently of his values and goals: 'It was necessary to abolish the fez, which sat on our heads as a sign of ignorance, of fanaticism, of hatred to progress and civilization, and to adopt in its place the hat, the customary headdress of the whole civilized world …' (McNeill and Waldman, 1973, 446)
- Polygyny was outlawed and men and women were given equal rights in divorce. Women were given equality in education and employment, and were given the vote in national elections.
- Arabic script was replaced with Latin script for writing Turkish (1928). Practically this had the effect of cutting off later generations from direct access to their written heritage. Also, Arabic script is closely identified with Islam, so that the change of script powerfully signals a turn from Islam to the West.
- History was rewritten to stress the continuity of Anatolian/Turkish civilization back to the Hittites and Sumerians, a typically nationalist move.

Obviously these measures are not secular in the sense of separating "mosque" from state. They clearly subordinate "mosque" to state. In doing this they constitute the final step in a development that had been going on for a century. At the same time,

Figure 16.1 Statue of Atatürk and Turkish flag. Courtesy of Shutterstock

Islam is and continues to be an essential part of Turkish identity, so much so that in common parlance no one is called a Turk who is not a Muslim, at least by cultural background. A non-Muslim may be a citizen of the Turkish Republic but not a Turk. Thus, for all that Kemalism seems anti-religious, Islam viewed as a cultural tradition is part of it and can contribute to the nationalist project, while religion as a purely private affair is acceptable to it. On the other hand, it is possible in this context to be an atheist Muslim just as it is possible to be an atheist Jew. In fact, Atatürk is said to have been agnostic in his personal beliefs.

Atatürk's statements illustrate the identification of "civilization" and "progress" with Western civilization and the use of these as almost religious symbols, typical of much secularism. "Modernity" likewise is identified as Western. He stated to a journalist, "Our aim is to establish a modern, therefore a Western state in Turkey" (Toprak, 1981, 144).

There is also a case for considering the ideology of Atatürk and his followers, called Kemalism, a kind of religion itself. There is some tendency to deify the nation or the state in the constitution (1983) since it speaks of the "Eternal Turkish nation", "sacred Turkish state", and "absolute supremacy of the national will", though this is, of course, found in other nationalisms. It has been suggested that for Kemalism today Atatürk is a "virtual deity", the military and political elite its clergy and Atatürk's Mausoleum in Ankara its Mecca. Certainly Atatürk's picture and sayings are everywhere to be seen in Turkey. It has also been suggested that his published sayings are functionally comparable to the *Hadith* of Muhammad, although one might also compare them to something like the sayings of Chairman Mao. There is unquestionably material here for any discussion about the relation of nationalism to religion or idolatry.

Partial retreat from secularism from about 1950

While Kemalism was the ideology of the ruling elite, it did not capture the hearts of most Turks. Outside the cities women remained veiled, Sufi orders continued underground and older ways generally prevailed. When, in 1945, the government decided to allow the formation of other political parties and to hold elections, it was found expedient to relax some of the restrictions on religion and to take some measures encouraging it. These were not sufficient to prevent the defeat of the Republican People's Party when the elections took place in 1950. The succeeding government was more favorable to religion and, generally, public religious expression has increasingly been allowed over the years, while religion has sometimes been something of a political football. Sufi *tariqas* have had considerable behind-the-scenes political influence and have owned a number of media outlets.

Still, governments have remained committed to secularism and to maintaining considerable control over religious expression. The military remains firmly committed to Kemalism and has been the ultimate arbiter in politics until recently. Four times it has intervened in civilian politics (1960–61, 1971–73, 1980–83, 1997) when the generals felt things were out of control, the first three times forming a government of its own for a period of time. Not all of the reasons have been related to religion but some have.

Among the measures favorable to religion have been the appointment of military chaplains (1941), permission to get foreign currency to go on *Hajj* (1948), recitation of the *adhan* in Arabic, the airing of religious radio programs (1950), teaching of religion in primary schools, initially as an elective (1949) but near compulsory later, the opening of schools for *imams* and preachers (1949) and the establishment of a Faculty of Divinity in Ankara University and later elsewhere. In the 1960s politicians began to mention God in their speeches. Turkey has been a member of the Organization of the Islamic Conference since its founding in 1969. Women's head coverings appeared in the 1970s and have been a source of considerable debate, being banned in the universities and the government service. The state-run *imam* and preachers' schools have become something of a parallel system to the regular

Figure 16.2 Mevlevis ("whirling dervishes") and musicians perform for visitors in the event hall of the Sirkeci Train Station – Istanbul, Turkey (2005). Courtesy of Shutterstock

state schools since their graduates were eventually able to get jobs in state schools and government service. With these schools and the theological faculties the state has sought, with some success, to train *'ulama'* who are attuned to secularism. From 1983 to 1993 Turgat Özal, known to be a practicing Muslim in his personal life and a Naqshandi follower, was president. He relaxed state control of society to some degree and this opened more room for religious activities.

In 1969 an Islamist party was formed under the leadership of Necmettin Erbakan, first called the National Order Party and then the National Salvation Party. It has had a close relationship to the Naqshbandi *tariqa* and has adhered to an ideology its founder called National Vision (*milli görüş*). It has called for a "just order", which may be taken as the Shari'a or simply as less corruption. This ambiguity is presumably intentional since it would not be permitted to call openly for the Shari'a or even to have Islam in its name. One member has described the party as Islamic with a "secularist overcoat". It uses considerable nationalist rhetoric and calls for industrialization. It draws support from technically educated people and business communities in the provinces. Erbakan has a background in industrial technology. The source of its support is typical of Islamism generally but its nationalism and Sufi connection are not. Although usually labelled Islamist it has been described as neo-Ottoman and, strictly speaking, should probably be considered neo-traditionalist.

The party has periodically been banned and resurfaced under a different name. It has polled roughly 10 to 20 percent of the vote and participated in some governments. Of all the parties it has apparently been the best at grass roots organization and women have played an important role here. In the 1970s it, along with the National Action (fascist) Party and leftist parties, was involved in considerable political violence that led to the military intervention in 1980. In 1995 as the Welfare Party it gained the largest number of votes and Erbakan became prime minister in coalition with a secularist party. He was forced out by the military after two years on the grounds of his presumed Islamist agenda and the party was again banned, to resurface as the Virtue Party, which was banned in 2001. It appears that much of the party's vote has been a protest vote. A researcher reports one voter as saying he voted for the Welfare Party because of government corruption, inflation, unemployment and inadequate public services. When asked if he wanted the Shari'a enforced he said he was sure that the generals would prevent that.

After the last ban, the party split and the more liberal group took the name of Justice and Development Party (AKP), which is often called "post-Islamist". It supports secularism understood as the relative impartiality of the state toward different religious and philosophical beliefs, in contrast to the more aggressive secularism of the Kemalists, but, on two major flashpoints, it favors more support to Muslim religious education (which is supported and run by the state) and opposes the ban on women's headscarfs in universities. Its detractors question the sincerity or at least the wholeheartedness of its secularism. It was elected to power in 2002 and has been reelected twice. In its early years it enacted measures, such as the abolition of the death penalty, greater freedom for the media, limited cultural rights for minorities, such as the Kurds, that can be described as liberal but not as distinctively Islamic. Unlike Erbakan's party, it actively seeks membership in the European Union. It has also sought to improve relations with its Muslim neighbors. For example, it allowed a Turkish ship to try to break the Israeli blockade of Gaza in 2010. It has drastically diminished the power of the military, long the ultimate authority in politics and bulwark of secularism.

In recent years, however, the prime minister, Recep Tayyip Erdoğan has appeared to many to become dictatorial and intolerant of opposition, among other things intimidating and arresting journalists and political enemies. On 28 May 2013 a small protest began against a plan to cut down trees in an Istanbul park for new buildings. After a harsh police response and an uncompromising stance by Erdoğan it swelled into massive demonstrations in many cities calling for the resignation of the government. While the majority of demonstrators are young and apparently secular, a very wide range of political and religious views is represented. It has not been not a secularist attack on (post-)Islamism nor a rejection of the political system as such, but is focused on the perceived failings of a particular government. The demonstrations have galvanized opposition to the government but seem unlikely to remove it since it still has considerable support. The outcome of these events is still not clear at the time of writing (August 2013).

The Nurcu and Gülen movements

A movement with Sufi roots and wide influence is the Nurcu movement, based on the teachings of Badiuzzaman Said Nursi (1876–1960). Nursi was an educational reformer before the First World War concerned especially to combine modern science and religion in the curriculum but found Atatürk's aggressive secularism unacceptable and withdrew from public life, being exiled by the government for some time. His main achievement during this time was a vast commentary on the Qur'an, *Risala-i Nur,* which covers a wide range of topics and particularly seeks to show that the Qur'an is consistent with modern science and technology. While he hoped eventually for a Shari'a-based society, his immediate goal was to strengthen and enlighten the faith of individuals. He developed a following that consisted of a large network of people who meet in study sessions to discuss his writings. Since his death the movement has grown considerably both in Turkey and worldwide. Its emphasis is not political although it has supported different political parties over the years and many secularists are suspicious of it.

One offshoot of the Nurcu is an apparently loosely organized movement led (or at least inspired) by Fathullah Gülen (1941–). It includes a network of businesses, media outlets and charitable organizations and sponsors conferences that involve many respected scholars, but is especially known for its schools, both in Turkey and abroad. In these Islamic ethics and ethos are taught "by example" but there are no classes in Islamic doctrine. Gülen is revered by his followers as an inspirational and moderate leader and the movement stresses openness and tolerance but its detractors claim it is secretive and suspect it of political ambitions and an Islamist agenda. It is said to place its supporters in key government and business positions. In 1999 Gülen was threatened with prosecution for opposing secularism. He moved to the United States and the movement has prospered there. In recent years it has supported the AKP but there have also been tensions between them.

Alevi revival

The Alevis comprise 15 to 25 percent of the population of Turkey but have been largely invisible to outsiders. They were persecuted under the Ottomans and hence resorted to ***taqiya***. They supported Atatürk's movement, which ended persecution but could not eliminate popular prejudice against them. Moreover, the cultural uniformity enforced by the republican government worked against their maintaining their distinctive customs and practices. In politics they have tended to support left-wing parties, and to become very secular. All of this resulted in a situation in which their esoteric religious teachings, traditionally passed on personal instruction by spiritual teachers known as *dedes*, were in danger of being lost. Since the 1980s there has been a considerable cultural revival among them and also an effort to revive spiritual teachings and practices and put them in more modern form.

The Turkish experience

There are some interesting anomalies in the Turkish experience. For example, it is said that the politicians took the decision to allow the *adhan* in Arabic over cocktails. In one town alcohol was prohibited near Atatürk's statue (Atatürk was a heavy drinker) and I saw people at Atatürk's mausoleum reciting the ***Fatiha*** for him. As for attitudes toward political Islam, in a survey in 2000 some 60 percent opposed the existence of a religiously based party although 46 percent reported that they pray five times a day, 84 percent of the men reported that they attend mosque for Friday *salah*, and 91 percent give ***zakat***. In general, the Turks have come to accept both secularism and Islam, but they are still trying to work out exactly how to relate them.

Key points

- The Ottomans were one of the first Muslim states to experience the growing power of Europe.
- Their response was to undertake Westernizing reforms while retaining their Islamic faith and institutions, but the result was significant changes in these institutions.
- The reforms did not, finally, save the empire but they did prepare the way for the next stage, that of nationalism and secularism.
- Turkish secularism does not mean separation of "mosque" and state but state domination of "mosque".
- Turkey has had an active Islamist party and the present governing party (2013) is derived from it.
- Sufi orders are still strong, though officially banned, and the Nurcu and Gülen movements, partly derived from Sufism, are popular and active. The Gülen movement is especially active in education and has spread beyond Turkey.
- The people of Turkey remained largely religious but most seek to be secular also.

Discussion questions

1. Based on the Turkish experience and your knowledge of other situations, would you say that nationalism is idolatry?
2. In the 1950s Wilfred Cantwell Smith thought the Turks represented the most successful Muslim response to imperialism and modernization, spiritually as well as materially. Do you agree for the 1950s? For the present?
3. On the basis of what you know, why did the Turks treat the Armenians so harshly?
4. In what ways are the Alevis important? Why do outsiders know so little about them?
5. Do you think the AKP represents the view of most Turks on the question of secularism?

Critical thinking box 16.1

The following comes from an interview with Fathullah Gülen published in the *New York Times*, Friday, 18 February 2011. How and where do these ideas fit into the Turkish ideological scene today?

> In our times, democracy is still trying to perfect itself. We should try to develop a democracy that is going to be able to respond to all the demands of humanity – a humanity that will not find fulfillment in anything other than God's favor and the promise of eternity.
>
> This issue should be put out on the table and opened up for discussion. I think that democracy should be encompassing enough to fulfill humanity's material and spiritual longings. Human beings should be able to live freely in accordance with what they believe, and democracy has to prepare such an environment for them.
>
> If you like, you can call this "democracy with a spiritual dimension". This means a democracy that includes respect toward the rights and freedoms of human beings and that ensures freedom of religion and at the same time prepares an environment where people can practice their beliefs freely and pursue a life of their own conscience. Furthermore, this means a democracy that assists people in fulfilling their desires concerning eternity.

http://rumiforum.blogspot.com/2011/02/new-york-times-full-interview-with.html#ixzz2WkGyxxUo (accessed 27 August 2013)

Critical thinking box 16.2

This chapter ends with the words, "The Turks have come to accept both secularism and Islam, but they are still trying to work out exactly how to relate them." Do you agree? If so, what do you see as the possibilities? Can you specify how particular individuals or groups relate them? If you disagree with the statement, why?

Companion website

Includes population figures, quotes from Atatürk, selections from the 1982 constitution, a comment on Sufi practices and weblinks for various individuals and movements.

Further reading

Berkes, N. (1964) *The Development of Secularism in Modern Turkey.* Montreal: McGill University Press. (A major study, detailed and still useful. Secularist point of view.)

Toprak, B. (1981) *Islam and Political Development in Turkey.* Leiden: Brill. (Both informative and perceptive, also still useful.)

White, Jenny, B. (2002) *Islamist Mobilization in Turkey: A Study in Vernacular Politics.* Seattle, WA: University of Washington Press. (Presents the practical, "on the ground" aspects of Islamism as well as the larger pictures. Very perceptive.)

Kinzer, Stephen (2001) *Crescent and Star: Turkey Between Two Worlds.* New York: Farrar, Straus & Giroux. (Well written study by a journalist that effectively portrays the reality of modern Turkey up to 2000. Author stresses the need for more democracy.)

Pope, Nicole and Pope, Hugh (1997) *Turkey Unveiled: Atatürk and After.* London: John Murray. (Journalistic account, perceptive with interesting details, not profound. Chapter 18 is good on religion.)

Yavuz, M. Hakan and Esposito, John L. (eds.) (2003) *Turkish Islam and the Secular State: The Gülen Movement.* Syracuse, NY: Syracuse University Press. (Background on Nurcus as well as a good, generally favorable, account of the teachings and policies of the Gülen movement.)

See also: Voll, *Islam: Continuity and Change* [15].

17 *Ideology and politics in Egypt*

Between secularism and Islamism

> Islam in Egypt is Islam without fanaticism, Islam without extremism ... Indeed, the Egyptian personality is moderate in its religiosity and behavior, middle-of-the-road in its thought and practice, neither excessive nor negligent, and from here were the riches of civilization.
>
> (From a high school textbook)

While Turkish leaders responded to the Western challenge in the most dramatic way, it is fair to say that the Egyptians have provided for the whole *umma* more leadership and inspiration across the ideological spectrum than any other one nation and have attracted more academic attention. Partly for this reason I deal with Egypt in greater detail. Like Turkey, the Egyptians have secularized, but to a lesser degree and less definitively; their retreat from secularization has been greater but more ambiguous. Also, whereas Turkey virtually eliminated its non-Muslim minorities, Egypt still has a strong Coptic Christian community comprising about 10 percent of the population that is culturally homogeneous with the majority.

In this chapter

- The beginnings of modernization and secularization in the nineteenth century
- Muhammad 'Abduh and Islamic modernism
- Nationalism and secularization in the early twentieth century
- The beginnings of Islamism; the Muslim Brothers
- Revolution: support, control and repression
- Resurgence of Islam
- The "Arab spring" in Egypt

The beginnings of modernization and secularization

Egypt became part of the Ottoman Empire in 1517, but the **Mamlukes**, who had ruled previously, continued to run the country under the loose control of the Ottoman governor. During the last decades of the eighteenth century Mamluke rule degenerated into considerable anarchy as the Mamluke leaders fought with each other, but economic activity was strong. Sufi ***tariqas*** flourished, as did the ***'ulama'***, who often mediated between the people and the rulers. More than a fifth of the land was held by ***awqaf***, which were managed by *'ulama'* and often used for the benefit of their institutions.

The French occupation from 1798 to 1801, described in chapter 15, effectively destroyed Mamluke authority and left a power gap. The *'ulama'*, who had led revolts against the French, briefly stepped into this gap and then supported the choice of Muhammad 'Ali (r. 1805–49), an Albanian officer in the Ottoman army, as governor. His ambition was evidently to take control of the Ottoman Empire using Egypt as his base. To do this he had to remove or neutralize those who might threaten his control and also to institute a number of modernizing reforms. He dealt with the Mamlukes in 1811 by inviting their leaders to a ceremony and having them all slaughtered.

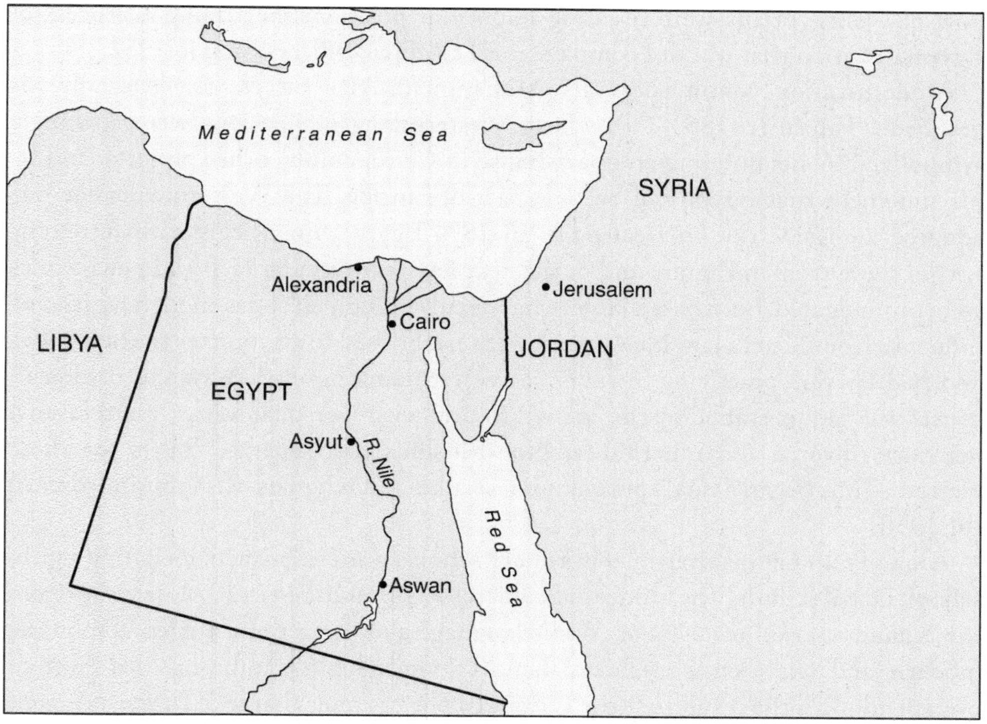

Map 9 Egypt

He attacked the power and independence of the *'ulama'* by exiling some of the most influential and by attacking their economic base. He confiscated the *awqaf* that provided their institutions with income, replacing these with government grants at a lower level. He also replaced the *iltizam* (tax farming), in which many *'ulama'* participated, with direct taxation. The result of this was a decline in the ***madrasas*** and other *'ulama'*-run institutions during the nineteenth century. He never openly violated the Shari'a but also showed little respect for the *'ulama'*'s views. Authority over the *tariqas* and their shrines was given to the ***shaykh*** of the Bakriyya *tariqa*. This authority was somewhat amorphous at first and never complete, but served to increase government influence on the *tariqas*. At this time virtually all adult male Muslims were connected with a *tariqa*.

Modernizing reforms included the establishment of specialist schools for the military in subjects such as language, medicine and engineering, with many of the teachers being Europeans. Muhammad 'Ali's designs on the **Ottoman** sultanate were eventually stymied by the Europeans but he had started a modernization process that had sufficient momentum to keep going. Today he is respected as the "Great Modernizer" but is loved by few, if any.

In 1850 the Ottoman commercial code, based on the French code, took effect in Egypt and in 1855 the law abolishing ***jizya*** and granting legal equality to religious minorities also took effect. The political elite had been Turkish-speaking but now native Egyptians were reaching important positions, beginning a process of Egyptianization that was not complete until the Free Officers coup in 1952.

Modernization continued under Muhammad 'Ali's successors, especially his grandson, Isma'il (r. 1863–79), whose Westernizing inclinations were strikingly symbolized by his building an opera house in Cairo, among other projects, and by his statement that Egypt had become part of Europe. The Western calendar was adopted alongside the ***hijri*** calendar. In 1874 Egypt gained legislative autonomy within the Ottoman Empire and in the next few years secular civil and penal codes were promulgated, both based largely and openly on French codes though with some influence from Shari'a law. New courts were established to administer the new codes and had lawyers practicing in them, a Westernizing novelty. A system of Shari'a courts was set up, staffed by the *'ulama'*, to deal with "personal status" matters such marriage, divorce and inheritance. Non-Muslims had separate courts for these matters. Thus began a dual court system, secular and religious, that continued until the 1950s.

A small number of government primary schools was established, including a girls' school. Dar al-'Ulum (The House of Sciences) was established in 1872, separate from the **Azhar**, to train teachers of Arabic language and, for a time, judges, combining modern and traditional methods. Isma'il's modernizing ambitions led him to overspend, with the result that the European powers took charge of the government finances and got Isma'il removed.

Figure 17.1 Skyline of Cairo, known as the city of a thousand minarets (those pictured here are of Mamluke style). Courtesy of iStockphoto

This situation prompted army officers led by Ahmad 'Urabi to demand a constitution that would limit the ruler's powers. Their grievances included preference given to Turkish-speaking officers over Arabic-speaking officers in the army and the European intervention. This movement was described by its partisans as a ***jihad***. The British responded in 1882 by sending in military forces and occupying the country, an occupation that lasted for forty years. They did not remove the existing government but British "advisors" largely determined policies and made a number of administrative and economic reforms. State and private (non-*'ulama'*) schools continued to develop, though most Egyptians believe that the British did not encourage education enough.

Muhammad 'Abduh and Islamic modernism

One of 'Urabi's supporters was Muhammad 'Abduh (1842–1905), an Azhari who had been a close disciple of al-Afghani (see chapter 15) when the latter was in Cairo in the 1870s. He was exiled after the 'Urabi movement and collaborated with al-Afghani in Paris in 1884 on a short-lived but influential newspaper. His path diverged from al-Afghani's, however, when he became convinced that the struggle for Egyptian independence was premature and that Egypt needed a period of European tutelage before she could become truly a part of the modern world. He returned to Egypt in 1888, where he became a judge in the new courts and was appointed to the

Legislative Council, an advisory group to the government. He was also appointed to the administrative council of al-Azhar where he worked with partial success for administrative reforms. He was appointed ***mufti*** of Egypt, in which capacity he worked for reforms of the Shari'a courts and gave ***fatwas*** on matters of public interest. He also responded to requests for *fatwas* from outside of Egypt. He was a "liberal" ***salafi*** (as described in chapter 15) in the sense of wanting to revive the spirit of early Islam while flexibly meeting current needs. ***Ijtihad*** should be bound only by the Qur'an and the best attested ***hadiths*** and should follow *maslaha,* the interest of the community, broadly interpreted. In his *fatwas* he ruled, for example, that Muslims could eat meat slaughtered by Jews and Christians and take bank interest.

He claimed that Islam is a rational religion, de-emphasizing miracles but not going quite as far in this as Sayyid Ahmad Khan. As for the miracles ascribed to ***walis,*** he says that no one is obliged to believe them, a position that may seem cautious but was fairly radical, given that many Egyptians believed that anyone who denied such miracles was a ***kafir.*** Right and wrong can largely be discovered by human reason, though prophets are needed for some matters and to provide certainty and full authority. Muhammad's message provides the final revelation that a rationally mature humanity needs. He contrasts the rationality of Islam with what he sees as the miracle mongering and authoritarianism of Christianity. He interprets the ideas of *qadar* (predestination) and *kasb* (acquisition) in the direction of genuine human choice rather than predestination, while recognizing the ultimate divine control over all things. His positions were often close to those of the **Mu'tazila.** He also opposed *takfir,* the practice of declaring people *kafir* because of sectarian or doctrinal differences. He is probably the best known and most influential of the modernist reformers, both in Egypt and beyond.

Nationalism and secularization in the early twentieth century

By 1900 Egypt was divided between a small "effendi" class, who lived a Europeanized life style and a large "traditional" population. The numerical difference is suggested by statistics from 1899 indicating that there were 7,735 students in state schools and 180,000 students in the ***kuttabs*** of the *'ulama'.* The effendi class, however, had disproportionate political and cultural influence and saw itself as the wave of the future. Among these were many who were keen to end the British occupation. Mustafa Kamil, a charismatic (or demagogic, according to his critics) politician called for the immediate departure of the British from Egypt but died in 1908, before he could accomplish much. His interpretation of Islam was modernist, identifying the "real" Islam with patriotism, justice and tolerance, but his main focus was Egyptian patriotism.

Qasim Amin (1865–1908), a disciple of 'Abduh, stirred up considerable controversy with two books on the emancipation of women, the first argued in a modernist manner from the Islamic sources but the second argued in a secular manner from science, freedom, progress and civilization. In both he stated that women must be given at least a primary education and be freed from the veil and seclusion so that they can properly manage their families and raise successful children. Only by following the West in these matters could the nation become strong. Effectively he called for the replacement of the existing form of male dominance with a Western form of male dominance. Other reformers in the following decades also argued that the emancipation of women was necessary for the welfare of the nation, an argument to be made by many others.

Nationalist and patriotic feeling increased in Egypt during the First World War and led to a movement for independence under a former colleague of 'Abduh, Sa'd Zaghlul (1857–1927). A popular revolt in 1919 led to the end of the British occupation in 1922, although the British retained certain privileges, including control of the Suez Canal. This revolt was in a secular nationalist mode, with Muslims and Christians cooperating. One of its slogans was, "Religion is for God but the fatherland is for all." On independence the ruler from the line of Muhammad 'Ali took the title king and a parliament was elected. The constitution stated that all authority stems from the nation, that Islam is the religion of state, but that there is freedom of religious belief and all Egyptians are equal before the law.

Women played a prominent role in the 1919 revolt and in 1923 an upper-class woman, Hoda Sha'rawi, founded the Egyptian Feminist Union and prominently discarded her veil, as other women of the effendi class soon did. The feminist movement at this time was both strongly nationalist and strongly Westernizing.

After independence there was a considerable expansion of state education at all levels, while the traditional *kuttabs* and the Azhar system lost ground. By 1970 there were some five million students in secular primary and secondary schools while students of the same level in religious schools, now organized under the Azhar, numbered only about 83,000. In 1966 religion constituted about 11 percent of the state primary curriculum. The first university was founded in 1908 as a private institution and was taken over by the government in 1925. Other universities were established from 1942. Reform of the Azhar itself was limited since the *'ulama'* resisted losing control, but it still continued to draw students from throughout the Muslim world. Education for women increased dramatically from the 1920s and the first women entered university toward the end of that decade.

Atatürk's abolition of the caliphate in 1924 occasioned much debate in Egypt. Out of the debate came the best known defense of secularism on Islamic grounds, *Islam and the Bases of Government* (*Al-islām wa-uṣūl al-ḥukm*), written by 'Ali 'Abd al-Rāziq (1888–1966) in 1925. Its argument is that the caliphate is not clearly stipulated in the Qur'an or the ***Sunna***, a point generally recognized, that there had never been a true ***ijma'*** on it, and that this particular form of government could not be shown to be necessary for the welfare of the community (*maslaha*). Moreover, the mission of Muhammad did not include politics. Admittedly he had the elements of government, the appointment of governors and judges, the collection of taxes, etc., but these were done in an *ad hoc* fashion and only as necessary actions to sustain his preaching. In any case, a prophet's authority is spiritual rather than material. Muhammad's mission was to unify humankind, something that might be possible religiously but not politically. The book raised a storm and was condemned by the *'ulama'* of the Azhar, and its author lost his status as an ***'alim***. Still, many educated people in the following decades have held views similar to his.

During the 1920s and 1930s there was a lively literary and intellectual life, many of whose participants articulated secularist and nationalist views. At first the emphasis was on Egyptian nationalism, as it had been earlier. By the 1930s, however, there was more interest in pan-Arab nationalism. The latter, we may note, is easier to square with Islamic sensibilities, since the Arabs and the Arabic language have always had a special place in Islam. The early Arab heroes and the early heroes of Islam are the same people. By contrast, the ancient Egyptians were pagans and Pharaoh is a great villain in the Qur'an. In the 1930s and 1940s several leading literary figures wrote studies of Muhammad and other early Islamic figures, some of which have been discussed in chapter 2. These signal a partial retreat from secularism but are still secularist insofar as they treat their subjects as heroes and Islam as heritage.

Another storm was raised in 1926 by a book on ***jahili*** poetry by Taha Hussein, probably the greatest modern Egyptian literary figure and one whose influence goes beyond Egypt, because it denied the historicity of some events recounted in the Qur'an. Combined with politics this caused the author to lose his university position for a time. In the 1940s there was another controversy over a doctoral dissertation by Muhammad Khalafallah, on the Qur'anic stories of the prophets, that argued that they were not meant to give precise historical information. These events, along with the case of Abu Zayd mentioned below, signaled a line not to be lightly crossed.

The beginnings of Islamism: the Muslim Brothers

If some of Muhammad 'Abduh's successors took his legacy in a secularist direction, others took it in an Islamist direction. Rashid Rida (1865–1935), a close associate of 'Abduh, developed his doctrine of *salafiyya* in a conservative direction, partly influenced by the success of the **Wahhabis** in Arabia. His interpretations included the view that *jihad* is defensive and that interest on loans was acceptable because of necessity but he favored the traditional predominance of men over women and justified polygyny. He contributed to the debate over the caliphate with a book, *The Caliphate or the Great Imamate*, attacking the idea of a "spiritual" caliphate, which the Turks instituted between 1922 and 1924. A true caliph should have material as well as spiritual authority and should be a ***mujtahid***, although a caliph of necessity would be acceptable for a time. Legislative power is authorized by God and confided to

Figure 17.2 Hasan al-Banna. Courtesy of AFP/Getty Images

the *umma*, which through consultation (*shura*) and *ijma'* makes enforceable decisions that the caliph cannot overturn. *Ijma'* here becomes an active and intentional process rather than the *ex post facto* recognition of what was already the case, as it traditionally was.

One who was influenced by Rashid Rida was Hasan al-Banna (1906–49), a young graduate of Dar al-'Ulum and a state school teacher. In 1928 he founded the Muslim Brothers (*al-Ikhwān al-Muslimūn*), initially a social and educational group but soon a mass movement articulating a political message. The ultimate goal was an "Islamic Order", in which Islam would be followed in all areas of life, if possible by convincing the government to implement this. Their focus, however, continued to be on educational, social and economic activities, including youth groups and women's activities. Modern methods of propaganda were used to spread the message. The organization had a strong leadership structure, and al-Banna, who was a member of a Sufi *tariqa* although he criticized many current Sufi practices, ran the organization with something of the manner of a Sufi *shaykh*. The membership was largely middle class, members of the effendi sector of society, though efforts were made to reach workers and peasants. The movement spread to other Arab countries after the Second World War and provided some of the best fighters on the Arab side in the 1948 war in Palestine. Politics in Egypt after the war was chaotic and violent and the Brothers were one of the strongest forces, but in 1948 a Brother assassinated the prime minister and Hasan al-Banna was killed in retaliation, and the movement was banned until 1951.

Revolution: support, control and repression

In 1952 a group of army officers, some of whom had had contact with the Brothers, took control of the government under the leadership of Gamal Abdel Nasser. However, while Abdel Nasser and others were probably more personally pious than previous leaders, they adopted secular Arab nationalism as their ideology, and then Arab Socialism from 1961. These ideologies have a place for Islam, but not as central a place as Islamists demand. In a small book entitled "The Philosophy of the Revolution" Abdel Nasser speaks of Egypt as part of three circles, an Arab circle, which is the most important, then an African circle, and finally an Islamic circle, in the context of which he speaks of the ***Hajj*** as potentially a congress of Muslim leaders in a pan-Islamic mode. Elsewhere in response to criticism he describes socialism as the law of God. With the Coptic minority in mind he describes his government as adhering to "religion", Muslims to their religion and Christians to theirs.

Far from separating religion from government, his government undertook to incorporate and reform the religious institutions. Separate religious courts were abolished in 1956 though the distinctive religious laws remained. *Awqaf* (many had been created since Muhammad 'Ali's time) that supported institutions such as mosques were put under the control or the Ministry of *Awqaf* (or Ministry of Religious Affairs). In 1961 the Azhar and its system of feeder schools were brought more firmly under state control and new faculties were added to the Azhar, including business administration, medicine and engineering. It was argued that in this context religion could be made more relevant to worldly affairs but some have questioned the quality of these courses. The Shaykh of the Azhar (the leading figure in the religious establishment) gave *fatwas* supporting the regime's socialist measures, arguing, among other things, that while private property is permitted, the Prophet said, "All people partake in three things, water, pasture and fire", and this is taken to justify state ownership of comparable modern necessities such as electricity and transport.

The Brothers at first supported this regime, hoping that it would implement their program, but then turned away from it. In 1954 after an assassination attempt against Abdel Nasser that was blamed on the Brothers, the organization was again banned. A few of its leaders were executed and many of the members were given long prison sentences. Others left Egypt. The prison experience radicalized some of them.

Among these was Sayyid Qutb (1906–66), who had been one of the secular literary elite for two decades, then adopted an Islamist position, joined the Brothers and become their chief ideologue. He was influenced by **Mawdudi**, but was to go beyond both Mawdudi and Banna in his Islamism. He presented his ideas in a number of writings, of which the most important is his multi-volume commentary to the Qur'an *In the Shade of the Qur'an* (*Fī ẓilāl al-Qur'ān*) and the best known and most radical is *Milestones* (*Ma'ālim fī al-ṭarīq*), which circulated in manuscript form in prison and was published in 1964. In his later thinking the difference between good and evil, faith and unbelief is stark and uncompromising. There can be no mixture or compromise between a society run by God's laws and one run by human laws. The latter are *jahili* societies, and *jahiliyya* is not just non-Islamic, it is actively anti-Islamic. According to Qutb all societies in his time were *jahili*, including those that called themselves Muslim and very much including Abdel Nasser's Egypt (though he could not quite say this openly in print). Mawdudi had spoken of these societies as mixtures of Islam and *jahiliyya*, but Qutb would not allow this compromise. Given this, the only way to establish an Islamic society is by *jihad*, which in Qutb's interpretation meant a revolutionary takeover after a long period of preparation and then a long struggle. His picture of the process was patterned after the Prophet Muhammad's experience but probably also influenced by Marxist ideas. Qutb had other ideas of significance but these were his most radical ideas and they were to inspire a number of extremists in the decades to come. Qutb himself was released from prison in 1964, rearrested in 1965 on charges of conspiring against the government and executed in 1966, thus adding the power of martyrdom to his ideas.

Through the nineteenth and early twentieth centuries the Sufi *tariqas* continued to be important, though not as all-encompassing as before. It is said that the height of their activity was in the last two decades of the nineteenth century. Criticism from both secularists and *salafis* has led to the decrease of some of the more spectacular activities of the *tariqas*. Their numbers declined in the first half of the twentieth century in the face of the secularization of society but have risen since then. To a significant degree they have been able to develop a middle-class urban following. The system of organizing the orders and bringing them under some degree of government jurisdiction was strengthened with the creation of the Sufi Council in 1895, and this system has continued, although many *tariqas* are not part of it. The *tariqas* were involved in politics at the level of seeking favors from politicians and providing them with support. The government of Abdel Nasser gave support to the *tariqas*, in part as a counterbalance to the Islamists, and used them for propaganda, as have later governments. Abdel Nasser himself is said to have had a Sufi *shaykh* as a spiritual advisor.

Resurgence of Islam

The defeat in 1967 at the hands of the Israelis in the "Six Day War" was devastating to the prestige and the ideology of the Abdel Nasser government although Abdel Nasser remained personally popular. After his death in 1970, his successor, Anwar al-Sadat removed his left-wing colleagues and opened Egypt to a greater degree of capitalism and trade with the West, a policy known as *infitāḥ* (opening). In part as a counterbalance to the left-wing he gave more of a place to religion; he referred to his government as "the government of science and religion" and to himself as "the believer president". He released the members of the Muslim Brothers who were in prison and allowed them to reorganize and publish a magazine but did not grant them legal status. The Brothers renounced violence and sought to work within the system for their vision of an Islamic society. With the help of the government, Islamist groups were able to take over the university student councils from the leftists and control them for several years. In 1972 the constitution was amended to state that "the principles of the Islamic Shari'a are a principal source of legislation". In 1980 this was amended to read " ... *the* principal source of legislation". This comes close to the Islamist position (which would presumably say "the source of legislation") but it did not have too much effect on actual legislation. When Sadat went to war with Israel in 1973 he called it "Operation Badr", after the Prophet's famous battle. On the other hand, on one occasion when Sadat was criticized by Islamist organizations he responded "no religion in politics and no politics in religion". Without denying his personal sincerity, it is probably fair to say that he desired the authority religious symbols would give him but not the restraints religion would impose.

The 1970s saw the beginning of the "re-veiling" phenomenon. Young women, mainly university students, many of whose grandmothers had removed the veil in the 1920s and 1930s, began to wear "Islamic garb", which covered all but their faces and hands and was different from traditional forms of Muslim garb. Since then this has spread and become more varied, including for some the *niqāb*, which covers the face. It has become a visible marker of Islamism, although not all who use it are strictly speaking Islamists nor are all who do not use it secularists. Since the 1950s women had made considerable progress in education and employment but the family laws pertaining to them changed little until, to the tune of much controversy, a series of decrees and laws between 1979 and 2000, among other things, gave a woman the right to divorce if her husband took another wife (see chapter 21, pp. 348–49).

Some of the younger Islamists, radicalized in prison, formed potentially violent groups and there were two prominent incidents in the 1970s. In 1974 one group took over the Military Academy as part of a failed coup d'état. Another, popularly known as "*Takfir* and *Hijra*" was suppressed by the government in 1978, after kidnapping and killing a former government minister. The popular name reflects the group's ideology, which was an extreme variant of Sayyid Qutb's ideas. They held that the whole of society was *kafir* (*takfir* means to declare someone a *kafir*) and that true believers should withdraw physically from it (*hijra*) to prepare for a time when they could take it over. In declaring the whole of society *kafir* they were close to Qutb's view but went further than other extremist groups, who believed that only the leaders were *kafir* and that society would follow them once the leaders were removed. The popular label also alludes to the **Kharijis** of the early years of Islam, and in fact critics of the extreme Islamists frequently refer to them as Kharijis.

In 1979 Sadat made a peace treaty with Israel, getting a *fatwa* from the Shaykh of the Azhar in support of it, but attracting violent criticism from many quarters, leftist, Islamist and others, leading him to imprison many of the critics and ban the many Islamist groups of students and others that he had earlier supported. Out of these Islamists were formed several extremist groups of which two, Egyptian Islamic Jihad and the Islamic Group (*al-jamāʿa al-islāmiyya*) have been the most prominent. Members of Islamic Jihad assassinated Sadat in 1981, hoping to spark a revolt that did not materialize. One of their leaders, Abd al-Salam Faraj wrote a booklet, *The Neglected Duty* (Jansen, below), explaining their views. *Jihad*, in the sense of fighting, is an obligation and it should be directed at the "near enemy", i.e. the *kafir* leadership of Egypt, before the "far enemy", i.e. Israel. He used the *fatwas* of **Ibn Taymiyya** against the Mongols to make the case that a ruler who claims to be Muslim but does not rule according to the Shari'a is a *kafir*. The Azhar produced a lengthy rebuttal.

Sadat was replaced as president by Husni Mubarak, whose government was secularist but walked an uneasy tightrope between the demands of the Islamists and those of the secularists. It attended sometimes to one side and sometimes to another, banning liquor sales (except in tourist areas!) and books that offended Islamists but also destroying Islamist books for schools and replacing them with secularist books.

The Azhar largely supported the government but became more assertive and critical and more successful in getting its way on specific matters. It produced a draft Islamic constitution in 1979. It also provides *fatwas* for individuals on a wide range of issues mainly relating to the family. In 2007 the Shaykh of the Azhar gave a *fatwa* approving the government's appointment of female judges over the disapproval of many Islamists.

Attendance at mosques has increased since 1970 and more women have attended *salat al-jum'a*. There has also been a proliferation of religious associations, many not political in orientation. The Ministry of *Awqaf* has set itself the target of supervising all of the mosques in the country, partly because extremist groups often center on private mosques, but it has not had the resources to do this. In 1999 it was claimed that about 41,000 of 67,000 mosques were supervised. Religious books and tapes of popular preachers sell well and there have been a number of religious "personalities", both male and female, such as Shaykh Sha'rawi, who combined a fairly traditionalist message with a very dramatic presentation and had a popular television program. A certain number of well-known secular intellectuals have publicly changed from a secularist to a modernist or Islamist position. A number of Islamic financial institutions have come into existence and regular banks often have Islamic sections. There was something of a "bubble" in these institutions in the late 1980s that burst, causing many people to lose money.

The Sufi movement has continued to grow. Official figures calculated three to five million Sufis (not counting women) in 1989 but a Sufi *shaykh* claimed that as many as half of all Egyptians have some sort of connection with a *tariqa*. There have been a number of *walis* recognized in recent decades. One is said to have been refused passage on a Nile ferry because he was impolitely criticizing the morals of the tourists, so he crossed the river on his handkerchief.

The Muslim Brothers, still unrecognized legally and often harassed by the government, were the main opposition group. They participated, under other labels or as independents, in all of the parliamentary elections from 1984 but one and they did relatively well, given that Egyptian elections are engineered to return a large majority for the ruling party. In 2005 they won 88 of the 454 seats. The Brothers and other Islamists also sought with some success to gain control of professional associations (or syndicates). Between 1987 and 1992 they were successful with the lawyers, physicians and engineers' syndicates and the Cairo University Faculty Club, but the government soon found ways to reverse most of these. More recently they have been satisfied with representation on the governing boards of syndicates without control. Islamists continue to engage in education and social service. During an earthquake in Cairo in 1992 they embarrassed the government by providing aid faster and more effectively than it did. The Brothers now speak favorably of democracy and claim it is consistent with Islam. In 1996 a group of Brothers broke away to form the Wasat (Middle-of-the-Road) Party, taking a more liberal position, but they have not been allowed to register as a political party. Their ideology may possibly be compared to that of the Justice and Development Party in Turkey.

The late 1980s to the late 1990s saw considerable political violence involving Egyptian Islamic Jihad and the Islamic Group. This included the assassinations of the speaker of parliament and of a prominent secularist writer, and attempts on the life of President Mubarak and of the Nobel Prize winner Neguib Mahfouz. There was violence against Copts and attacks on tourists. The police response was likewise violent and a number of Islamists and others were killed. In 1997 the leaders of the Islamic Group called for an end to the violence. Many of the leaders of Islamic Jihad followed the same path a couple of years later, while others, following Ayman al-Zawahiri, merged with **al-Qaeda** in 2001 (see chapter 20). Violence against tourists reflects to some extent the fact that many tourists dress and act in a manner that is offensive to many Egyptians (not just Islamists) and also the fact that tourists symbolize the imbalance between the West and Islam that lies at the heart of the modern problem. Still, Egypt depends heavily on tourists and such actions were rejected by the average Egyptian.

While the Muslim Brothers and their violent offshoots may be considered *salafi* in a relatively broad sense of the term, religiously stricter but non-political *salafi* groups also exist in Egypt. Among the best known are Al-Jam'iyya al-Shar'iyya li-l-'amilin bi-l-kitab wa-l-sunna (Shari'a Association of Those Who Adhere to the Book and the Sunna) founded in 1912 and Anṣār al-Sunna al-Muḥammadiya (Association of Supporters of Muhammad's Sunna) founded in 1926. These actively propagate their views and carry out social service activities. In the late 1970s al-Da'wa al-Salafiyya and other groups were formed by younger people who had split from the Islamic Group. It was quite active but strictly non-political until 2011. These have often been in contact with like-minded counterparts in Saudi Arabia and this has led to their being accused of "Wahhabism" by their critics.

This same period saw a major controversy over the case of Nasr Muhammad Hamid Abu Zayd, a professor at the University of Cairo, whose critical theories of the Qur'an, emphasizing its human dimension, prompted an Islamist lawyer in 1993 to sue in the courts to have his marriage dissolved on the grounds that his views made him a *kafir*, and a *kafir* cannot be married to a Muslim. The suit was first denied, then upheld on appeal, and then later the law was changed, but by that time Abu Zayd had left Egypt because of the threats he had received. The case can be compared to those of Taha Hussein and Khalafallah, but the consequences were more serious for Abu Zayd (see chapter 20).

In spite of all this, the majority of Egyptians were probably not Islamist in their views. The government continued to be secularist and entrenched in power. It had also become authoritarian and corrupt, an oligarchy of military men and wealthy capitalists. A protest movement against it in 2004–5, called "Enough" (*Kifaya*), was also predominantly secular. There were still spokespeople for secularist and modernist views, though preferring not to use the label "secularist"(see text box on "Tendentious terms" in chapter 15). A prominent example is the retired judge, Sa'id al-Ashmawy. He has criticized what he and others call "political Islam" quite trenchantly. Among other things he argues that those who call for the application of the Shari'a are really calling for the application of *fiqh*, which is human opinion. In fact, Western law and Islamic law are related and in adopting Western laws the Egyptians have not violated the Shari'a. A true "government of God" is only possible during the life of the Prophet. While the resurgence of Islam in Egypt had definitely swung the cultural balance away from secularism it had not produced an Islamic government and the secular elite was still very influential.

The "Arab spring" in Egypt

An observer in 2010 would be forgiven for having thought that Husni Mubarak's regime, having quelled the violent Islamists, sidelined the secular liberals, largely coopted the Azhar and kept the Muslim Brothers at bay, would make a successful transition to a new leader. Events outside Egypt were to complicate matters.

The hopeful wave of demonstrations and revolts known as the "Arab spring" that began in Tunisia in December 2010 reached Egypt in the form of massive demonstrations in Tahrir Square in Cairo beginning 25 January 2011, led mainly by secular youth calling for the end of Mubarak's regime. The president resigned in February. The military, who then took charge, were at first perceived as protectors of the revolution but later as seeking to continue the old regime. Islamists were not prominent in the early stages of the movement but they proved stronger than the secularists at the ballot boxes. In the parliamentary elections in January 2012

Figure 17.3 The flags of Tunisia, Libya and Egypt fly at a demonstration in Tahrir Square, Cairo (February 2011). Courtesy of iStockphoto

parties associated with the Muslim Brothers gained almost half of the seats while three *salafī* parties, including one associated with al-Da'wa al-Salafiyya, abandoned their apolitical position and gained almost a quarter. In the presidential elections the secular liberal candidates were eliminated in the first round and in the second round, in June, Muhammad Mursi, connected with the Muslim Brothers, defeated the candidate associated with the old regime.

The military attempted to retain its power but failed as Mursi replaced the top military leaders and also placed his decisions above review by the (mainly secularist) judiciary. In December a constitution, technically no less secular than the 1980 constitution but with more attention to religion, was approved in a controversial referendum. Mursi's popularity declined over time as he was accused of concentrating power in his own hands and those of the Muslim Brothers, acting arbitrarily and failing to deal with the disastrous condition of the economy.

A campaign by a group of younger secularists called Tamarrud (Rebellion) led to massive demonstrations against Mursi on 30 June 2013 and three days later the military leaders deposed him and installed a provisional president. All of this was accompanied by violence on various sides, culminating on 14 August when police violently dispersed two pro-Mursi demonstrations and this was followed by further clashes and the burning of churches. The death toll, mainly of Islamists, was reportedly over 600.

Considerable controversy attends both the details and the significance of these events. Did the military have to step in to save the nation from an Islamist dictatorship? Or did the military, with the support of many who are considered "liberals", violate democracy by ousting an elected president? Given the fear and hatred of many secularists for the Muslim Brothers, could the Brothers be included in a future democracy? But could there be a democracy without them? Would they entrust their fate to the ballot box again? Such questions and others are posed at the time of writing (August 2013). The future is murky, and not very promising.

Key points

- In Egypt both the *'ulama'* and the Sufis were influential in the eighteenth century, lost ground especially in the upper levels of society in the nineteenth and early twentieth centuries, but seem to have regained some influence since about 1970.
- Modernization led to a dualism between "modern" and "traditional" in many areas of society, e.g. law, education, dress, but this has decreased in recent decades.
- Secularism has been strong but much less aggressive in Egypt than in Turkey.
- The state has sought to control religious expression but with only partial success.
- Islamism has taken both moderate and violent forms.
- Egypt has had major secularist, Islamic modernist and radically Islamist thinkers.
- Egyptians may think of themselves as Egyptians and/or as Arabs. The latter fits better with Islam.
- As of 2013 Egypt is undergoing major political developments that may or may not change the balance between secularism and Islamism.

Discussion questions

1. Why does an emphasis on Arab identity accord better with Islam than an emphasis on Egyptian identity?
2. Egyptians like to say that they are essentially religious and opposed to violence. Does the evidence of this chapter lead you to agree?
3. How have the relations between Muslims and non-Muslims developed in Turkey and Egypt?
4. How secular is Egypt today?
5. Construct a debate between Ali Abd al-Raziq and Sayyid Qutb.
6. Who today best represents the heritage of Muhammad 'Abduh?

Critical thinking box 17.1

On the website there are selections from a number of writers or groups, including Taha Hussein, Hasan al-Banna, Ibrahim Jum'a, Abdel Nasser, Mahmud Shaltut, Sayyid Qutb, The Wasat Party. Taking any two or three of these analyze and compare what they have to say on the relationship between religion and society or on the relationship between religion and nationalism.

Critical thinking box 17.2

Sayyid Qutb writes:

> If we insist on calling Islamic Jihad a defensive movement, then we must change the meaning of the word "defense" and mean by it "the defense of man" against all those elements which limit his freedom. These elements take the form of beliefs and concepts, as well as of political systems, based on economic, racial or class distinctions. When Islam first came into existence, the world was full of such systems, and the present-day Jahiliyyah also has various kinds of such systems.
>
> (Qutb, 1978, 111)

Compare this understanding of *jihad* with others of which you are aware, and also with the understanding of *jihad* found in al-Jabarti's description of the uprising against the French found on the website.

Critical thinking box 17.3

The following was written by a leading American scholar of the Middle East about the (alleged) conspiracy by members of the Muslim Brothers in Egypt in 1965:

> It was the predictable eruption of the continuing tension caused by an ever-dwindling activist fringe of individuals dedicated to an increasingly less relevant Muslim "position" about society; and of professional malcontents. Our feeling, for some time now shared by others, is that the essentially secular reform nationalism now in vogue in the Arab world will continue to operate to end the earlier appeal of this organization.
>
> (Mitchell, 1969, vii)

Why did he and so many others get it so wrong, if indeed they did get it wrong? (The website contains this extract and another, similar one, along with two more perceptive ones.)

Companion website

Features population figures, quotes material on the French occupation, quotes from many of the thinkers and ideologues mentioned in the chapter, especially Sayyid Qutb, several further readings and weblinks for some important figures.

Further reading

'Abduh, Muhammad (1966) *The Theology of Unity*, trans. I. Masa'ad and K. Cragg. London: Allen & Unwin. ('Abduh's main book on theology and the most accessible of his works in translation.)

Hourani, A. (1970) *Arabic Thought in the Liberal Age*. London: Oxford University Press. (The classic work on Arab political, social and religious thought to 1939, giving considerable attention to Egypt; relied on heavily by all scholars.)

Mitchell, R.P. (1969) *The Society of the Muslim Brothers*. London: Oxford University Press. (A detailed study of the Brothers to 1954; probably the most relied on.)

Qutb, Sayyid (1978) *Milestones*. Beirut and Damascus: Holy Koran Publishing House. (Qutb's most popular work, a "revolutionary manifesto". Translation is acceptable. There are one or two other translations.)

Calvert, John (2010) *Sayyid Qutb and the Origins of Radical Islamism*. New York: Columbia University Press. (Excellent study of Qutb's activities and writings during both his secularist and Islamist periods; with helpful information on the social and political background and a survey of later "Qutbists".)

Jansen, J.J.G. (1986) *The Neglected Duty: The Creed of Sadat's Assassins and Islamic Resurgence in the Middle East*. New York: Macmillan. (Includes a translation of *The Neglected Duty* by 'Abd al-Salam Faraj, a very important source. The title of Faraj's book is variously translated, e.g. *The Forgotten Obligation*.)

Kenney, Jeffrey T. (2006), *Muslim Rebels: Kharijites and the Politics of Extremism in Egypt*. Oxford: Oxford University Press. (A good discussion of the Kharijites as a political symbol in modern Egypt.)

Wickham, Carrie Rosefsky (2002) *Mobilizing Islam: Religion, Activism and Political Change in Egypt*. New York: Columbia University Press. (A well-informed and perceptive study of the "moderate" Islamists in the early 1980s, with attention to ideology and forms of mobilization.)

Gaffney, P.D. (1994) *The Prophet's Pulpit: Islamic Preaching in Contemporary Egypt*. Berkeley, CA: University of California Press. (Anthropological study of mosques and preachers, interesting "on the ground" information.)

Starrett, Gregory (1998) *Putting Islam to Work: Education, Politics and Religious Transformation in Egypt*. Berkeley, CA: University of California Press. (Based on research done from 1987 to 1993; good information on education and on the general religious situation with some very perceptive observations.)

See also: Voll, *Islam: Continuity and Change* [15].

18 *Ideology and politics in Iran*

From secularism to Islamic republic

> Some said that "the King is God's representative on earth and the Prophet's in guiding the people; and that the Sadr and all other clerics must not interfere in the government or politics."
>
> (Recorded by seventeenth-century French traveler, Jean Chardin, in Martin, 1989, 17, minor correction)

> Our kings being iniquitous and unjust men, their domination is a tyranny to which God has subjected us to punish us, after having withdrawn from the world the legitimate successor of His Prophet. The supreme Throne of the universe belongs only to a Mujtahid, a man who possesses sanctity and science above ordinary men. It is true that since the Mujtahid is holy, and consequently a peaceful man, there must be a king who carries a sword for the exercise of justice; but he must only be like his minister, and dependent upon him.
>
> (Jean Chardin in Keddie, 1972, 222, corrected)

If Turkey in the twentieth century opted dramatically for secularism and Egypt walked an uncomfortable path between secularism and Islamism, Iran first opted for a path like Turkey's and then made a dramatic about face with its Islamic revolution. This chapter will follow this dramatic history including the secularist reforms of Reza Shah and his son and the Islamic revolution led by Khomeini and its aftermath. Much of this history turns on the relations between the *'ulama'* and the rulers; contrasting opinions on this appear in the preceding quotations.

In this chapter

- The Qajars: religion, foreign interference, constitution
- The Pahlavis: Reza Shah and Iranian nationalism
- The Pahlavis: Muhammad Reza Shah – White Revolution
- Islamic opposition and revolution

- Islamic republic
- After Khomeini

The Qajars: religion, foreign interference, constitution

As we have seen in chapter 4, Iran became predominantly Shi'i under the Safavid dynasty (1501–1736). This dynasty was followed by two short-lived dynasties and then by the Qajar dynasty, which lasted into the twentieth century (c. 1779/1794–1925). Qajar control over the whole country, however, was tenuous at best and tribal chiefs and other local leaders were often virtually independent. The Qajars made only limited efforts at the sort of centralizing and modernizing reforms undertaken by the **Tanzimat** in the Ottoman Empire and Muhammad 'Ali and his successors in Egypt. They did not, for example, create a unified army under their control. They lost the Caucasus and Armenia to Russia in two wars in 1804–13 and 1826–28 and their central Asian provinces between 1864 and 1885. In the second half of the century there was increasing Western economic penetration and political meddling, especially by Russia and Great Britain, until in 1907 the country was formally divided into Russian and British spheres of influence. There was sufficient reform and Westernization to create a small class of modernizing intelligentsia, calling themselves "enlightened thinkers".

Map 10 Iran

The *'ulama'* had been largely dominated by the government under the early **Safavids** but later they became more independent and influential. Under the Qajars their influence with both the people and the government increased. In addition to being spiritual leaders, judges, and administrators of ***awqaf***, some *'ulama'* were local power brokers, landowners and traders. They were often viewed as protectors of the people against unjust government action. Their authority was strengthened by the victory of the **Uṣūlīs** over the **Akhbārīs** at the end of the eighteenth century and the development through the nineteenth century of the Usuli system of ***ijtihad***, according to which each believer should follow a *marja'-i taqlid* ("source of emulation", see chapter 10). Usually there have been several *marja's* with at any one time more or less equal status, though during at least three periods, in the 1860s, 1890s and 1940s–1960s, there has been just one for the whole Shi'i world. The *'ulama'* regularly opposed foreign influence. They urged the government to engage in ***jihad*** against the Russians in 1826 with disastrous results. They later successfully opposed, with Russian assistance, extensive economic concessions given to the British entrepreneur Baron de Reuter in 1872. It was about this time that an alliance with the bazaar merchants developed, based on common interest and often on family ties. It has continued to the present.

Views of the relationship between government and religion varied, as they did in the earlier periods. Some saw the shah as appointed by God. Some saw all worldly government as in some measure usurping the rights of the Twelfth ***Imam*** but as necessary during the time of **Occultation**. Probably most common was the idea of "dual agency", according to which the *'ulama'* were the general agents of the *Imam* for guiding (*vilayat*) the ***umma*** and the shah was the special agent of the *Imam* for enforcing order in the world. Besides the courts of the *'ulama'*, which administered Shari'a law, there were the ***'urf*** courts, run by government officials under the shah's authority. Shari'a courts generally dealt with civil cases and *'urf* courts with criminal cases, but there was some overlap and thus some competition between them. *'Urf* law was not written law and varied from place to place, but both kinds of law were fairly unsystematic. The establishment of a Ministry of Justice in the 1850s did not change this much.

Actual relations between the *'ulama'* and government varied according to circumstances but were not devoid of tension. Muhammad Shah (r. 1834–48), for example, favored the Sufis and sought to limit the *'ulama'*. The Shi'i *'ulama'* have generally opposed the Sufis for reasons mentioned in chapter 12 and they were severely persecuted under the Safavids, but the Dhahabi and Ni'matullahi ***tariqas*** re-established themselves in the later eighteenth century and the Ni'matullahis have been able to attract a number of government officials and upper-class people. The spread of Sufism has been limited, however, by *'ulama'* opposition.

A greater danger to the *'ulama'* came from the three related "heterodox" movements, the Shaykhis, the Babis and the Baha'is. The first was founded by Shaykh Ahmad

Ahsa'i (1753–1826), whose most controversial claim was that the occulted Twelfth *Imam* is not located in the material world but in an intermediate spiritual realm called *hurqulya* (this is also the realm where resurrection, heaven and hell take place) and he communicates with the world through inspiration to one representative, a "Perfect Shi'a" or "Gate (*Bab*)" to the *Imam*. There is always one such person in the world. He is not publicly announced but Shaykh Ahsa'i's followers were convinced that he and his successor were this figure. This represented a clear challenge to the authority of the *'ulama'*, who persecuted the Shaykhis although the Qajars generally protected them. The movement exists in small numbers to the present but has modified its doctrine in an orthodox direction.

The year 1844 marked the 1,000th anniversary of the occultation of the Twelfth *Imam* and many expected his return. In this year a member of the Shaykhi movement, Sayyid Ali Muhammad Shirazi (1819–50), claimed to be the Bab (Gate of the *Imam*) and gained a number of followers. Later he claimed to be the Twelfth *Imam* (more precisely, a human figure corresponding to the archetypal *Imam* in *hurqulya*) and announced the abrogation of the Islamic *Shari'a* and the beginning of a new dispensation, which, among other things, would not have *'ulama'* and would grant a higher place to women. He raised a revolt against the shah's government but was defeated and in 1850 was executed. The Bab had promised the advent of another figure, "Him whom God shall make manifest", and in 1863 Mirza Husayn Ali (1817–92) claimed to be this figure and took the title Baha'ullah (Splendor of God) and was followed by the majority of the Babis. He came to be seen as a new prophet following in the line of Buddha, Zarathushtra, Moses, Jesus and Muhammad so that Baha'ism came to be a separate religion. Baha'ism has spread worldwide and become Westernized in its expression. For these reasons Baha'is have often been persecuted in Iran. The remaining Babis came to be known as Azalis and some of these became active in later reform movements.

As mentioned in chapter 8, the practices connected with the ***ta'ziya*** gained in popularity during the Qajar period and were supported, sometimes lavishly, by the Qajar shahs. The *'ulama'*, however, generally opposed the more extreme practices involved.

In 1890 the shah granted a concession to a British company for a monopoly over the production, sale and export of tobacco. The result was a growing number of protests on the part of growers, merchants and city mobs, led or at least fronted by the *'ulama'*. Allied to them were modernizing reformers such as Jamal al-Din Asadabadi (Afghani), many of whom put secular reform ideas into traditional religious language to appeal to the people. Opposition was based not only on economic concerns but also resentment against Western influence and a fear that non-Muslims handling tobacco would make it ritually impure. The protests came to a head when a *fatwa* banning the use of tobacco was solicited and gained from Ayatollah Mirza Hasan Shirazi, who was the sole *marja'* of the time and resident in Samarra, in Iraq, beyond the reach of the shah. The response was so overwhelming that the shah was forced to cancel the concession. This was the first nationwide protest of this sort. It strengthened the position of the *'ulama'* and forged an alliance between them and the modernizing intelligentsia. It is worth noting that the success was made possible by a modern invention, the telegraph, used to communicate with Ayatollah Shirazi. Unfortunately, the Persian government went into debt for the first time to pay the indemnity to the concessionaire. This was followed by other borrowing and by 1900 most of the country's resources were mortgaged to British and Russian creditors.

The tobacco protest was a forerunner of the Constitutional Revolution that began in 1905 and plunged the country into civil war for several years. Protests by some *'ulama'*, merchants and intellectuals forced the shah in 1906 to call a *majles* (parliament) and accept a constitution modeled after that of Belgium. Many of the *'ulama'* appear not to have understood at first the difference between the secular constitution desired by the modernists and government by the Shari'a. When this became clear many *'ulama'* turned against the constitution, although a supplementary law added the next year provided for a committee of five ***mujtahids*** that could veto bills that contravened the Shari'a. The constitution in fact sought to combine the Islamic and the secular. Twelver Shi'ism was declared the religion of state and sovereignty was described as a "trust, confided, by the grace of God, to the person of the shah, by the nation". Elsewhere it says that "the powers of the state are derived from the nation" and grants equal rights to all inhabitants. The continuing civil war, followed by the occupation of Iran during the First World War by the British and Russians, meant that the constitution had little chance to operate at that time, but it remained on the books until 1979. The committee of *mujtahids* was never actually established.

The best known defense of the constitution on Islamic grounds was the book *The Admonition and Refinement of the People* by Mirza Muhammad Husayn Na'ini (1860–1936). He argued that all human government usurps the authority of the Twelfth *Imam*, but tyranny also usurps the right of the people while constitutional government does not. Moreover, if the *'ulama'*, as agents of the *Imam*, approve of it, then it does not usurp the *Imam's* authority either. This book disappeared from circulation soon after 1910 but was republished in 1955, when its ideas were still relevant. The leading anti-constitutionalist was Shaykh Fadlullah Nuri (1842–1909). He argued that laws are made by God, not by humans, and it is not for the majority of people to interpret these laws but for those specialized in them. Moreover, justice does not mean equal rights for all but recognizes distinctions, as between minors and adults, sane and insane, healthy and ill, slave and free, father and son, wife and husband, learned and ignorant, *mujtahid* and follower (*muqallid*), Muslim and ***kafir***, and so on.

The Pahlavis: Reza Shah and Iranian nationalism

Years of civil war and occupation left Iran in a weak and anarchical situation. Into this situation came the man who was to be in many respects the "Muhammad Ali" of Iran. Reza Khan was the commander of the Cossack Regiment, the only strong and disciplined military force in the country. He became minister of war in 1921 and shah in 1925, deposing the last Qajar shah. He took the dynastic name Pahlavi, which means "heroic", but is also the name of the pre-Islamic Persian language. Influenced by the example of **Atatürk**, he espoused Iranian nationalism and sought to unify Iran and make it strong. He introduced conscription, forced tribes to sedentarize, strengthened the administration, improved communications and established a national bank. These and other measures unified Iran as never before. He also forced a revision of the oil concession that the British had held since 1914, although he did not get as good terms as he might have.

At first Reza Shah sought the support of the *'ulama'*. He followed their advice against setting up a republic and expressed a desire to implement the Shari'a. Soon, however, he acted to weaken their influence and diminish their place in society. He expanded the state school system (without adequately funding it) at the expense of the *maktabs* (Persian for ***kuttab***), which were eliminated by about 1950, although the upper-level ***madrasas*** survived with decreasing numbers and largely maintained their independence. He introduced new civil, commercial and criminal codes that included some provisions of Shari'a law (especially on issues of gender) along with French-derived laws and set requirements for judges that excluded most *'ulama'*. Registration of documents was taken out of the hands of the *'ulama'* and given to the secular courts. Government control of *awqaf* was increased. He dictated "modern" dress for men and commanded women to abandon the *chador* (as the traditional all-covering garb is called in Iran), though with limited success. He also attempted to suppress the *ta'ziya* rituals. His nationalist ideology glorified the pre-Islamic period and people were encouraged to take names from that period, such as Cyrus or Darius. This had considerable success since, unlike Egyptians, Iranians had always retained a significant awareness of their pre-Islamic past. He made the Persian solar calendar official with the Persian names for the months and a modified Islamic calendar, based on the solar year and called solar *hijri* (e.g. 2012 CE is 1433 *hijri* and 1391 solar *hijri*, see also Appendix III). He also declared the name of the country to be Iran (related to the word *Aryan*), which he saw as associated with the glories of ancient Iran rather than the weakness of recent times. While the *'ulama'* were forced to be quiet politically, the learning center at Qom was re-established and became the main center in Iran. Here the future leader, Ayatollah Khomeini, was trained along with many of his colleagues.

In many respects Reza Shah accomplished in a generation what took a century in Turkey and Egypt, but this was done in a highly authoritarian and often brutal manner. One result was to create a considerable cultural and economic gap between the "traditional" sector of society, consisting of the lower classes and the "traditional" middle class (*bazaaris*), and the smaller "modern" sector, consisting of the upper class and the "modern" middle class. This was to prove significant in the 1970s. His achievements were not enough to prevent the Russians and British from occupying the country in 1941 and forcing him to abdicate because of his pro-German sympathies.

Muhammad Reza Shah: White Revolution

Reza Shah was succeeded by his son, Muhammad Reza Shah, and for a time there was a lively and diverse political scene, including the Marxist Tudeh (Masses) party, moderate and radical nationalist parties and two religious groups, the Mujahidin-i Islam, led by Ayatollah Abol-Qasem Kashani, and the Fada'iyan-i Islam, led by Navvab Safavi. The latter was made up of younger and more lower-class people and was more radically Islamist. It had contacts with the Muslim Brothers in Egypt. It also engaged in assassinations. In 1951 the *majles* acted to nationalize Iranian oil, under the influence of the National Front, which included both nationalist parties and Kashani's party and was led by Muhammad Mossadegh, a secular nationalist with strong personal religious beliefs. This led to a standoff with the British and the Americans and the brief flight of the shah from the country in August 1953. Kashani abandoned Mossadegh when he felt that the communists were gaining too much power. Riots, partly arranged by the American CIA, led to the shah's return and Mossadegh's arrest. Oil was allowed to remain formally in Iranian hands but pricing and distribution were under the control of the British and Americans. The Americans were the winners in this since they gained access to Iranian oil!

After this the shah determined to rule with a strong hand and, among other things, created SAVAK, his secret police. He managed to eliminate or coopt most of the secular opposition but the *'ulama'*, though quiet, retained considerable independence and many were unreconciled. From 1947 to 1961 the Shi'i world had its third sole *marja'*, Grand Ayatollah Burujerdi. He generally cooperated with the shah and tried to persuade the *'ulama'* to stay out of politics, but he also improved the organization of the *'ulama'*'s activities. After his death there were again several *marja's*, among them Ayatollah Khomeini, who had for some time taught ***irfān*** but then shifted to ***fiqh***.

In 1963 the shah announced a "White Revolution" that included several measures opposed or feared by the *'ulama'*. These included land reform measures that the *'ulama'* feared would affect their *awqaf*, establishment of a literacy corps, which would undermine their authority in the villages, and electoral reforms giving the vote to women. These were in addition to a more general opposition to his dictatorial ways, his alliance with America and his support of Israel. Opposition was led by Khomeini and on 'Ashura he was arrested and a number of students killed; bloody demonstrations took place in several cities. All of this evoked the martyrdom of

Figure 18.1 Muhammad Reza Shah Pahlavi, from 1974 Iranian banknote. Courtesy of Shutterstock

Husayn. Khomeini was eventually exiled to the shrine city of Najaf in Iraq. For many Western observers this seemed to be a last gasp of ***mullah*** opposition to "progress", but events were to prove otherwise.

For some time, though, the shah appeared firmly in control and Iran an "island of stability" as the American President Jimmy Carter was to say. In 1967 the shah felt secure enough to have himself crowned, taking the title *aryamehr* (Light of the Aryans). His wife became the first empress or *shahbanou* since pre-Islamic times. Pre-Islamic symbolism was to the fore when he staged a lavish celebration of 2,500 years of Iranian monarchy in Persepolis in 1971 and when in 1976 he changed the official calendar from solar *hijri* to one dating from Cyrus the Great (1976 CE = 1355 HS became 2535 Iranian Imperial). Two family protection acts gave greater protection to wives in cases of polygyny and divorce. He claimed to be a faithful Shi'i but also saw Shi'ism as a patriotic matter. The *ta'ziya* passion plays were presented as folklore in the 1970s. He created a "religion corps" as a step toward "modernizing" religion. He claimed to have had visions of some of the Shi'i *Imams* and to have a sense of divine protection and guidance.

Islamic opposition and revolution

During this time, however, a significant Islamically oriented opposition was developing, not only among the *'ulama'* but also among the lay intellectuals. By the mid-1960s people were speaking of "Islamic ideology" and were soon to give an activist interpretation to Husayn, as a revolutionary martyr whose sacrifice delegitimated tyranny for all time. Among the *'ulama'* people such as Sayyid Mahmud Taleqani (1910–79) and Morteza Muttahari (1920–79) sought to engage with modern Western thinking. The former, who had been connected with the Fadai'yan-i Islam, provided a somewhat "socialist" interpretation of the Qur'an and a progressive view of history to undergird revolutionary action. The latter developed a traditional but rational Islamic critique of Marxism and other Western ideologies. Among the secular intelligentsia, Jelal Al-e Ahmad (1923–69) was a one-time Marxist who found cultural authenticity in Shi'i Islam, though he could not quite accept it as faith. He coined the term *gharbzadegi* ("Westoxication"), for the tendency of Iranians to adopt Western ideas and practices indiscriminately, and this term became quite popular. Mehdi Bazargan, an engineer and former adherent of the National Front, held an Islamic version of liberal nationalism. With Ayatollah Taleqani he founded the Freedom Movement in 1961. About 1965 a group of university graduates founded the Mujahidin-i Khalq (People's Freedom Fighters), who undertook a campaign of "armed operations" (aka "terrorist attacks") that got their leaders arrested or killed by the mid-1970s. In their ideology Islam was interpreted very much in Marxist terms, aiming at what they called a *"tawhidi"* society, interpreting the key term, *tawḥīd*, to mean a "classless" society as well as the worship of one God.

By far the most influential of these ideologues was Ali Shariati (1933–77). Son of an *'alim*, he studied in Paris in the early 1960s and was influenced by the Algerian struggle and by writers such as Marx, Durkheim, Sartre, Franz Fanon and Louis Massignon, a well-known academic scholar of Sufism. On his return he lectured widely and his ideas caught the attention of many university students. In his interpretation Islam becomes a populist, third-world revolutionary ideology. 'Ali and Husayn become symbols of the struggle for justice and there is a strong feeling for the *mustazafin*, the Qur'anic term for the oppressed (4:75). When the Qur'an speaks of social matters "the people" becomes almost synonymous with "God". Thus, "Rule belongs to God" effectively means "Rule belongs to the people". The true "enlightened thinker" is not the university-educated intellectual or the traditionally trained *'alim* but the ideologically committed activist (not mujtahid but **mujahid**). He also popularized the phrase "Everywhere is Karbala' and every day is Ashura", later to be a revolutionary slogan. Shariati was exiled and died of a heart attack in London in 1977, though many thought he was poisoned by SAVAK.

Ayatollah Khomeini continued to criticize the shah from his exile in Najaf. In 1970 he gave a series of lectures on Islamic government that was later transcribed from student notes and published. The argumentation is fairly traditional and scholastic in form but modern in its concerns. He blames imperialism for many of the current problems and responds to the challenge of Western science, arguing in a manner typical of many apologists that Westerners may go to the moon but they lack the moral laws Islam provides. His central argument is that Islam is concerned with the whole of society, not just purity rituals for individuals (with which Shi'is have traditionally been especially concerned) and its rules are meant not just to be taught but implemented. In the absence of the *Imam*, those who are qualified to do this are the *'ulama'*, either one or a group of them. He rejects kingship as un-Islamic in principle, something neither he nor others had done before. This is *vilayat-i faqih*, the governance or guardianship of the *faqih*, and was to become the slogan and ideology of the revolutionary government. The phrase itself was not new: it had been used for the guardianship of minors, the supervising of mosque or *waqf* property, general moral guidance and good government in general. As Khomeini uses it here, however, it is definitely an innovation, probably the greatest of the century.

In the 1970s revolutionary tinder was accumulating. The oil boom beginning in 1973 increased the pressure of Westernization and the gap between the rich and the poor, while there was also a revival of traditional religious practice in Iran as elsewhere. Some of the thousands of informal circles that characterize Iranian society were undoubtedly discussing the revolutionary ideas mentioned earlier. The spark was struck in January 1978 when a scurrilous newspaper article against Khomeini, published at the government's behest, provoked demonstrations in which many were killed. This was followed by continuing unrest and violence through the year as revolutionary anger and momentum mounted. The shah was depicted as the "**Yazid** of the age" while the demonstrators were in the role of Husayn. Many women donned the *chador* in protest. Khomeini came increasingly to prominence, now incorporating the language of the lay ideologues such as Shariati. People began to call him *Imam*, a title sometimes given to Arab Shi'i leaders but never before to an Iranian. In October Khomeini was forced to leave Iraq and went to Paris, from where, paradoxically, he was better able to communicate with his followers via telephone and tape recorder (as in the Constitutional Revolution, modern technology played a crucial role). The ***dastas*** of the last two days of the Ashura period (10–11 December) turned into massive demonstrations against the shah's government. In January 1979 the shah left Iran for a "holiday" and in February Khomeini returned to Iran and established a government with Mehdi Bazargan as prime minister.

Islamic republic

The disparate factions that briefly united to make the revolution had quite incompatible visions for society. So it is not surprising that they soon fell out and that this revolution, like many others, consumed many of its children. The Bazargan government had to resign in November 1979 after activists took American diplomats hostage at the "Den of Spies" (aka U.S. embassy), setting off a major confrontation with the U.S. The revived National Front and other secular parties, including the Tudeh, which had declared its allegiance to Khomeini, were banned in 1981 and 1982. The Mujahidin-i Khalq demonstrated and engaged in assassinations, including "suicide bombings", and many of them were imprisoned and executed (martyred like Husayn, in their view). Their leader was forced to flee the country, along with the first president, Bani Sadr, an economist interested in Islamic economics, who was impeached in 1981. They continued their activities from exile.

The ruling group that emerged was organized as the Islamic Republican Party and included *'ulama'*, many of them students of Khomeini, along with sympathetic laymen. They too suffered. In 1981 "seventy-two" leaders of the ruling party were killed at one time in a bomb blast (actually more, but seventy-two is the number of Husayn's companions at Karbala' and thus the number published) and later both the president and the prime minister were assassinated. Karbala' seemed truly to be "everywhere" and "every day". Many *'ulama'*, including all of the *marja's* except Khomeini, were opposed to or ambivalent about the government, but kept silent. One who did not, Grand Ayatollah Shariatmadari, was effectively "defrocked".

During this period a constitution was established by plebiscite. It included much that is typical of Western constitutions, such as an elected president and *majles* (parliament), but it also asserts the sovereignty of God, who makes man responsible for his social destiny following the continuous *ijtihad* of the ***faqihs***. It provides for a " just and pious *faqih*" and *marja'* to be the leader and highest authority and also a Guardian Council, half of whose members are *'ulama'*, and these determine whether laws passed by the *majles* accord with Islam. The position of leader is somewhat reminiscent of Plato's "philosopher king", a concept Khomeini would have known from his studies.

In 1980 Iraq invaded Iran, thinking to take advantage of the disruption there but underestimating the power of religious and revolutionary zeal. The result was an eight-year war that ended inconclusively but cost both sides dearly. The willingness of its youth for martyrdom saved Iran from defeat. The dictum that "Everywhere is Karbala' and every day is Ashura" was illustrated again and again through the revolution and the war. During this period many hoped for the imminent return of the Twelfth *Imam* and a popular slogan was "O God, O God, preserve Khomeini until the revolution of the *mahdi*". Khomeini himself stated that the Islamic Republic was a preparation for the return of the ***mahdi***.

The ruling group turned out to be quite fractious. It is common to divide them into moderates, conservatives and/or radicals, but the reality is much more complex. To a considerable degree the divisions are based on personal relations (as are the relations among the *'ulama'* generally) but one may note several ideological issues. These include a stricter or looser interpretation of the Shari'a, a greater or lesser acceptance of freedom of expression and other human rights, preference for a state-run or free market economy, and preference for a more or less aggressive foreign policy (including whether or not to "export the revolution"). An individual might hold a "liberal" position on one issue and a "conservative" one on another and might change his position. Khomeini has been quoted as forbidding music and later

Figure 18.2 Celebration marking the eighteenth anniversary of the death of Ayatollah Ruhollah Khomeini (L), at his mausoleum in Tehran (June 2007). On the right is a poster of Iran's current supreme leader, Ayatollah Ali Khamene'i. Courtesy of ATTA KENARE/AFP/Getty Images

permitting it. Khomeini generally remained above the factional fighting, seeking to reconcile and intervening when necessary.

In 1982 Khomeini declared secular laws invalid. A very traditional criminal code was passed and the shah's Family Protection laws were rescinded. Women were largely expected to accept traditional roles but still allowed some activity in politics and encouraged to get educated. (As of 2012 there were more women in universities than men.) The substance of many laws, however, continued from the previous period, presumably judged as not conflicting with Islam (i.e. *mubah*, neutral, in terms of the Shari'a). The Guardian Council has been very conservative and vetoed many bills of the *majles*. In 1988 this led Khomeini to speak of the absolute *vilayat-i faqih*, i.e. that the needs of the Islamic state take precedence over all other obligations, even ***salah***, fasting and ***Hajj***. This led some observers to claim that Khomeini had put the state above Islam, but in fact it involved changing the priority of various elements within Islam, one of which is the state, and is explicit or implicit in most radical Islamist thinking. It can be seen as an application of the *fiqh* principle of ***maslaha***, which Khomeini accepted. It could imply, paradoxically, that the *'ulama'* would have less independence of the state, now that it was "Islamic". The term, however, does not appear to have been much used since Khomeini's death. That Khomeini considered the revolution a success is clear from his spiritual testament in which he states that the

Iranian masses are better than the people of the Prophet Muhammad's time, since the latter disobeyed the Prophet and the Imams, a statement that would hardly be possible for a Sunni and may reflect some influence from Western ideas of "progress".

After Khomeini

For all its fractiousness, the ruling establishment made a calm transition of leadership when Khomeini died in June 1989. It was claimed that Khomeini had designated the president, Ali Khamane'i, as his successor, even though Khamane'i was not even an ayatollah, much less a *marja'*. He was immediately recognized as an ayatollah but has never fully established himself as *marja'* in Iran, though the Hizbollah in Lebanon accept him as such. The same year a revised constitution removed the requirement for a *marja'*. Khamane'i has held this position to the present (2013) and strengthened his authority.

Over the last thirty years the record of the Islamic Republic has been decidedly mixed. The revolution has not actually been exported but Iran has spread its influence in the region and effectively supported Shi'i Islamist movements in Lebanon and Iraq, as well Hamas in Palestine. It is certainly taken far more seriously on the international scene, both by friends and enemies, than the shah's regime was.

At home, the power of the state and its bureaucracy has been extended (paradoxically achieving a goal aimed at by the Pahlavis) and the regime has done much to bring modernization to the countryside. On the other hand, the economy has been in bad condition, partly due to an American boycott, leading to a high level of unemployment, especially among youth, and corruption and human rights violations may be worse than under the shah. Thus many of the youth have been alienated, as well as some important thinkers.

Politics has been lively and at least formally democratic, though within somewhat narrow ideological limits enforced by the Guardian Council, who have the power to reject candidates for the *majles* and use that power extensively. Elections are often unpredictable, as with those of Muhammad Khatami in 1997 and Mahmud Ahmadinejad in 2005. These two illustrate the extremes of acceptable ideology. Khatami is a "moderate" who spoke of a "dialogue of civilizations" and sought to liberalize the system somewhat but was largely stymied by the Guardian Council and other entrenched conservatives. Ahmadinejad, who is not an *'alim*, is populist in style and appears to have considerable following in the rural areas and among the urban poor. He stands for a strict interpretation of the Shari'a, state intervention to help the poor and an aggressive foreign policy but has gotten onto bad terms with the conservative *'ulama'*. He has become notorious in the West for his denial of the Jewish Holocaust (at a time when Iranian state television was airing a mini-series on the Holocaust!) and his refusal to accept limitation on Iran's quest for nuclear capacity, a point on which most Iranians certainly agree with him.

Figure 18.3 Inside Khomeini's mausoleum, 1999. Sermon is being given by Khomeini's grandson. Large pictures are of Khomeini and Khamane'i, the current leader. Courtesy of the author

In June 2009 Ahmadinejad won a second term in an election that had many signs of fraud. The result was dramatic street demonstrations by a wide segment of the population, particularly the young. If the tobacco protests were facilitated by the telegraph and the Islamic Revolution by the cassette tape, now it was the turn of the cellular phone and Twitter. The demonstrators were not opposing the Islamic Republic as such, however, but the conservatives and hardliners currently in power. The main opposing candidate, Mir Husayn Mousavi, a former prime minister with impeccable revolutionary credentials, provided a focus for the demonstrations but not aggressive leadership. The government dealt forcefully and successfully with the demonstrations (something the shah had achieved in 1963 but not in 1979!). Opposition continued, especially among the young and educated, but was expressed cautiously and often via the internet. In spite of massive economic problems and notable government failings, Ahmadinejad did appeal to many, especially among the poorer levels of society. The pressure from the Americans and Israelis over Iran's nuclear development and other things undoubtedly strengthened his "revolutionary" credentials.

The "Arab spring" did not spark a similar effort in Iran and most expected the presidential elections of June 2013 to produce nothing significantly new. Indeed, the Western media largely ignored it. Surprisingly, last-minute efforts by supporters of reform produced a victory for Hasan Rowhani. Rowhani is a highly placed member of the *'ulama'* and has been a leading negotiator on the nuclear issue. Though he had opposed the 2009 demonstrations, he took a reformist stance on matters such as human rights, freedom of speech and gender issues, and had the support of former presidents Rafsajani and Khatami. One is inclined to see in him a very "pragmatic" reformer but at this stage it is impossible to know just how he will act or how effective he will be. The least the election shows is that the forces for reform are still very much alive, in spite of the discouragements of the previous eight years.

Key points

- Iranian Shi'ism has a number of characteristics that are relevant to politics, especially the authority of the *'ulama'* and the story of Husayn and Karbala'.
- The *'ulama'* were very influential in the nineteenth century, lost much of their influence through much of the twentieth century and then regained it with the revolution.
- Modernization was pushed very fast under the Pahlavis, resulting in social imbalances.
- "Lay" ideologues played an important role in the lead up to the revolution.
- Since the Islamic revolution Iran has in principle been governed according to the Shari'a but with divergent interpretations and considerable factionalism.
- Despite its problems, the Islamic Republic appears firmly established and likely to continue for some time though its policies may change.

Discussion questions

1. Why did Iran have an Islamic revolution and Egypt and Turkey did not?
2. Do you think it would be more accurate to compare Reza Shah Pahlavi to Atatürk in Turkey or to Muhammad Ali in Egypt?
3. Which represents a greater break with previous history, the reforms of Reza Shah or the Islamic revolution?
4. Is it appropriate to call the Islamic revolution in Iran a Shi'i revolution?
5. Is is appropriate to speak of a "Turkish spring" and an "Iranian spring" along with an "Arab spring"?
6. What judgment might you make on the Islamic republic in Iran at this point in time? By what standards might you judge?

Critical thinking box 18.1

The two quotations at the beginning of this chapter represent two different attitudes toward the relationship between religion and government. Trace these as they appear in modern Iranian history, along with any other attitudes of which you are aware.

Critical thinking box 18.2

Compare, contrast and analyze the conception of political leadership contained in the following two passages (both are taken from material on the website):

> Or is it rather that government is necessary, and ... is still enjoined upon us by God after the Occultation even though He has appointed no particular individual to that function? The two qualities of knowledge of the law and justice are present in countless *fuqaha* of the present age. If they would come together, they could establish a government of universal justice in the world. If a worthy individual possessing these two qualities arises and establishes a government, he will possess the same authority as the Most Noble Messenger (upon whom be peace and blessings) in the administration of society, and it will be the duty of all people to obey him.
>
> (Khomeini, 1981, 61–62; part of a longer passage on the website.)

> In the affairs of society, therefore, in all that concerns the social system, but not in creedal matters such as the order of the cosmos, the words *al-nas* and Allah belong together. Thus when it is said, "Rule belongs to God", the meaning is that rule belongs to the people. ... When it is said, "Property belongs to God," the meaning is that capital belongs to the people as a whole. ... The political philosophy and the form of regime of the *umma* is not the democracy of heads, not irresponsible and directionless liberalism ... It consists rather of "purity of leadership" (not the leader, for that would be fascism) committed and revolutionary leadership, responsible for the movement and growth of society on the basis of its world view and ideology, and for the realization of the divine destiny of man in the plan of creation. This is the true meaning of imamate!
>
> (Shariati, 1979, 116–17, 119–20)

Critical thinking box 18.3

An example of Western scholarship misjudging the situation (cf. critical thinking box 17.3) is the following from a leading scholar of Iran.

> The position of the *'ulama'* seems bound to continue in general to decline as literacy, secular schools and scientific education spread; as Islamic practices regarding the relations of the sexes and other matters are increasingly ignored, and insofar as some of the *'ulama'* can be identified with a self-seeking opposition to reform.
>
> (N. Keddie, "The Iranian Power Structure and Social Change, 1800–1969: An Overview", 1971, *International Journal of Middle East Studies,* 2(1): 3–20)

Why did she "get it wrong", if indeed she did? Are there any factors distinctive to Iran?

Companion website

Features population figures, the supplementary law to the 1906–7 Constitution, quotes from Muhammad Reza Shah, Ali Shariati, Khomeini, Constitution of the Islamic Republic, thoughts on the missile crisis, links to books by Shariati (under further reading) and other weblinks.

Further reading

Mottahedeh, Roy (1986) *The Mantle of the Prophet: Politics and Religion in Iran.* London: Chatto & Windus. (Excellent introduction to the varied aspects of Iranian religion, culture, education and the events leading up to the revolution, using the life-story of a contemporary mullah as a framework.)

Gheissari, Ali and Nasr, Vali (2006) *Democracy in Iran: History and the Quest for Liberty.* Oxford: Oxford University Press.

Milani, Mohsen, M. (1988) *The Making of Iran's Islamic Revolution: From Monarchy to Islamic Republic.* Boulder, CO: Westview Press. (Covers developments from about 1900 to the 1980s, with primary attention to developments from 1963.)

Dabashi, Hamid (1993) *Theology of Discontent.* New York: New York University Press. (Chapters on all of the main Islamic opposition figures.)

Fischer, M.M.J. (1980) *Iran, from Religious Dispute to Revolution.* Cambridge, MA: Harvard University Press. (Perceptive discussion of the Revolution and surrounding events by an anthropologist.)

Khomeini, R.M. (1981) *Islam and Revolution, Writings and Declarations of Imam Khomeini*, trans. H. Algar. Berkeley, CA: Mizan Press. (Collection of Khomeini's writings and statements from 1941 to 1980 including his lectures on *vilayat-i faqih*.)

Shariati, Ali (1979) *On the Sociology of Islam*, trans. H. Algar. Berkeley, CA: Mizan Press. (Some of his popular lectures. Introduction has a short biography.)

Loeffler, Reinhold (1988) *Islam in Practice: Religious Beliefs in a Persian Village*. Albany, NY: SUNY Press. (A study of popular attitudes based on anthrological field work done before and after the Revolution.)

Abrahamian, Ervand (1993) *Khomeinism: Essays on the Islamic Republic*. Berkeley, CA: University of California Press. (A detailed study of the thinking of Khomeini and some of his followers, includes the changes over time.)

Abrahamian, Ervand (1989) *Radical Islam: The Iranian Mojahedin*. London: Tauris. (The main monograph on them that I know of.)

Brumberg, Daniel (2001) *Reinventing Khomeini: The Struggle for Reform in Iran*. Chicago, IL: Chicago University Press. (A detailed study of the first two decades, mainly oriented toward politics.)

See also: Richard, *Shi'ite Islam* [8]; Halm, *Shiism* [8]; Enayat, *Modern Islamic Political Thought* [15]; Rahmena, *Pioneers of Islamic Revival* [15]; Voll, *Islam: Continuity and Change* [15].

Online resources (accessed 28 August 2013)

Iran Chamber Society. (Has a very wide range of historical and cultural information about Iran.): http://www.iranchamber.com/about_us/about_us.php

The Hajj, by Ali Shariati. (A revolutionary interpretation (also available as a book).): http://www.al-islam.org/hajj/shariati

Fatima Is Fatima, by Ali Shariati. http://www.al-islam.org/fatimaisfatima

"Patterns of Discontent: Will History Repeat in Iran?" by Michael Rubin and Patrick Clawson. (Good survey of events from the Revolution to 2006.): http://www.meforum.org/921/patterns-of-discontent-will-history-repeat-in-iran

19 *Ideology and politics in Indonesia*

Islamic society or Islamic state?

Unity in Diversity
(Indonesian national motto)

Indonesia is the largest Muslim country in the world today in terms of population and its diverse cultural background is different from that of the countries of the Middle East. It became Muslim later than Turkey, Iran or Egypt, experienced colonial rule more directly and gained independence more recently. Like Egypt, it has sought to find a way between secularism and Islamism, but its path has been somewhat different. This chapter will outline the background and trace the path during the last century.

In this chapter

- Islamization of Java, Sumatra and other islands
- Dutch imperialism and continuing Islamization
- Twentieth-century movements
- Independence and the issue of an Islamic state
- The events of 1965 and Suharto's regime
- Post-Suharto: election; violent Islamism, and beyond

Islamization of Java, Sumatra and other islands

Indonesia consists of some 6,000 inhabited islands and its various areas differ considerably from each other in language, culture and historical background. The present political boundaries were created by Dutch imperialism in the nineteenth century. Before that there were a number of autonomous political entities in the area. While it is predominantly Muslim, about ten percent of its population is Christian or Hindu. More than half of the population lives on Java, and there has been a tendency for Java to dominate the other areas, resulting in a complex and sometimes

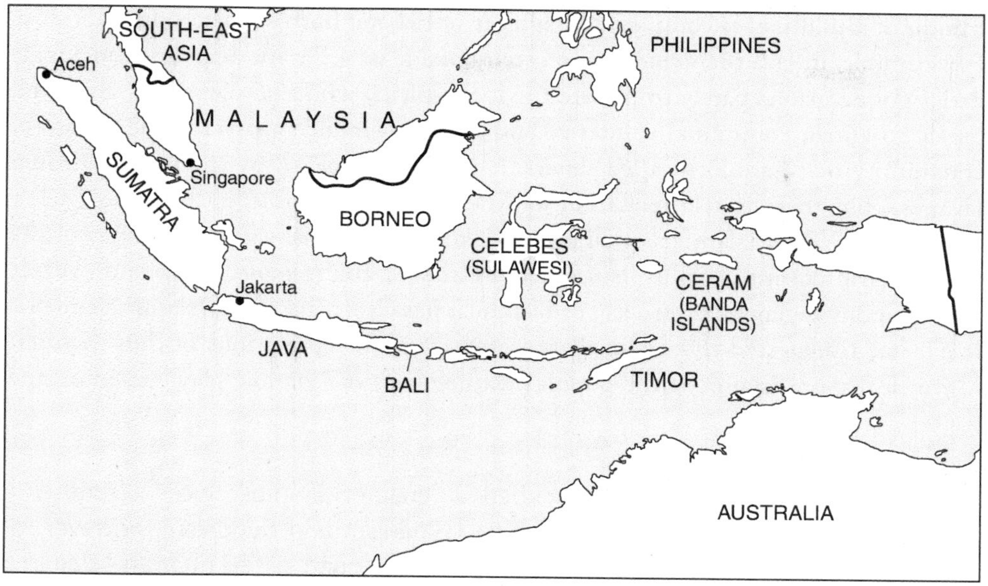

Map 11 Indonesia

tense relationship with them. This chapter will unavoidably focus more on Java than elsewhere and ignore some areas completely.

As mentioned in chapter 4, Islam was brought to the area by traders and independent teachers, many of them Sufis. It is unclear when it first arrived but there were Muslim rulers in the north of Sumatra before 1300. Over the previous millennium Java and Sumatra had had major Hindu–Buddhist kingdoms. The last of these, Majapahit, collapsed about 1525 and was replaced by the Muslim kingdom of Mataram. Islamization took place first in the coastal areas and then proceeded inland. This process was largely if superficially complete by the late eighteenth century but in some places it continued into the twentieth. In central Java the Hindu Code of Manu continued in use until 1768. Bali remains Hindu to the present. The Islam that came was strongly Sufi; Javanese tradition speaks of nine ***walis*** who brought Islam there and the miraculous, that is, Sufi ***baraka***, features significantly in their stories and other conversion accounts. Undoubtedly the perception that the Muslim teachers had more *baraka* than the local spirits, gods and mediums played an important role in conversion. Several Sufi ***tariqas*** took hold, especially the **Qadiriyya**, the **Naqshbandiyya** and the Shattariyya. Sufi theosophy appeared with Hamza Fansuri (d. c. 1600) who propagated the teachings of **Ibn Arabi**, and with Nur al-Din al-Raniri (fl. c. 1637–44) who opposed Ibn Arabi's doctrine of ***wahdat al-wujud***.

For most people becoming Muslim meant adding some Muslim symbols and practices to the ones they already had, possibly modifying the latter. In many cases the actual relationship between Islam and the pre-Islamic traditions, whether folk,

Hindu or Buddhist, is complex and subject to debate, both scholarly and political. For example, in Java the *slametan* is a ceremonial feast given for neighbors on a wide variety of occasions partly to placate the local spirits, who also partake of the food, partly to affirm communal solidarity and partly to induce a psychological state of equanimity or tranquility called *slamet*. It includes a speech by the host in formal Javanese, but there is also recitation in Arabic including passages from the Qur'an and this is held on Islamic as well as non-Islamic occasions, e.g. the birthday of the Prophet. Moreover the name, *slamet*, derives from Arabic (*salāma*, well-being). While the ceremony is generally seen as pre-Islamic it has clearly taken on Islamic elements. It has been suggested that its goals represent local interpretations of Sufi theories. More clearly pre-Islamic is the popular *wayang kulit* or "shadow play" based on the

In terms of the Axial Age, described in chapter 2, most local Javanese practices would be considered pre-Axial. Hinduism and Buddhism, however, are considered post-Axial but in ways that are quite different from Islam, Christianity, Judaism and Zoroastrianism. Here I will mention the most salient differences, bearing in mind the dangers of generalizing since these religions are quite diverse.

For both Hinduism and Buddhism ultimate reality is one and transcends the world, but for Buddhists it is not conceived as a personal creator God. Buddha is a teacher but not the Creator. Many Hindus do believe in a single creator God, but this God has different forms, while some believe in a supra-personal Brahman of which the personal God is a lower form. Lower-level gods and spirits may be devotees or manifestations of the one God, or followers of the Buddha, and are accorded some form of worship. *Shirk* is not a problem.

A cosmic struggle between good and evil is recognized, but ultimate reality stands beyond this distinction. The universe is infinite in past and future time and goes through cycles of evolution and devolution. Beings are born, die and are reborn again and again as humans, gods, animals and beings in heaven or hell (neither of which is permanent), depending on the *karma* accumulated from good or bad deeds. This round of rebirth represents a kind of alienation and escape from it (*moksha* in Hindu parlance, *nirvana* in Buddhist parlance) is the ultimate spiritual goal, sometimes conceived as merging with the Ultimate. The law of *karma* explains human inequality, justifying the caste system among Hindus. Buddhism is a universal religion and has spread quite widely. Hinduism is more identified with India, though it did spread to what is now Indonesia.

The most obvious contrasts to Islam are the conception of ultimate reality, the greater tolerance of diversity and the idea of *karma* and rebirth. On the first two the Sufis are closer to them than the Shari'a minded.

Hindu classics, the Mahabharata and the Ramayana. Many Javanese, especially in the upper classes, have a strong awareness of and pride in their Hindu–Buddhist heritage and some follow distinctive spiritual traditions often referred to as "Javanese mysticism" (*kejawen* or *kebatinan*), aimed at an awareness of the divinity within and without and a concentrated state of *slamet*. But this is not so different from the Sufi sense of *wahdat al-wujud* and may be influenced by it. Hindu–Buddhist kings had been viewed as having access to cosmic powers; their Muslim successors were viewed as "shadows of God", "God's caliph", as having *wahyu* (literally revelation but here a divine energy) and even as *walis*. In the legal and political sphere *adat* (custom) was recognized and played a large role (an example from Aceh is mentioned in chapter 10).

Important to Islamization were the Islamic boarding schools known in Java as *pesantrens* (see chapter 9). These, interestingly, are a continuation of pre-Islamic schools and the name derives from Sanskrit. They particularly taught Sufism and their teachers, known as *kiais*, would have seemed similar to the gurus of the Hindu period.

Dutch imperialism and continuing Islamization

Europeans appeared on the scene while the process of Islamization was still under way. The Portuguese took Malacca in 1511 and were a significant trading and naval force in the area for about a century. They were then replaced by the Dutch, who founded Batavia (now Jakarta) in 1619 and by the middle of the eighteenth century had established bases throughout the area and forced local rulers to grant them trading monopolies. It was only in the nineteenth century that they began to take direct control of the inland areas, often in the face of popular armed resistance, stimulated in part by economic arrangements that disadvantaged the peasants. This resistance included the Java War of 1825–30, led by Prince Dipanegara, who came to be seen as a hero of Indonesian independence, and also the Padri Wars in Sumatra, 1821–37, endemic resistance in West Java from 1820 to 1869 and a major insurrection in 1888, and war followed by guerrilla resistance in Aceh from 1871 to about 1910. All of these were peasant revolts that were seen as ***jihads*** and were largely led by ***'ulama'***, while the local chiefs and nobles often sided with the Dutch.

Although the revolts failed, they deepened the Islamic identity of those involved and helped to spread Islam. The *'ulama'* tended to become identified with resistance to Dutch, in the minds of both the local people and of the Dutch. Improved internal communications also aided the spread of Islamic teaching and practice. Improved external communications facilitated the ***Hajj*** and other overseas travel and many returned with a wider sense of the ***umma*** and a commitment to a more **Shari'a**-oriented version of Islam. As a result *pesantrens* began to give more attention to ***fiqh***. Often Islamic reform efforts and resistance to the Dutch went together. In the legal area, the Dutch had a policy of retaining *adat* law but also introduced considerable

Dutch statute law. In 1900 they introduced the "Ethical Policy", according to which the colonial government would seek paternalistically to improve the condition of its subjects. As part of this Islam was not to be viewed simply as the enemy; Islam as a religion was acceptable but Islam as political doctrine was not. This, of course, amounted to promoting secularism as defined in this book.

Since the later nineteenth century it has been common in discussing Indonesia, and particularly Java, to distinguish three groups, *abangan*, *santri* and *priyayi*. The *abangans* are sometimes called "statistical Muslims", since they identify themselves as Muslims but do not follow Islamic practices very much. They are usually more interested in local spirits and rituals related to them, including the *slametan* mentioned earlier. They are found among the peasants and lower classes generally. The *santris* are the "practicing Muslims" and have tended to be strong particularly among the merchants and wealthier peasants. (The term *santri* refers, in the first instance, to students of the *pesantrens*.) The reform movements and *jihads* of the nineteenth century strengthened this group. As scholars returned from places such as Egypt in the early twentieth century the *santris* came to be divided between the *kaum muda* (young group), who accepted the ideas of modernist reformers such as **Jamal al-Din al-Afghani** and **Muhammad 'Abduh**, and the *kaum tua* (old group), who did not. The *priyayis* were the old nobility, particularly in Java. Some were practicing Muslims, thus also *santris*, but more of them gave primary value and allegiance to the heritage and ethos believed to derive from the pre-Islamic civilization and from the religious point of view may be considered *abangan*. The *priyayis* lost political power as the result of Dutch imperialism but compensated by becoming public servants under the Dutch. It was *priyayis* who had access to the limited number of European-style schools that were available to Indonesians before 1900. They were, therefore, the most Westernized of the three groups.

Twentieth-century movements

In the twentieth century the *jihad* resistance movements were replaced by modern social and political associations. This was facilitated by the extension of Western-style education at all levels after 1900. Some of these, such as the Budi Utomo ("Noble Endeavor"), founded in 1908, and the Taman Siswa ("Garden of Learning"), founded in 1922, were secular and took a particular interest in Javanese culture. Also secular was the Indonesian National Party (PNI), founded in 1927 under the leadership of Sukarno, who became the primary spokesperson for the independence movement. The first labor union was founded in 1905 and the Indonesian Communist Party (PKI) was founded in 1920; it was banned in 1927 and went underground after provoking a series of strikes and revolts but emerged as a major force after 1945.

The first Islamic association was Muhammadiyah, founded in 1912 and by 1920 had spread to almost all cities and towns in Java. It took a modernist position along the lines of the teachings of Muhammad 'Abduh and **Rashid Rida** and opposed many customary practices, such as the *slametan* and other spirit-related rituals and also visits to the tombs of *walis*. It did not recognize the four ***madhhabs*** but to some extent developed a *fiqh* of its own. It calls for a truly Islamic society but does not participate directly in politics. It engages in ***dakwa*** and has established a large network of schools, clinics, hospitals and orphanages. Unlike the *pesantrens*, the schools have been organized on modern lines and teach religion along with a considerable range of secular subjects. It also has organizations for women and youth. Muhammadiyah has been one of the two largest Islamic associations and has for some time been active throughout Indonesia.

More political was Sarakat Islam, founded about the same time as Muhammadiyah. It called for political and social reforms, while its charismatic leader was viewed by many as the *ratu adil* (just king), a kind of Javanese ***mahdi***. It attracted peasants, merchants and also radical socialists and for a brief time was a mass movement. It could not, however, hold these disparate groups together and declined after the radicals were expelled in 1921. Its leaders sought to root socialist principles in the Qur'an.

Somewhat along the lines of Muhammadiyah but more radically Islamist is Persatuan Islam (Persis), founded in 1923. Initially it was non-political though holding a political point of view; during the 1940s and 1950s it was involved in politics but later withdrew and now concentrates on educational and *dakwa* activities. It calls for a society and state that will implement the Shari'a and sees loyalty to the worldwide *umma* as taking precedence over loyalty to the nation-state. It does not totally reject *adat* but this must never take precedence over the Shari'a. It sees a form of democracy as compatible with Islam and does not advocate violence to further its aims. Its long-term goals can be compared to those of the Muslim Brothers in Egypt and Mawdudi in India/Pakistan. Since it was founded before either of these it can be considered the first Islamist group in the world, although it has never been as influential as they.

In conscious response to the modernists, the traditionalist Nahdlatul Ulama (NU) was founded in Java in 1926. It was, and is, based on the network of *pesantrens* and their *kiais* and is the largest of the Islamic associations in Indonesia but with its strength mainly in Java and has more of a rural constituency than Muhammadiyah or Persis. It has explicitly defended such things as the four *madhhabs* and visits to tombs, along with other activities opposed by the modernists, but it uses modern methods of organization and publicity to defend them. Many of the *pesantrens* have added modern schools to their activities. Nahdlatul Ulama people generally value local traditions, quite self-consciously in recent decades, but would not favor *adat* where it is seen to contradict Islam. Some have even spoken of the "Indonesianization" of Islam as opposed to the Islamization of Indonesia. They wish to influence government and were involved in party politics from 1945 until 1984, favoring an

Figure 19.1 Pesantren Pabelan, Java; *salah* at the mosque. Courtesy of the author

Islamic state, but then formally withdrew and no longer favor an Islamic state. In general they have found it easier to cooperate with secular nationalists than have the modernist groups since they tend to follow the long-standing Sunni approach that accepts much less than perfect rulers on the grounds of necessity.

Some smaller Muslim groups called for independence from the Dutch but it was the secular nationalists, especially the PNI under Sukarno, who took the lead in the independence movement. Sukarno had some involvement with Muhammadiya but believed in the separation of religion from state. During the Second World War the Japanese occupied Indonesia from 1942 to 1945 and sought to use Islam to gain support. They created an Office of Religious Affairs, which laid a basis for the later Ministry of Religious Affairs, and they brought the various Islamic groups, including Muhammadiya and Nahdlatul Ulama, into a single organization, Masyumi (Supreme Indonesian Council of Islam). This brought *santris* closer to government than they had been under the Dutch and gave them expectations and political instruments that would make a difference in the future.

Independence and the issue of an Islamic state

After the Japanese defeat, Indonesian independence was declared but it took five years to fight off the Dutch effort to return. In general *abangans, santris, priyayis* and non-Muslims all participated in this effort, but a number of Muslim leaders declared it a *jihad*. After victory, one of the contentious issues was whether the new state would be Islamic. It was finally decided to base the state on "five principles" (*pancasila*), of which the first was "belief in the one and only Divinity". An earlier version added "with the obligation for the adherents of Islam to practice the Shari'a" but after considerable debate these "seven words", as they are often called (they are seven words in Indonesian), were deleted along with some other references to Islam in the interest of national unity.

A Ministry of Religious Affairs was created that deals with all religions but primarily oversees and supports Islamic institutions such as mosques, state-funded Islamic schools, Shari'a courts, arrangements for the *Hajj* and promotional literature for *dakwa*. It also provides a source of patronage for the Islamic movements. It has sometimes been called an Islamic "state within the state". Both *pancasila* and the Ministry of Religious Affairs represent a distinctive Indonesian compromise between secularism and Islamism.

The Masyumi continued as one of the main political parties in the new state but the NU withdrew in 1952 to form a separate party, leaving the Masyumi primarily associated with Muhammadiya. There were two main secular parties, Sukarno's PNI and the PKI (Communist). There was a national election in 1955, in which PNI gained 22.3 percent of the vote, the largest of any single party, the Islamic parties gained 42.5 percent of the vote among them, less than they had expected, and the PKI gained 16.4 percent. The result was unstable government and in 1959 Sukarno introduced his authoritarian "Guided Democracy", in which the nationalists, the religious groups, the communists and, increasingly, the army were all to have a major role. The communists were well organized and feared by many, not least by the Muslim groups. There were clashes between Muslim and communist youth.

Sukarno's religious views are hard to pin down but worth noting. He presented himself as the son of a father whose Islam was mixed with Javanese religion and a Balinese mother whose Hinduism was mixed with Buddhism. He believed in God in what he called a "pantheist" way (though panentheist may be more accurate) and was concerned for the current backwardness of Muslims, who must not look to the past but "run forward, catching up with the time" and follow "the spirit of Islam", not "the spirit of the *pesantren*" (Boland, 1971, 126–29).

During this period there were at least three Islamist revolts labeled "Dar al-Islam" seeking to set up Islamic states. A movement in West Java began in 1948 and continued until 1962. It proclaimed itself the Islamic State of Indonesia. One in South Sulawesi was initially concerned with regional grievances and later became Islamist and proclaimed itself the Indonesian Islamic Republic. It lasted from 1950 to 1965. The third movement, in West Sumatra and elsewhere from 1958 to 1961, called itself the Revolutionary Government of the Republic of Indonesia but was actually an attempt to change the government in Jakarta. Some of the Masyumi leaders were implicated in the last two of these and this, added to the fact that they had been strongly criticizing Sukarno's move toward guided democracy, led to the banning of the Masyumi party in 1960 and the arrest of its leaders. The NU, more flexible in such matters, remained in the Sukarno government to the end.

The events of 1965 and Suharto's regime

On 30 September 1965 several army generals were killed in an attempted coup d'etat ascribed to the communists. The coup was quickly put down by General Suharto but the aftermath was an extensive pogrom throughout the country of communists and those who might be associated with them (often settling personal scores). As many as half a million may have died, though many put the number lower. The communist movement, which was now outlawed, never recovered. Many Muslims saw the events as a great victory for Islam. Muhammadiya had declared them a *jihad* (but not justifying the excesses) and much of the killing was done by members of NU, convinced it was a religious duty. The effects on individuals and communities continue to this day and can hardly be underestimated.

The following year Suharto took control of the government and in 1968 officially became the president of the republic. He was to rule, effectively as a dictator though with democratic trappings, until 1998. After the events of 1965 all Indonesians were required to declare themselves adherents of one of five religions: Islam, Roman Catholicism, Protestantism, Hinduism or Buddhism. The groups adhering to Javanese mysticism have sought but failed to get themselves considered a recognized religion.

Although he had disposed of the communist threat Suharto gave little joy to the Islamists for the first twenty years of his rule. Suharto himself is said to have been inclined toward Javanese mysticism and the higher echelons of the army during this period were largely *abangan* or non-Muslim. From 1983 to 1988 the head of the army was a Roman Catholic who was considerably suspect in Muslim eyes. The Masyumi Party was not reinstated and in 1973 Suharto decided to coalesce all parties into three. Golkar was the government party and always destined to win. The Muslim parties, including NU and those who had been part of Masyumi, were joined together into the United Development Party (PPP) and closely regulated by the government. Although it could not win, how well it did was noted. Many radical Islamists were imprisoned for violent activities in the 1970s and for the riots at the Jakarta port of Tanjung Priok in 1984. Religious, cultural and economic factors led to a revolt in Aceh, a very strongly *santri* area, that began in 1976 and continued off and on until 2005, becoming particular bloody just after Suharto's departure.

In the early 1980s the government undertook to make *pancasila* a more substantial ideology than it had been and demanded that all organizations, religious and social as well as political, accept *pancasila* as their "sole basis". Nahdlatul Ulama already accepted *pancasila* as the basis for society, but this went further. How could a

Muslim group (or a Christian one) accept something as vague as *pancasila* as its *sole* basis? The pressure was put on, however, and all of the groups fell into line, Muhammadiya being the last to do so. Some took the position that "belief in the one and only Divinity" could be interpreted as ***tawhid***.

The Suharto government was not, in fact, anti-Islamic where it could control Islamic activities and where they were not political. The Ministry of Education promoted Muslim religious education and provided materials. Religious instruction continued to be compulsory in state schools and universities as it had been since about 1960. The State Institutes of Islamic Religion (IAIN) were expanded. These offer upper-level theological education to *pesantren* graduates as well as others and include modernists on their faculties. About 1978 the Council of Indonesian Ulama (MUI) was established to provide *fatwas* for the government but some describe it as a "cynical creation" of the regime. The government appears to have encouraged non-political *dakwa* in areas where *santri* Islam was weak and in fact many *abangan* and *priyayi* became *santri* during this period. To its critics, Suharto's policy looked like the Dutch "Ethical Policy".

Apart from the government there was considerable and varied Islamic activity, including Muhammadiya, NU and other groups mentioned earlier. More radically Islamist was the Dakwah Council (Dewan Dakwah) founded by Mohammad Natsir, a former leader of Masyumi, in 1967 and linked to the Saudi-based World Muslim League (*Rābiṭat al-ʿĀlam al-Islāmī*). There were strict ***salafi*** groups linked to the Saudis that were apolitical but formed separate communities. The groups connected with the Indonesian Students Association (HMI) were quite active and diverse. Some of these took a radically Islamist position, particularly stimulated by the example of the Iranian revolution, but most were apolitical and stressed individual moral improvement.

A numerically small but influential group calls itself "neo-modernist". Its most prominent representatives have been Nurcholish Madjid (1939–2005) and Abdurrahman Wahid (1940–2009), both of whom came from a *pesantren* background. After his *pesantren* studies Nurcholish Madjid attended the IAIN in Jakarta and was active in the student movement in the 1960s and 1970s. Initially close to Masyumi, he soon took the position "Islam, yes! Islamic parties, no!" From 1978 to 1984 he studied for a Ph.D. in the United States under Fazlur Rahman, the Pakistani scholar by then teaching in Chicago, who had labeled his own views "neo-modernist". Later Nurcholish taught at an IAIN and founded Paramadina, an educational and social foundation appealing to middle- and upper-class Muslims. Abdurrahman Wahid was born into a highly respected NU family and had a wide cultural exposure in addition to his *pesantren* education. From 1964 to 1971 he was in the Middle East, studying first at al-Azhar in Cairo and then at Baghdad University. On his return he became active in institutions related to the *pesantrens* and the NU. In 1984 he became general chairman of the NU. He played an important role in taking the organization out of party politics and getting it to accept *pancasila* as the sole basis. Later he was to become president of Indonesia for a brief period, as we shall see. From the 1970s a number of NU activists engaged in rural development projects, seeking to involve the *pesantrens* and, especially from the late 1980s, to express their goals in terms that the *kiais* could appreciate.

In general, neo-modernists see themselves as "progressive", looking to the future rather than to the past greatness of Islam. They are more favorable than most to Western culture and give considerable value to democracy, tolerance, pluralism and human rights. Religion and state should be separate; some speak of "Islamic values" or "Islamic society" rather than Islamic state. Nurcholish Madjid has stated that Islamic values are essentially the same as universal human values and are to be made concrete in the Indonesian context. Abdurrahman Wahid has said he wants not an "Islamic society" but an "Indonesian society" in which the Muslims are functioning well. The Shari'a does not contain a blueprint for society but general principles that must be applied flexibly to each situation. Abdurrahman particularly is concerned to respect and build on local traditions. At the same time ***ijtihad*** should be systematic and well grounded in traditional Islamic scholarship. Although the neo-modernists were often critical of Suharto, their position is quite consistent with *pancasila*. In terms of the types presented in chapter 15, neo-modernism is secularist but with clear neo-traditionalist roots.

In the late 1980s Indonesian Islam could be described as politically weak but culturally vigorous, with various groups engaged in social, educational and *dakwa* activities. About 1989 Suharto changed his stance to one more favorable to Islam. In 1991 he prominently went on *Hajj*. Shari'a courts were given a higher status and a government-sponsored Islamic bank was established. Women were permitted to wear Islamic head-covering in state schools. More *santri* were appointed to the higher echelons of the army. Suharto also encouraged the formation of the Indonesian Association of Muslim Intellectuals (ICMI) under the leadership of the vice-president, inviting a number of activists to join it who had previously been out of favor. Many intellectuals and civil servants joined it, at least nominally, and it drew in conservatives also. Abdurrahman Wahid criticized it, fearing that it would be a political tool for the government and would foster sectarianism. He and others formed the interfaith Democratic Forum (*Forum Democrasi*).

Post-Suharto: elections; violent Islamism

It was economic collapse that finally brought down the Suharto government in 1998. After a transition period under the vice-president the first free election was held since 1955. Some 48 parties took part. In addition to the PPP, there were parties backed by the NU and by Muhammadiya respectively and several smaller Islamist parties. The Muslim parties got a total of 38 percent of the vote, not much worse than in 1955, but the major Muslim parties in 1955 could all be considered Islamist while the parties backed by the Muhammadiya and the NU in 1999 are not. "Back room" negotiations led to the choice of Abdurrahman Wahid as president but he lasted only two years, defeated by the difficulties of the situation and, in part, by his own outspokenness and erratic style.

The post-Suharto period has seen a number of religious developments. While Sufi *tariqas* have always been present and in recent decades some intellectuals have taken a greater interest in Sufism, more recently its popularity has increased, featuring, among other things, mass communal ***dhikrs*** led by popular preachers.

"Progressive" Muslims have continued their efforts but have faced serious resistance from conservatives and Islamists, who have become much more active and gained considerable media attention. The leadership of the Muhammadiyah and the NU have become more conservative and the Council of Indonesian Ulama has become independent of the government and has given conservative *fatwas*, including one declaring secularism, pluralism and religious liberalism un-Islamic. A number of small but very radical groups have appeared. Radical Islamists organized a Mujahidin

Figure 19.2 Indonesian police check members of Jemaah Islamiya outside a court in Jakarta where Abu Bakar Ba'asyir is on trial for treason (May 2003). Courtesy of CHOO YOUN-KONG/AFP/Getty Images

Congress in Yogyakarta in 2000 and established the Indonesian Mujahidin Council (MMI), dedicated to the goal of a new international caliphate. The international movement, Hizb al-Tahrir (see next chapter), which has a similar goal, has gained increasing influence in Indonesia.

Intercommunal violence increased for a time, including the bombing of churches at Christmas time in 2000. There has also been serious violence against Ahmadis more recently. The Laskar Jihad was formed in 2000 and became known for its attacks on Christians and general exacerbation of communal tensions in some of the outer islands. It claimed that its mission was to defend Muslims by attacking "belligerent" ***kafirs***. It was accused of receiving support from elements in the army and harboring al-Qaeda cells, though it denied both of these charges. It derived from the *salafi* groups that had appeared earlier, though many of them opposed it, and was disbanded in 2002.

The most infamous of the violent groups was the Jemaah Islamiya, whose members bombed the night club in Bali on 12 October 2002, the Marriott Hotel in Jakarta in 2003, the Australian Embassy in 2004 and possibly sites in Kuta in 2005. While it has connections with the international *jihad* movement to be discussed in the next chapter, its main roots are within Indonesia. Its leader, Abu Bakar Ba'asyir, and others had been members of the youth wing of the Masyumi and then were involved in the Dar al-Islam movements. Later they spent time in prison for violent Islamist activities. Some of the leaders were in Afghanistan between 1985 and 1995 and Ba'asyir came into contact with the Egyptian Jama'a Islamiyya (Islamic Group) in the mid-1990s. He was an organizer of the Mujahidin Congress and the MMI, mentioned earlier.

For all of this, Islamist forces are far from dominating Indonesian politics. In the parliamentary elections of 2009 the Islamically oriented parties (including those not Islamist) lost ground, having gained 38 percent of the vote in 2004 but only 24 percent in 2009. Abdurrrahman Wahid was succeeded as president first by the daughter of Sukarno, Megawati Sukarnoputri (2001–4), and then by Susilo Bambang Yudhoyono, a retired army general with reform interests (2004–). Both are of *priyayi* background and relatively secular orientation, although Yudhoyono has publicly affiliated with a Sufi *tariqa*.

Indonesian Islam continues to be intellectually and culturally vigorous, perhaps more so than at any time in the past, but it is also the focus of severe communal and ideological tensions. Islam in Indonesia has the reputation of being more tolerant and flexible than in most other places, but the events of 1965, the activities of the Jemaah Islamiya and many other things remind us that it has considerable potential for radicalism and violence.

Key points

- Islam penetrated the area that is now Indonesia gradually and mixed with earlier practices.
- The Dutch presence served to strengthen Islam and particularly Shari'a-oriented forms of Islam.
- It is common to distinguish three groups, *abangan*, *santri* and *priyayi* in discussing Indonesia.
- The twentieth century saw the creation of several Islamic movements, of which Muhammadiya and Nahdlatul Ulama are the largest.
- The struggle for independence was led by Sukarno and the secularist Indonesian National Party but the Muslim groups participated.
- *Pancasila* became the ideological basis of the new Indonesian state.
- The communist movement was destroyed after the pogrom of 1965, in which many Muslims participated.
- Suharto's government generally favored secularists but took on a more Islamic coloring from about 1989.
- A small but influential movement has been that of the "neo-Modernists".
- There have been several violent movements over the years, the most recent including the Jemaah Islamiya, responsible for the Bali bombing in 2002 and others.

Discussion questions

1. Indonesian Islam is commonly seen as particularly tolerant and flexible. To what extent does the material in this chapter seem to justify this claim?
2. How has the presence of non-Muslims and *abangans* influenced Indonesian developments in relation to Islam?
3. Compare the role of Sukarno in Indonesia with that of Atatürk in Turkey and/or Reza Shah in Iran.
4. Compare the attitudes toward Islamic movements of the Suharto regime and of the Mubarak regime in Egypt.
5. Indonesian Islam in the late 1980s has been described as politically enfeebled but culturally vigorous. Is this true? If so, why? Was it still true as of 2010?
6. Why have "liberal" or "secular" forms of Islam arisen from among the NU members?

Critical thinking box 19.1

The official slogan of Indonesia is "unity in diversity". In what ways have Indonesians sought to create unity in diversity, particularly in the realm of religion? How successful do you think they have been? You may, if you wish, compare Indonesia with one or more other countries, Muslim or non-Muslim.

Critical thinking box 19.2

Is it appropriate for a Muslim to participate in a *slametan*? (Geertz (below) has an important discussion of the *slametan* and Woodward (below) has useful comments. There are further suggestions on the website.)

Companion website

Features population figures, information on various customs, *pancasila*, Sukarno's beliefs, neo-modernists and Laskar Jihad, also some further reading and websites for various figures and groups.

Further reading

Geertz, Clifford (1960) *The Religion of Java*. Glencoe, NY: Free Press. (The seminal work on the subject, by a highly respected anthropologist.)

Woodward, Mark R. (1989) *Islam in Java: Normative Piety and Mysticism in the Sultanate of Yogyakarta*. Tucson, AZ: University of Arizona Press. (Detailed study of Javanese Islam, both courtly and popular; sees Hindu and Buddhist elements as thoroughly incorporated into the Islamic matrix.)

Boland, B.J. (1971) *The Struggle of Islam in Modern Indonesia*. The Hague: Nijhoff. (An excellent study of the political involvements of Muslims in the twentieth century.)

Nakamura, Mitsuo (1983) *The Crescent Arises Over The Banyan Tree: A Study of the Muhammadiyah Movement in a Central Javanese Town*. Yogyakarta: Gadja Mada University Press. (Anthropological study of Muhammadiyah in a particular town, stressing the degree to which the organization fits into its Javanese environment. There is also a second, enlarged, edition published in 2012 by the Institute of Southeast Asian Studies in Singapore.)

Federspiel, Howard M. (1970) *Persatuan Islam: Islamic Reform in Twentieth Century Indonesia*. Ithaca, NY: Modern Indonesian Project, Southeast Asia Program,

Cornell University. (The most thorough monograph on this organization that I know of.)

Barton, Greg and Fealy, Greg (eds.) (1996) *Nahdlatul Ulama, Traditional Islam and Modernity in Indonesia*. Clayton, Victoria: Monash Asia Institute, Monash University. (A collection of articles on this organization.)

Woodward, Mark R. (ed.) (1996) *Toward a New Paradigm: Recent Developments in Indonesian Islamic Thought*. Tempe, Arizona, AZ: Arizona State University Program for Southeast Asian Studies. (Articles on a range of topics, including Dewan Dakwah, banking, considerable attention to neo-modernists.)

Barton, Greg (2005) *Indonesia's Struggle: Jemaah Islamiyah and the Soul of Islam*. Sydney: University of New South Wales Press. (Study of this and similar groups set in their larger religious and political context.)

Hilmy, Masdar (2010) *Islamism and Democracy in Indonesia; Piety and Pragmatism*. Singapore: Institute of Southeast Asian Studies. (Studies three small contemporary Islamist parties with attention to their attitudes toward democracy but also deals with wider issues. At points not so well written.)

See also: Martin, Woodward and Atmaja, *Defenders of Reason in Islam* [11].

20 *Globalization*

Challenge and opportunity

The "globalization" of human society in recent decades has influenced Muslims and their understanding and practice of Islam in diverse ways. This chapter will consider three of them: the development of a "global *jihad*", exemplified and symbolized by the destruction of the Twin Towers in New York, the creation of a Muslim "diaspora" as Muslims have emigrated to Western countries largely for economic reasons, and activities of a number of liberal or "progressive" Muslims both in the Muslim world and in the diaspora.

In this chapter

- Globalization, various examples
- Global *jihad*
- Why martyrdom operations?
- Muslim diaspora in the West
- Liberal/progressive Islam

Globalization: meaning and examples

The term globalization commonly refers to the fact that organizations, institutions and individuals increasingly function on a worldwide level little inhibited by distance or even national boundaries. Science, technology, ideas and fashions spread quickly from their sources to other parts of the world. Multinational corporations source raw material in one country, produce in another, are managed in a third and market almost everywhere. Political events in one place can influence almost immediately what happens on the other side of the world. All of this has been made possible by advances in transportation and communication, most recently such developments as satellite communication and the internet. In a sense globalization is not new. The term is sometimes used for the spread of the European-based political and economic system around the globe in the nineteenth and twentieth centuries, and before that there is a history that goes back, presumably, to the invention of the wheel. But the last few decades have witnessed what seems like a quantum leap. Today we can more literally speak of a global society than ever before.

The history of Islam can also be seen as a process of globalization. The ***umma*** was global in intent from the earliest conquests and has never stopped spreading geographically. Even though it was soon divided politically people, ideas and goods could travel relatively unobstructed by political boundaries. Some Sufi ***tariqas*** spread throughout much of the Muslim world. The ***Hajj*** was probably the greatest symbol and manifestation of this global tendency.

If European imperialism has been a form of globalization many Muslim political and ideological responses have also been global. The pan-Islamic movement of the late nineteenth century attempted to give a global response to imperialism. The ideas of Muhammad 'Abduh spread from Morocco to Indonesia, as did the influence of Atatürk's reforms and the ideas of Islamist groups such as the Muslim Brothers and the Jama'at-i Islami. The awareness of the Palestine problem spread to other Muslim countries from the 1930s. Some Sufi *tariqas*, such as Inayat Khan's (1882–1927) Sufi Order International, the **Ni'matullahis** under Javad Nurbakhsh (1927–2008) and the **Naqshbandis** have spread to the West, as have other forms of ***da'wa***. The Islamic revolution in Iran very quickly had repercussions throughout the world as did the events of 9/11.

Islam and Muslims are involved in the current phase of globalization in many ways, of which several will be mentioned briefly here and then a few dealt with in more detail. Science and technology are obviously globalized and Muslims participate, mostly as recipients but some developments take place in Muslim countries and a number of Muslim scientists work in the West. Popular culture and the media provide many examples of globalization. The "Barbie" doll was mentioned in chapter 15 and another example is the "I ♥ New York" sticker, which has spawned among other things "I ♥ Islam". Television, whether private or government-controlled, conveys much Western material. I remember watching the American sit-com "Love Boat" in Egypt in the 1980s, for example. Even if the government tries to exercise control, satellite dishes and the internet may make it easier for people to by-pass government controls. Of course, individuals and all sorts of Muslim groups and movements make use of the worldwide web. Almost every organization has its website and one can find many sites where, for example, one can seek a ***fatwa*** or a Muslim marriage partner. Much of this is done in English, so that English is becoming a major Muslim language. Much, though not all, of this globalization can be seen as examples of "cultural imperialism". At the same time much of it undoubtedly strengthens the awareness of a worldwide *umma* as opposed to local forms of it.

There is also the growth of worldwide Muslim organizations. The Organization of Islamic Cooperation (OIC, formerly the Organization of the Islamic Conference) is an intergovernmental agency formed in 1969 at the instance of the Saudi king. It has fifty-seven member states and seeks to promote Islamic values and cooperation among its members and the welfare of their peoples. The Muslim World League (Rābiṭat al-ʿĀlam al-Islāmī), a non-governmental organization supported primarily by Saudi Arabia, was founded in Mecca in 1962 and actively supports a wide range of activities throughout the world. Its orientation can be described as ***salafi*** and many claim that it propagates a **Wahhabi** form of Islam. A connection with Indonesia has been mentioned (see chapter 19).

Two very widespread movements that can also be considered *salafi*, though with different ideological orientations, are the Tablighi Jamaat and the Ḥizb al-Taḥrīr. The former was founded in India in the 1920s and its main goal is to get Muslims to perform regularly the basic obligations such as ***salah***. Groups of volunteers travel from place to place, both within countries and internationally, spreading their message. They do not involve themselves in politics. They have a presence in some eighty countries, both Muslim and diaspora. Hizb al-Tahrir (The Liberation Party) was founded in 1952 by the Palestinian judge, Taqi al-Din al-Nabhani (1909–77) and aims to create a caliphate governing the whole of the *umma* by the Shariʿa. It rejects the present system of states, which it considers to be the abode of unbelief (*Dar al-**kufr***) though "unbelief" applies to the governments, not all of the people. Both the doctrine and the organization are highly structured and Nabhani wrote a detailed constitution for the caliphate. While its goal is radical its actions have not been violent. It hopes to come to power through a bloodless coup d'état and made several unsuccessful attempts in several Arab countries between 1968 and 1983. It has spread to over forty countries, including several Western countries. It is usually controversial and has been banned in most Arab and central Asian countries and restricted in Germany. We have noticed its presence in Indonesia (chapter 19).

Global jihad

One of the most dramatic forms of globalization has been what is often referred to as "global *jihad*" or "global terrorism". We will consider here only that strand of it that is connected with Afghanistan and al-Qaeda, which is the most globalized. Afghanistan successfully resisted British and Russians imperialism in the nineteenth century and entered the twentieth century as one of the few Muslim countries not subject to European control, but in the second half of the century it was caught up in the pressures of the Cold War. In 1978 the Afghan communists seized power but infighting among the leaders, along with other factors, led the Soviets to send in troops in 1979. The same year a number of Afghan groups mounted ***jihad*** against them.

This *jihad* forced the Soviets to withdraw in 1989 though the Afghan communist president managed to hold on until 1992. From the Soviet point of view the whole campaign was a major disaster, worse than the American experience in Vietnam, and was soon followed by the dissolution of its empire. The ***mujahidin*** groups were quite diverse ethnically, ideologically and in other ways. Most were Sunni but some were Shi'i. Some were traditionalist; at least one was secularist and several were Islamist, influenced by Hasan al-Banna, Sayyid Qutb and/or Abul 'Ala' Mawdudi. Many of the Islamist fighters had been in refugee camps and many had studied in the ***madrasas*** in Pakistan that have sprung up in recent years, usually having roots in the Deobandi movement though not necessary directly connected with it. The *mujahidin* received assistance from various sources including the United States government. They were also joined by one to three thousand young men from various parts of the Muslim world who came to fight in the *jihad* (somewhat reminiscent of leftist youth who fought in the Spanish Civil War in the 1930s). These were called "Arab Afghans", although many were not Arabs. Some of them went to fight in Bosnia and Chechnya in the following decade, and others went back to their home countries, such as Egypt, Algeria and Indonesia, to participate in violent Islamist activities there. The Afghan *jihad* also had enormous psychological repercussions throughout the Muslim world. For many it destroyed the "myth" of superpower invincibility. If the Soviet Union was vulnerable, why not the United States?

Unfortunately, the *mujahidin* groups could not form a stable government in Afghanistan after their victory. In reaction to their squabbling and corruption an ultra-traditionalist group, also connected with the Deobandi tradition, known as the Taleban (the word refers to *madrasa* students) was formed by Mullah Omar in 1994. According to one account this happened after a local *mujahid* commander had abducted two teenage girls and Mullah Omar and his students rescued them, acquiring weapons in the process. After considerable fighting they gained control of most of the country by 1996. They managed to impose order and make the country safer than it had been, but they did so with a very conservative interpretation of the Shari'a and *pushtunwala* (the local form of customary law). Their harsh restrictions on women have received considerable international attention. In 2001, after the events of 9/11, the Americans and their allies invaded Afghanistan and forced the Taleban out because of their support for al-Qaeda (see below). They retreated to the mountains and to the adjacent areas of Pakistan, where many of their followers had been students in *madrasas*. Since 2006 they have made a significant comeback to control parts of the country as well as having an organized presence in northwest Pakistan. Efforts by the United States and its allies to defeat them militarily have so far (2013) failed.

Among the "Arab Afghans" in Afghanistan in the 1980s were Abdullah Azzam (1941–89), Usama Bin Laden (1957–2011) and Ayman al-Zawahiri (1951–), leader of the Egyptian Islamic Jihad (see chapter 17). Azzam was a Palestinian and a passionate ideologue who preached that *jihad* is as important as *salah* and is *fard 'ayn* (individual obligation) so long as ***kafirs*** occupy or threaten Muslim lands. He was the mentor of Bin Laden, who was a Saudi, from a wealthy family of Yemeni origin, and a successful businessman in his own right. Together they gathered a small

Figure 20.1 Screenshot from video broadcast showing Usama Bin Laden as he calls on Muslims all around the world to support him and the al-Qaeda network in *jihad*, or holy war, against the US (November 2001). Courtesy of Salah Malkawi/Getty Images

number of fighters, mostly Egyptian followers of al-Zawahiri, to form the group that would become known as al-Qaeda. After the Russians left Afghanistan Bin Laden returned to Saudi Arabia. When the Iraqis invaded Kuwait, he offered to organize a force of "Arab Afghans" to protect the kingdom but the royal family rejected this and opted for American troops, getting a *fatwa* from the leading Saudi ***'ulama'*** to justify this. This appears to have been crucial in deciding Bin Laden's future direction. He went to the Sudan for several years and then, in 1996, returned to Afghanistan and reorganized al-Qaeda. The precise meaning of this term is debated. It may mean "base" (as in a military base), or "principle", or "foundation" in the sense of a "strong foundation (*qaeda*) for the expected victory" as Abdullah 'Azzam had termed it (Burke, 2004, 8). Later al-Zawahiri wrote of *qaedat al-jihad*.

Al-Zawahiri has been seen as the brains behind the organization and his followers a key element within it, while Bin Laden was the spokesperson and financier. In February 1998 these two, along with others, issued the document entitled "World Islamic Front against Jews and Crusaders", attacking American activities. On 7 August 1998 "martyrdom operations" (aka "suicide attacks") were carried out against the American embassies in Nairobi, Kenya and Dar es Salaam, Tanzania and on 20 August the Americans retaliated with missile attacks, dubbed "Infinite Reach", on targets in Afghanistan and the Sudan, destroying a pharmaceutical factory in the latter country.

Mullah Omar had granted protection to Bin Laden and his group when they came to Afghanistan but the relationship was very uneasy. The Taleban were extremely traditionalist, rigid on matters of authority and interpretation but somewhat accepting of local custom, and localized in their interests. By contrast, the radically Islamist al-Qaeda were more "modern" in their thinking, more global in their interests and more flexible in matters of authority and interpretation. Among other things, Mullah Omar felt that Bin Laden, who is not an ***'alim***, exceeded his authority in some of his statements. It is claimed that "Infinite Reach" led Mullah Omar to continue his protection of al-Qaeda when he had been considering withdrawing it. In later years, however, under the influence of al-Qaeda and also of circumstances the Taleban would become more sophisticated in the use of modern methods, including "martyrdom operations" and show a more international orientation.

In 2000 "martyrdom operations" were continued with an attack on the warship U.S.S. Cole by a small powerboat laden with explosives. On 11 September 2001 the best known operations took place as airplanes crashed into the Twin Towers of the World Trade Center in New York and into the Pentagon in Washington D.C., giving Bin Laden worldwide recognition. A number of later operations have been connected or said to be connected with al-Qaeda, including the bombing of a nightclub in Bali in 2002 (see chapter 19), the bombing of a commuter train in Madrid in 2004 and the bombings in London on 7 July 2005.

The level of al-Qaeda's involvement has varied, however. Al-Qaeda is loosely organized and appears to have become more so since 2001. It may be pictured as concentric circles. The inner circle is the hard core group. The next circle consists of people recruited for specific operations and other militant groups ("affiliates") related to it in various ways and to various degrees. Such individuals or groups may suggest operations and seek al-Qaeda's assistance. Beyond this are sympathizers influenced by al-Qaeda but not necessarily in touch with it. The hard core were involved in the operations mentioned above in 1998, 2000 and 2001. Since then many of the hard core have been killed or captured and most operations have been carried out by affiliated groups or sympathizers. For example, those who carried out the Bali bombings may be considered an affiliated group and are said to have been funded to a considerable degree by al-Qaeda. Richard Reid, who was caught with a bomb in his shoe during an airplane flight in December 2001, is an example of an individual recruited by al-Qaeda. Late in 2004 Bin Laden recognized Abu Mus'ab al-Zarqawi, the leading "terrorist" in Iraq, as effectively an affiliate. Despite initial claims that the London bombers were connected with al-Qaeda, the official report concluded they were not, though they were influenced by it. Likewise, investigations have indicated that the Madrid bombers were inspired by al-Qaeda but did not have direct links with it and the same is true of other cases where claims of al-Qaeda involvement were made at some point. Al-Qaeda need not be directly involved for its influence to be deadly. At the same time, because it has become a prime symbol of terrorism and because of its leaders' high profile, its influence is almost certainly perceived to be greater than it is.

As is often the case among radical Islamists, many of those connected with al-Qaeda come from middle-class backgrounds or better and have had higher education, especially in technical subjects. Ayman al-Zawahiri is a medical doctor. Muhammad Atta, the leader of the group that flew the airplanes into the Twin Towers, came from a family of professionals, had a degree in architectural engineering and had studied town planning in Germany. Bin Laden comes from a wealthy family and had studied business administration at university though without completing a degree. By contrast, Richard Reid came from a broken family and had a prison background.

Al-Qaeda is a network as fully globalized as is probably possible. Since the American invasion of Afghanistan in 2001 its geographical base has been problematic, but its leaders have been able to get their videotapes on television and its members can still communicate with each other. Many of these members are "globalized" in the sense that they have moved around a lot and lack firm roots anywhere. Their loyalty is less to a geographical homeland or a geographical *umma* than to an ideal *umma* that exists mainly in their minds. Al-Qaeda affiliates, in addition to those mentioned earlier, include al-Qaeda in the Arabian Peninsula, headed by the Yemeni-American Anwar al-Awlaki (Awlaqi) until he was killed by the Americans in 2011, and al-Qaeda in the Islamic Maghreb, derived from the Algerian Islamist movements of the 1990s. Other groups, such as Hizbollah in Lebanon and Hamas in Palestine, have considerable international support but are nationally based and focused in their efforts. Al-Qaeda is certainly the most globalized of the *jihadi* groups.

Increasing pressure from the Americans has caused al-Qaeda to become even more diffuse than it was and less able to publicize itself. After a long effort American special forces finally killed Bin Laden on 2 May 2011. Al-Zawahiri eventually succeeded him as leader but at present it is hard to judge the condition of al-Qaeda or predict its future.

In very general terms, al-Qaeda's campaign may be seen as a particularly extreme response to the basic problem of modern Islam outlined in chapter 15: why has God permitted the Western *kafirs* to dominate Muslims and what should be done about it? More immediately, it represents a response to the failure of violent *jihad* in particular countries, especially Egypt and Algeria, in the 1990s. Most of those involved have recanted or become quiescent, but Bin Laden and his followers have shifted the focus from the "near enemy" to the "far enemy" (using the terms of Abd al-Salam Faraj, one of the leaders of Egyptian Islamic Jihad), and particularly the greatest of them, the U.S., which supports the "near enemy".

Bin Laden's message has been, in the first place, to stress the danger of the West as a direct physical threat to the Muslims and also a moral threat because of its immoral lifestyle. The labels "crusaders" and "Jews/Zionists" evoke notable examples of Western assaults, past and present, and suggest that Westerners are all the same and unchanging (as orientalists have often presented the Muslim world). This threat must be dealt with by violent *jihad* since the West is using violence and, in fact, only understands force (a point often made by others who are far less extreme). Bin Laden believed that *jihad*, whether offensive or defensive, is a continuing obligation for Muslims, but he appeared to see the present struggle as a defensive one, in which the Muslims are fighting for their survival. Therefore participation is incumbent on all people (i.e. is *fard 'ayn*) and more desperate measures may be used. The death of Bin Laden does not change the force of these arguments.

Why martyrdom operations?

"Martyrdom operations" have seemed particularly horrendous to non-Muslims and to most Muslims, but a number of points are made in their defense. (Note that more attention is given here to these points than to their refutations since it is assumed that most readers will find it harder to empathize with the former than the latter.)

First, martyrdom is a value in and of itself since it is done for God and receives an immediate heavenly reward whatever the outcome of the operation. "Say not of those slain in the way of Allah that they are dead; in fact they are living, but you are unaware" (2:154).

Second, the fight against imperialism is just. All people honor soldiers who sacrifice themselves for a just cause. One person's terrorist is another person's freedom fighter.

Third, Muslims are not strong enough to engage in conventional warfare against the West, but martyrdom operations require relatively few resources and are particularly hard to counter. "Terrorism" is generally the strategy of the weak. There is something like David and Goliath here. About the attack on the U.S.S. Cole Bin Laden composed a poem:

> A destroyer, even the brave fear its might,
> It inspires horror in the harbour and in the open sea,
> She sails into the waves
> Flanked by arrogance, haughtiness and false power,
> To her doom she moves slowly,
> A dinghy awaits her, riding the waves.
>
> (Lawrence, 2005, 149)

Fourth, such operations can achieve concrete results. Martyrdom operations by Hizbollah in Lebanon drove out the American and French "peacekeepers" in 1983 and played a major role in the Israeli army's withdrawal in 2000. The bombing of the commuter train in Spain was followed by Spain's withdrawal of troops from Iraq. Can the U.S. be brought down by such operations? God knows best. Though outwardly strong, the U.S. is inwardly corrupt and weak, according to Bin Laden, just as the Soviet Union proved to be in 1989. In the 9/11 attacks a mere nineteen *mujahids* "shook America's throne, struck its economy right in the heart, and dealt the biggest military power a mighty blow ... " (*ibid.*).

Fifth, even if they do not bring down the U.S. they encourage the Muslims of the world by demonstrating U.S. vulnerability. Here the symbolism of the action is important. The Twin Towers and the Pentagon symbolize the economic and military power of the United States.

Sixth, they provide effective publicity. Bin Laden said that they were "speeches that overshadowed all other speeches made everywhere else in the world. The speeches are understood by Arabs and non-Arabs – even Chinese". (Burke, 2004, 38). Donations to radical Islamist movements increased after 11 September.

Seventh, they are revenge for what the West has done and thus tend to restore the honor of the *umma*. The Qur'an permits revenge so long as it is proportionate. It is proportionate when one considers how many more have been killed by "legal" Western imperialism and wars than by all the Muslim "terrorist" acts.

Eighth, they are a warning to the West. One of the London "martyrs" said: "Until we feel security you will be our targets. Until you stop the bombing, gassing, imprisonment and torture of my people we will not stop this fight. We are at war and I am a soldier" (Sadiq, 2005, no page).

Most *'ulama'* and other spokespeople, including the main international Muslim organizations, were prompt to express their horror and disapproval of al-Qaeda's actions on 9/11. In addition to asserting that Islam is about peace and tolerance and that murder and suicide are forbidden, they have underlined the point that in war it is forbidden to kill non-combatants. Some also have argued that the traditional procedures for declaring *jihad* were not followed and particularly that the Americans have not directly attacked Muslims in such a way as to call for *jihad*. Moveover, it is immoral and impractical to attack directly such a strong country as the United States, provoking a retaliation that harms many Muslims and strengthening anti-Muslim feeling in the West. In general these actions sully the name of Islam and are against the welfare of the *umma*.

Bin Laden and his associates answer the first objection by saying that it is clear from the Qur'an and the ***Sunna*** that the way to peace is often through violence, especially when the enemy is as insistent and threatening as the West is. They further argue that it is traditionally acceptable to kill non-combatants, including women and children, in situations where they cannot be distinguished from combatants in a legitimate target. This also applies to Muslims who may be killed, many of whom are allied with the West and thus apostates in Bin Laden's view. Also, Americans are not innocent since they choose their leaders and approve their policies. As for suicide, there are no precise precedents for the martyrdom operations but these are analogous to those who plunged to certain death in battle or chose death rather than apostasy or dishonor, and these were approved by the Prophet so long as the motive was to serve God. Bin Laden also noted that some of the *'ulama'* who criticize al-Qaeda on these grounds approve comparable actions by Hamas against Israel. These arguments do not persuade most Muslims but they do have some force and many who disapprove of the actions probably still have a certain admiration for the group.

Muslim diaspora in the West

Although there were some Muslims living in the West before 1950, many more have emigrated to Western countries since then either to get jobs or to seek refuge from political turmoil. In many cases they have come from former colonies of the Western countries to which they have gone. In Great Britain the largest number have come from the Indian subcontinent, while in France most have come from North Africa, especially Algeria and Morocco. In 1962 an agreement between the German and the Turkish governments provided for Turkish "guest workers" to work in Germany. Most of those coming to these three countries took unskilled jobs in industry although some professionals and business people also came. For reasons of space, we will consider mainly these countries along with the United States, though there are Muslim immigrants in many other countries, as well.

Along with their Muslim identity the immigrants have also had an ethnic identity, and at first the ethnic identity has generally been given priority by both the immigrants and the host countries. It has been common for the men to come alone first and only some years later to bring their families. The first generation has usually not tried to adapt fully to the new environment, in part because many expected to return eventually to their homeland, although only a few have. The second generation, those raised and educated in the new country, stand between the culture of their parents and that of their environment. They have to decide about their identity, including whether and how they will be Muslim (see below).

The United States saw a considerable increase in Muslim immigration after the repeal of restrictive legislation in 1965. Most of these were professionals and business people, who have found it easier than less-educated people to adapt in the first generation although they still have issues relating to religion and identity.

Most Western countries have also had significant numbers of Muslim students temporarily resident who carry the effects of their stay back to their home country. This may include exposure to transnational Islamist groups.

In the early stages the immigrants' religious practices have tended to be limited to the basics and they would meet in homes or rented premises. Later buildings have been bought and converted to mosques; less often purpose-built mosques have been

Figure 20.2 The Islamic Center of America in Dearborn, Michigan. Opened in 2005, it is the largest mosque in North America. Courtesy of Shutterstock

constructed. These mosques take on more of a community center function than is usual in the home countries. Such matters as ***halal*** food and space in cemeteries are also arranged. In general the first generation has sought to replicate, to the extent possible, the traditional forms of Islam they knew at home. When the need is felt to pass on the tradition to the children, this may first be done by more or less formal "after school" classes in the mosques. In time some day schools are built, usually following the state curriculum along with Muslim religious education, and sometimes with state funding, but most children will go to state schools.

Trained religious leaders, *imams*, mostly come from the old country and often do not understand the Western culture well enough to meet many of the needs of their people. Efforts to provide training for religious leaders in Western countries are at a very early stage. Regional and national associations have been formed but they do not usually represent all of the existing groups and associations. The immigrants face the challenge of organizing all of this with little or no state support and guidance (Turks excepted to some extent). At the same time, they have more freedom than in the home country. Many feel it is safest to avoid involvement in politics, but many do vote and some stand for political office. They also petition the government when they feel Muslim interests are at risk or in relation to developments abroad. Muslims in Great Britain and Denmark, respectively, played major roles in the protests against Salman

Rushdie's novel, *The Satanic Verses*, in 1988 and the "Danish Cartoons" depicting Muhammad in 2005, protests that quickly became worldwide and undoubtedly like other forms of globalization have strengthened the feeling of a worldwide *umma*.

Various international Islamic groups involve themselves with Muslim immigrants to the West and with students. The Tablighis and Hizb al-Tahrir have been mentioned. Others, such as the Jama'at-i Islami, the Muslim Brothers and the Muslim World League are active. The Saudi government in particular provides considerable funding for mosques and other needs, and encourages a *salafi* version of Islam. The Turkish government provides *imams* and other support for Turkish diaspora communities. ***Milli Görüş*** (an ideology in Turkey but an organizational name in the diaspora) and the **Nurcus** are also active in these communities.

All of this is very much influenced by the attitude of the host country, both official and unofficial. Germany for some time tried to keep the immigrants separate. Citizenship has been hard to get and most of the second generation are not citizens. France seeks assimilation to secular French values. England officially espouses "multiculturalism". The United States has seen itself as a land of immigrants and has been religiously pluralist but also has a strong sense of American values. All of these recognize the legitimacy of Islam in some way. In America there is some willingness to extend the "Protestant–Catholic–Jew" paradigm to include Muslims and others. At the popular level in all of the countries there has been suspicion of Islam and Muslims and, especially in Europe, an awareness of the antagonistic history between Christendom and Islam. There is often local opposition to the building of mosques. Female ***hijab*** has been a major issue in France, sometimes an issue elsewhere. There have been claims of discrimination in various forms, including employment. International events, such as the Iranian revolution, the Palestinian–Israeli struggle and "9/11" have roused anti-Muslim feeling. The last resulted in restrictive actions in the United States.

As stated earlier, the second generation has to decide about its Islam. The traditional forms followed by their parents often do not appeal, since their exposure to the host culture is too deep. Some seek to assimilate, reducing their Islamic identity and practice to an absolute minimum. Others will give their Islamic identity priority over their ethnic identity, partly because the Islamic identity is more universal. These may find some form of *salafi* Islam attractive, since it strips away the cultural "accretions" of their parents' religion and allows them to believe that they are practicing a "purer" form. This may be a radically Islamist form, through which they may channel any anger they feel toward the host society. At the extreme they may become involved in terrorist activities. This seems to have been the case with those who carried out the 7/7 attacks in London. The fact that many Muslims live in a ghettoized situation in Britain seems to have played a role there. An alternative option is a more liberal version of *salafism*, which would replace the traditional "accretions" with more Western material. Such people may speak of creating a

"French Islam" or a "European Islam". Western converts to Islam, who are few in number but often important, are likely to prefer this approach. (See Tariq Ramadan below and on the website.)

The American situation is distinctive in that 20 percent of the Muslim community consists of African-Americans who are not immigrants but are connected with movements originating in America, such as Elijah Muhammad's "Nation of Islam". Elijah Muhammad (1897–1975) preached that the blacks were the original human beings and were originally Muslims and intrinsically righteous while whites were "devils". This mirrored the prevalent white racism and provided a powerfully positive sense of identity, especially for the most alienated, such as prisoners. After the death of Elijah Muhammad his son, Warith Deen, quickly steered the movement into orthodox Sunni channels and sought a positive integration with American society. In 1979, however, Louis Farrakhan broke away to form a new "Nation of Islam", retaining Elijah Muhammad's oppositional stance and many of his doctrines. He has gained a significant following and considerable publicity.

The African-American Muslims and the immigrant groups have had difficulty working together because of their different backgrounds and different needs, but a recent study shows that both tend to have a positive view of American society and share the "American dream", albeit a morally conservative version of it. This moral conservatism is largely true of Muslims in other Western countries.

As Muslims have had to adapt to their host countries, the host countries have also been influenced by the Muslim presence. In some cases they have had to become aware of cultural and religious diversity in new ways and had their own sense of identity challenged. The response has sometimes been negative, as noted in relation to mosques and *hijab* above. There are some who express fears about *halal* food, fear it may be sold without being identified. More broadly, some journalists and other writers are prepared to present Islam as a threat to "(Western) civilization" and the immigrants as its fifth column. This kind of reaction has been labeled "Islamophobia". At the same time, there is no shortage of people prepared to assist and befriend Muslims, dialogue with them, help them seek their rights and counteract the attacks on them.

Of interest in this connection is the question of whether the Shari'a can be applied in the West. In fact those parts relating to ritual, including food laws, are generally applied since they require little or no government involvement. In family matters they are sometimes recognized in law or applied informally, where they do not contravene Western legal or ethical norms. Explicit discussion of the role of the Shari'a can be quite emotive, as indicated by the response to the tentative and rather obscure suggestions of the Archbishop of Canterbury in 2008 that Shari'a might have a place in Britain. Fears about the introduction of the Shari'a are a common focus for Islamophobia. Resolution of this issue will require mutual adjustment on the part of Muslims and the host societies.

Islamophobia

Islamophobia, a recently coined term, means an irrational or extreme fear of Islam and represents one Western reaction to the resurgence of Islam, the activities of terrorists and Muslim immigration to the West. It characterizes certain journalistic and academic writings and is present in other media such as television, movies, radio talk back, letters to the editors and internet blogs, as well as influencing more moderate discourse. For extreme Islamophobes Muslims ultimately want to take control of the world and proximately to weaken Western countries, whether by terrorism or political means, and replace the Western way of life with theirs. Immigrants are seen as a fifth column, harboring terrorists and seeking to introduce the Shari'a, which is identified with such things as polygamy, imposing the veil on women and killing apostates. Islamophobes ignore as much as possible the diversity of Muslims, identifying them all with what they see as Islam's worst traits and worst representatives. For example, a recent article in New Zealand writes first of the shooting of the Afghani teenager Malala Yousafzai and then continues, "What makes the Muslims so loathe their women; what powers of ignorance are at play, what juices are squeezed in their brains to make them want to commit such atrocities?" (*Waikato Times*, 10 November 2012).

To some extent Islamophobia is rooted in the fears of Christians during earlier centuries of Muslim–Christian conflict. These fears contributed to imperialism but seemed to recede as Western dominance was achieved and then taken for granted. They have reappeared with the highly publicized resurgence of Islam and a certain loss of confidence in some Western circles. Also, with the end of the communist threat many Westerners, especially Americans, seem to need a new enemy and resurgent Islam provides it.

Diaspora Muslims face the challenge of how to be Muslim in non-Muslim societies that do not merely tolerate them but hold out the (at least apparent) promise of equal participation. The host countries face the challenge of how to fulfill this promise. This situation has hardly existed in the past and there is reason to expect distinctive developments in the future.

Liberal/progressive Islam

There are a number of intellectuals, mostly not trained as *'ulama'* and often with degrees from Western universities, who have undertaken or are undertaking radical reinterpretations of Islam. They are often referred to as "liberal" or "progressive" Muslims and represent continuations of the secularist and modernist tendencies (described in chapter 15) under contemporary globalized conditions. Many live in the diaspora, often having been forced out of their countries of origin. They have global concerns and relate to each other across national boundaries. They undertake substantial reinterpretations of the Qur'an and the *Sunna*, engage in radical forms of ***ijtihad*** and are particularly concerned with human rights, gender issues and religious pluralism. Most of their writing is for fellow intellectuals and is often better received internationally than in their Muslim countries of origin. Thus their popular influence has been limited but their accomplishments may be very important for the future. Here I mention just a few of them.

The doyen of these thinkers is perhaps Fazlur Rahman (1919–88, see chapters 6 and 15), who headed the Central Institute of Islamic Research in Pakistan in the early 1960s but was forced out for religious and political reasons. From 1968 he was a professor at the University of Chicago. He has been very influential in the field of Islamic Studies, both through his writings and through his students, many of whom are leading scholars in the field today. Among other things, he argued that Muslims must learn to see the Qur'an as both the verbatim word of God and the word of Muhammad, who at the moments of revelation became one with the moral law. He also argued that the *Sunna* of the Prophet was at first mostly transmitted "silently", i.e. in behavior, and that most of the ***hadiths*** in their existing form are later than the Prophet's time. *Ijtihad* should proceed (as noted in chapter 15) by studying the specific commands of the Qur'an in the light of their historical background and the overall teachings of the Qur'an to discover the ethical principles they illustrate and then applying these principles to contemporary cases. This approach has been very influential among progressive Muslim thinkers, some of whom would describe it as prioritizing the spirit of the Qur'an over the letter.

Another scholar who has had to leave his country because of his views is Nasr Abu Zayd (1943–2010), as mentioned in chapter 17 on Egypt. From 1995 he was resident in the Netherlands. He appears to go a bit further than Fazlur Rahman when he claims the text of the Qur'an is a human manifestation of the Word of God and, being human, it reflects the practices of its particular time. Justice and freedom are the central teachings of the Qur'an but the particular form in which it presents them is not necessarily to be followed today. He sees himself as heir to the Mu'tazili ideas of the created Qur'an and metaphorical interpretation.

A scholar who calls himself a neo-Mu'tazili is Abdolkarim Soroush (1945–), an Iranian philosopher. He was an active supporter of the Islamic Revolution and participated in the effort to Islamicize university education, but he soon became disillusioned and became one of the most vocal critics of the regime from within the country. Since 2000 he has been a visiting scholar at various universities outside Iran. He distinguishes between religion, which is divinely revealed, and religious knowledge, which is fallible. He believes with the Mu'tazila that the Qur'an is created but goes beyond them to say that it is created by Muhammad as well as God.

As revealed by God the Qur'an is beyond words; the Prophet puts it into words and it thereby becomes human, potentially fallible and influenced by its culture. The Mu'tazila held that ethical values can be known apart from revelation and for Soroush this means that "primary" values such as reason, liberty, freedom and democracy do not depend on religious support. These sorts of ideas provide a basis for religious pluralism and political secularism.

Abdullahi An-Na'im (1946–) was a follower of the Sudanese reformer Mahmud Muhammad Taha and left the Sudan to work in the United States after Taha was executed in 1985. He has especially been a campaigner for human rights. He affirms the view of his mentor that only the Meccan part of the Qur'an contains permanent teachings, but does not seem to stress this. He also holds that the interpretation of the Qur'an and *Sunna* are human and thus historically conditioned, so that new interpretations are needed in the light of today's realities. He argues that Islam and the state must be kept separate, while maintaining the connection between Islam and politics. Muslims may work to have Islamic principles implemented by the state, not on the basis of their divine origin, but by democratic decision and subject to constitutional and human rights safeguards. He calls this "secularism" or "pluralism".

Tariq Ramadan (1962–) is the grandson of Hasan al-Banna, the founder of the Muslim Brothers, but was born in Switzerland and is a Swiss citizen. He is particularly associated with the idea of a European Islam. His attitude to the Qur'an and *Sunna* is more conservative than that of the others discussed here, but he accepts *'urf* (custom) as a source of Islamic law. Europe, he says, is not *dār al-ḥarb* but *dār al-da'wa* or *dār al-shahāda*, a place where the *shahada* can be pronounced and Islam witnessed to. European Muslims can and must integrate into the local society while maintaining their Islamic practice. There should be a dynamic and dialectic movement between the sources of Islam and the environment. Oddly, Tariq Ramadan was refused entry to the United States in 2004 on the grounds of having donated to charities that supported terrorism (before they had been officially designated as such, however). This action was reversed in 2010 after court action by his American sympathizers.

These are only a few of the figures who might have been mentioned here. Others include Muhammad Arkoun, a highly respected Algerian–French scholar; Khaled Abou El Fadl, a legal expert, originally from Egypt, now in the United States; Farid Esack, a South African social activist; Chandra Muzaffar, a Malaysian known for human rights concerns; Ziauddin Sardar, who has pondered the future of Islam; and several mentioned elsewhere in this book, such as Fethullah Gülen (Turkey), Nurcholish Madjid (Indonesia) and Muhammad 'Ashmawi (Egypt).

It will be clear from the material in this chapter that globalization, like all the gifts of technology, has its good and its bad aspects. It will clearly make a significant difference for Islam and Muslims, although what that difference will be in the long run is hard to say. The *umma* will continue with the basic witness, "There is no god but God; Muhammad is the Messenger of God", and the other Pillars will remain. One predicts with caution, however, what forms it will take.

Key points

- Globalization of a sort has long characterized the world in general and the Muslim world in particular, but the present globalization represents a "quantum leap" that influences the Muslim world at many levels.
- It is reflected in governmental organizations such as the OIC and non-government groups such as the Tablighi Movement.
- The "global *jihad*", illustrated by al-Qaeda, represents a particularly intense response to the "great reversal" presented in chapter 15.
- Considerable Muslim immigration to Western countries has produced communities that face a distinctive situation and may make distinctive contributions to the *umma*.
- A number of intellectuals, many living in the West, are rethinking the nature of the Qur'an and the *Sunna* and producing radically new interpretations that could have significance for the future.

Discussion questions

1. What are the main opportunities and challenges that globalization offers Muslims?
2. Can you think of other manifestations of globalization not mentioned here?
3. Is the "war on terrorism" an appropriate response to the examples of "terrorism" mentioned in this book?
4. To what extent do the challenges faced by Muslims in diaspora differ from those faced by Muslims in Muslim majority countries? How do they differ in different Western countries?
5. What might Muslim diaspora communities have to offer the *umma* as a whole?
6. Could one say that the "progressive" Muslims have simply sold out to the West?

Critical thinking box 20.1

Consider the arguments presented for "martyrdom operations" point by point. Can you refute them? Do the arguments presented in the text satisfactorily refute them? Can you find others? If possible, make use of the methods of *fiqh* described in chapter 10. (There is relevant material in the readings and on the website.)

Critical thinking box 20.2

What would it or could it mean to introduce the Shari'a into Great Britain or the United States (or other Western country)? Consider the various theoretical and practical issues involved.

Companion website

Features definitions of globalization, material and thoughts on terrorism and on Muslims in Western countries, quotes from various neo-modernists, and limited additional reading and websites for various topics, groups and individuals.

Further reading

Globalization

Cooke, Miriam and Lawrence, Bruce B. (eds.) (2005) *Muslim Networks from Hajj to HipHop*. Chapel Hill, NC: University of North Carolina Press. (Articles on various kinds of networks, include art, music, internet, mosques, women, etc., all but one modern.)

Roy, Olivier (2004) *Globalized Islam: The Search for a New Ummah*. London: Hurst. (Discusses the implications of globalization for Muslims and Muslim societies and its relation to disporas, Islamism, terrorism and other phenomena.)

Husain, Ed (2007) *The Islamist: Why I Joined Radical Islam in Britain, What I Saw Inside and Why I Left*. London: Penguin. (Personal account of a former member of Hizb al-Tahrir and other Islamist groups, interesting and informative.)

See also: Herrera and Bayat, *Being Young and Muslim* [14].

Jihad *and martyrdom*

Victor, Barbara (2003) *Army of Roses: Inside the World of Palestinian Women Suicide Bombers*. Emmaus, PA: Rodale. (Details on seven women "martyrs" or would-be "martyrs", showing their diversity and motivations.)

Burke, Jason (2004) *Al-Qaeda: Casting A Shadow of Terror*, revised ed. London: Penguin Books. (Excellent journalism. Best book I know of on al-Qaeda to the date of publication.)

Burke, Jason (2011) *The 9/11 Wars*. London: Allen Lane. (Analyzes the various battles and terrorist activities following 9/11 in Afghanistan, Iraq and Pakistan.)

Ibrahim, Raymond (ed.) (2007) *The Al Qaeda Reader.* New York: Doubleday. (Selection of statements by Bin Laden and al-Zawahiri, including on offensive and defensive *jihad.*)

Kepel, Gilles and Milleli, Jean-Pierre (eds.) (2008) *Al-Qaeda in its Own Words.* Cambridge, MA and London: Belknap Press.

Lawrence, Bruce (ed.) (2005) *Messages to the World: The Statements of Osama Bin Laden,* trans. James Howarth. London: Verso. (Biography and twenty-four statements of Bin Laden, from 1994 to 2004.)

Diaspora

Haddad, Yvonne Yazbeck and Smith, Jane I. (eds.) (2002) *Muslim Minorities in the West: Visible and Invisible.* Walnut Creek, CA: Altamira Press. (Several articles on the U.S., also France, Norway, Germany, Australia, New Zealand, South Africa, the Caribbean.)

Ramadan, Tariq (1999) *To be a European Muslim: A Study of Islamic Sources in the European Context.* Leicester: The Islamic Foundation. (Sometimes controversial Muslim leader seeks to reconcile authenticity with integration, is optimistic.)

Turner, Richard Brent (2003) *Islam in the African-America Experience,* 2nd ed. Bloomington, IN: Indiana University Press. (Good survey of the whole history of Muslim African-Americans from the time of slavery on.)

See also: Esposito, *The Oxford History of Islam* (Ch. 14) [F].

Liberal/progressive Islam

Esack, Farid (1999) *On Being a Muslim: Finding a Religious Path in the World Today.* Oxford: One World Publications. (A "liberation theologian" seeks to reconcile the Qur'an and Hadith with his contemporary experience.)

Sadri, M. and Sadri, A. (eds.) (2000) *Reason, Freedom and Democracy in Islam, Essential Writings of Abdolkarim Soroush.* New York: Oxford University Press.

Kurzman, Charles (ed.) (1998) *Liberal Islam: A Sourcebook.* New York and Oxford: Oxford University Press. (Selections from a wide range of mainly modernist writers, including most of those mentioned in this chapter and many mentioned in earlier chapters.)

Kamrava, Mehran (ed.) (2006) *The New Voices of Islam: Reforming Politics and Modernity: A Reader.* London & New York: I.B.Tauris. (Includes many of those in Kurzman but some others, e.g. Nasr Abu Zayd.)

Noor, Farish A. (ed.) (2002) *New Voices of Islam.* Leiden: International Institute for the Study of Islam in the Modern World (ISIM). (Interviews with "progressive" thinkers, including many in Kurzman and Kamrava: Na'im, Soroush, Moosa,

Ali Asghar Engineer, Madjid, Muzaffar.) Online: https://openaccess.leidenuniv.nl/bitstream/handle/1887/10069/paper_noor.pdf?sequence = 1 (accessed 28 August 2013).

Safi, Omid (ed.) (2003) *Progressive Muslims: On Gender, Justice and Pluralism*. Oxford: Oneworld. (Collection of articles mainly by prominent "progressives" including Khaled Abou El Fadl, Farid Esack and Amina Wadud.)

See also: Esack, *The Qur'an: A Short Introduction* [5]; Vogt, Larsen and Moe, *New Directions* [21]; Esposito, *The Oxford History of Islam* (Ch. 14) [F]; Knysh, *Islam in Historical Perspective* (Chs 24–25) [F]; Ernst, *Following Muhammad* (Ch. 4, Postscript) [1].

Online resources

Euro-Islam.Info (Has considerable information on European Muslims. See, e.g., Country Profiles and Latest News.): http://www.euro-islam.info/about_us (accessed 28 Aug 2013).

Muslims for Progressive Values (An American website that links to liberal groups and various material.): http://www.mpvusa.org (accessed 28 Aug 2013).

21 *Three cultural flashpoints*

Gender, democracy and human rights

> We hold these truths to be self evident, that all men are created equal, that they are endowed by their Creator with certain inalienable rights, that among these are life, liberty and the pursuit of happiness.
>
> (Preamble to the United States Declaration of Independence)

In this chapter we deal with three timely and tendentious issues, gender, democracy and human rights, in relation to Islam and Muslim societies. All three stir up passionate convictions and people often respond with shock, horror or derision to opposing positions. Empathetic understanding is hard to achieve and may even seem immoral, but is all the more important for that reason. Here I shall not attempt to provide a thorough or balanced coverage of these subjects but rather to frame issues and suggest approaches, attempting to provide enough information for these purposes. My own views will be more evident here than in previous chapters.

In this chapter

- Gender issues in the West and Islam
- Democracy and the potential for it in Islam
- Human rights: Western and Muslim views
- The "myth" of equality

Gender, democracy and human rights are closely related to each other. Much that is discussed under the heading of gender is also properly discussed under the heading of human rights while human rights are commonly seen as part of democracy and as requiring democracy for their realization. All three concerns are Western generated in the sense that in their current form they arose in the West and in response to Western historical experience. They can be seen as aspects of Western "cultural imperialism" but arguably as desirable aspects of it.

In each case I shall provide a working definition of the issue, review the modern Western experience, present relevant material from Islamic doctrine and history and consider the Western challenge and the Muslim response.

I shall argue that the differences between Islam and Christendom were not so great before the modern transformation and that one should not assume that Muslim society is incapable of a similar transformation drawing to a considerable degree on its own cultural resources. I shall try not to assume that adopting the West's positions either is or is not the best course for Muslims.

Gender

It is common to discuss this issue under a heading such as "Women in Islam". Along with many others, however, I prefer to speak of "gender", because virtually all so-called women's issues involve men also and the relations between women and men.

If one observed the Muslim and Christian worlds from their beginnings to about 1700 CE one would conclude that both were "patriarchal", run largely by and for men with women in a supportive and protected role. There were, of course, differences between the two civilizations at particular points. Christians were tantalized and repelled by veils and harems while Muslims often felt the uncivilized "Franks" gave too much license to their women. There were also considerable variations within each civilization. But speaking in general terms from today's perspective at least, the similarities were greater than the differences. In both women were "second class" citizens in many respects.

The developments that would challenge this situation in a major way began in some Western countries in the nineteenth century, with movements for women's suffrage achieving success in many countries in the early twentieth century and major involvement by women in various social reform movements such as prohibition, settlement houses, planned parenthood, etc. A second wave of "feminism" from the 1960s has worked for practical and legal equality with men in virtually all areas, though with some ambivalence around traditional female priorities in family matters and definite lags in practice. Perhaps the ultimate symbols of this are the "right" of women to engage in military combat and the appearance of the idea and reality of "house husbands". There has also been a concern about gendered language (such as "man" in the Declaration of Independence cited above). In this area, and also with democracy and human rights, Western expectations and standards have been constantly changing, thus complicating the Muslim responses to them. These responses have been varied but can roughly fit into the categories used in chapter 15, (neo-)traditionalist, modernist, secularist and Islamist.

Before going into this, however, we must first outline something of the "traditional" Muslim views on gender, with an occasional glance at "traditional" Christian views, recognizing that this will hardly do justice to a large and complex field.

In this area as in others the Qur'an, the ***Sunna*** and the practices of the early generations of Muslims provide the basic guidelines. It is common to say that these improved the lot of women over the previous ***jahiliyya*** period in Arabia, but the matter is complicated because the *jahiliyya* practices were diverse. On one hand we hear of female infanticide and wives being inherited, both of which the Qur'an forbids. On the other hand, some marriages in the *jahiliyya* were matrilocal and some women could easily divorce their husbands. The position of Khadija, Muhammad's first wife, suggests that there were considerable economic opportunities for at least some women in the *jahiliyya*. At a more basic level the Qur'an makes women and men equal as humans. Both are called to submit (*islam*) to God and both are to be rewarded or punished in the afterlife for their deeds (Qur'an 33:35), but paradise is depicted very much in male-friendly terms. As mentioned in chapter 5, women raised questions about this and received assurance about their reward in the afterlife but the pictures of paradise remained male-oriented.

On the other hand there is an oft-mentioned ***hadith*** according to which the majority of people in hell are women and women are deficient in religion. Unlike the Bible, which has Eve tempting Adam in the Garden of Eden, in the Qur'an the men are equally responsible for the sin that causes the fall. But the Biblical version does appear in *hadith* and other early sources. In the Qur'anic stories of previous prophets and nations all the prophets are male, though there are some important female figures, and the ***'ulama'*** concluded that all prophets are male. The Bible has rather more major female figures though the majority are male and some females are called prophets. It should be noted that three women, Khadija, 'A'isha and Fatima played important roles in Muhammad's life. By comparison we may note the importance of women in the life of Jesus and the earliest church. In neither case did this provide much of a model for the future.

At the practical level, the Qur'an allows men four wives and unlimited concubines but nothing comparable for women. (The West did not have polygamy but did have concubinage and "mistresses".) Rules for inheritance are complex but generally give the male twice what the female receives, and two women equal one man as witnesses in court. Marriage is assymetrical: the wife mainly owes obedience and the husband owes support and protection. The following oft-discussed passage makes the point.

> Men are managers and protectors (or supporters and maintainers, Arabic: *qawwamūn*) of women, in that (or since) God has preferred some people over the others, and in that (or since) they have expended of their property. Righteous women are therefore obedient, guarding what God would have them guard. And those you fear may be rebellious admonish; refuse to share their beds, and beat them. If they then obey you, look not for any way against them; God is All-high, All-great.
>
> (4:34)

The New Testament, of course, likewise has passages calling on wives to be submissive to their husbands and the Christian fathers have some quite harsh things to say, such as the following from Chrysostom, "What else is woman but a foe to friendship, an inescapable punishment, a necessary evil, a natural temptation, a desirable calamity, a delectable detriment, and evil nature, painted with fair colors?" (Phillips, 1984, 22).

Divorce is easier for the husband, although some controls are put in place, which may have been an improvement over some *jahiliyya* situations. In much of the Christian world divorce has been equally available to husband and wife, i.e. forbidden to both. The rules around purity limit women more than men, because men's impurities can always be eliminated by ***wudu'*** or ***ghusl*** but impurities such as menstruation (which the Qur'an calls a "sickness") have to run their course. While the Pillars are equally incumbent on men and women, there are times when women cannot perform some of them, such ***salah*** and the Fast of **Ramadan**.

If the Qur'an teaches the basic equality of men and women but qualifies it to some extent, the later tradition, both ***fiqh*** and custom, carries the qualifications further. Arranged marriages have been the norm in most Muslim cultures mainly because concern for the family takes precedence over concern for the individual. The *fiqh* rules generally presume and encourage this. Again, Christendom was not so different at this point. Although in some interpretations an adult woman may choose her own husband, in most cases the bride's family makes this decision and the marriage contract is between the ***wali***, usually the father, and the groom. The woman must indicate her acceptance, but this may be done by keeping silent. *Fiqh* interpretation recognizes several forms of divorce, one of which, *talaq al-**bid'a***, in which a man may irrevocably divorce his wife by pronouncing the divorce formula three times on one occasion, is considered reprehensible but valid. A woman's ability to initiate divorce is much more limited and involves sacrificing certain rights. A woman is allowed to retain her own property in marriage and is not required to use it for her basic sustenance, since that is the husband's responsibility. By contrast, English common law did not allow wives to own property before the nineteenth century, a point often mentioned by Muslim apologists. Also, a woman normally keeps her maiden name after marriage, a practice relatively recent in the West under feminist inspiration and far from universal.

The Qur'an calls for men and women to dress modestly (24:31), but its provision for women's garb is open to interpretation. *Fiqh* interpretaton generally calls for covering of everything but the hands and face, but custom has varied, sometimes more liberal, sometimes veiling all but the eyes (*niqab*) sometimes covering everything, as with the *burqa*. Qur'an called for a degree of seclusion of the prophet's wives due to circumstances (33:53) but in later times many women were secluded, mainly among the upper classes (also true of heavy veiling). In a sense, therefore, seclusion was a mark of privilege. Veiling and seclusion apparently already existed among some Arabs as well as Byzantines and Iranians. Sexual immorality (*zina*) is harshly punished but in principle equally for men and women. The Qur'an stipulated the virtually impossible condition of four witnesses, but confession is accepted and sometimes pregnancy; in the last case one presumes women would suffer punishment more often than men. So-called female "circumcision" is not mentioned in the Qur'an and hardly in the *Hadith*, and is practiced only in some places, e.g. the Nile Valley. Where it is practiced it is usually seen as part of Islam and as important for a woman's chastity and honor.

Learning has been largely the province of men, but women have participated to some degree. As mentioned earlier, both **Ibn Arabi** and **Ibn Taymiyya** had female teachers. Muhammad's wife, A'isha, is recognized for the large number of *hadiths* she reported. Wealthy women have often contributed by funding ***madrasas*** and other social institutions.

The realm of government has been mainly the preserve of men, both in the Islamic world and in the West. The prophet is reported to have said that a nation ruled by a woman will not prosper. There have been some women rulers, such as "Sayyida" and Shajarat al-Durr (see chapter 4 and text box in chapter 13), but they mostly had to rule through sons or husbands and thus are exceptions that prove the rule. Still, their influence was palpable and there were undoubtedly many others who significantly influenced government in this way. The situation in the pre-modern West was not so different, but to my knowledge the Muslim world had no women rulers of the stature of Elizabeth I of England or Catherine the Great of Russia.

The Sufi movement is often seen as more woman friendly. While the vast majority of *walis*, ***shaykhs*** and ***murids*** have been males, women have participated quite avidly in Sufi practices, especially those related to the tombs of *walis*. There have been a number of important female adepts, of whom the best known is Rabi'a al-Adawiya, of whom a biographer says "When a woman becomes a 'man' in the path of God, she is a man and one cannot any more call her a woman" (Attar, 1979, 40). Patriarchy finds a way! Interestingly, these words are paralleled by the following from St. Jerome, "But when [a woman] wishes to serve Christ more than the world, then she will cease to be a woman, and she will be called man" (Phillips, 1984, 146).

Modern developments

Muslims have responded diversely to the pressure and example of the West in the nineteenth and early twentieth centuries both ideologically and practically. Secularists have generally accepted many Western practices with some concession to tradition, while traditionalists have defended existing practice with some concession to change. Modernists and Islamists have responded with both apologetic defense and reinterpretation.

For example, some defend the polygamy of Muhammad's time on the grounds of circumstance and necessity. The wars of the time led to a shortage of men and polygyny was the only way to provide for the widows, a point made particularly in relation to some of Muhammad's marriages. Some say that since this situation recurs from time to time polygyny should always be a possibility. The point is made that this was the situation in Europe after the world wars and, in the absence of legal polygyny, there was an increase in sexual immorality.

Others reinterpret the Qur'an. The passage permitting polygyny is ambiguous (it may just apply to orphans) and calls for equal treatment of wives, but another passage says that such treatment is impossible (4:3; 4:129, cf. chapter 6, p. 94). Therefore, the true (or preferred) teaching of the Qur'an is monogamy. The Qur'an took the ***umma*** as far as it could go in this direction at that time and now it is possible and therefore obligatory to complete that move. Similar arguments are applied to veil, seclusion and slavery (concubines are always slaves). The arguments are liberal ***salafi*** ones. True Islam is to be found in the spirit of the Qur'anic teachings and the *Sunna*, not necessarily the letter, and is dynamic, moving with the times. In practice it tends to be close to what is approved by Westerners.

Perhaps the most challenging of all Qur'anic passages for such interpretation is the one quoted above, "Men are *qawwamun* of women, in that God has preferred some people over the others ... and beat them ... " (4:34). *Qawwamun* suggests support, control and/or protection and translators vary in their emphases. Also, the phrase "in that" may be interpreted "because" or "to the extent that", so that men's control of women is conditioned on their financial support of them. Also, the phrase "preferred some people over the others" may mean that only some men are preferred over some women. The word "beat" seems straightforward in Arabic but at least one translator renders it "abandon (i.e. for a time)" (Bakhtiar, 2007). Some claim that the Prophetic *sunna* has effectively abrogated beating since the Prophet never beat his wives. Progressive Muslims argue that a passage like this must be interpreted in the light of the general principles of equality and compassion found in the Qur'an (cf. Fazlur Rahman's method, pp. 238, 336). The verse, some say, was meant to moderate violence in a very violent society by making it a last resort, but the general message of the Qur'an as well as contemporary circumstances make beating a wife wrong. Malaysian Sisters in Islam "found that the dominant interpretation of Verse 4:34 (as one that justified domestic violence) was inconsistent with the overall Qur'anic ethos of justice and compassion, and that there were other equally valid interpretations of 4:34 that were not premised on the permission of domestic violence" ("SIS Story", no page).

Reform efforts

Early practical reforms focused very much on developing schools for girls, both private and state-run, and getting girls to attend them. For example, in Egypt the first government girls' schools were opened in the 1870s and primary education was made compulsory in principle for all in 1925. Women began attending university shortly before 1930. Early marriage was discouraged and in many countries a minimum age was set (e.g. 16 for girls in Egypt from 1923). Changes have been sought and to some extent made in relation to polygyny, divorce, maintenance, husband's control over wives, custody of children and inheritance. In Turkey and Tunisia polygamy was abolished and husbands and wives put on equal footing in divorce.

In most countries, other than Turkey, family matters are under the Shari'a and liberal *fiqh* procedures, such as drawing from different ***madhhabs*** are used for reform. The process has usually been slow, and even slower in achieving effective enforcement. Gender and family issues stand at the core of a culture and change is likely to be resisted, especially when the model for it is foreign, indeed ***kafir***. Traditionalists might grant that under current conditions Muslims had to copy *kafirs* in science and technology, but to follow them in these basic elements of society would surely mean ceasing to be Muslim. It is in precisely these areas that the Shari'a provisions had been most consistently followed down through the centuries, so that the moral authority of tradition was highest here. For traditionalists these changes also threatened the well-being of the family and thus the whole structure of social authority. And one did not have to look long at Western society to find the signs of social breakdown and sexual immorality that Muslims would want to avoid. This became more the case with the second wave of feminism in the West and with the "sexual revolution" of the 1960s.

In the immensely symbolic area of clothing, the Egyptian feminist, Hoda Sha'rawi, having been persuaded by her French mentor that "the veil stood in the way of their [Egytian women's] advancement" (Ahmed, 1992, 176) famously removed her veil in 1923 and most upper- and middle-class women in Egypt and elsewhere soon followed suit. In Turkey the veil was forbidden. By the 1950s and 1960s in many countries upper- and middle-class women were wearing Western garb (as were men) though somewhat conservative by some Western standards (the mini-skirt never caught on). All of this did not mean a change in the basic idea that the woman's place is in the home (an idea still dominant in the West at mid-century and by no means dead today). Rather, it was expected that educated and liberated women would raise children to be better citizens and thus strengthen the nation. The reformers found one of the secrets of Western strength to be its treatment of women and sought to emulate it, at least selectively.

Movement in this area was partly reversed, but only partly, with the "resurgence" of Islam and the prominence of Islamism beginning about 1970. The most obvious example would be the reversal of some of the reforms under the Pahlavis after the Islamic revolution in Iran. Family law in Malaysia, relatively liberal when enacted in 1984, was changed in the 1990s to make polygyny and divorce easier for men. In Egypt after virtually no legal change in this area since 1929, president Sadat promulgated by decree a law that would, among other things, have given a woman the right to divorce if her husband took another wife. This aroused considerable opposition and was labeled "Jihan's law", after the president's wife, who had worked for it. The law was declared unconstitutional in 1985 but then enacted in a slightly more restrictive form by parliament the same year. In 2000, in the context of considerable debate, a law was passed making divorce easier for women. On the other hand, education has generally increased for women and in some places there are more women in universities than men. More women also hold jobs outside the home, though this is mainly due to economic conditions that require more middle-class and working-class women to work.

Again, clothing has been the main symbol of "resurgence". Many of the daughters and granddaughters of women who had abandoned the veil put on "Islamic garb" or *hijab*, which covers all but the hands and face. Some have gone further and donned the *niqab*, which covers the face too. The veil they put on is not, however, the veil their grandmothers took off. The *hijab* is not, sartorially, the same as the traditional forms of dress, nor are the motives all the same. It is a statement of Muslim faith and modesty in the face of strong secular and "immodest" trends and thus has an element of rebellion or assertiveness that the earlier veil did not have. Sometimes it has been a political statement, as when otherwise secular women donned it in the Iranian revolution and the Algerian war of independence. It can be a criticism of capitalism and consumerism. As the movement has progressed, however, many have undoubtedly donned it from motives of conformity or because of male pressure. *Muhajjabas* (those wearing *hijab*) are usually relatively well educated and believe in education. While they generally believe that a woman's first responsibility is to home and family, many expect to have a career also. It should be noted that the *hijab* is not impervious to fashion, and a whole

Figure 21.1 Muslim women in *niqab* with stroller in Birmingham, UK. Courtesy of Shutterstock

Figure 21.2 Women outside Blue Mosque in Mazar-i Sharif; two are in *burqa* and two in *hijab*, Afghanistan. Courtesy of iStockphoto

industry has developed around this. It should also be noted that not all *muhajjabas* are Islamists. Some may be modernist or even secularist in political or other areas.

The "resurgence" also gave rise to an "Islamic" feminism contrasting with "secular" feminism. These feminists seek to be authentically Islamic while opposing the abuses of tradition and seeking a more active and public role for women in both society and religious institutions. Many are Islamist and active in connection with the women's wings of Islamist organizations such as the Muslim Brothers. They generally stick to the sorts of social and educational activities traditionally associated with women but some are involved in political activities and some take active leadership and organizational roles in what they do. Most, I think, see their activities as being in support of what the men are doing. On issues such as polygyny they hold to existing interpretations of the Shari'a but probably stress more than most such protections as these afford. They usually pray at the mosques more than traditional women have (usually in separate rooms).

Others, while strongly emphasizing their Islamic character and likely to be *muhajjaba*, take a more modernist approach to the issues, invoking a radical reinterpretation of the

Islamic sources, along lines mentioned earlier, to come to positions at variance with tradition. For example, the American scholar Amina Wadud (1952–) gives a feminist reading of the Qur'an explicitly using Fazlur Rahman's method of ***ijtihad***. She has been controversial and particularly stirred debate when she led a mixed congregation in *salat al-jum'a* in New York in 2005. She has been associated with the Malaysian group, the Sisters in Islam, mentioned earlier.

Of course, many women have continued along a secular path and press for reform in its secularist form. Many affirm the equality demanded by the "second wave" of feminism. While not using *hijab* they will usually dress modestly by Western standards, whether out of preference or prudence. One result of this, potentially at least, is to create a greater divide in society.

Varying situations

What has been said so far applies generally to much of the Arab world, I think, along with Malaysia and Indonesia to a considerable degree. In Turkey matters are different because the *hijab* has been forbidden by law in many contexts and has become a point of major contention between secularist and Islamists (including "post-Islamists"). In Iran, on the other hand, the *hijab* is enforced. It takes two forms, the *chodor*, which is a traditional all enveloping garb that leaves hands and face exposed, and what looks like a raincoat and headscarf (often pushed back as much as possible), which signals a more secular attitude. Afghanistan has a particularly marked divide between a small urban partly secularized population and the remainder who are quite traditional. The Taleban are extremely traditional and their harsh attitude toward women partly reflects their *pushtunwala* tradition and partly the vastness of the gap between them and the more secularized group.

Gender and family issues of course are also important for Muslims in *diaspora*, where they are in direct contact with the Western practices that others experience at more of a distance. Some Muslim practices are forbidden by law (e.g. polygyny, female "circumcision", *hijab* in France, early marriage and possibly arranged marriage) while others are socially discouraged. Some Muslims are happy to integrate into Western ways and find them liberating, but others see severe threats to their moral and ethnic ways and seek ways to resist or isolate themselves, such as providing separate education for their children where they can.

Further considerations

It is important to recognize that in many gender issues what is at stake is the relative importance of the individual and the family. Western feminism is very much based on individualism. The individual woman should make her way in life without being impeded by family, state or social attitudes simply because she is a woman. Solidarity among women is also important, but the ultimate goal for most is the well-being of individual women. For Muslim traditionalists (and most other traditionalists) the family is much more important. The family is the basic unit of society. Without it the individual could not come into existence or survive. Moreover, in societies dominated by corrupt and autocratic elites, as is the case in many modern Muslim societies, the family is often the only source of support and protection the individual has. It is also often the means of acquiring wealth or power. It is worth mentioning that most of the women prime ministers of Muslim countries in modern times have been the daughters or wives of previous (male) prime ministers or presidents.

Consider also the case of arranged marriages. Surely it is the height of madness to allow a young person, driven by hormones and lacking in experience, to choose a lifelong mate. Wiser heads are much more likely to make a choice that will in the long term strengthen the family and be conducive to the well-being of the young people. Of course arranged marriages are open to abuses, and it is these that Westerners hear about in the media and from human rights groups. But it is a reasonable guess that there are at least as many happy and successful marriages among arranged marriages as among marriages based on the choice of individuals. All this cuts against the grain of Western ideas of marriage-based romantic love, but for the traditionalists (not just Muslim ones) their view is just as obvious as the Western view is to Westerners.

Gender issues are not so clear cut as most activists for any particular view would like us to believe. But without activists there would be no reform.

Democracy

Since about the middle of the twentieth century democracy has been the most potent of political concepts and symbols. Most people are in favor of democracy although ideas of what it means vary considerably. As a concept it has been described as a "rich mosaic rather than a simple paradigm" (Esposito and Voll, 1996, 193). Nevertheless, we will begin by defining it here as a system of government in which the majority rules, but with safeguards for minorities. The form of democracy considered here is representative democracy, in which majority rule is carried out through a parliament whose members are elected by the people and an executive either elected by the parliament or directly by the people. Minority rights may be protected by an independent judiciary and/or a fixed constitution. Populism, in contrast to democracy, is here understood to mean majority rule without necessarily protecting minorities. It often involves a charismatic leader who in some sense "embodies" the people and may be chosen by direct action of some sort without set electoral procedures. In the light of the "Arab spring" and other recent events observers have spoken of "illiberal democracy" or "majoritarian democracy" where governments are elected but do not protect the rights of minorities or the opposition.

Of course no actual governments are perfect democracies; corruption, procedural issues and other factors may frustrate majority rule or minority protection. Many governments have the trappings of democracy but are actually oligarchies or dictatorships. So there is often room for debate as to whether a particular government is a democracy and we may speak of degrees of democracy.

Democracy in the West

Democracy as defined here is a relatively recent Western development, conditioned by Western experience and especially by the forms of autocracy against which its protagonists struggled. While the word and some of the reality goes back to ancient Greece, and aspects and precursors may be found later (e.g the Magna Carta and pre-modern parliaments and assemblies), it is only in the nineteenth century that it comes fully to light. In 1800 most people in the West and elsewhere would have thought it patently absurd to imagine that the common people could rule themselves. They would have seen order as a greater concern and probably agreed with the Muslim dictum that "Thirty years of tyranny are better than one day of anarchy" (chapter 8, p. 130).

Even in the United States, commonly seen as the first democracy, the term and the ideal were fully accepted only in the Jacksonian period (1820s and 1830s), while slaves were emancipated only in the 1860s and women gained the vote at the national level only in 1920. As late as the 1940s fascism was a strong competitor to democracy in the minds of many in the West, prioritising order as it did, while the communist version of "people's democracies", which hardly fits the preceding definition, had a strong ideological hold in many places until the 1980s. Also, the definition and expectations of democracy have developed over time, so that now not only full adult suffrage but also certain economic rights are expected in the concept of "social democracy". It is well to remember that, even today, democracy is in some ways a "new boy on the block."

For all this, democracy has not only become a central political concept but the word "democracy" has become one of the most positive and powerful of political symbols and slogans. Today most rulers and governments lay claim to the label of democracy, whether or not they fit the definition given here or genuinely aspire to do so, since this will gain them approval in most circles in the West and in many outside the West.

Islamic concepts and democracy

It is common for Muslims of modernist or Islamist inclination to claim that the earliest Islamic polity was a democracy, indeed the best democracy ever. It is said to be found in the concepts and practices of *bay'a*, allegiance, and *shura*, consultation.

While Muhammad, having been made a prophet by God, was not an elected leader, he nevertheless was "elected" to the extent that he received freely chosen *bay'a* from his followers, and this would hold to some extent for the earliest caliphs too. **Abu Bakr** was chosen as successor (caliph) in a confused and contentious meeting when **'Umar** pre-empted the situation by giving him *bay'a* and others followed suit. This was a kind of democracy but perhaps more like populism. Likewise, Ali was chosen by acclamation by the people of Medina, though not by the whole *umma*. By contrast, Umar was chosen by his predecessor and **Uthman** by a council (called *shura*) chosen by his predecessor.

The Qur'an says "Those who respond to their Lord ... conduct their affairs by mutual consultation" (*shura*; 42:38, cf. 3:159). Both Muhammad and the early caliphs consulted with their followers on many matters and so did many later rulers, and this consultation is often presented as the element of democracy in early Islam. Those consulted were not elected by ballot but were presumably the close followers of the caliph or leaders of factions, clans or families, or other highly respected people, sometimes described as "the people of binding and loosing" (*ahl al-ḥall wa-l-'aqd*). Also, the leader was not usually bound to follow the advice of those he consulted, although on some occasions Muhammad did follow this advice. Thus the early *shura* did not fit the definition of democracy given here but probably represents a precursor of democracy comparable to the councils and parliaments of early Western monarchs, though less formalized.

With the victory of Mu'awiya and the Umayyads, according to a common view, autocracy came to dominate the Muslim world. Rulers were generally military men relying on their troops or they were descendants of bureaucratic dynasties originally founded by military might. There was usually a sense that the ruler was in some way seen as chosen by God and that obedience to God entailed obedience to the ruler. Nevertheless, many of these rulers also engaged in consultation. Most Western dynasties were also founded by military means and the divine right of kings came to be an extremely strong ideology against which democracy had to fight.

One can also find precursors to democracy in the roles of the Shari'a and *'ulama'*. The Shari'a represents a form of the rule of a law above and independent of the rulers. The *'ulama'*, as the interpreters of the Shari'a, could sometimes act as a brake on the rulers, though their power was mainly moral. They typically represented and defended the people to the rulers and represented and defended the rulers to the people.

The relative lack of racism was another factor favoring democracy. While Arabs claimed a certain pre-eminence in relation to the caliphate, people of all races and ethnicities comprised the *umma* and actually achieved power. A sense of solidarity and mutual responsibility (*takāful*) and at least spiritual equality in the *umma* can be seen as another factor.

The main minority groups were marked off by religion. The *dhimma* provided protection for Jews and Christians, though it also required a level of social and political subordination that would in principle be unacceptable in a modern democracy. Other groups, such as Zoroastrians and Hindus sometimes benefited from the *dhimma* though their position was less clear or secure. Nevertheless, the *dhimma* probably provided better protection for minorities such as the Jews than Europe did before the nineteenth century or even later in some cases (Nazi Germany being the extreme example).

Modern efforts toward democracy

In modern times many Muslim reformers have found in democracy one of the secrets of Western strength, as well as being morally attracted to it, although this has not been universally the case, since Western forms of autocracy, including fascism, have had some appeal. The concept of *shura* has been particularly evoked, with the argument that whatever its forms in the past, parliamentary government is its appropriate form today. It is also seen as a means of strengthening the solidarity of the *umma* (whether conceived as the whole Muslim community or as the nation). In this connection the later "social democracy" of the West has had considerable appeal. "Socialism" of various sorts has abounded in the Muslim world, particularly in the third quarter of the twentieth century, in the immediate aftermath of the independence of many Muslim countries and when it was also at its most popular in the West. In many places the *dhimma* has been legally replaced by equality before the law, although older attitudes persist and some Islamists, including Mawdudi, would like to restore it.

It is, however, perhaps among Muslims that democracy as a symbol is most called into question, since it seems to contradict the basic meaning of Islam. Democracy is the rule of the people but Islam is the rule of God. In democracy the people, not God, make the laws. Is this not the height of *shirk* and *kufr*? Many traditionalists and radical Islamists think so. Khomeini refused to allow "The Democratic Islamic Republic of Iran" as the name of his revolutionary republic for this reason. Nevertheless, it is possible to think of the people ruling themselves within the framework of the Shari'a, just as Western democracies generally recognize some moral law, divine or natural, that transcends their legislatures. The United States, for example, claims to be a democracy but also to be "under God". Even if rulers must rule by the Shari'a, there would seem to be no reason why they cannot be chosen by the people. Legislatures can make rules in the areas where the Shari'a is silent or allows diversity. Both rulers and legislators will inevitably interpret the Shari'a, and courts may judge their actions by the standard of the Sharia. Mawdudi, one of the leading Islamists, proposed something like this, describing it as "theodemocracy". He argued that the ***khilafa***, given by God to Adam according to the Qur'an (2:30) now belongs to the whole Muslim *umma*. "The entire Muslim population runs the state in accordance with the Book of God and the practice of His Prophet" (Mawdudi, 1960, 132).

Figure 21.3 Women cast their vote on a new constitution at a polling station in Cairo (December 2012). Courtesy of MARCO LONGARI/AFP/Getty Images

Iqbal, a modernist, and others have argued that the function of *ijtihad*, traditionally the interpretation of *fiqh* by properly qualified *'ulama'*, could be vested in legislatures. Iqbal interpreted the early reforms in Turkey under Atatürk in these terms. Such rulers, legislatures and courts exist in Iran today (though not with Iqbal's interpretation of *ijtihad*). Khomeini not withstanding, some Iranians have claimed that the Islamic Republic has "presented a new definition of democracy" (Esposito and Voll, 1996, 76). How democratic Iran is in fact today may be debated, but observers generally agree that Iran is closer to democracy (or perhaps populism) than most Muslim governments.

One of the ironies of the present scene for liberal and secular democrats is that as the common people in the Muslim world have gained more political influence, politics has become more Islamic. The "common people" are generally more Islamic than the elite, among whom most liberals and secularists are to be found and who think to rule them for their own good. For this reason many secular liberals in Egypt abetted the military takeover in July 2013, and it has been said that liberals there are not democrats and democrats are not liberal.

In my view enough of the ingredients of democracy are to be found in the Islamic texts and Islamic history so that one may hope that a recognizable form of democracy, imperfect to be sure, may in time predominate in the Islamic world. One already can see this in Turkey, Indonesia and Malaysia, and perhaps Iran and Pakistan, and one still hopes the "Arab spring" might produce other examples. Elements of democracy, such as a parliament, exist in most countries. One observing Western Europe in 1650 would hardly have predicted something like democracy as an important part of its future. The fact that the West has come to democracy first has positive and negative sides. On the positive side, it has demonstrated the possibility of democracy and provided models of it, diverse and imperfect as they are, for others to follow. Negatively, aspects of those models may not be suitable for the Muslim world and the history of imperialism tends to associate the name of democracy with the "enemy". Still, the basic idea behind democracy, government of, by and for the people, appears to have appeal everywhere.

Human rights

Like democracy, the current concept of human rights has its roots in the West. The American "Declaration of Independence" (1776) and "Bill of Rights" (1791), and the French "Declaration of the Rights of Man" (1789), all based on eighteenth-century Enlightment thinking, are commonly seen as the first major milestones and exemplars, although they themselves are the culmination of a long struggle for rights and the concept of rights in one form or another goes back to ancient Greece and Rome or earlier. Today the Universal Declaration of Human Rights (UDHR), enacted by the United Nations in 1948, when the majority of its members were Western, along with various other UN-sponsored treaties and conventions since then, is taken by most human rights activists as the standard statement. These statements, of course, reflect the circumstances under which they were produced and the abuses against which they were directed. For instance, the American Bill of Rights protects people from having soldiers forcibly quartered in their homes, a practice of their former British rulers. The UDHR includes the right to asylum for refugees, reflecting a need arising out of the Second World War and the events leading up to it. It is important to note that the concept of human rights developed in tandem with secularism (in the sense of drawing one's values from this worldly experience rather than other worldly revelation) and pluralism.

In principle human rights belong to humans simply by virtue of being humans, without regard to gender, race, ethnicity, class, wealth, educational level or other markers of distinction. In the words of the UDHR. "All human beings are born free and equal in dignity and rights". Human rights may be divided into two types, negative and positive. "Negative" rights involve freedom from undue restriction, e.g. freedom of speech, press, religion, etc.; freedom from arbitrary imprisonment, cruel and unusual punishment. Positive rights include the right to an adequate livelihood, employment, medical care and the like. The earlier statements of rights focused more on the negative rights while the positive rights have come to the fore in more recent times, and are stressed in the later articles (23 on) of the UDHR.

The rights are primarily rights of individuals and the ideal reflects to a considerable degree the individualism of modern Western society. Group rights are also recognized, to some degree, particularly of family and minority groups. These will be particularly important to any groups that feel under threat. It should also be noted that most human rights discourse is related to the modern state with its considerably expanded powers. It is usually from the state that "negative" rights need to be protected and it is usually the state that is to provide or create the conditions for the "positive" rights.

For many rights activists human rights comes close to being an absolute concern, having virtually a religious force. Rights are, perforce, limited in certain ways, however, e.g. children cannot engage in certain activities, the rights of convicted criminals are abridged, etc. Rights of individuals may conflict. My neighbor's right to have a loud party may conflict with my right to sleep. Rights of groups may conflict with those of individuals, as in the case of the young person who wants to marry against the family's wishes. Exercise of some rights under some circumstances may be against the well-being of society. It has been pointed out that one does not have the right to falsely cry "Fire!" in a crowded theatre and cause a stampede. The right of free speech is likely to be curtailed in wartime or crisis. The actions of the U.S. government in holding suspected terrorists at Guantanamo Base illustrates the issues and tensions involved here. The concept of rights has also been extended over time. In the past "cruel and unusual punishment" was not seen to include capital punishment but now in many jurisdictions it is.

In spite of these qualifications, there is still a certain sense of absoluteness that attaches to human rights for those who believe in them, and thus a certain sacredness.

And this is probably appropriate. When we come to the practical question of how to get governments and other wielders of power to respect human rights when their material or political interests incline them otherwise, one part of the answer is to create an atmosphere in which human rights are seen as sacred.

Islamic grounds for human rights

The Western origin of the current human rights movement obviously presents issues for Muslims and Muslim societies. These values come from sources that are viewed with considerable ambivalence and often seen as religiously wrong, morally dangerous and materially threatening. Moreover, the Western states that propound them can be seen as quite hypocritical, since their actions often belie their high-sounding words.

The concept of rights is, of course, not absent from traditional Muslim thinking. It is usually attached closely to duty, however, and also is usually related to social location (as it was in the pre-modern West). Children have rights vis-à-vis their parents, wives have rights vis-à-vis their husbands, subjects have rights vis-à-vis rulers, and vice versa in each case; but all this is equally well put in terms of duty: parents have duties to their children, etc. The five Shari'a valuations discussed by *fiqh* (obligatory, recommended, neutral, disapproved, forbidden, see pp. 147–48) can be seen as varying degrees of duty. Justice, also, is a central concept and is expected of rulers, parents, husbands, etc. Both duty and justice may be said to imply corresponding rights.

The basic Qur'anic affirmation of the spiritual equality of humans as creatures of God also seems to provide a ground for rights vis-à-vis each other and for the idea that God has granted these rights. The Qur'an specifically calls for tolerance of difference in certain situations, especially in the case of *dhimmis*, as mentioned earlier. Some passages suggest full equality: "Surely those who believe, and those who are Jews, Christians and Sabeans, whoever believes in God and the Last Day, and does righteous deeds – shall have their reward with their Lord, and no fear shall be on them, neither shall they sorrow" (2:62; cf. 5:69) although others do not (e.g. 9:29). The concern for the poor and for community solidarity, both in the Qur'an and in later tradition, provides a basis for concern for the "positive" human rights. The Prophet said "The one who strives to sponsor a widow or a poor person is like the one who strives in *jihad* in the cause of Allah, the Mighty and Sublime" (Nasa'i, Bukhari). In fact, Muslims are often quicker to affirm these than the "negative" rights. One may argue that this is no less fertile ground than the Bible.

On the other hand, a strong sense of contrast between right and wrong along with a strong sense of being on the right side has characterized much Muslim thinking and certainly characterizes the Qur'an. "Truth has come and falsehood has vanished; falsehood is ever bound to vanish" (Qur'an 17:81). The terms referring to unbelievers or heretics, *kufr, shirk, zandaqa*, etc., are extremely strong terms. This makes it hard to tolerate those who are in the wrong, especially when not only earthly welfare but eternal felicity is at stake. One of the fundamental bases of human rights is what we may term "the right to be wrong", not only tolerating those we "know" to be wrong but defending their rights, as when the American Civil Liberties Union has upon occasion defended the rights of neo-Nazis. Of course the Christian tradition has for the most part had much the same sense of rightness and from it persecution has often flowed, probably even more than among Muslims. For the modern West secularism and pluralism have tempered the sense of rightness and thus have been major enabling factors for human rights. Must this be the case for Muslims?

The sacred is central to religion and both Muslims and Christians, as well as followers of other religions, can have very strong reactions when this is perceived to be violated. This has been illustrated dramatically in the case of Muslims in recent years by the events surrounding Rushdie's *Satanic Verses* and the Danish Jyllands Posten cartoons of Muhammad. Some Muslims feel obligated to respond forcefully when the honor of the Prophet, in particular, is violated. Comparable cases can be found among Christians and others. Is the sacred inconsistent with full human rights?

Some would argue that a diminished sense of the sacred, an aspect of secularization, makes tolerance and thus the recognition of the rights of dissenters easier. On the other hand, we have noted that human rights have a degree of sacredness for many. How tolerant are human rights activists of those who oppose rights they consider important? Some are, such as with the American Civil Liberties Union defense of the neo-Nazis, but perhaps not so many. The reader is encouraged to reflect on these issues.

Also, historical conditions both past and present have given Muslims a strong fear of *fitna* (disorder, civil war) and a corresponding strong desire for order. The first century of Islam was characterized by considerable *fitna* and this early experience has imprinted itself on the later tradition. Later eras have also had their share of *fitna*, as has the modern period. This leads to the attitude enshrined in the supposed *hadith*, "One day of *fitna* is worse than a thousand years of tyranny". For such an attitude rights are dangerous and will often be sacrificed on the altar of order. Certainly many of the results of the extension of rights and freedom in the West look like *fitna* to many Muslims today, a *fitna* that would weaken the *umma* if it accepted them.

When it comes to specifics, both the Qur'an and Shari'a as interpreted by the *'ulama'* have a lot that violates current conceptions of human rights, most prominently such things as cutting off the hand of a thief, stoning or flogging for *zina*, taking life for life as well as matters relating to gender, discussed earlier. Modernist interpretation may moderate some of this, by claiming that they were relevant to conditions of Muhammad's time that no longer exist, that they violate the spirit of the Qur'an or that they have usually not been enforced in the past, but such interpretation may not go far enough or have sufficient moral authority.

As has been mentioned, communities in danger or in crisis are likely to restrict rights. The Muslim *umma* has seen itself under siege from the West for over two centuries. Moreover, human rights as now presented have their source in the West and those who espouse them most prominently are highly Westernized. It is not surprising that many Muslims see human rights as a kind of device to weaken their will and solidarity.

Muslim moves toward human rights and some criticisms

In spite of all this, human rights have an inherent appeal that may ultimately overcome the obstacles. Those who have suffered abuse along with their families and friends, and also all who are concerned for justice, form a reservoir of support. Another potential source of support is the Muslim diaspora, since Muslims there have often benefited from the assistance of human rights activists when faced with discrimination. Muslim human rights advocates are freer to express their views there than in most Muslim countries and many Muslim have fled to the West when their rights were being violated in their home countries.

Added to this is the prestige of the West (which is as important as its threatening nature) and the diminished prestige of many of the post-colonial Muslim states. As noted earlier, human rights concerns tend to focus on the modern state. In most places the Muslim modern state is a fairly recent phenomenon and was initially seen as the fruit of independence, a means of improving the lot of the people and defending against continuing imperialism. This made criticism of it difficult. Since most Muslim states have failed to fulfil their promise, however, criticism has become easier.

Beginning as early as the 1960s human rights organizations have been formed in a number Muslim countries, including Bahrain, Palestine, Syria, Egypt, Nigeria, Yemen, Pakistan, Malaysia, Indonesia and Bangladesh (the last four connected with the Asian Forum for Human Rights and Development). The Egyptian Organization for Human Rights, founded in 1985, has defended Islamists who oppose its views. The presence of a significant desire for human rights has been illustrated by the demonstrations accompanying the "Arab spring", and also by the earlier demonstrations in Iran, even where they have not (yet?) achieved their goals.

Human rights are sufficiently prestigious so that even conservative Muslim groups have produced statements of human rights. One of these is the Cairo Declaration on Human Rights in Islam, a fairly traditionalist statement endorsed by the Organization of the Islamic Conference in 1990. It is more or less patterned after UDHR, covering largely the same topics but with Islamically inspired modifications and fairly frequent references to the Shari'a. On freedom of religion, for example, where the UDHR speaks of freedom to change one's religion (Article 18), the Cairo Declaration says, "Islam is the religion of unspoiled nature. It is prohibited to exercise any form of compulsion on man or to exploit his poverty or ignorance in order to convert him to another religion or to atheism" (Article 10). The following statements on the family also illustrate the contrast:

Cairo Declaration Article 5

(a) The family is the foundation of society, and marriage is the basis of its formation. Men and women have the right to marriage, and no restrictions stemming from race, colour or nationality shall prevent them from enjoying this right.
(b) Society and the State shall remove all obstacles to marriage and shall facilitate marital procedure. They shall ensure family protection and welfare.

UDHR Article 16

(1) Men and women of full age, without any limitation due to race, nationality or religion, have the right to marry and to found a family. They are entitled to equal rights as to marriage, during marriage and at its dissolution.

> (2) Marriage shall be entered into only with the free and full consent of the intending spouses.

The UDHR ends with the statement that no state or person may do anything "aimed at the destruction of any of the the rights and freedoms it sets forth herein". The Cairo declaration states that "all the rights and freedoms stipulated in this Declaration are subject to the Islamic Shari'a".

These differences are justified by many on the grounds that human rights in any Muslim country must take a distinctively Islamic form if it is to have sufficient moral authority in the minds of the people so that they will defend them and act on them in the face of repression. Human rights, as mentioned earlier, depends very heavily on moral authority. Such a form would presumably be more conservative on personal morals and would privilege groups such as the family more than the UDHR does.

This view is decried as "cultural relativism" by some Western human rights proponents. Ann Mayer, another important writer on human rights, argues that human rights as enshrined in the UDHR are universal and that Muslim countries, most of whom have ratified it, cannot opt out. She criticizes the references to the Shari'a in statements such as the Cairo Declaration as vague, since the Shari'a is diversely interpreted. She does express the hope that a modern form of Islam may prevail that interprets it in a manner consistent with human rights, but Muslims must adapt themselves to the UDHR version of human rights, not adapt the UDHR to their views.

Anthony Chase takes a different tack and argues that Islam and human rights fall into different categories. Islam is rarely directly connected with human rights violations; rather the causes are politics and political structure. This view would presumably be congenial to the more radical Muslim secularists, since it assumes a separation between religion and society. But this would be theoretically unacceptable to most Muslims and rarely obtains in practice in the Muslim world. Some form of Islam influences most political and social actors, even relatively secular ones.

A modernist who has devoted a considerable amount of effort to the issues of human rights is Abdullahi An-Naim, a Sudanese scholar and former follower of **Mahmud Muhammad Taha**, who was executed by the Sudanese government. He argues that religion is necessarily exclusive but that various religions can come to an "overlapping" consensus on a set of human rights, each coming at it from its own angle so to speak. Religion, secularism (here seen as safeguarding pluralism) and human rights are mutually supportive. Religion needs secularism and human rights so as to be able to transform itself over time. Secularism needs sufficient moral content to serve as a basis for human rights and human rights needs the support of religion to be accepted by religious people, who are the majority.

Islamists generally take a hard line where the traditional interpretation of the Shari'a does. On cutting off the hand of a thief some would say that this should only be done when there is an Islamic state since in the immoral and unjust atmosphere of other states someone may need to steal to live. On the *dhimma,* Mawdudi says that an Islamic state is an "ideological state" and that therefore only those who accept the ideology can have full political rights, as we have seen earlier. Others have the rights the Shari'a gives to *dhimmis,* a category which he does not seem to limit to Jews and Christians. He claims that national states say all of their citizens are equal, but hypocritically deny this equality to minorities in practice (Mawdudi, 1960, 65, 139–40, 177–78, cf. p. 247).

Western imposition ... or dialogue?

For some Muslims views such as those of Anne Mayer and Anthony Chase represent an arrogant Western imposition on societies for which they are not appropriate. Is this so? Or are human rights something that accords and meets the needs of basic human nature, as human rights advocates hold? Are they perhaps like the truths of current physical science, which have been discovered in the West but are agreed to be equally true for all people? In the first case one would look for a distinctively Muslim form of human rights in a world more pluralist than most Westerners have imagined. In the latter case they will probably be accepted eventually by the Muslim world, but Muslims may play a role in their further development and change, as some of them do in physical science. As mentioned earlier, a Muslim form of human rights is likely to give more weight to groups and be more conservative in sexual and other personal morality. It is also likely to put duties and rights more in balance. It would also be less secular and might demonstrate that human rights are possible without complete secularization. There are many in the West who would not be averse to this.

We like to speak of dialogue in inter-cultural relations but tend to forget that in a real dialogue both sides have roughly equal standing and usually influence each other. So far human rights has been more of a monologue, in which Westerners speak and Muslims respond diversely. To have dialogue Westerners would have to take Muslim positions more seriously and probably adopt some of them. Here is a possible example. People in the West have begun to talk about victims' rights, recognizing that victims are too often sidelined in criminal court cases. Here we might consider Shari'a law as it applies to murder and some other crimes, where the family of the victim decides the punishment: physical punishment, monetary compensation or forgiveness. Westerners may not want to adopt precisely this practice but could certainly learn something from it.

On all three issues discussed here there is much to be said for developing a genuine two-way dialogue, one might say a higher pluralism, rather than a clash of civilizations.

Concluding problematic postscript: the myth of equality

In all of the issues discussed in this chapter human equality is a fundamental assumption. But the proposition that "all men are created equal", if taken as a statement of fact, is patently false. Some people are born strong and healthy and some are born with congenital defects, some are born with high intelligence and some with low, some are born into prosperous families and some into poor families, some are born into loving families and some into violent families, and so on. What is meant, of course, is that all people are of equal intrinsic value. But on what basis can this be said? The religious person can assert that they are equal in God's sight, as the writers of the Declaration of Independence said and as at the most basic level both the Bible and the Qur'an say.

But on what basis does the secularist who does not believe in God assert this? Some might argue from natural law, though the examples given here would put this in question. Post-modernist secularists could hardly even evoke natural law. Going purely on empirical facts, a better case can probably be made for inequality than equality. In fact most people down through the ages have believed that God ordains inequality and nature illustrates it. In the words of a hymn Christians used to sing:

> The rich man in his castle
> The poor man at his gate
> He made them High and lowly
> He ordered their estate

Must one then not only be religious but also adhere to certain modern forms of religion to have a firm foundation for equality, and thus human rights? Many who read and teach this book would certainly not agree.

In fact, we may say that human equality is a myth, in two senses of the word. It is a myth in the common meaning of being untrue. It is also a myth in the sense frequent in Religious Studies, that is, a story or idea that may be literally false but that points to a more important social, moral or spiritual truth, and does so in a way that activates strong feelings and forceful actions. All great religious stories and ideas are myths in this sense (even though some are true). There are also secular myths, such as those connected with nationalism. Perhaps human equality is the greatest and best of all modern myths. The reader is invited to reflect on this.

Key points

- Concern for gender equality, democracy and human rights in their current form developed in the West and are on offer to the Muslim world as part of the general spread of Western ideas.
- They have attraction for many Muslims but are also suspect because of their connection with Western imperialism.
- Muslim traditionalists, secularists, modernists and Islamists respond diversely to all of these.
- Comparing the culture and religious history of Christendom and Islam, there appears no compelling reason why Muslim society cannot adopt these Western practices.
- Nevertheless, there is a case to be made that Muslims should not adopt them in precisely their Western form but should develop their own forms.

Discussion questions

1. How convincing are the modernist interpretations of the Qur'an in relation to the three topics discussed in this chapter?
2. How has the "resurgence" of Islam since about 1970 affected the situation of Muslim women?
3. What are the elements in early or traditional Islam that may support the development of democracy in Muslim countries today?
4. Are human rights as presented in the UDHR universal?
5. Are Western countries hypocritical in urging gender reform, democracy and human rights on Muslims?
6. Must one believe in God in order to believe in human equality?

Critical thinking box 21.1

Compare in detail the United Nations' Universal Declaration of Human Rights with the new Egyptian constitution. What are the most important differences and what is their significance? (Selections from both are on the website along with internet links to the full documents.)

Critical thinking box 21.2

How would Ibn Sina, Al-Ghazali and/or Ibn Taymiyya react to the Universal Declaration of Human Rights? Would this have any implication for the claim that human rights is a form of cultural imperialism?

Critical thinking box 21.3

Analyze the quotation from Fathullah Gülen in critical thinking box 16.1 in terms of a general definition of democracy such as the one given in this chapter.

Critical thinking box 21.4

Interpretation of Qur'an 4: 34. Locate commentaries to this verse and write a brief essay on how it has been and may be interpreted. (Information will be placed on the website.)

Critical thinking box 21.5

In an article entitled "A Region at War with its History" (*Time*, 16 April 2012, p. 16) Fareed Zacharia asks why there is a "democracy deficit" in the Arab world today. Assess his general argument and the accuracy of his statements about Islam and Islamic history. (Available online: http://www.time.com/time/magazine/article/0,9171,2111248,00.html [accessed 29 August 2013].)

Companion website

Features Qur'anic and other traditional material on gender, information on a woman Sufi saint, material on issues relating to democracy, selections from human rights documents, websites for these documents and gender issues and limited further reading.

Further reading

Gender

Ahmed, Leila (1992) *Women and Gender in Islam: Historical Roots of a Modern Debate.* New Haven, CT and London: Yale University Press. (Thorough historical study, something of a "classic", largely limited to the Middle East.)

Brooks, Geraldine (1995) *Nine Parts of Desire: The Hidden World of Islamic Women.* New York: Doubleday. (Attractively written, covers diverse situations with a good appreciation of differing positions.)

Mernissi, Fatima (1985) *Beyond the Veil*, rev. ed. London: Al-Saqi Books. (Early work by one of the best known modernist feminist writers.)

Wadud, Amina (1999, originally 1991) *Qur'an and Woman: Rereading the Sacred Text from a Woman's Perspective.* New York: Oxford University Press. (Good modernist treatment.)

Vogt, Kari, Larsen, Lena and Moe, Christian, (eds.) (2009) *New Directions in Islamic Thought: Exploring reform and Muslim Traditions.* London, New York: I.B. Tauris. (Some general articles, e.g. by Soroush and Kadivar, but most related to gender.)

Singerman, Diane and Hoodfar, Homa (eds.) (1996) *Development, Change, and Gender in Cairo: A View from the Household.* Bloomington and Indianapolis: Indiana University Press. (Anthropological studies of low-income families; very enlightening about the realities of women's lives.)

Joseph, Suad (ed.) (2003) *Encyclopedia of Women and Islamic Cultures*, 6 vols. Leiden: Brill.

See also: as-Sulamī, *Early Sufi Women* [12]; Esposito, *Women in Muslim Family Law* [10].

Democracy

Esposito, John L. and Voll, John O. (1996) *Islam and Democracy.* Oxford University Press. (General study followed by chapters on Iran, Sudan, Pakistan, Malaysia, Algeria and Egypt.)

Abou El Fadl, Khaled (2004) *Islam and the Challenge of Democracy.* Princeton, NJ: Princeton University Press. (An interesting and well-argued defense of democracy by an Islamic modernist, with comments by other scholars.)

See also: Esposito, *The Oxford History of Islam* (Ch. 15) [F].

Human rights

Chase, Anthony and Hamzawy, Amr (eds.) (2006) *Human Rights in the Arab World: Independent Voices*. Philadelphia: University of Pennsylvania Press. (Several articles, see especially Chase's contribution.)

Mayer, Ann Elizabeth (1991) *Islam and Human Rights: Tradition and Politics*. 3rd ed. Boulder, CO : Westview Press. (In some ways the "standard" Western work. Vigorously defends universality of human rights over against cultural relativism. Argues that Islam is diverse and thus not necessarily opposed to human rights.)

Safi, Louay (2003) *Tensions and Transitions in the Muslim World*. Lahnam, MD: University Press of America. (See especially chapters 7 and 8 for an interesting discussion of human rights; criticizes Mayer, among others)

Abdullahi, An-Na'im (2010) *Islam and Human Rights: Selected Essays of Abdullahi An-Na'im*, ed Mashood A. Baderin. Farnham: Ashgate.

Haddad, Yvonne Yazbeck and Esposito, John L. (eds.) (1998) *Islam, Gender and Social Change*. New York: Oxford University Press. (Has an article on Qur'anic interpretation and others on specific countries and areas.)

See also: Robinson, *The Cambridge Illustrated History of the Islamic World* [F]; Safi, *Progressive Muslims* [20]; Kurzman, *Liberal Islam* [20]; Noor, *New Voices of Islam* [20]; Knysh, *Islam in Historical Perspective* (Ch. 19) [F]; Ernst, *Following Muhammad* (Ch. 4, Postscript) [1].

Appendix I

Glossary of names and terms

Abangan Javanese Muslims who do not follow Islamic prescriptions strictly and follow many traditional Javanese customs; often called "statistical Muslims".

Abbasid caliphate (750–1258) Line of caliphs claiming descent from Muḥammad's uncle with their capital in Baghdad; the early period was one of the high points of Muslim political power, while the whole dynasty saw major cultural achievements. A shadow line of Abbasids continued until 1517 in Egypt.

'Abd al-Rāziq, 'Alī (1888–1966) Wrote a controversial but influential book defending secularism on Islamic grounds in Egypt in 1925.

'Abduh, Muḥammad (1842–1905) Egyptian modernist reformer, influential throughout the Muslim world.

Abū Bakr (d. 634) The first caliph or successor to Muḥammad as leader of the *umma*.

Abū Ḥanīfa (d. 767) One of leading early *faqīhs* (jurists); understood to be the founder of the Ḥanafī *madhhab*.

***'Āda* (or *adat*)** Custom; may be seen as a source of *fiqh* or as an alternative or complement to the Sharī'a, also called *'urf*.

Adab Proper manners and behaviour, especially of the courtier or bureaucrat; literature, *belles lettres*. There is also an *adab* for Ṣūfīs, *faqīhs* and other groups.

Adam The first man according to the Qur'ān; also understood to be the first prophet.

Adhān The call to *ṣalāh* (prayer) five times a day.

Ahl al-ḥadīth Among the early *'ulamā'*, those who insisted on basing their view and judgments on *ḥadīth*, as opposed to ahl al-ra'y, who based their views on considered opinion and reason. Ahl al-ḥadīth include Ibn Ḥanbal and al-Shāfi'ī. Often called traditionalists.

Ahl al-sunna wa-l-jamā 'a The Sunnīs, as opposed to the Shī'is, literally: the people of the *sunna* and the (mainstream) community.

Ahl-i Ḥadīth Movement in South Asia, dating from the late nineteenth century, who hold strictly to the Quran and *ḥadīth* as authority; today generally considered *salafī*.

Aḥmad al-Badawī (1200?–76) The most popular of the Sufi *walīs* ("saints") in Egypt and founder of the Ahmadiyya Badawiyya *ṭarīqa*. His *mawlid* ("birthday" festival) attracts vast numbers each October to Tanta in the Nile Delta.

Ahmadiyya or **Ahmadiyya Badawiyya.** Very popular *ṭarīqa* in Egypt, see Aḥmad al-Badawi.

Ahmadiyya Followers of the Indian reformer, Ghulam Ahmad (1835–1908), thought to be a prophet by some of his followers. For this reason they are often persecuted by other Muslims. The movement is an actively proselyting one. No connection with the Egyptian Ahmadiyya.

Akbar (r. 1556–1605) Ruler of the Mughal Empire at its height; open minded toward other religions and philosophies.

Akhbārī Twelver Shī'ī school of *fiqh* that emphasizes the authority of the *akhbār* (reports of Muḥammad and the *Imāms*).

AKP Turkish acronym for the Justice and Development Party (Adalet ve Kalkinma Partisi), a "post-Islamist" party formed by younger members who split from Erbaken's Islamist party. Combines a moderate secularism with an Islamic ethos.

'Alawīs (or Nuṣayrīs) Sect recognizing 'Alī as the highest manifestation of the divine; currently dominating the government of Syria. Distinct from the Alevis.

Alevis Sect recognizing 'Alī as the highest manifestation of the divine; located in Turkey, experiencing a cultural revival since the 1980s.

'Alī ibn Abī Ṭālib (d. 661) Cousin and son-in-law of the Prophet Muḥammad, fourth caliph in the Sunnī reckoning and first *Imām* in the Shī 'ī reckoning.

'Ālim Singular of *'ulamā'*, q.v.

Al-Kulaynī (d. 940) Compiler of the main collection of Twelver Shī'ī *Ḥadīth* and *akhbār*.

Allāh Arabic word for the One God and the one mostly used by Muslims; used in other Islamic languages beside Arabic.

Ameer Ali (1849–1928) Indian modernist, whose book *The Spirit of Islām* has been quite influential.

Amīr Military commander; title of some rulers; in modern times often means prince (heir apparent to a king), can be used for religious leaders.

Amīr al-mu'minīn "Commander of the faithful", title of caliphs and other rulers, usually implying a serious commitment to religion.

Andalus Areas of Spain and Portugal under Muslim rule from 711 to 1492. Site of a flourishing and relatively tolerant civilization.

Anṣār "Helpers", the Medinan supporters of Muḥammad; name also taken by other groups, e.g. the supporters of the Sudanese Mahdī. See also ***Muhājir.***

Aramaic A group of Semitic languages widely spoken (by Jews and others) in Western Asia in the centuries before Islam. Syriac is a form of Aramaic used by Christians.

Ash'arīs (Ash'arites or Ash'ariyya) The most prominent school of Sunnī *kalām* (theology), founded by Abū al-Ḥasan 'Alī al-Ash'arī (d. 935), who sought to demonstrate traditionalist theses by rational methods.

'Ashūrā' Tenth day of Muḥarram, the first month of the Muslim year; the death of Ḥusayn on this day is commemorated by Shī 'īs.

Atatürk, Mustafa Kemal (1881–1938) Founder of the Turkish Republic; instituted far-reaching secularist reforms. The title Atatürk means "Father of the Turks".

Awqāf See *waqf.*

Āya "Sign", verse of the Qur'ān; also used in the Qur'ān for the signs of nature that point to God and for some miracles.

Ayatollah "Sign of God", title given to high-ranking Shī'ī *'ulamā'* in the Uṣūli school of *fiqh*; Grand Ayatollah (*Ayatollah 'Uzma*) is the title given to those with the highest rank (see *marja'-i taqlid*).

Azhar, al- Mosque and *madrasa*, now University, in Cairo. Founded in the tenth century CE, it has long been considered the greatest traditional *madrasa*/university, drawing students from throughout the Muslim world. It is considered the most authoritative official Islamic institution in Egypt.

Baha'is Followers of Baha'ullah (1817–92), who in 1863 claimed to be the one promised by God, effectively the next prophet after Muḥammad. The movement began among Iranian Shī 'īs but is now a separate, worldwide religion.

Baraka "Blessing"; a sacred power, derived from Allāh, believed to be present in the Qur'ān, the actions and tombs of Ṣūfī saints (*walīs*) and elsewhere.

Bektashis Ṣūfī *ṭarīqa*, eclectic in doctrine and practice, closely associated with the Janissaries in the Ottoman Empire, suppressed in the 1820s.

Bid'a "Innovation", something not practiced in the earliest days of Islām and therefore viewed as heresy; some, however, recognize "good innovations".

al-Bukhārī, Muḥammad ibn Ismā'īl (d. 870) Compiler of one of the two most authoritative collections of *Ḥadīth*, known as *Ṣaḥīḥ Bukhārī.*

Buyid, Buwayhid Dynasty of Twelver Shi'i *amīrs* ruling in Baghdad under Sunni Abbasid caliphs from 945 to 1045. They supported Shi'i interests and patronized Shi'i scholarship.

Byzantine Empire The later Roman Empire with its capital at Constantinople; Greek-speaking and Christian, it lost territory to the first wave of Muslim conquest, then held out until conquered by the Ottomans in 1453.

Caliphs Sunnī rulers, at least in name, of the whole Islamic empire until 1258 (see Abbasid, Umayyad); title claimed by Ottoman *sulṭāns* in the nineteenth and early twentieth centuries. See *khalīfa*.

Chishtis (Chishtiyya) Ṣūfī *tariqa* widespread in India; the tomb of its founder, Mu'in al-Din Chishti (d. 1236), is a popular site for pilgrimage (*ziyāra*).

Christ (Ar: Masīḥ) In the Muslim view the last of the prophets before Muḥammad, Christ's revelation is the *Injīl* (Gospel) and he is often referred to as Jesus, the son of Mary ('Īsā ibn Maryam).

Crusades A series of expeditions by Western Christians ("Franks") beginning in 1099 against the Muslims in the Near East with the initial goal of reconquering the Holy Land; today Islamists often refer to Western imperialists as Crusaders.

Dār al harb See Dār al-Islām.

Dār al-Islām The "Abode of Islam", the whole geographical area ruled by Muslims, traditionally contrasted with *dār al-ḥarb*, "the abode of war". Some have recognized an intermediate position, *dār al-ṣulḥ* or *dār al-ahd*, "Abode of treaty" (viz. with a non-Muslim ruler or state). In modern times areas that have passed out of Muslim rule but where Muslims can still practice their religion are considered part of Dār al-Islām by most. The term is also used for certain movements in Indonesia between 1948 and 1965.

***Darwish* (or *dervish*)** Persian word for "poor" or "poor in spirit"; a term used for a Ṣūfī.

Dasta Procession of Shi'i young men who flagellate themselves to demonstrate their support for Husayn, especially during the period of 'Ashura, q.v.

Da'wa, Dakwa Inviting people to Islam, whether non-Muslims to become Muslims or Muslims to become better and more active Muslims.

Deobandi A modern traditionalist movement based on the *madrasa* at Deoband in India (founded in 1867).

Dhawq "Taste", the experience of the divine that Ṣūfīs seek and some have.

Dhikr (zikr) "Remembering"; awareness of God; the rituals used by Ṣūfīs to achieve this awareness.

Dhimmīs (zimmis) Non-Muslims with a covenant of protection (*dhimma*) that allows them to live in a Muslim society under specified conditions; particularly Christians and Jews but others often have this status in practice.

Druze A sect who believe that the Fatimid ruler of Egypt, al-Hakim, was the earthly manifestation of God. They live mainly in Lebanon, some live in Israel and some in diaspora.

Du'ā' Prayer other than *ṣalāh*, may be free prayer or formal.

Elijah Muhammad (1897–1975) Founder of the "Nation of Islam" movement in the United States, commonly known as the "Black Muslims".

Erbakan, Necmettin (1926–2011) Founder of the *milli görüş* (national vision) ideology in Turkey and several political parties associated with it, e.g. the Welfare Party.

Falsafa Philosophy, the neo-Platonic and Aristotelian philosophy received from late antiquity and developed and taught by Muslim philosophers (*faylasūfs*). See also *ḥikma*.

Fanā' Annihilation or passing away in God, the Ṣūfī experience of union with God; some say it is to be followed by *baqā'*, continuance in God.

Faqīh Expert in *fiqh* (law, jurisprudence).

Faqīr Poor, poor in spirit, term for a Ṣūfī, cf. *darwish*.

al-Farabi (c. 870–950) One of the early Muslim philosophers.

Farḍ Obligatory, one of the five Sharī'a valuations (*aḥkām*); also called *wājib*.

Farḍ 'ayn An obligation that applies to every individual under the Sharī'a.

Farḍ kifāya An obligation that applies to a "sufficient number", e.g. teaching; until there are enough teachers in a community everyone is under obligation to become one; when there are enough the obligation is lifted from the rest.

Fātiḥa The opening *sūra* or chapter of the Qur'ān; recited on many occasions.

Fāṭima Daughter of Muḥammad and wife of 'Alī ibn Abī Ṭālib; she was the mother of the next two Shī'ī *Imāms* and ancestress of the others and is considered *ma'sūm* (protected from sin) by Shī'īs. She is highly respected by all Muslims.

Fatimid Dynasty Ismā'īlī dynasty that ruled Egypt from 969 to 1171.

Fatwa An advisory opinion by a qualified *faqīh* stating whether an action is permitted or forbidden by the Sharī'a.

Fez A brimless hat worn by Muslim men in Turkey from 1826 to 1925 and in other countries for some time after that; not much used today.

Fiqh "Understanding", viz. of the Sharī'a; working out the details of commands and prohibitions through the sources (see *uṣūl al-fiqh*); the substance of the law so worked out.

Fiṭra The created nature of humans that leads them to seek God.

Firdowsi (d. c. 1020) Author of the *Shahnameh* (*Book of Kings*), a long epic poem about the pre-Islamic Persian kings; one of the first works in the revival of Persian literature after the Muslim conquest and one of the greatest works of Persian literature.

Ghayba Disappearance or occultation of the twelfth Shīʿī *Imām*; during the Lesser Occultation (872–939) he was in contact with people through deputies; during the Greater Occultation he is in the world but out of touch with people until his return as the *mahdī*.

al-Ghazālī, Abū Ḥāmid Muḥammad (1058–1111) One of the greatest Muslim scholars of all time; he played a major role in reconciling the streams of *fiqh*, theology and Ṣūfism and selectively adopting *falsafa*.

Ghāzī Warrior who engages in *jihād*, usually on the frontiers of Dar al-Islam.

Ghaznavids (961–1186) A Sunnī dynasty ruling in Afghanistan and sometimes much of Iran and northwest India. They patronized scholars such as Firdowsi.

Ghusl Complete washing of the body for ablution from major pollution.

Gülen, Fathullah Leader of a branch of the Nurcu movement in Turkey and elsewhere; stressing tolerance in its teachings, it has a network of businesses, media outlets and charitable organizations but is known especially for its schools, which are non-sectarian in their teaching.

Ḥadd Special class of penalties specifically imposed by God in the Qur'ān or *Sunna*, e.g. cutting off of the hand of a thief.

Ḥadīth A report of something the prophet said, did or approved of, or the sum total of these reports. See also *Sunna* and Akhbārī.

Ḥadīth Qudsī *Ḥadith* whose words are ascribed to God rather than to the Prophet.

Ḥāfiẓ One who has memorized the whole of the Qur'ān.

Ḥajj Annual pilgrimage to Mecca; to be done at least once in a lifetime if possible. One of the five Pillars.

***Ḥājj* or** *Ḥajjī* One who has performed the *Ḥajj*.

Ḥalāl Permitted, includes all of the Sharīʿa valuations except forbidden; also specifically used for food that may be eaten.

Ḥamās Acronym (in Arabic) for "Islamic Resistance Movement", the main Islamist movement among the Palestinians; appeared in 1988 and currently (2013) controls Gaza.

Ḥanafī (or Hanafite) Follower of the *madhhab* of Abū Ḥanīfa.

Ḥanbalī Follower of the *madhhab* of Ibn Ḥanbal.

Ḥanīfs Figures mentioned in the Qur'ān, taken to be pre-Islamic monotheists in Arabia; also used for any practicer of pure monotheistic worship, e. g. the prophet Ibrāhīm.

Ḥarām Forbidden, one of the five Sharī'a valuations (*aḥkām*). Also used for things in that category, e.g. food.

Ḥijāb The most general term for female "Islamic" garb, which according to conservative interpretation must cover all of the body but the hands and the face; sometimes used particularly for the head covering.

Hijra The emigration or flight of Muḥammad and his followers from Mecca to Medina in 622. The year in which it occurred is the first year of the Muslim or *hijrī* calendar. See also *muhājir.*

Ḥikma "Wisdom"; may refer to Islamic Philosophy (*falsafa*) or to the later "theosophy" partly based on it; the term may also be used for a "wise saying" or for the reason something is done, especially something done by God.

Ḥizb al-Taḥrīr (Liberation Party) Islamist organization founded in 1952 by the Palestinian judge, Taqī al-Dīn al-Nabhānī (1909–77); it seeks to restore the caliphate, is active in many countries and banned in many.

Ḥizbollah "Party of God"; name of several Islamist groups in modern times; the best known is the Shī 'ī Islamist party in Lebanon, which is currently (2013) a strong force there.

***Ḥukm* (pl. *aḥkām*)** "Judgment, valuation, governance", here particularly used for the valuation placed by the Sharī'a on actions; thus there are five *aḥkām*, commanded (*farḍ*), recommended, permitted (neutral), disapproved, forbidden (*ḥarām*).

Ḥusayn ibn 'Alī (d. 680) The younger son of 'Alī and Fāṭima; was martyred at Karbalā' by the forces of the Umayyad caliph Yazīd; focus of intense Shī'ī piety and considered a symbol of self-sacrifice in the cause of justice.

***'Ibādāt* (sing. *'ibāda*)** "Acts of worship", those actions, such as *ṣalāh*, done specifically for God, in contrast to *mu'āmalāt*, duties owed to other humans. More generally, *'ibāda* refers to any action, whether ritual or ethical, and may be translated as "service". It is related to the word *'abd*, servant or slave.

Ibn 'Abd al-Wahhāb, Muḥammad (1703–92) Reformer in Central Arabia and founder of the movement called "Wahhābī".

Ibn 'Arabī, Muḥyī al-Dīn (1166–1240) Considered the greatest of the Sunnī Ṣūfī theosophers, known among other things for his controversial doctrine of *waḥdat al-wujūd* (the unity of existence).

Ibn Ḥanbal, Aḥmad (d. 855) *Ḥadīth* scholar and traditionalist opponent of the Mu'tazila, held that the Qur'ān is uncreated and that the divine attributes and actions in the Qur'ān should be accepted *bilā kayf* (without asking how), i.e. without metaphorical explanation. He suffered for his beliefs in the *miḥna* (inquisition).

Ibn Isḥaq (d. 770) Author of the best known *sīra* (biography) of Muḥammad; extant in the form revised and edited by Ibn Hishām (d. 833).

Ibn Khaldūn (1332–1406) West African scholar and author of a universal history, *Kitāb al-'Ibar* (Book of (historical) Lessons), whose introduction presents a highly regarded theory of political history focusing on *'aṣabiyya*, group solidarity.

Ibn Rushd (Averroes) (1126–98) Spanish Islamic philosopher and judge; presented the most purely Aristotelian version of Islamic philosophy; wrote a refutation of al-Ghazālī's refutation of philosophy; influential in the West.

Ibn Sīnā, Abū 'Alī (Avicenna) (980–1037) Perhaps the greatest of the Islamic philosophers (*faylasūf*).

Ibn Taymiyya, Taqī al-Dīn (1263–1328) Hanbali reformer during the Mamluke period who criticized many popular religious practices as *shirk* and defended the traditionalist position in theology. Has provided inspiration for many modern reformers.

Ibrāhīm Qur'ānic prophet, the biblical Abraham. Possibly viewed as the most important figure in the preaching of *tawḥīd* (monotheism) before Muḥammad; his near sacrifice of his son is commemorated on 'Īd al-Aḍḥā.

'Īd al-Aḍḥā One of the two major festivals in the Muslim year; commemorates Ibrāhīm's near sacrifice of his son with the sacrifice of an animal and distribution of its meat; done by those on *Ḥajj* on the tenth of Dhū al-Ḥijja, and by Muslims everywhere.

'Īd al-Fiṭr The other major festival of the Muslim year; one to three day celebration after the fast of Ramaḍān.

Ifṭār Evening meal after the daily fast in Ramaḍān.

Iḥrām Garment consisting of two pieces of plain cloth worn by men during the *Hajj*.

Ijāza "Permission"; the authorization given by a teacher to a student to teach one or more books the student has studied under him.

Ijmā' "Consensus", in its fullest form, the unanimous agreement of all the *mujtahids* of a given age on a point of law; traditionally according to Sunnīs binding on future generations, but modernists disagree. In fact, the consensus is usually within a given *madhhab*.

Ijtihād "Effort", specifically the effort of the *faqīh* to discover the Sharī'a judgment on a matter. Absolute *ijtihād* involves going directly to the Qur'ān and *Sunna* for this. More restricted *ijtihād* involves following the principles of one's *madhhab*. In Uṣūlī Shī'ī *fiqh*, *ijtihād* is the effort to derive judgments from all of the sources of *fiqh* (*uṣūl al-fiqh*). See also *taqlīd*.

Ilhām Inspiration or revelation that may come to Ṣūfīs, as distinct from *waḥy*, which comes only to prophets.

'Ilm Knowledge, learning, science; basically knowledge of the Qur'ān and the *Sunna* and thence of the disciplines such as *fiqh* and *kalām* based on them; also exoteric knowledge as opposed to esoteric knowledge, *ma'rifa*. See also *'ulamā'*.

'Ilm al-tawḥīd Science of *tawḥīd*, theology; cf. *kalām*.

Imām "Leader"; leader at the performance of *ṣalāh*; according to Shī'īs the divinely chosen leader of the *umma*; in Sunnī usage a synonym for caliph; title of respect for a great religious scholar.

Īmān Faith, true faith in God. See also *mu'min*.

Intoxication (*sukr*) Among Ṣūfīs, the state of ecstasy in which the Ṣūfī does not have rational control of himself but is presumably caught up in God. Contrasted with "sobriety" (*ṣaḥwa*).

Iqbal, Muhammad (1876–1938) Indian Muslim poet and philosopher, probably the greatest of the Indian modernists; also viewed as the spiritual father of Pakistan.

Iran(ian), Persia(n) These terms are used more or less interchangeably in most of this book, except that Persian is always used for the language and literature and Iran(ian) is always used after this became the official name of the country under Reza Shah in the twentieth century.

'Irfān A form of philosophical mysticism, practiced especially by Iranian Shi'i scholars; considered distinct from Sufism.

'Īsā (Jesus) See Christ.

'Ishq Passionate love; used by many Ṣūfīs to describe their love of God; contrasted with *ḥubb* or *maḥabba*, which suggests something more restrained.

Islām Submission or commitment to God, specifically in accordance with the teaching of Muḥammad. The one who submits is a Muslim.

Islamic law Used in this book to refer in a general way to *fiqh*, Shari'a or both.

Islamicist Academic scholar who studies about Islām; to be distinguished from Islamist.

Islamist Modern Muslim activist for whom Islām is a political and social ideology covering all areas of life. Islamists criticize modernists for accepting too many Western ways and usually call for an "Islamic state".

'Iṣma Protection, viz. from error or sin; according to Sunnīs the prophets have *'iṣma* (i.e. are *ma'ṣūm*); according to Shī'īs the *Imāms* and Fāṭima are also *ma'ṣūm*.

Ismā'īl Son of Ibrāhīm, the biblical Ishmael. Muslims believe that it was he, not Isḥaq (Isaac), who was almost sacrificed at God's command.

Ismā'īlīs Division of the Shī'a (q.v.) that accepts Ismā'īl the son of Ja'far as the next *Imām* and a continuing line of *Imāms* after him, often in concealment. One group, the Qarmatis, was in power in Bahrain from c. 900 to 1077 and another, the Fatimids, was in power in Egypt from 969 to 1171. Two lines that continue today are the Nizāris (q.v.), the followers of the Agha Khan, and the Bohras.

Jahiliyya "Ignorance" or "time of ignorance". Conventionally the period of Arabian history before Muhammad's mission. Some modern writers, such as Sayyid Qutb and Mawdudi consider all societies that do not follow the Shari'a to be partly or entirely *jahili*.

Jamā'a Islāmiyya (Islamic Group) Name of several Islamist groups in Egypt, including student groups in the 1970s and a group under the guidance of Omar Abdel Rahman involved in the violence of the 1990s. The same phrase in its Indonesian spelling, Jemaah Islamiyah, refers to the Islamist group responsible for the Bali bombings in 2002 and later.

Jama'at-i Islami (Islamic Society) Islamist movement in India and Pakistan, founded in 1941 by Abul 'Ala' Mawdudi, has been ideologically influential but had limited success in Pakistani politics.

Jamāl al-Dīn "al-Afghānī", known as "Asadabadi" in Iran (1838–97) Modernist reformer and anti-imperialist activist, mentor of Muḥammad 'Abduh and extremely influential on a wide range of Muslim movements since his time.

Jihād "Striving", i.e. striving in the way of God. Usually applied to warfare in a perceived religious cause, including anti-imperialist struggles in modern times, but also applied to striving against the individual's anti-ethical tendencies (the "greater *jihād*") and striving to build society (e.g. *jihād* for construction).

***Jinn* (sing. *Jinnī*)** Invisible beings, made of fire according to the Qur'ān, more powerful than humans, usually evil but capable of good and of faith in God.

Jizya Head tax paid by *dhimmīs* to the Muslim ruler or state, in part in return for not doing military service but also a sign of subordination.

Jum'a Congregation, gathering, also Friday; short for *ṣalāt al-jum'a*, the Friday noon *ṣalāh*, to be done in congregation.

Ka'ba Square building in Mecca toward which *ṣalāh* is made and which is circumambulated during the *Ḥajj*; believed to have been built, or rebuilt, by Ibrāhīm and Ismā'īl; believed also to be a copy of the heavenly *Ka'ba* circumambulated by angels.

Kāfir See *kufr, takfīr.*

Kalām "Words", theology. *Mutakallim* is a theologian.

Karbalā' Place in Iraq where Ḥusayn was martyred; a shrine city for Shī'īs today.

Khalīfa "Successor, deputy". In the Qur'ān Adam (and thus humanity) is *khalīfa* of God on earth; a Muslim ruler as successor of the Prophet or Deputy of God; deputy to the *shaykh* of a Ṣūfī *ṭarīqa*. *Khilāfa* means caliphate.

Khan, Sir Sayyid Ahmad (1817–98) Early Indian modernist reformer; sought to improve the Muslims' relations with their British rulers and learn from them.

***Khanqah* (or *khanaqah*, etc.)** Ṣūfī hostel or retreat center, with facilities for *dhikr*, retreat, accommodation for some. Also called *tekke* (Turkish), *zāwiya* (Arabic).

Khārijī (pl. *khawārij*) "Seceders, rebels". Party that broke with 'Ali over the arbitration with Mu'awiya. Held that the leader could be of any descent but must be chosen by the community and be free of serious sin. Formed various oppositional and even "terrorist" groups in the early centuries. A moderate branch, the 'Ibadis, continues in small numbers to the present. The term is often used today as a pejorative label for radical Islamists.

Khilāfa See *khalīfa*.

Khomeini, Ayatollah Ruhollah Musavi (1902–89) Grand Ayatollah and leader of the Islamic Revolution in Iran in 1979.

Khul' A form of divorce requested by the wife in return for compensation, such as renouncing her right to the unpaid part of the *mahr.*

Khums A tax of one-fifth of one's income paid by Shī'īs to the descendants of the Prophet and to the *'ulamā'* as representatives of the twelfth *Imām*.

Khuṭba Sermon given at *ṣalāt al-jum'a*; may cover a range of topics but somewhat more formalized than the usual Christian sermon.

Kiai (or kiyayi) Traditional *'ālim* in Java; commonly head of a *pesantren*.

Kufic "From Kufa (a city in Iraq)". Refers to an early form of Arabic script, squarish rather than rounded.

Kufr Unbelief, refusal to submit to God, with a connotation of ingratitude. Opposite of *īmān*, faith.

Kuttāb Traditional Islamic elementary school, primarily for reciting the Qurān. Called *maktab* in some places.

Madhhab School or tradition of *fiqh* or *kalām*, but the term is usually used for *fiqh*; there are four Sunnī *madhhabs* of *fiqh* that are today recognized as equally valid.

***Madrasa* (*medrese* in Turkish)** Upper-level school primarily for the teaching of *fiqh*, but other subjects are also taught. In Arabic the term often refers to a secular school today.

***Mahdī* (*Mehdi* in some languages)** "Guided", for Sunnīs usually refers to a figure appointed by God as a reformer or the one who will destroy evil at the end of time; for Shī'īs the Twelfth *Imām* on his return.

Mahmud Muhammad Taha (1909–85) Sudanese reformer who held that the Meccan part of the Qur'an is the permanent message of Islam, while the Medinan part represents a temporary position responding to the social realities of the time. He was executed by the government in 1985.

Mahr Sum of money paid by husband to wife, usually part at the time of marriage and part later, e.g. upon divorce or death.

Mālik ibn Anas (d. 795) Early scholar and *faqīh*, based in Medina, and considered the founder of the Mālikī *madhhab*.

Mālikī *Madhhab* of Sunnī *fiqh*, named for Mālik ibn Anas.

Mamlukes "Owned". Slaves trained to serve the ruling dynasty and often becoming rulers themselves; particularly the Mamlukes of Egypt (1250–1517), whose influence continued under the aegis of the Ottomans, but there were other examples of this in the Islamic world.

Manicheism Dualistic Iranian religion founded by Mani (d. c. 275), considered matter to be evil; often called *zindīqs* in Islamic times (though this term came to be applied more indiscriminately) and severely persecuted.

Ma'rifa "Knowledge", particularly direct personal knowledge as claimed by the Ṣūfīs and contrasted with *'ilm*, seen as second hand knowledge from books or reports.

***Marja'-i taqlid* (*Ar. marja' al-taqlīd*)** "Source of emulation", in Uṣūlī Shī'īsm, a leading *'ālim* who has a following of people who accept his *fiqh* judgments; has the title of Grand Ayatollah.

Maṣlaḥa "Welfare, benefit". In *fiqh*, the welfare or benefit of the community as grounds for a judgment (*ḥukm*).

Ma'ṣūm Protected from error or sins; characteristic of prophets; according to Shī'īs, characteristic also of *Imāms* and Fāṭima. The precise interpretation of this concept varies.

Matn The substantive part of a *ḥadīth*; see also *sanad*.

Māturīdīs *Madhhab* of *kalām*, founded by Abū Manṣūr al-Māturīdī (d. 944), popular among Ḥanafīs; their teachings are similar to those of the Ash'arīs but they are more inclined to allow for rational knowledge of ethical duties and human free will.

Mawdudi, Abul 'Ala' (1903–79) Leader of the Jama'at-i Islami in India and Pakistan and possibly the most influential Islamist thinker.

Mawlid **(or** ***mulid*****)** Birthday celebration of the Prophet Muḥammad or Ṣūfī saints. Very popular but criticized by some reformers.

Mecca (or Makka) Birthplace of the Prophet Muḥammad and place where his mission began. Location of the *Ka'ba*.

Medina (or Madina) Short for *madīnat al-nabī*, city of the Prophet; city to which the Prophet moved in the *Hijra* when forced to leave Mecca and where he established the first Islamic polity; originally called Yathrib.

Mevlevi (Ar. Mawlawī) Ṣūfī *tariqa* founded by Jalal al-Din Rumi (d. 1273); also known as the Whirling Dervishes.

Miḥna "Trial, inquisition", refers usually to the effort of the Abbasid caliph al-Ma'mūn and his successors (c. 833–50) to compel the *'ulamā'* to accept the doctrine of the created Qur'ān. See also Ibn Ḥanbal.

Miḥrāb Niche in the inner wall of a mosque indicating the direction to Mecca.

Millet Communities into which *dhimmīs* were organized in the Ottoman Empire; later formed the basis for some Eastern European nations.

Milli Görüş (National Vision) Islamist ideology of Erbakan and of several Turkish political parties led by him; name of several organizations following this ideology in the Turkish diaspora.

Minaret Tower connected with a mosque from which the *adhān* is given.

Minbar Pulpit in the mosque from which the *khuṭba* is given.

Mosque (Ar. ***masjid*****)** "Place for prostration in prayer", place where Muslims gather for *ṣalāh* and other communal purposes.

Mu'āmalāt Duties owed to other people, in contrast to *'ibādāt*, duties owed specifically to God.

Mu'āwiya ibn Abī Sufyān (d. 680) First Umayyad caliph, viewed by many as turning the Islamic caliphate into a worldly kingdom.

Muezzin (Ar. ***mu'adhdhin*****)** Person who gives the *adhān*, or call to *ṣalāh*.

Muftī *Faqīh* qualified to give a *fatwa*, an advisory opinion in *fiqh*.

Mughul Empire (1526–1858) Muslim Empire ruling most of India at its height, under Akbar (r. 1556–1605).

Muhājir Emigrant, one who makes *Hijra*; especially Muḥammad's Meccan followers who moved to Medina when he did; later groups also, e.g. the Indian Muslims who moved to Pakistan at the time of partition. See also *Anṣār*.

Muḥammad ibn Abdallāh (c. 570–632) Last prophet and messenger of God (*rasūl allāh*), first leader of the Muslim *umma*.

Muḥammad 'Alī Ottoman governor and *de facto* ruler of Egypt from 1805 to 1849, began the process of modernization.

Muhammadiya Influential modernist movement in Indonesia founded in 1912.

Mujāhid Person who engages in *jihād*; "freedom fighter" often in the modern context.

Mujtahid *Faqīh* qualified to make *fiqh* judgments on his own, i.e. to practice *ijtihād*; generally given the title Ayatollah among *Uṣūlī* Shī'īs, especially in Iran.

Mullah Title often given to *'ulamā'*, especially outside the Arab world; suggests a lower-level *'ālim*.

Mu'min "Believer, person of faith"; Muslims more commonly call themselves *mu'min* than *muslim*.

Muqallid One who is not a *mujtahid* and who therefore follows a present or past *mujtahid*.

Murid Follower or disciple of a Sufi *shaykh*. Shaykh–murid relationship is basic to Sufism.

Mūsā Qur'anic prophet, the biblical Moses, prophet of the people of Israel.

Muṣalla "Place for *ṣalāh*", small mosque not used for *ṣalāt al-jum'a*.

Muslim One who submits or commits him- or herself to God, a member of the Muslim *umma*.

Muslim Brothers (Ar. *al-ikhwān al-muslimūn*) The leading Islamist organization in Egypt, founded by Ḥasan al-Bannā in 1928.

Muslim ibn al-Ḥajjāj (d. 875) Compiler of one of the two most authoritative Sunnī collections of *Ḥadīth*, commonly known as *Ṣaḥīḥ Muslim*.

***Mustazafin* (Ar. *Mustaḍ'afīn*)** "Oppressed", Qur'anic term (4:75) used in modern ideological contexts.

Mut'a "Pleasure", a marriage contracted for a limited period of time, valid in Shī'ī *fiqh*.

Mutawātir *Ḥadīth* with more than one sound line of transmitters (*sanad*), considered to be certain.

Mu'tazila Rationalist *madhhab* in *kalām*, called themselves the "people of *tawḥīd* (monotheism) and justice"; taught that the Qur'ān is created, among other things. Their views were rejected by the Sunnīs but have been influential among the Shī'īs.

Muwaḥḥidūn People of *tawḥīd*, name used by a number of reform groups, such as the Almohads in Morocco and Spain in the twelfth and thirteenth centuries and the Wahhābīs in Arabia from the eighteenth.

Nabī Prophet, one who receives divine revelation (*waḥy*). According to traditional thinking there have been thousands sent before Muḥammad's time, one to every community or nation (*umma*); only a few are mentioned in the Qur'ān. Muḥammad is the "seal of the prophets". See also *rasūl*.

Nahdlatul Ulama "Awakening of the *'Ulamā'*"; very influential traditionalist movement in Indonesia founded in 1926.

Naqshbandiyya Widespread Sufi *ṭarīqa* named after Baha' al-Din Naqshband (d. 1390), traces its *silsila* to Abu Bakr and noted for its "silent" *dhikr*, strong in Turkey and has spread to the West.

Naṣṣ Authoritative text, i.e. the Qur'ān and the *Ḥadīth*. In Shī'īsm, an *Imām's* designation of his successor.

Nasta'liq A very flowing form of Arabic script developed in Iran.

"Nation of Islam" American movement led by Elijah Muhammad, claims to return African-Americans to their original religion and true identity. Name now used by Louis Farrakhan's wing of the movement.

Ni'matullahis Iranian Shi'i Sufi *ṭarīqa* that has spread to the West under Javad Nurbakhsh (1927–2008).

Nizaris Revolutionary Isma'ili movement, eleventh to thirteenth centuries, famous for its assassinations; continues today as the followers of Aga Khan.

Nūḥ Qur'anic prophet, the biblical Noah, model of a prophet whose people reject his message and are destroyed.

Nurcus Followers of Said Nursi, q.v.

"Occasions of revelation" (Ar. *asbāb al-nuzūl*) The circumstances in which a particular verse or verses of the Qur'ān were revealed; useful for interpreting these verses.

Occultation See *ghayba*.

Ottoman (or Osmanli) Empire (1281–1924) Sunnī empire ruling much of the Arab, Greek and Balkan world for several centuries; strong vis-à-vis Europe for some time but in the nineteenth century the "sick man of Europe". Terminated by Atatürk's reforms.

Pancasila The "five principles" of the Indonesian constitution: belief in one God, humanity, national unity, democracy, social justice.

People of the Book (Ar. *ahl al-kitāb*) People who follow the scripture of a prophet before Muḥammad, i.e. Jews and Christians. These scriptures are thought to have been corrupted and superseded but those who follow them have a higher status than those without a scripture and are qualified to be *dhimmīs*.

Perennialism A movement among some Western intellectuals claiming to teach the "perennial philosophy" underlying all religions; partly derived from Sufism. Sometimes called "traditionalism" or "primordialism".

Pesantrens Islamic boarding schools in Java.

Pillars of Islām The most important obligations of Islām: *shahāda*, *ṣalāh*, fast of Ramaḍān, *Ḥājj*, *zakāh*.

Plotinus (205–c. 270 CE) Neo-Platonist philosopher and a major influence on Islamic philosophy.

Polygyny Marriage in which one husband has two or more wives. Polyandry is where one wife has two or more husbands and polygamy is the general term covering both.

Priyayi The old nobility of Java, strongly attuned to the Javanese traditions going back to pre-Islamic times.

Qadiriyya Oldest of the Sufi *ṭarīqas*, tracing its lineage to 'Abd al-Qadir Jilani (d. 1166), spread worldwide.

Qāḍī Judge, particularly for Sharī'a law; appointed by the caliph or other ruler or government; may take advice from a *muftī*.

al-Qaeda (*al-qā'ida*, literally "the base") Islamist organization or network carrying out or supporting "martyrdom" attacks on the West, such as the one on the Twin Towers, "9/11". Led by Usama Bin Laden until his death in 2011 and then by Ayman al-Zawahiri.

Qaṣīda Ode, popular form of poetry in pre-Islamic Arabia and among Muslims.

Qibla The direction to Mecca. See also *miḥrāb*.

Qiyās Analogy, for Sunnīs the most acceptable form of reasoning in *fiqh*; not acceptable to Shī'īs.

Qur'ān "Recitation", the revelations that came from God to Muḥammad between 610 and 632; memorizing and reciting the Qur'ān is one of the most important religious activities for Muslims.

Quraysh Muḥammad's tribe; Sunnī caliphs were expected to be descended from this tribe.

Quṭb, Sayyid (1906–66) Egyptian Islamist and martyr whose views on Islām, *jāhiliyya* and *jihād* have influenced many, including the violent activists of groups such as al-Qaeda. Quṭb was influenced by Mawdudi but became more radical.

Rahman, Fazlur (1919–88) Pakistani scholar who later taught in the U.S.A.; one of the leading modernists who has influenced other modernists and many Islamicists.

Rak'a A series of actions, including recitations, bowing and prostration, that constitute one cycle of *ṣalāh*. A *ṣalāh* usually consists of more than one *rak'a*.

Ramaḍān The ninth month of the Muslim year, when Muslims fast during the daytime.

Rashīd Riḍā (1865–1935) Disciple of Muḥammad 'Abduh, interpreted his teachings in a more conservative direction, preparing the way for the Islamism of Ḥasan al-Bannā and others.

Rasūl "Messenger", specifically Muḥammad as *rasūl allāh*, the Messenger of God. The terms *rasūl* and *nabī* overlap in meaning in the Qur'ān; generally there are understood to be fewer *rasūls* than *nabīs*; Muḥammad is both.

Ra'y "Opinion", specifically the considered opinion (in the absence of more formal criteria) of an experienced *faqīh* in making a judgment; accepted in the earlier centuries, viewed as too arbitrary later.

"Rightly Guided Caliphs" (Ar. *al-Khulafā' al-Rāshidūn*) In Sunnī thinking the first four successors to Muḥammad, viewed as the highest examples of proper leadership of the *umma*.

Rumi, Jalal al-Din (1207–73) Generally considered the greatest of the Persian Ṣūfī adepts, author of several mystical poems including the *Mathnawi* and founder of the Mevlevi *ṭarīqa*.

Ṣadaqa Free-will offering, alms beyond the required *zakāh*.

Safa and Marwa Two hills in Mecca that the pilgrims run between in imitation of Hagar seeking water for Isma'il.

Safavids Dynasty ruling Iran from 1501 to 1736; imposed Twelver Shi'ism, particularly strong in the sixteenth century.

Ṣaḥīḥ "Sound", used for a *ḥadīth* whose *sanad* (chain of transmitters) is strong at all points; also, the informal title of collections of such *ḥadīths*, e.g. *Ṣaḥīḥ Bukhārī* and *Ṣaḥīḥ Muslim*.

Said Nursi, Badiuzzaman (1876–1960) Author of a major commentary on the Qur'ān studied by his followers, the Nurcus. His immediate aim was to strengthen individual faith but the movement has had some involvement in Turkish politics. Gülen (q.v.) movement is a branch of the Nurcus.

Salafī Modern reform tendencies that seek to follow the model of the *salaf*, the righteous leaders of the early Islamic centuries; oppose *bid'a* (innovation); tend to be strict in interpretation, may or may not be politically oriented; vary in the degree of willingness to accept modern/Western ideas and practices. Some are modernist, others strongly traditionalist or Islamist. Generally look back to the inspiration of Ibn Taymiyya.

***Ṣalāh* (or *salat*)** The formal prayer or worship that is to be done five times a day and on other occasions; consists of set movements and recitations. One of the Pillars of Islām.

Ṣalāḥ al-Dīn al-Ayyūbī (d. 1193) Muslim leader who recaptured Jerusalem from the Crusaders (1187) and re-established Sunnī rule in Egypt. Viewed as a hero by Arab nationalists and Islamists. Also known as Saladin.

Ṣalāt al-jum'a Congregational *ṣalāh* on Friday at noon; obligatory for men.

***Samā'* (or *sema*)** "Hearing", sessions of music and dance that are part of some Ṣūfī rituals.

Samanid dynasty Independent Persian dynasty (900–999) in Iran that encouraged the renaissance of Persian language and literature.

***Sanad* (or isnād)** Chain of transmitters that guarantees the authenticity of a *ḥadīth*; to be sound (*ṣaḥīḥ*) the chain must be unbroken back to Muḥammad and the transmitters must have been knowledgeable and trustworthy. See also *mutawātir*.

Santri In Indonesia, a practicing Muslim. Contrast *abangan*.

Sasanian Empire (226–651) Pre-Islamic Iranian empire, destroyed in the early Muslim conquests but generally viewed in a positive light by later Iranian Muslims.

Shāfi'ī (or Shafi'ite) Follower of the *madhhab* of al-Shāfi'ī.

al-Shāfi'ī, Muḥammad ibn Idrīs (d. 819) One of the leading early *faqīhs*; important in establishing the importance of *Ḥadīth* in *fiqh* and in setting the main outlines of *fiqh* procedure (*uṣūl al-fiqh*) for Sunnīs; considered the founder of the Shāfi'ī *madhhab*.

Shahāda The Formula of Witness, "There is no god but God; Muḥammad is the Messenger of God", by which a Muslim witnesses to his or her faith and a non-Muslim becomes a Muslim. The word also means "martyrdom".

***Shahnameh* (*Book of Kings*)** See Firdowsi.

Sharī'a "Path leading to water"; the law or way of life laid out by God for human life; in principle covers all areas of life; involves the classification of actions as commanded, recommended, permitted (neutral), disapproved, or forbidden;

Sharī'a law is any law (e.g by a modern legislature) that bases itself on the Sharī'a. Islamists typically call for the "application of the Sharī'a". See *ḥukm; fiqh.*

Shariati, Ali (1933–77) Iranian Islamic ideologue, influenced by Marx and "Third World" radicalism; played a major role in preparing the people, especially the youth, for the Islamic revolution.

Shaṭḥ "Theopathic utterances", strange and often heretic statements made by Sufis in a state of ecstasy, e.g. Al-Hallaj's statement, *Anā al ḥaqq* (I am the Truth).

Shaykh "Elder", may refer to various sorts of leaders, such as a tribal leader, a highly respected teacher or, especially, a Ṣūfī teacher and guide.

Shī'īs (or *Shi'a* or *shi'at 'Alī*) The Party of 'Alī; those who believed that 'Alī should have succeeded Muḥammad as leader of the *umma* and whose movement developed into a separate division (or sect) of Islām over against the Sunnīs. They are divided into Imāmīs or Twelvers, Ismā'īlīs or Seveners, and Zaydīs or Fivers.

Shirk Associating anything with God in worship or obedience; outward *shirk* may be worshipping a god or an idol; inward shirk may be giving too much attention to possessions, family or ambitions. *Salafīs* see many popular customs as *shirk*. Islamists see secular government as *shirk* (obeying humans rather than God).

Shūrā Consultation; the Muslim ruler is expected to consult with the leaders of the community; modernists interpret this as the basis for parliamentary government.

***Sibḥa* (also pronounced *subḥa*) (or *misbaḥa*)** String of beads used to count a recitation of the names of God or prayer formulae; a Muslim "rosary".

Silsila "Chain", among Ṣūfīs, the chain of teachers and disciples that links a given teacher back to the founder of the *ṭarīqa* and thence to Muḥammad.

Sīra A heroic biography, especially that of the Prophet. See Ibn Isḥaq.

Sirhindi, Ahmad (d. 1664) Indian reformer and theosopher; criticized Ibn 'Arabi's *waḥdat al-wujūd*, claimed to be the "renewer" of the Islamic tradition after the first thousand years.

Siyāsa "Governance, politics", actions taken by a government for practical reasons that may be viewed as an alternative to the Sharī'a or as under the general permission of the Sharī'a.

Slametan Feast given by Javanese *abangans* to placate spirits and achieve a state of tranquillity (*slamet*).

Ṣūfī Follower of the mystical or devotional movement called Ṣūfism or *taṣawwuf*; at the highest level one seeks a direct knowledge of God (called *ma'rifa*, q.v.) through exercises called *dhikr*, q.v.

Suhrawardi, Shihab al-Din al- (1153–91) Sufi "theosopher" who taught a philosophy of "illumination" and focused on light as the true nature of all existence.

Suhrawardi, Abu Hafs al- (1145–1234) Founder of the Suhrawardiyya *ṭarīqa*, more willing than most to deal with political rulers.

***Suḥūr* (or *saḥūr*)** Meal taken in the early morning before fasting in Ramaḍān.

Sulṭān "Authority, holder of authority", title of many Muslim rulers; implies less of a religious claim than caliph or *amīr al-mu'minīn*.

***Sunna*, viz. *Sunna* of the Prophet** Authoritative teaching and example of the Prophet Muḥammad, as found in the *Ḥadīth*; one of the sources of *fiqh* (see *uṣūl al-fiqh*).

Sunnīs Majority division of Muslims, as opposed to Shī'īs. See *Ahl al-sunna wa-l-jamā'a*.

Sūra Chapter of the Qur'ān; it is usually noted whether a *sūra* was revealed in Mecca or Medina.

Syria Until after the First World War refers to the area currently including Syria, Lebanon, Jordan and Israel/Palestine, sometimes called "Greater Syria".

al-Ṭabarī, Ibn Jarīr (d. 922) Author of one of the best known commentaries (*tafṣīrs*) to the Qur'ān.

Tablighi *Salafī* movement started in India in the 1920s and now worldwide; emphasizes the faithful practice of the basic obligations of Islām; is not political and is less strict than some *salafis*.

Tafṣīr Interpretation of the Qur'ān, exoteric in contrast to *ta'wīl*.

Ṭaha, Maḥmūd Muḥammad (d. 1985) Leader of the Republican Brothers in the Sudan; taught that the Meccan *sūras* supersede the Medinan *sūras* today; executed in 1985; his follower, Abdullah al-Na'im, is active in human rights concerns in the U.S. today.

Taha Hussein (1889–1973) Leading Egyptian educator and literary figure; wrote a book on *jāhilī* poetry that questioned its authenticity; wrote a biographical study of Muḥammad and other books on Islām, generally secularist with an appreciation of Islamic culture and civilization.

Tajwīd A relatively elaborate and "musical" recitation of the Qur'ān, see also *tar'tīl*.

Takfīr Declaration that someone is *kāfir*, no longer a Muslim.

Takfīr wa-Hijra Label given to a group in Egypt active in the 1970s that declared the whole of society *kāfir* and sought to separate from it in the hope of eventually taking it over. Disbanded by the government after assassinating a former government minister.

Taleban "Students"; very traditionalist movement in Afghanistan founded by Mullah Omar in 1994; ruled Afghanistan from 1996 to 2001; became associated with al-Qaeda; they have continued to struggle after being forced out of government by U.S. intervention.

Tanzimat Series of reforms in the Ottoman Empire in the mid-nineteenth century, designed to modernize and strengthen the central government's power.

Taqiya "Prudent dissimulation"; keeping silent about one's true views when they would endanger oneself or one's community; obligatory for Shī'īs in certain circumstances.

Taqlīd Following the decision of another when one is not a *mujtahid*; in modernist parlance often a blind conservatism.

Tarāwīḥ Extra *ṣalāhs* performed at night in Ramaḍān by Sunnīs.

Ṭarīqa "Path"; Ṣūfī practice. Ṣūfī lineage or "order" looking back to a particular founder and with distinctive practices; many are large and popular.

Tartīl Slower and more measured recitation of the Qur'ān, in comparison to *tajwīd*.

Ṭawāf Circumambulation of the *Ka'ba* during the *Ḥajj*.

Tawḥīd The affirmation of the unity of God, monotheism. See also *muwaḥḥidūn* and *'ilm al-tawḥīd*. *'Ilm al-tawḥīd* is one name for theology.

Ta'wīl Esoteric interpretation of the Qur'ān, in contrast to *tafṣīr*.

Tayammum Purification with sand rather than water.

Ta'ziya (lit.: consolation) or ***Shabīh*** Play reenacting the sufferings and death of Husayn and his followers at Karbala', performed during the celebrations leading up to 'Ashura (q.v.). It evokes highly emotional responses.

Tekke Ṣūfī hostel or retreat center, see *khanqah*.

Traditionalists In earlier times those such as Ibn Hanbal who wished to base interpretation as exclusively as possible on the Qur'ān and *Ḥadīth*; in modern times those who wish to hold to the existing tradition. See alsp *ahl al-ḥadīth*.

Traditionists (Ar. *muḥaddithūn*) Experts in *Ḥadīth*, to be distinguished from traditionalists.

Twelvers (or Imāmīs) Majority division of Shī 'a, that recognizes twelve *Imāms*, the last of whom is in occultation (*ghayba*).

'Ulamā' "Those who know"; scholars, experts in religious knowledge, roughly equivalent to clergy or rabbis. Singular is *'ālim*. See also *'ilm*.

'Umar ibn al-Khattāb Second of the Rightly Guided Caliphs, q.v. (r. 634–44).

Umayyad dynasty (Ar. Umawī) Dynasty of caliphs (661–750) in Damascus founded by Mu'āwiya, completed the first wave of conquests; Arab in orientation and style; a line of Umayyads continued in Spain after 750.

Umma The whole community or nation of Muslims worldwide. In the Qur'ān it may refer to the communities of earlier prophets. In modern times it may be used for nation in the modern sense.

'Umra "Lesser pilgrimage"; first part of the pilgrimage to Mecca, including the circumambulation of the *Ka'ba* and the running between Safa and Marwa; may be done separately from the *Ḥajj* at any time of the year.

'Urf See *'āda*.

Uṣūl al-fiqh "The sources or roots of *fiqh*"; the sources on which *fiqh* judgments are based; conventionally given by Sunnīs as the Qur'ān, *Sunna*, *qiyās* (or *ijtihād*) and *ijmā'*, with other sources, such as *'āda* or *maṣlaha* allowed by some. Uṣūlī Shī'īs give the sources as Qur'ān, *Sunna* (including the *Imāms*), *ijmā'* and reason.

Uṣūlī Twelver Shī'ī school of *fiqh* that recognizes the authority of *mujtahids*; predominant in most of the Twelver world for the last two centuries.

'Uthmān ibn 'Affān (r. 644–56) Third of the Rightly Guided Caliphs, q.v.

***Vilayat-i faqih* (Ar. *wilāyat al-faqīh*)** The doctrine that a leading *faqīh* should be the highest authority in the state; currently in effect in Iran.

Waḥdat al-wujūd Unity of existence, doctrine of Ibn 'Arabī.

Wahhābī Outsiders' name for the followers of Ibn 'Abd al-Wahhāb in Arabia and their successors; extremely strict *salafīs*, they call themselves *muwaḥḥidūn*.

Waḥy Revelation, that which comes to a prophet, as distinct from the *ilhām* that a Ṣūfī may receive.

Walī "Friend of God", "saint", Ṣūfī adept believed to have attained union with God and whose *baraka* can benefit others; visits are therefore made to his tomb; also, in *fiqh*, a guardian, e.g. of a minor or a bride.

Waliullah of Delhi, Shah (1701–62) Indian reformer who sought to heal the divisions within the Muslim community and encouraged *ijtihād*.

***Waqf* (pl. *awqāf*)** Trust under the Sharī'a, used to finance religious and community institutions; also used to protect family resources.

Wazīr (vizier) Person in charge of the adminstration in pre-modern states; in modern Arabic a government minister.

West (Western) The cultures and civilization of Western and Central Europe and their offshoots in the Americas and elsewhere. "The West" is commonly contrasted to "Islam", a contrast that is imprecise and often tendentious but unavoidable.

Wuḍū' Minor ablution, when *ghusl* is not necessary.

Yazīd Second Umayyad caliph, responsible for the death of Ḥusayn at Karbala'; especially for Shī'īs the symbol of an evil ruler.

***Zakāh* (or *Zakat*)** "Alms" or "poor tax"; a set portion of one's wealth to be given as a tax or charity for the poor and other specified recipients. One of the Pillars of Islām.

Zāwiya See *khanqah*.

Zaydīs Fiver Shī'īs; recognize Zayd ibn 'Alī Zayn al-'Ābidīn as fifth *Imām*; the *Imām* may be any descendant of 'Alī and Fāṭima who has knowledge and leads a revolt against Sunnī authorities.

Ziyāra "Visit"; pilgrimage to shrine or tomb other than Mecca.

Zoroastrianism Iranian religion going back to the prophet Zarathushtra; recognizing a creator God and an opposing cosmic force of evil; the state religion of the Sasanian Empire at the time of the Muslim conquests. Zoroastrians were generally treated as *dhimmīs*.

Appendix II

Chronology

331 BCE	Alexander the Great invades Iran.
322 BCE	Death of Aristotle.
226–651 CE	Sasanian Empire.
205–c. 270 CE	Plotinus.
c. 275	Death of Mani, founder of Manicheism.
313–92	Roman Empire becomes Christian; eastern half comes to be known as the Byzantine Empire.
400–800	Jewish Talmuds compiled.
451	Council of Chalcedon defines orthodox Christian doctrine of incarnation; Nestorians and Monophysites separate.
c. 500	Quraysh settle Mecca. *Jahiliyya* (c. 500–630).
c. 570	Ethopian governor of Yemen, Abraha's expedition against Mecca.
c. 575–631	Persians control Yemen.
578	Death of Mazdak.
603–28	War between Byzantines and Sasanians; Jerusalem captured and recaptured.
610	Muhammad's first revelation in the cave at Hira'.
615?	Hijra of some of Muhammad's followers to Ethiopia.
619	Death of Khadija and Muhammad's uncle and protector.
622	Hijra to Medina.
624	Battle of Badr.
625	Battle of Uhud.
627	Battle of the Trench.
628	Treaty of Hudaybiyya.
630	Mecca capitulates to Muhammad. Ka'ba cleansed of idols.

632	Farewell *Hajj*. Death of Muhammad.
632–4	Abu Bakr caliph. Wars of *ridda*.
634–44	'Umar caliph. Conquest of Syria, Egypt, Eastern Iran.
644–56	'Uthman caliph.
656–61	'Ali caliph in Medina. Mu'awiya opposes him: first *fitna*.
661–80	Mu'awiya caliph in Damascus, establishes the Umayyad dynasty.
680	Second *fitna*. Battle of Karbala'; Husayn ibn 'Ali killed.
681–92	Second *fitna*. Revolt of Ibn Zubayr, claimant to caliphate, in Mecca and Medina.
685–705	Caliphate of 'Abd al-Malik; administrative reforms; Dome of the Rock built.
712–13	Sind in India conquered.
642–728	Al-Hasan al-Basri, ascetic, preacher, critic of rulers.
750	Revolt against Umayyads brings Abbasid dynasty to power in Baghdad.
765	Death of Ja'far al-Sadiq, sixth Shi'i *Imam*. Divergence of Sevener and Twelver lines.
767	Death of Abu Hanifa, eponym of Hanafi *madhhab*.
770	Death of Ibn Ishaq, biographer of the Prophet.
795	Death of Malik ibn Anas, eponym of Maliki *madhhab*.
796–809	Harun al-Rashid caliph.
801	Death of Rabi'a al-Adawiya, best known female Sufi.
c. 815	Death of Abu Nuwas, poet.
819	Death of Muhammad ibn Idris al-Shafi'i, eponym of Shafi'i *madhhab*.
711–18	Al-Andalus (Spain) conquered.
833–48	*Mihna* (Inquisition).
855	Death of Ahmad ibn Hanbal, eponym of Hanbali *madhhab*.
868–906	Egypt autonomous under Ibn Tulun and his son.
870	Death of al-Bukhari, compiler of *Hadith* collection.
872	Occultation of the Twelfth *Imam*.
874	Death of Bayazid Bistami.
875	Death of Muslim, compiler of *Hadith* collection.
873–900	Saffarids stimulate renaissance of Persian literature.
897–1962	Zaydi state in Yemen.
900–1077	Qarmati (Isma'ili) republic in Bahrain.
910	Death of Abu al-Qasim al-Junayd, a leading Sufi.
922	Death of al-Tabari, Qur'an commentator.
922	Martyrdom of al-Hallaj, Sufi martyr.

935	Death of Abu al-Hasan al-Ash'ari, eponym of Ash'ari *madhhab* of *kalām*.
939	Beginning of Major Occultation for Twelver Shi'is.
940	Death of al-Kulayni, compiler of Shi'i *Hadith* collection.
944	Death of Abu Mansur al-Maturidi, eponym of Maturidi *madhhab* of *kalām*.
915–65	al-Mutanabbi, poet.
945–1055	Buyids (Twelver Shi'is) *amirs* in Baghdad.
961–1186	Ghaznavids (Sunnis) rule in Afghanistan and elsewhere. Patrons of scholarship.
969–1171	Fatimids (Isma'ili) rule Egypt.
c. 1020	Death of Firdowsi, author of *Shahnameh*.
980–1037	Ibn Sina, philosopher.
1055–1258	Saljuk Turks sultans in Baghdad.
1058	Death of al-Mawardi, author of treatise on caliphate.
1067	Nizamiyya Madrasa opened in Baghdad, sponsored by Nizam al-Mulk.
1071	Saljuks defeat Byzantines at Manzikert; Anatonia open to Muslims.
1085–1492	Christian reconquest of Spain and Portugal.
1094–1256	Nizari Isma'ilis ("Assassins") active, based at Alamut.
1099–1187	Crusaders control Jerusalem and much of the Holy Land.
1058–1111	Al-Ghazali, *faqih*, theologian, Sufi.
1048–1131	Omar Khayyam, mathematician and poet.
1166	Death of 'Abd al-Qadir Jilani, "founder" of the Qadiriyya *tariqa*.
1171–1250	Ayyubid dynasty in Egypt and Syria (Salah al-Din and successors).
1187	Salah al-Din recaptures Jerusalem.
1209	Sultanate of Delhi founded.
1240	Death of Ibn 'Arabi, the great theosophist.
1250–1517	Mamlukes rule Egypt and Syria.
1258	Mongols sack Baghdad, end Abbasid caliphate.
1260	Mongol advance stopped at Ain Jalut by Mamlukes.
1207–73	Jalal al-Din Rumi, founder of Mevlevi *tariqa*.
1281	Ottoman dynasty begins.
1291	Crusaders lose last hold in Holy Land.
1295	Mongol Il-Khan Ghazan converts to Islam.
1263–1328	Ibn Taymiyya, traditionalist reformer.
1379–1402	Campaigns of Timur.

1421	Death of Suleiman Chelebi, composer of the *Mevlidi Sherif*.
1453	Ottomans take Constantinople, end Byzantine Empire.
1501–1736	Safavid dynasty in Iran.
1516–17	Ottomans take Syria and Egypt.
1520–66	Suleyman the Magnificent, highpoint of Ottoman power.
c. 1525	Last Hindu state in Java ends; replaced by Muslim states.
1526–1858	Mughul Empire in India.
1529	Ottomans besiege Vienna.
1566–1605	High point of Mughul power under Akbar.
1588–1629	High point of Safavid power under Shah Abbas.
1640	Death of Mulla Sadra, proponent of *irfan*.
1683	Ottomans besiege Vienna.
1699	Treaty of Carlowitz.
1701–62	Shah Waliullah of Delhi, reformer.
1787	First recorded performance of *shabih*.
1703–92	Muhammad ibn 'Abd al-Wahhab, reformer in Arabia.
1798–1801	Napoleon and the French in Egypt.
Early 19th century	Dutch begin to take control of inland Indonesia, prompting resistance.
1805–49	Muhammad Ali rules Egypt, "great modernizer".
1839–77	Tanzimat reforms in Ottoman Empire.
1863	Mirza Husayn Ali takes title of Baha'ullah, beginning of Baha'i religion.
1876–1909	Abdul Hamid sultan of Ottoman Empire, pan-Islamic ideology.
1879	Deoband Madrasa founded.
1891	Tobacco protest in Iran.
1838–97	Jamal al-Din "al-Afghani", reformer.
1817–98	Sir Sayyid Ahmad Khan in India, reformer.
1842–1905	Muhammad Abduh, Egyptian reformer.
1905	Parliamentary Revolution in Iran.
1912	Muhammadiya founded in Indonesia.
1920–38	Mustafa Kemal Atatürk leads war against Greeks, establishes a republic and introduces major secularizing reforms.
1920s	Tablighi movement founded in India.
1925	Royal Egyptian edition of the Qur'an.
1925	'Ali 'Abd al-Raziq's book *Islam and the Bases of Government*.
1925–79	Pahlavi dynasty in Iran.

1926	Nahdlatul Ulama founded in Indonesia.
1928	Muslim Brothers founded in Egypt by Hasan al-Banna (1906–49).
1876–1938	Muhammad Iqbal, poet and philosopher in India.
1941	Jama'at-i Islami, founded in India in by Abul 'Ala' Mawdudi (1903–79).
1945–50	Indonesian struggle for independence.
1947	Independence and partition of India and Pakistan.
1948	State of Israel founded, successfully defends itself against Arabs.
1950–61	Dar al-Islam movements in Indonesia.
1952	Free Officers' coup in Egypt, Abdel Nasser comes to power.
1952	Hizb al-Tahrir (The Liberation Party) founded by the Palestinian judge, Taqi al-Din al-Nabhani (1909–77).
1876–1960	Badiuzzaman Said Nursi, founder of the Nurcu movement.
1962	Agreement between German and Turkish governments for Turkish "guest workers" to work in Germany.
1965	Violence in Indonesia kills many communists and others; communist party outlawed; citizens must declare themselves Muslim, Catholic, Protestant, Hindu or Buddhist.
1966	Execution of Sayyid Qutb (1906–66), radical Islamist.
1967	Arab defeat by Israelis in the "Six Day War"; a defeat for secularist ideologies.
1969	Organization of the Islamic Conference (OIC) formed.
1969	Islamist party founded in Turkey by Necmettin Erbakan.
1897–1975	Elijah Muhammad, founder of "Nation of Islam" in America.
1933–77	Ali Shariati, ideologue of Iranian revolution.
1978–89	Afghan *jihad* against Soviet occupation.
1979	Islamic revolution in Iran and Islamic republic led by Ayatollah Khomeini (1902–89).
1981	Assassination of Egyptian president by Islamist.
1983	Hezbollah "suicide bombers" induce U.S. and French peacekeepers to leave Lebanon.
1988	Hamas becomes active in Palestine.
1988	Rushdie's *Satanic Verses* published, provokes uproar.

c.1989–97	Violence by Islamist extremists in Egypt.
1991	Dissolution of the Soviet Union; several Central Asian Muslim states become independent.
1992	Algerian elections cancelled, leading to violence between Islamists and government.
1993	Nasr Abu Zayd accused of *kufr* by Islamist.
1996–2001	Taleban government in Afghanistan.
2000–2	Abdurrahman Wahid, NU leader, president of Indonesia.
2001	Twin Towers destroyed on 9/11 by al-Qaeda operatives.
2001	Americans and allies intervene in Afghanistan.
2002	Justice and Development Party elected to power in Turkey (post-Islamist?).
2002	Bombing of Bali nightclub by Jemaa Islamiya.
2003	Invasion of Iraq by (primarily) American forces.
2010	In Tunisia Muhammad Bouazizi immolates himself, 17 December, triggering the "Arab spring".

Appendix III

The Islamic calendar

The Islamic era is called *Hijri* and is abbreviated H or AH (Anno Hegirae). It begins with the year during which the *Hijra* occurred (there appears to be some debate as to whether this occurred in Muharram or Rabi' I). The decision on this was made in 638 CE, during the caliphate of 'Umar, because of the need to date official documents. The year of the *hijra* was chosen because this was when the Muslims gained political autonomy.

The *Hijri* year is a lunar year and consists of twelve months of 29 or 30 days, each beginning with the sighting of the new moon. It is therefore approximately 11 days shorter than the solar year, which is used in the West and elsewhere. As a result the Islamic months move backward, so to speak, as each Islamic month begins about 11 or 12 days earlier in relation to the Western calendar and to the (solar) seasons than the year before and makes a full cycle in about 33 years. Ramadan, therefore, cycles through the four seasons in this period.

The months of the Islamic years 1435 to 1438 (with the Western dates for the first day of the month corresponding for the years 2013–14 to 2016–17) are as follows:

Month	*1435H* *2013–14CE*	*1436H* *2014–15CE*	*1437H* *2015–16CE*	*1438H* *2016–17CE*
Muharram	5 Nov 2013	25 Oct 2014	14 Oct 2015	2 Oct 2016
Safar	4 Dec	23 Nov	13 Nov	1 Nov
Rabi I	2 Jan 2014	23 Dec	12 Dec	30 Nov
Rabi II	1 Feb	21 Jan 2015	11 Jan 2016	30 Dec
Jumada I	2 Mar	20 Feb	10 Feb	29 Jan 2017
Jumada II	1 Apr	21 Mar	10 March	28 Feb
Rajab	30 Apr	20 Apr	8 Apr	29 Mar
Sha'ban	30 May	19 May	8 May	27 Apr
Ramadan	28 June	19 June	6 June	27 May
Shawwal	28 July	17 July	6 July	25 June
Dhu al-Qa'da	27 Aug	16 Aug	4 Aug	24 July
Dhu al-Hijja	25 Sept	14 Sept	2 Sept	23 Aug

Source: Islamic Finder: http://www.islamicfinder.org/dateConversion.php?mode=hijger&day=1&month=7&year=1435&date_result=1 (accessed 6 September 2013).

Hijri months begin only when the new moon is actually sighted, so that calculations such as these could be off by a day. It is worth noting that the Muslim year 1429 fell entirely within the Western year 2008. This happens only once in about 33 years. Otherwise, the Western year spans two Muslim years. The Hijri year always spans two Western years and upon occasion three (2008 CE included a few days of 1428 H and 1430 H).

A formula for rough conversion from an Islamic date to a Western date is as follows: 1429 × 0.97 = 1386.13 + 622 = 2008.13

At present Muslim countries also use the Western dates, so that both a Western date and a *Hijri* date are often given.

Hijri *solar calendar* (Hijri shamsi)

This calendar begins with the *Hijra* but uses a solar year beginning at the (northern) Spring equinox, which is *Now Ruz*, the Persian New Year. The *Hijri Shamsi* year 1388 corresponds to the Western year 2009–10 and the Lunar *Hijri* year 1430–1. It is said to have been created by the Persian writer, Saadi (d. 1292 CE), and was made the official calendar for Iran by Reza Shah. Its use has continued, except for Islamic religious festivals, under the Islamic Republic. The same calendar is used in Afghanistan but with different names for the months.

The months in Iran are as follows:

Farvardin (21 March)
Ordibehesht (21 April)
Khordad (22 May)
Tir (22 June)
Mordad (23 July)
Shahrivar (23 August)
Mehr (23 September)
Aban (23 October)
Azar (22 November)
Day (22 December)
Bahman (21 January)
Esfand (20 February)

Appendix IV

Classical Arabic names

Arabic names prior to modern times were lengthy and conveyed considerable information. One may see different versions of a well-known person's name and in ordinary usage only a part of a person's full name would be used. Moreover, different parts of the same person's name might be used in different contexts or by different people; e.g. the great *'alim* and Sufi, al-Ghazali is usually referred to as al-Ghazali, but I have also seen him referred to as Abu Hamid.

Here is a version of al-Ghazali's full name: al-Imam Abu Hamid Muhammad ibn Muhammad ibn Ahmad al-Ghazali al-Tusi al-Shafi'i Hujjat al-Islam.

The elements of an Arabic name as exemplified here are as follows:

Ism — The given name, here Muhammad. This is the basic name, the one given by the parents. The *isms* often have meanings: Muhammad means most praised; Karim means noble or generous; Jamila means beautiful, etc. Often the *ism* is 'Abd (servant of) followed by a name of God; e.g. 'Abd al-Qadir means servant of the Powerful One; 'Abd al-Rahman (Abdurrahmam) means servant of the Merciful One; 'Abd Allah (Abdullah) means servant of Allah. Abdul means "servant of the" and appears to be a figment of the Western imagination.

Kunya — Refers to the first born son, here Abu (father of) Hamid. If the person is old enough to have a son but doesn't, a putative one may be given. For a woman *umm* (mother of) is used, e.g. Umm Kulthum.

Nasab — Refers to the father, here ibn Muhammad ibn Ahmad. As in this case it may go back more than one generation, but usually only the father is given. For a woman *bint* (daughter) is used; e.g. Fatima bint Muhammad.

Nisba	Indicates a relationship, here al-Ghazali (meaning uncertain, possibly spinner of yarn) al-Tusi (from the city of Tus) al-Shafi'i (follower of the Shafi'i *madhhab*). As with the *nasab*, usually only one is given but more may be given. It refers most commonly to the place one comes from, e.g. al-Masri (from Egypt), but may refer to a tribal connection, e.g. al-Adawiya (from the tribe of Adi) or occupation, e.g. al-Hallaj (the wool carder) or Khayyam (the tent-maker).
Laqab	Is an honorific, here al-Imam and Hujjat al-Islam (proof of Islam). These are most often religious, e.g. Salah al-Din (soundness of religion) or political, e.g. Nizam al-Mulk (order of the realm).

The order of these elements varies, but the most common order in my experience is *laqab, kunya, ism, nasab, nisba*. Abu Bakr is generally known by his *kunya* but 'Ali ibn Abi Talib is commonly referred to by *ism* and *nasab*. Note that the form *Abi* often occurs in transliterated names rather than *Abu* for grammatical reasons. Also note that the combination of *ism* with the father's *kunya* is common.

Non-Arab Muslim names may follow this form or something like it, e.g. Abu Yazid al-Bistami (*kunya* and *nisba*) becomes Bayazid Bistami in Persian.

Appendix V

Muhammad's wives

This is a topic often of interest to Westerners, though the concerns we bring to it are different from the concerns of Muhammad's contemporaries as well as many other Muslims. Muhammad was specifically permitted by God to have more than the four wives permitted to others. For many Muslims this is primarily an indication of his status as the Prophet and of his personal capacities. As modernists point out, the fact that he first married at age 25 to a woman 15 years older indicates that sexual passion was not the driving force. In fact, most of the marriages were either to cement alliances or to provide for the wife in a society that did not have social security. While there is some uncertainty in the historical records the following list (with the date of marriage, etc.) from W. Montgomery Watt represents something of a consensus (Watt, 1956, 395–99).

1. Khadija bint Khuwaylid, c. 595, aged 40. Widow. She is the only wife who bore Muhammad children that survived, four daughters, one of whom was Fatima, who married 'Ali and became the ancestress of the Shi'i *Imams*. See chapters 3 and 21.
2. Sawdah bint Zam'ah, c. 620, aged about 30. Widow of an early convert, she had participated in the *Hijra*.
3. 'A'isha bint Abi Bakr, 623, aged 9. Generally agreed to be Muhammad's favorite wife; her early age at marriage raises concerns among modern commentators but seems not to have concerned contemporaries very much; undoubtedly one motive was to cement the alliance with Abu Bakr. 'A'isha later became involved in the politics of the early community and still later an important transmitter of *hadith*, in which capacity she is sometimes said to be responsible for half of the Muslim religion. There was considerable hostility between A'isha and Fatima and some claim this played a role in the division between Sunnis and Shi'is.
4. Hafsah bint 'Umar ibn al-Khattab, 625, aged 18. Widow of a Muslim killed at Badr; daughter of another close companion of Muhammad. She is said later to have played a role in the transmission of the text of the Qur'an.

5. Umm Salamah bint al-Mughira, 626, aged 29. Widow of Meccan killed at Uhud.
6. Zaynab bint Khuzaymah, 626 or 625, aged about 30. Widowed and divorced, she died soon after her marriage to Muhammad.
7. Juwayriyyah, 627, aged 20. Daughter of the chief of an opposing tribe, captured in a raid, married to Muhammad when she professed Islam.
8. Zaynab bint Jahsh, 627, aged 38. A cousin of Muhammad and divorced from his adopted son Zayd, about which there was controversy and about which the Qur'an speaks (33:38).
9. Mariyah the Copt, 628 or earlier. A concubine, presented to Muhammad by the governor of Egypt, did not become a wife.
10. Umm Habibah bint Abi Sufyan, 628, aged 35. Widow, early convert who had gone to Ethiopia with her first husband.
11. Safiya bint Huyyay, 628, aged 17. Jewish, captured in a raid on the Jewish settlement at Khaybar.
12. Maymunah bint al-Harith, 629, aged 27. Sister of the wife of Muhammad's uncle, 'Abbas (claimed ancestor of the Abbasid dynasty), probably to cement alliance with him.
13. Rayhanah bint Zayd, 627, aged 17, died 632. Jewish, captured in the raid on the Banu Qurayza (probably a concubine).

The wives who survived Muhammad came to be known as the "mothers of the believers".

Further reading

Encyclopedias

Esposito, John L. et al. (eds.) (1995) *The Oxford Encyclopedia of the Modern Islamic World*, 4 vols., New York: Oxford University Press.

Gibb, H.A.R. et al. (eds.) (1960–) *The Encyclopaedia of Islam*, new ed., vols. 1–11, Leiden: Brill. (A third edition is in process; the earliest parts are available.)

Studies of Islamic civilization and history

Armstrong, Karen (2001) *Islam: A Short History*, London: Phoenix Press.

Esposito, John (ed.) (1999) *The Oxford History of Islam*, New York: Oxford University Press. (Articles on a wide variety of topics. Chapters 1, 8–11 deal with the pre-modern history the central lands, chapters 9–11 cover South and Central Asia, China, Africa.)

Fisher, W.B. et al. (eds.) (1968–91) *The Cambridge History of Iran*, Cambridge: Cambridge University Press.

Hodgson, Marshall G.S. (1974) *The Venture of Islam: Conscience and History in a World Civilization*, 3 vols., Chicago, IL: University of Chicago Press. ("Magisterial work", a major milestone in the development of Islamic studies.)

Holt, P.M., Lambton, A.K.S. and Lewis, B. (eds.) (1970) *Cambridge History of Islam*, 2 vols., Cambridge: Cambridge University Press.

Knysh, Alexander (2011) *Islam in Historical Perspective*, Boston, etc.: Prentice Hall. (Effectively blends historical and topical approaches, with considerable detail and extensive coverage.)

Lapidus, Ira M. (2002) *A History of Islamic Societies*, 2nd ed., Cambridge: Cambridge University Press. (Very detailed, highly regarded.)

Rippin, Andrew (ed.) (2008) *The Islamic World*, London and New York: Routledge.

Robinson, Francis (ed.) (1996) *The Cambridge Illustrated History of the Islamic World*, Cambridge: Cambridge University Press. (Chapters 1–3 have a good coverage of the Islamic history to the end of the eighteenth century.)

Anthologies

Cragg, K. and Speight, M. (eds.) (1980) *Islam from Within: Anthology of a Religion*, Belmont, CA: Wadsworth.

Jeffery, Arthur (ed.) (1958) *Islam: Muhammad and his Religion*, Indianapolis, IN and New York: Bobbs-Merrill.

Jeffery, Arthur (ed.) (1962) *A Reader on Islam*, 's-Gravenhage: Mouton & Co.

McNeill, William H. and Waldman, Marilyn R. (eds.) (1973) *The Islamic World*, New York: Oxford University Press.

Renard, John (ed.) (1996) *Seven Doors to Islam: Spirituality and the Religious Life of Muslims*, Berkeley, CA: University of California Press. (This and the following book have a wide variety of selections, many recently translated, focusing primarily on the spiritual dimension; chapter headings are the same in both books.)

Renard, John (ed.) (1998) *Windows on the House of Islam: Muslim Sources on Spirituality and Religious Life*, Berkeley, CA: University of California Press.

Rippin, Andrew and Knappert, Jan (eds.) (1990), *Textual Sources for the Study of Islam*, Chicago: University of Chicago Press.

Williams, J.A. (ed.) (1963) *Islam*, New York: Washington Square Press.

Textbooks and general studies

Brown, Daniel (2009) *A New Introduction to Islam*, 2nd ed., Malden, MA: Blackwell. (Well written and up to date. Chapters 2–3 and 7–8 reflect the critical and revisionist approaches.)

Denny, Fred (2006) *An Introduction to Islam*, 3rd ed., New York: Macmillan. (Readable though containing considerable detail.)

Nasr, Seyyed Hossein (2002) *Islam: Religion, History, and Civilization*, San Francisco, CA: Harper.

Rippin, Andrew (2005) *Muslims: Their Beliefs and Practices*, 3rd ed., London and New York: Routledge. (Widely used textbook, relatively advanced.)

Electronic resources

There is an enormous amount of information on the world wide web, though much of it must be used with caution. I have used *Wikipedia* to great advantage, but always with care. I find that on most topics it will have something worth looking at. If possible one should check its information with other sources, but this is true of many other websites, too.

The following sites list a large number of internet resources for the study of Islam and are largely complementary. (All accessed 29 August 2013.)

- Academic Islamic Studies and Middle East, Central Asian, and other Area Studies Sites. http://www.uga.edu/islam/MESCenters.html.
- Islamic Studies Digital Library. http://www.academicinfo.net/Islammeta.html.
- The American Muslim: Academic Islamic Studies Resources. http://www.theamericanmuslim.org/tam.php/tam/linkcategory/C12.
- The Pew Forum on Religion and Public Life is probably the most reliable source for statistical information and surveys. http://www.pewforum.org/topics/muslims-and-islam.
- Arab Media and Society (Has a number of interesting articles; earlier articles are archived and accessible.) http://www.arabmediasociety.com.

A number of scholars in the field have good websites. Here are three that I am aware of:

- http://www.uga.edu/islam maintained by Professor Alan Godlas of the University of Georgia; has a very wide range of articles and information.
- http://www.unc.edu/~cernst maintained by Professor Carl Ernst of the University of North Carolina at Chapel Hill; has a wide range of information and links to other sources including some other academic websites.
- http://www.fordham.edu/halsall/islam/islamsbook.html. *Internet Islamic History Sourcebook*, part of *Internet History Source Books Project*, edited by Paul Halsall; has a very wide range of material on Islam and Islamic history and culture. For index and copyright information see: http://www.fordham.edu/halsall/index.html.

References

The following is a list of books and articles from which the citations for quotations are taken. These citations are in the form of (Akhtar, 1989, 1).

Ahmed, Leila (1992) *Women and Gender in Islam: Historical Roots of a Modern Debate*, New Haven, CT and London: Yale University Press.

Akhtar, Shabbir (1989) *Be Careful with Muhammad*, London: Bellew Publishing.

Ammar, Hamed (1973) *Growing up in an Egyptian Village*, New York: Octagon.

'Aqqad, Abbas Mahmoud (n.d.) *'Abqariyat Muhammad (The Genius of Muhammad)*, revised ed., Cairo: Dar al-Kutub al-Haditha (in Arabic).

Arberry, A.J. (1970) *Sufism: An Account of the Mystics of Islam*, New York: Harper and Row.

Arnold, Thomas W. (1965) *Painting in Islam*, New York: Dover Publications.

Attar, Farid al-Din (1979) *Muslim Saints and Mystics*, trans. A.J. Arberry, reprint, London: Routledge and Kegan Paul.

Bakhtiar, Laleh, transl. (2007) *The Sublime Quran*, Chicago: Kazi Publications.

Boland, B.J. (1971) *The Struggle of Islam in Modern Indonesia*, The Hague: Nijhoff.

Brown, Jonathan A.C. (2009) *Hadith: Muhammad's Legacy in the Medieval and Modern World*, One World: Oxford.

Burke, Jason (2004) *Al-Qaeda: Casting A Shadow of Terror*, revised ed., London: Penguin Books.

Burckhardt, Titus (1976) *Art of Islam: Language and Meaning*, Westerham: World of Islam Festival Publishing Company.

Carlyle, Thomas (1910) *On Heroes and Hero Worship*, London: Ward, Lock & Co. First published 1841 under the title *Heroes, Hero Worship and the Heroic in History*.

Chelebi, Suleiman (1943) *The Mevlidi Sherif*, translated by F. Lyman MacCallum, London: John Murray.

Esposito, John L. and Voll, John O (1996) *Islam and Democracy*, New York: Oxford University Press, 1996.

Fischer, M.M.J. and Abedi, M. (1990) *Debating Muslims: Cultural Dialogues in Postmodernity and Tradition*, Madison, WI: University of Wisconsin Press.

Goodman, L.E. (1992) *Avicenna*, London: Routledge.

Graham, William (1977) *Divine Word and Prophetic Word in Early Islam*, The Hague: Mouton.

Grunebaum, Gustave E. von (1966) *Medieval Islam*, Sixth Phoenix Impression, Chicago, IL and London: University of Chicago Press; Toronto: University of Toronto Press.

Haeri, Shaykh Fadhalla (2004) *The Thoughtful Guide to Sufism*, New York: O Books.

Ibn al-'Arabi (1911) *The 'Tarjuman al-Ashwaq': A Collection of Mystical Odes*, ed. and trans. Reynold A. Nicholson, London: Royal Asiatic Society.

— (1980) *The Bezels of Wisdom*, trans. R.W.J. Austin, New York: Paulist Press.

Iqbal, Muhammad (1971) *The Reconstruction of Religious Thought in Islam*, reprint, Lahore: Ashraf.

— (1972) *The Secrets of the Self*, trans. R.A. Nicholson, Lahore: Sh. Muh. Ashraf.

Jeffery, Arthur (ed.) (1958) *Islam: Muhammad and his Religion*, Indianapolis, IN and New York: Bobbs-Merrill.

Johnson, Nels (1982) *Islam and the Politics of Meaning in Palestinian Nationalism*, London: Kegan Paul.

Keddie, Nikki (ed.) (1972) "The Roots of the 'Ulama's Power in Modern Iran", in *Scholars, Saints and Sufis*, N. Keddie, Berkeley, CA: University of California Press.

Khayyam, O. (1968) *Rubaiyyat of Omar Khayaam: A New Translation*, trans. Robert Avery and John Heath-Stubbs, London: Cassell.

Khomeini, R.M. (1981) *Islam and Revolution, Writings and Declarations of Imam Khomeini*, trans. H. Algar, Berkeley, CA: Mizan Press.

Kritzeck, James (ed.) (1964) *Anthology of Islamic Literature*, New York: New American Library.

Lawrence, Bruce (ed.) (2005) *Messages to the World: the Statements of Osama Bin Laden*, trans. James Howarth, London: Verso.

Lester, Toby (1999) "What Is the Koran?" *The Atlantic Monthly* 283/1 (January 1999): 43 (passim). Also online: http://www.theatlantic.com/doc/199901/koran (accessed 17 August 2013).

Lewis, B. (1961) *The Emergence of Modern Turkey*, London: Oxford University Press.

McNeill, W.H. and Waldman, M.R. (1973) *The Islamic World*, New York: Oxford University Press.

Mahfouz, Naguib (1975) *Midaq Alley*, trans. Trevor Le Gassick, London: Heinemann.

Makdisi, George (1981) *The Rise of Colleges: Institutions of Learning in Islam and the West*, Edinburgh: Edinburgh University Press.
Martin, Vanessa (1989) *Islam and Modernism: The Iranian Revolution of 1906*, London: Tauris.
Mawdudi (Maududi), Abul A'la (1960, reprint 1975) *The Islamic Law and Constitution*, revised edition, trans. Khurshid Ahmad, Lahore: Islamic Publications.
— (1981) *Selected Speeches and Writings of Maulana Maududi*, trans. S. Zakir Aijaz, 2 vols., Karachi: International Islamic Publishers.
Messick, Brinkley (1993) *The Calligraphic State: Textual Domination and History in a Muslim Society*, Berkeley, CA: University of California Press.
Mitchell, R.P. (1969) *The Society of the Muslim Brothers*, London: Oxford University Press.
Mottahedeh, Roy (1987) *The Mantle of the Prophet*, Harmondsworth: Penguin Books.
Nelson, Kristina (1985) *The Art of Reciting the Qur'an*, Austin, TX: University of Texas Press.
Nicholson, R.A. (ed.) (1950) *Rumi, Poet and Mystic*, London: Allen and Unwin.
— (1969) *A Literary History of the Arabs*, Cambridge: Cambridge University Press, first edition, 1907.
Nizam al-Mulk (1960) *The Book of Government or Rules for Kings*, 2nd ed., trans. Hubert Darke, London: Routledge and Kegan Paul.
Padwick, Constance (1961) *Muslim Devotions: A Study of Prayer-manuals in Common Use*, London: SPCK.
Phillips, John A. (1984) *Eve: The History of an Idea*. San Francisco, etc.: Harper and Row.
Qutb, Sayyid (1978) *Milestones*, Beirut and Damascus: Holy Koran Publishing House.
Reeves, Edward B. (1990) *The Hidden Government: Ritual, Clientelism and Legitimation in Northern Egypt*, Salt Lake City, UT: University of Utah Press.
Robinson, Francis (ed.) (1996) *The Cambridge Illustrated History of the Islamic World*, Cambridge: Cambridge University Press.
Sadiq (2005) "London Suicide Bomber Before 'Entering Gardens of Paradise,' and Ayman Al-Zawahiri's Threats of More Bombings in the West", http://www.memri.org/report/en/0/0/0/0/0/0/1465.htm (accessed 29 August 2013).
Sahih Muslim (1972) trans. Abdul Hamid Siddiqi, Lahore: Ashraf.
Schimmel, Annemarie (1963) *Gabriel's Wing*, Leiden: Brill.
— (1975) *Mystical Dimensions of Islam*, Chapel Hill, NC: University of North Carolina Press.
Shah, Idries (1968) *The Pleasantries of the Incredible Mulla Nasreddin*, London: Jonathan Cape.

Shariati, Ali (1979) *On the Sociology of Islam*, trans. H. Algar, Berkeley, CA: Mizan Press.

"SIS Story, The", Sisters in Islam: Empowering Voices for Change. http://www.sistersinislam.org.my/page.php?35 (accessed 29 August 2013).

Smith, Margaret (1972) *Readings from the Mystics of Islam*, London: Luzac.

Smith, W.C. (1957) *Islam in Modern History*, New York: New American Library.

Stetkevych, Jaroslav (1996) *Muhammad and the Golden Bough: Reconstructing Arabian Myth*. Bloomington, IN: Indiana University Press.

Tabataba'i, A.S.M.H. (1977) *Shi'ite Islam*, 2nd ed., Albany, NY: State University of New York Press.

al-Taftazani, Mas'ud ibn 'Umar (1980) *A Commentary on the Creed of Islam*, trans. Earl Edgar Elder, New York: Books for Libraries.

Toprak, B. (1981) *Islam and Political Development in Turkey*, Leiden: Brill.

Watt, W. Montgomery (1956) *Muhammad at Medina*, Oxford: Clarendon Press.

— (1970) *Bell's Introduction to the Qur'an*, Edinburgh: Edinburgh University Press.

Williams, J.A. (ed.) (1963) *Islam*, New York: Washington Square Press.

Yarshater, Ehsan (ed.) (1983) *Cambridge History of Iran*, vol. III/2. Cambridge: Cambridge University Press.

Zaehner, R.C. (1961) *The Dawn and Twilight of Zoroastrianism*, London: Weidenfeld and Nicolson.

Zilfi, Madeline C. (1988) *The Politics of Piety: The Ottoman Ulema in the Postclassical Age (1600–1800)*, Minneapolis, MN: Bibliotheca Islamica.

Index

Items with a star (*) refer to Glossary entries. Other mentions of the item in the Glossary are listed but not starred. Items in parentheses after the entry are explanatory; those not in parentheses are alternative words that sometimes appear in the text instead of the entry word.